The Marching Wind

by

Leonard Clark

The Long Riders' Guild Press

www.thelongridersguild.com

ISBN: 1-59048-060-0

To the Reader:

The editors and publishers of The Long Riders' Guild Press faced significant technical and financial difficulties in bringing this and the other titles in the Equestrian Travel Classics collection to the light of day.

Though the authors represented in this international series envisioned their stories being shared for generations to come, all too often that was not the case. Sadly, many of the books now being published by The Long Riders' Guild Press were discovered gracing the bookshelves of rare book dealers, adorned with princely prices that placed them out of financial reach of the common reader. The remainder were found lying neglected on the scrap heap of history, their once-proud stories forgotten, their once-glorious covers stained by the toil of time and a host of indifferent previous owners.

However The Long Riders' Guild Press passionately believes that this book, and its literary sisters, remain of global interest and importance. We stand committed, therefore, to bringing our readers the best copy of these classics at the most affordable price. The copy which you now hold may have small blemishes originating from the master text.

We apologize in advance for any defects of this nature.

To my brother
Laurence
In memory of Borneo days

Foreword

FORCED to leave Peking by the advance of the Communist armies in the winter of 1948, I went to western China to continue my archaeological studies and eventually reached Lanchow in northwestern China in March of 1949 where I planned to investigate neolithic sites. On the advice of the friendly German missionaries there I visited the agent of General Ma Pu-fang and obtained permission from him, after a thorough questioning, to proceed to the General's headquarters in Sining, the capital of Ching-hai province on the northern border of Tibet.

In this Mohammedan Chinese city of Central Asiatic architecture there were two official hostels for officials and guests of the General. One of them, an attempt at a western hotel, was the one in which I was invited to stay. The food was very poor and the army cot in my room reminded me of the bed in my college fraternity. Around midnight of the second of my uncomfortable nights there, there suddenly came a great banging at my door. This was caused by Leonard Clark, the American adventurer, and his companion, Prince Dorje, and I have reason to be grateful to them for interrupting my fitful sleep. They had heard that another American was in Sining and that he was lodged in the wrong hostel. The next day I moved to the native inn where Clark and Dorje were staying and found it much more comfortable than the big western style residence, and the cook at this smaller place was one of the best in all of northwestern China.

Here I spent about three weeks in the pleasant companionship of Clark and Dorje and had ample time to become acquainted with them and to observe the type of preparations they were making. During the frosty nights we would go over maps, discuss previous expeditions, argue, and attend government functions; during the daytime we would go on field trips or examine newly arrived equipment. During this time I became rather impressed with Clark's ability and seriousness and with Dorje's academic background. There was no detail in the way of preparation that did not receive Clark's closest personal attention, and there was no local service or equipment that was not made available to him. This last item was most important and I attribute the Government's splendid cooperation to his tact and patience.

As some of us escorted Clark a short distance beyond the walls of Sining on the day that he finally set out for Amne Machin, I had a feeling of confidence in this well equipped and ably led expedition, I felt that the trip would be successful and that the information brought back by them would be reliable.

R. C. RUDOLPH

University of California
Los Angeles

Author's Note

I THINK I'll take the bull by the horns right here. Not everybody agrees with my own estimate of the height of the Amne Machin mountain range. There has been criticism of the whole performance in its treatment in a magazine article (*Life,* October, 1949). In the following pages, then, is the full report, simply told, of my expedition to that mountain range of mystery. Prince Dorje, Solomon Ma, and I have verified the existence of Amne Machin peak, a mountain already reported as a rival of Mount Everest by General Pereira, Dr. Rock, Mr. Reynolds, various Hump pilots and others, none of whom has left a book-length report. The best reason, other than death in some cases, is that many armchair explorers and experts have called them liars and other equally hard and unfair names. All of them, in my opinion, were and are honorable men, and they were correct in their belief of the mountain's existence and its great height. I hope other expeditions will validate what I myself believe about the whole matter.

In this introductory note I will not recapitulate the full account which is told in the body of the book, but will cover only a few specific points.

Source material is from field notes, sketch maps, photographs and letters not burned at Lanchow when the Communists occupied that city after the expedition to Tibet was complete, and from memory. It is as accurate as I can make it.

Spelling of place names, personal names, native terms, etc., often a sore point with scholars, follows common usage in English, and when any doubt whatever exists I have introduced other spellings used among Europeans, Americans, and various Asians. Reference to map usage on our Moslem military Chinese maps are in English, Tibetan, Mongolian, and Romanized Cantonese and other Chinese spellings. While this may cause disputes as to the proper spellings, I believe no amount of hairsplitting will confuse the geographic points themselves.

Cross-checking of field material has been almost impossible for me due to Communist occupation of the strategic places in the regions concerned, and since most of my view of the expedition was through interpreters, I record these with whatever accuracy is possible to me.

Whether this book adds anything to the world's already great knowledge of Tibet is not for me to say, though all our findings and reports were handed over to the Tungans in Lanchow just prior to the Communist seizure of that city.

About conversations as recorded: these are approximations only and not exact word-for-word reportage, an obvious impossibility on a journey such as this one.

All characters in the report have their own true names. Since all political and military information not absolutely necessary to an explanation of the expedition's origin and field journey has been deleted, they have nothing to fear from either Nationalist or Communist sources, though I personally have enemies even among the first faction.

This book is not for the scholar, but for the public, and especially for the young man who will one day penetrate to Amne Machin and confirm or refute the findings made by myself and others who pioneered before me. This account is offered in good faith, and with the hope that some among the experts who care to read it will use the information it contains as a means for reaching the objective themselves.

A great deal of misinformation about this expedition is abroad. I have on hand some rather bulky complaints by mountain and other specialists who claim there is something "fishy" about me and this alleged expedition into Tibet and to Amne Machin in particular, and still other reports on estimates by experts denying the height claimed after their studies of snowlines in photographs.

In a recent authoritative book about mountains (*The Story of Mountains,* by Ferdinand C. Lane), my trip is reported to have been made from Sining to Amne Machin by motor trucks, and other inaccuracies are included. To my attention too come all sorts of fantastic tales, none of them true, including one to the effect that I was planning for the United States the destruction of the Communists in central Asia and launching an underground into Siberia and Russia. I had not intended writing this journal at all, but because of such legends, I have decided to release once and for all the full story and clear up the "mystery" and I might add, the actual "hatred" now apparently quite widely spread.

I must add somewhere, and it might just as well be here, that the United States was not aware of my very slight aid to Governor Ma Pu-fang, the backer of the expedition in his fighting the Communists, and particularly Lin-Pao, for control of central Asia, and that whatever I have done was upon my own responsibility as a private American citizen.

Since, due to lack of seconds' measurements on the instrument used by Prince Dorje, my surveyor, and to the United States Geologic Survey's conclusions (as reported in *Life*) that Amne Machin's height could therefore only be determined to within 2,500 feet, the mountain could be that much higher—or lower—than Dorje calculated in Tibet. I did not know these particulars in beseiged Lanchow, from where the first report was sent to my brother Laurence, in California. Had I known the inadequacy of this instrument, borrowed from the Sining Tungans, I should very likely not even have mentioned the mountains on my return home. Therefore, the expedition's findings are, in my considered opinion, indecisive, and will have to await further measurement by someone more competent and better equipped. This, then, is a guide to some traveler of the future through the western reaches of the Amne Machin Range. I wish him well, and all good luck. May he confirm the mountains' existence and vindicate the opinion of the great height of the central peaks held by others who have seen them from great distances, but which Dorje, Solomon and I penetrated in person.

That every explorer, flyer, and adventurer, has suffered misfortune in one form or another, not to say death, after even briefly sighting this so-called god mountain, need not mean fatal disaster to those who will accept the challenge of Amne Machin—including (who knows?) some reader of this account.

LEONARD CLARK

San Francisco
January, 1954

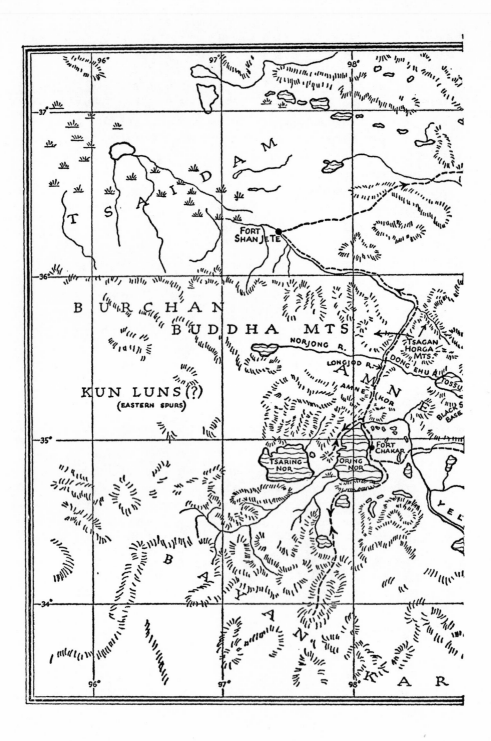

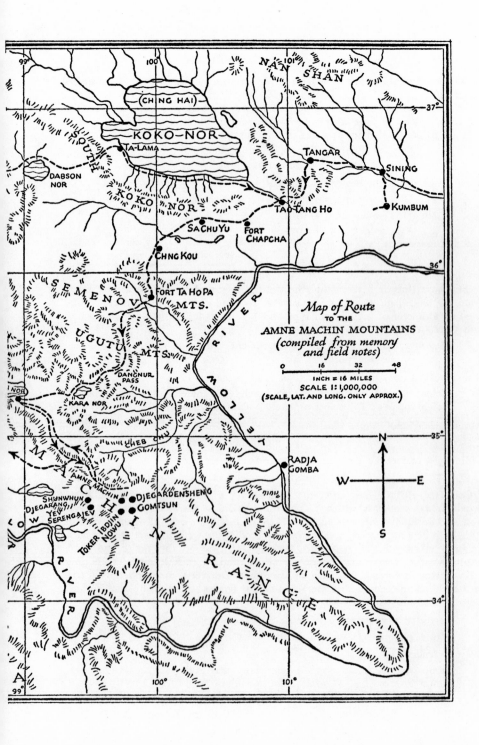

Map of Route
TO THE
AMNE MACHIN MOUNTAINS
(compiled from memory
and field notes)

0   16   32   48

INCH ≡ 16 MILES
SCALE 1:1,000,000
(SCALE, LAT. AND LONG. ONLY APPROX.)

MEASUREMENT of AMNE MACHIN PEAK
Refer to page 181 for illustration

This triangulation, one of several (with variations no greater than 50 meters) from different locations and other varied ranges on the west and north flanks of Amne Machin Peak, was made and recorded on May 6, 1949. A base line of 1000 meters by tape measure was laid down on a surveyed level ground straight to the southernmost point on the summit.

$$\text{First reading at point B} \quad 5° \; 6'$$
$$\text{At the end of the base line} \quad 5° \; 12'$$

Relative height of the peak is calculated:

$$h = \frac{\text{baseline} \times \sin b \times \sin d}{\sin (180° - b - 180° - d)}$$

$$= \frac{1000 \times \sin 5° \, 6' \times \sin 5° \, 12'}{\sin 0° \, 6'}$$

log 1000	3.00000
log sin 5° 6'	8.94887 — 10
log sin 5° 12'	8.95728 — 10
	20.90615 — 20
log sin 0° 6'	7.24188 — 10
Relative height: log 4616	3.66427

The base line or instrument (theodolite) height above sea level was taken from the official military highway survey, Jyekundo to Sining. The expedition used an altimeter of the aneroid type and a Centigrade thermometer (American and German respectively).

Readings: Altimeter at point instrument *OB:* 3800 meters
Boiling point   "   "   *OB:* 87° C.;

which worked out approximately 3850 to 3870 meters.

Height of *OB* point above sea level: 3860 meters (uncompensated)
Height of peak from instrument   4616 meters

Absolute height of Amne Machin:

$$3860 + 4616 = 8476 \text{ meters, or } 27{,}808 \text{ feet;}$$

adding 565 meters for instrument correction:

$$9041 \text{ meters, or } 29{,}661 \text{ feet}$$

Corrected altitude base line: the road survey of the Chinese and Chinghai provincial governments, which backed the expedition, shows the sea level elevation at our base camp at Chang Shih Tou meadow (west of Amne Machin Range) to be 4665 meters, a check on our readings of 4100 meters. On ten such readings taken on the Jyekundo Military Highway in the range the same results, weather remaining consistent, were found in each instance, with only a few meters difference one way or the other. Difference between our instruments (thermometer and altimeter) and official figures (surveyed by English and German instruments) was —565 meters.

Corrected reading for barometric pressure:
$$4616 + 4425 = 9041 \text{ meters, or } 29{,}661 \text{ feet.}$$

Summary:

Amne Machin Peak   29,661 feet above sea level
Mount Everest   29,144 feet above sea level
Amne Machine Peak is   *517 feet higher* than Everest

LEONARD FRANCIS CLARK

xiv

Contents

NOTE: Facing the title page is a reproduction of the original bilingual letter introducing Prince Dorje, Solomon Ma, and Colonel Leonard Clark, under the hand and seal of the Panchen Lama.

The Marching Wind

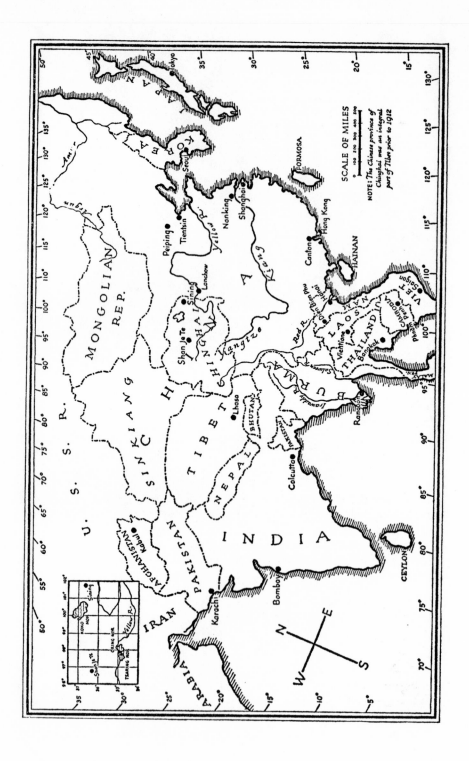

1

Ma Pu-fang and the Panchen Lama

THE YEAR was 1948 and time had come for another expedition; the conviction that I had stayed at home long enough was growing more intense with every passing day. There was, too, no question in my mind about where to go. All my life I had wanted to get into Tibet, not merely because it is remote and because entry to it is strictly forbidden, but because it is the highest tableland on earth, an isolated plateau in the heart of the least explored area of Asia. Even defining its location suggests how remote it is—north of India, west of China, east of Afghanistan and the U.S.S.R. (Turkestan), and south of Sinkiang, Siberia, and Mongolia. My previous years in China had given me some notion of how difficult a goal Tibet would prove to be, but it had also sharpened my appetite for a try at a land which seemed to be the very citadel of isolation.

The first thing, of course, would be to find out as much as possible about the country before setting out. Fortunately I was living near the University of California, and a visit there confirmed what I had already supposed. A few—a very few—Americans and a few hundred Europeans had been to Lhasa, the capital city. Most of them had got there along the treaty trail running north from the hill state of Sikkim in India. But of the Americans, only one seemed to have left an explorer's record of the country and his expedition to it. This was a man named W. W. Rockhill, who had traveled in eastern Tibet between the years 1889 and 1892. No one seemed to know much about him, and even his diary, which had been published fifty years before, had appeared in London rather than the United States. He had, of course, died long since.

There was, though, one man to whom I could go, my friend Colonel Nicol Smith, whom I had known for fifteen years. We had done exploration together on Hainan Island, off the coast of French Indochina, and I knew that he had recently completed a trip across Ladakh, a province west of Tibet proper. We talked long hours during the two weeks' visit I paid him in his Sierra Nevada fishing camp. He knew a great deal about the western Tibetans, but he repeatedly impressed upon me that while he had first-hand knowledge of the western Himalayan region, he had never been to Tibet itself. As background information this was naturally invaluable, but I knew that there could be no substitute for on-the-spot knowledge.

When I got back to San Francisco from Nicol's camp, however, I repaired to the Public Library and went through the standard books on Tibet which were available. The principal material was the work of the famous Swedish explorer, Sven Hedin, but there was a good deal else beside, and one report in particular augmented my already eager resolve. This was Dr. Joseph F. Rock's account of seeing, from a great distance, a Tibetan mountain which he believed to be over 28,000 feet high and hence a rival of Everest. His article, published in the February, 1930 issue of the *National Geographic Magazine,* was entitled "Seeking the Mountains of Mystery," but it seemed to me almost equally mysterious that in the intervening years no one had apparently done any further successful exploration, even with such a tremendous goal in view.

Dr. Rock's view of the peak had occurred while he was in west China, but I now recalled a series of newspaper stories about American pilots who, during World War II, had also caught glimpses of this mystery mountain. Momentarily full of hope I set about locating these fliers, only to learn that every one who professed to have seen it had died, from one cause or another, shortly afterward. It was almost as if there were a curse on the men who reported the peak, but curse or not, I soon found out that it had another kind of unpopularity. Most of the experts and interested members of the general public did not believe in the existence of such a mountain at all. Everyone was agreed on discrediting the reports of Dr. Rock and the pilot officers. This disbelief was virtually unanimous.

Such a reluctance to believe in the possible height of a mountain is something that still puzzles me. Everest has been considered the world's highest mountain for over a century, ever since the surveyors of the Indian Trigonometrical Survey had determined that it was the highest of the Himalayan peaks. Since the Himalayas are the highest mountains in the world, Everest must be the highest peak. Or must it? Not unless every other very high mountain had been carefully surveyed. This Tibetan peak had not, so much my research made abundantly clear.

With this final incentive of a tremendous mountain as one of the goals of my trip, the die was irrevocably cast. Tibet it was to be. The absence of capital, which was one of the features of my situation at the moment, did not deter me. The little money I did have would have to do. I purchased a ticket as a passenger on the *Vilja*, a small motor cargo ship of the Pacific Orient Express Line. After paying my fare, I had in my wallet only $1,200 with which to meet all the other costs of the entire expedition to Tibet and return home. But a man is very short-sighted to let the lack of money forestall him in any undertaking.

On the evening of January 13, 1949, the *Vilja* sailed without incident out of San Francisco bay. On the 2nd February we dropped general cargo at Manila, and, putting out to sea again, presently approached a barren point of land on the south coast of China— beyond which appeared the British Crown colony of Hong Kong. It was then the 5th of February, 1949.

A great many rusty, flag-flying ships were at anchor here in dirty water, and between them and the Kowloon mainland and the tall, house-stacked, green island of Victoria, were plying fleets of bat-winged cargo *junks* with eyes painted on their bows. After finishing with the immigration, customs, and medical officers, I disembarked and took a *sampan* ashore across to Victoria.

Beginning with the Hong Kong Hotel, I discovered that every hostelry was filled. Eventually I wound up in a small Chinese hotel on a smelly sidestreet.

All around the entrance were signs in huge Chinese characters, and crowds of pajama-clad and foreign-clothed refugees and locals, peddlers, and the noisy hurlyburly of any Chinese city—bicycles, rickshaws, and honking little automobiles. My room had a chair, a bamboo screen, a washbasin and pitcher (with bugs floating in the lukewarm water), and a rotting muslin tent to keep out mosquitoes suspended over a sagging brass bed.

But such quarters caused me no great concern, for I had already made four trips previously to China and had been in and out of Hong Kong itself perhaps twenty times. The first time had been on a hunting trip (to Borneo and elsewhere) with my brother in 1932; the second had been during the Chinese civil war when I had traveled in the interior of the central provinces during that early period when the Nationalists were fighting with the Reds, stationed then in Fukien and Chekiang; the third to explore Hainan Island in 1937 with Nicol Smith; and the fourth had been for 26 months during World War II on army duty with the OSS behind the Japanese lines.

Because of the last stages of the current Communist-Nationalist civil war, I now found it necessary to see a Mr. Kwok, Commissioner for Kwangtung and Kwangsi provinces, parts of which still remained free of Reds. I found Mr. Kwok at the Chinese Ministry of Foreign Affairs, in a smoke-filled upstairs office. Mr. Kwok was surrounded by agitated assistants who interrupted every few seconds. He proved to be a blunt, Westernized Chinese, without the usual manners of his people, who wondered why an American would want to be going into China at this time when everybody with any sense was trying to get out?

Mr. Kwok had a sort of bamboo version of a British accent, and Mr. Kwok didn't like the cut of my Yankee jib. Was I a Communist sympathizer? I kept the edge of my voice ground down, and answered "No." Was I buying gold? No. Was I trying to get in so that I could sell guns or airplanes to the Communists? No. I certainly wasn't a missionary? No. Then what conceivable excuse could I have for wanting to go into China during this time of war, when even part of the Nationalist capital itself had been forced to move from Chungking to Canton?

I didn't tell Mr. Kwok that sometimes the best chance to get into forbidden country (such as Tibet) was to go during times of great unrest such as a civil war. Instead, I told him I just wanted to travel to be traveling, like any tourist. That was it, there was no mystery about it. Well, Mr. Kwok finally decided he didn't give a damn whether I got into China or not, and said so, bustling outside into the corridor in company with his flunkies, elbowing through the long lines of patient Chinese, and foreigners such as missionaries, all trying to get visas like myself.

After leaving the hectic Ministry of Foreign Affairs and Mr. Kwok, I crossed over to the Alien's Registration Office, Police Headquarters, New Oriental Building, 2 Connaught Road. Here I signed up as British law required. Although I had been instrumental in helping save this juicy colony for England, I was now peremptorily given four days in which to get out, as there was no room here except for the British and the Chinese refugees.

I called on various people such as the American Consul; Mr. James A. Nelson of the American Express; and Mr. Jerry G. O'Donnell of Pan-American, who after learning I was not in the market for an outbound plane ticket, warned there was no way to get into China. All of which added up to the fact that I would find it impossible to get up to Lanchow in northwest China due to the unsettled conditions everywhere in the country. No visa could possibly be obtained from the all-powerful Mr. Kwok.

Still visa-hunting, I proceeded eighty miles west to Canton. A British passenger plane operated by Hong Kong Air Ways, Ltd., hedgehopped off the Kaitak Airdrome and flew junk-mast-high along the Pearl River finally to land me, together with a load of Chinese passengers, at the White Cloud Airdrome (where OSS agents had burned many a Jap plane). After slipping the Chinese immigration officer a hundred Nationalist *yuan,* I took a taxi into teeming Canton to one of the arched bridges leading over to tree-shaded Shameen Island.

Machine-gun nests and barbed wire were all over the streets, but I made my way along without being challenged. Here, from the Chinese Foreign Office of the Nationalist Government, I hoped to obtain somehow an interior visa into west China. I put on a bold front and a smile and walked past the guards holding Tommy guns at port position, and tramped up the stairs and into the main building. But this visa business proved not so difficult, because the young English-speaking official who eventually took me in charge, seemed devoted to one Major Leo Karwaski and one Major Joe Lazarsky, both of whom had been American guerrillas of the OSS. I thought I recognized this Chinese as one of their agents. "You know Karwaski and Lazarsky, don't you?"

"Ah!" he cried out, adjusting his horn-rimmed spectacles, "Do I! And how are my old side-kicks Lawaski and Karzarsky?"

"Probably digging coal in Pittsburgh," I ventured.

"Not at all," he informed me, "I hear on the bamboo telegraph that Leo is a big-shot in the Pentagon and Joe is making millions in the slot-machine business!"

While this patter was going on, my passport was being chopped all over with big red Chinese seals, and a special Chinese passport prepared as well.

"Well, here you are Colonel!" beamed the Foreign Office man, shaking hands. "After your trip into China, and when you get home, look up Joe and Leo and Nick Smith, and tell them 'hello' for me!" *

I stayed in Canton that night, and back in Hong Kong next day lost no time buying a ticket on a CNAC (China National Airways Co.) plane for HK$300, leaving on Friday, February 11, at 7 A.M., arriving at Chungking in west China (via dusty, sleepy Kunming—how it has changed since Flying Tigers' and OSS days!) at 5 P.M. next day. After six delightful days with Jimmy Houston, a young Scotchman met on the plane, I left Chungking on Friday, 18th, in a battered CAT (Civil Air Transport) Chennault cargo plane carrying ammunition, landing on the freezing dusty field at Lanchow, at 4 P.M.

I walked down the ladder and stood blinking in the dust. I had arrived at the end of nowhere in northwest China, and knew not a solitary soul. The plane's crew, a very fat and surly American pilot and his Chinese co-pilot, dropped me off with my suitcase at a high-walled mission compound inside the city. I picked up my suitcase and turned toward a small side door next to a very large bolted entrance. A Chinese in black pajamas came forward, and he spoke a halting brand of English mixed with Chinese. This place, I learned, was the Catholic Mission of Lanchow, the Apostolic Vicariate of Kansu Province, the Rt. Rev. Mgr. Buddenbrock, the Vicar Apostolic. The mission was called by the gateman, the "t'ien chu t'ang."

I slipped him five yuan, and walked on through the open doorway. A tall, burly priest in a black gown with a high Chinese collar came striding toward me, out of a garden, but instead of throwing me out he smiled. He introduced himself as Father Senge, a German.

Father Senge brought me immediately to see the Bishop of Kansu, Chinghai, Sinkiang, and Inner Mongolia, Mgr. Buddenbrock, a wonderful red-cheeked old man with a long beard, a chuckle, and a cane. I sat in his office, which was lined with books, and we talked in pidgin English, pidgin Chinese, and pidgin German. We got nowhere, but it was finally decided I would stay here for the time being, with the 25 or 30 priests and lay brothers, all Germans.

---

* Thanks—wherever you are—for the visa which ultimately led me into Tibet.

That very first evening, after dinner, the jolly Father Senġe came along for me, and together we passed swiftly down long stone-arched courtyards and bare-limbed gardens to the refectory where there was a table, some chairs, and a fire. Here I was introduced to a Prince Tsedan Dorje, a small man with a winning grin, who dressed in an old brown European sack suit which could stand not only a pressing but could have done with a patch or two as well. In perfect English, Dorje said:

"I say, Clark, it is delightful to know you at last. I knew of you during the war when I was with the Nationalist underground in Mongolia, and you were in charge of United States Intelligence and Guerrilla activities for North China, and were stationed behind the Yellow River lines with Marshal Yen Shih-son. The fathers, you know, understand almost no English, and are completely mystified as to why you have come to this place. With your consent I should like to have your story and I'll relay it along to them. Please sit down by the fire and warm yourself."

Dorje and I soon had our pipes going, and after explanations were finished (minus the OSS implications), Senġe said I must plan to stay a few days. And as they were now going to the church, would I care to come along and make my confession?

Through Dorje (whose brown eyes twinkled as he relayed this information) I said that for the present my multitudinous sins were as yet unorganized in my mind, but later in due time would undoubtedly prepare myself and comply all at once.

After the fathers had left for church we sat there, sizing each other up, wondering what part the other would play in the days to come, until the fire went out, and then we got up and walked back to my room where a few embers still glowed among the ashes in the brass brazier. Here we talked late that night, and as near as I can recall, the conversation went something like this:

"What are you a prince of—the Lanchow beggars' guild?"

He chuckled. "I am a Torgut Mongol, a refugee from the Communists in Peking. I make my living here by doing translating for the Fathers, who are interested in exact Mongolian and Chinese classics. My people call me a 'Tsagan Yasse,' White Bones, noble of the first class." Dorje balanced his over-run heels on the edge of the brazier and stared into the coals.

"Kind of tough on the Mongols when Genghis lost his shirt," I observed.

He glanced up and smiled quickly. "Do you know why I like an occasional American better than anyone else?"

"No. Do you?"

"Because, while they laugh at everybody else in the whole world, they are the only men today who can laugh also at themselves. Do you realize that the Mongols once ruled all the civilized world? Americans know nothing of Asian history, of course, or they would laugh softly hereabouts."

I might not know a lot about Mongol history, but I quite suddenly remembered for one thing that his brother, Minchur Tsewan Dorje, was, so I knew from OSS days in the 12th and 2nd War Zones of north China and Inner Mongolia, a leading prince among the western Mongols of the almost unknown Fifth Khanate established in west Gobi by Genghis Khan, then master of the world from the Arctic Sea to Singapore, from China to what is now Germany, from Siberia to India, Arabia and Egypt in Africa.

"The Russians and the Chinese Communists and the Nationalists have pretty well destroyed the Mongols north of us, have they not?" I asked.

"They are practically liquidated," he answered. "However, the Mongol Leagues and Banners, part of the residue of the Mongol invasions of Lhasa in 1637, still operate west of here, intact throughout Chinghai Province" (or Tsinghai according to the authorized Nationalist pronunciation).

This I knew was where Amne Machin was located in northeast Tibet. In talking further I recalled that Dorje's sister was the distinguished Torgut Princess Mme. Bréal, wife of the French Consul in Peking. Dorje was a very close friend of the Danish explorer Henning Haslund, among the greatest of Mongolian explorers, recently killed (so I was then informed to my surprise) entering Tibet.

"What is your official status now?" I asked of Dorje.

"I am representative from Peking to the National Legislative Yuan." *

Further talk revealed that he fluently spoke and wrote German, French, Russian, Mongolian, Chinese, Latin, Greek, and English. In addition he dallied with several dialects of central Asia.

---

* Same as the Congress of the United States, or the British Parliament.

"I have studied in Europe, and until recently have been a professor at Turin University in Peking."

About midnight Dorje got up and walked to the door where he read the thermometer.

"It's 14° below zero," he laughed, "haven't you any warmer clothes to put on?"

It was true, I was wearing a pair of slacks, a thin shirt, and a Harris tweed jacket. I put the last few pieces of charcoal on the coals, and sat back in my chair, the kind monks must sit on when they are doing penance. I had just made a very important decision, and so I put it up to him this way—

"Dorje, how about joining up with me for a journey into Tibet. Your knowledge of the country, the people, and the languages, would be invaluable."

He came back and took his chair on the other side of the coals. Leaning forward he held up the nubbin of candle which he had meanwhile lit, looking at me for about two long silent minutes. Finally he blew out the candle to save it, settled back, and asked:

"And, what do *you* contribute?"

"Me."

His mouth fell open, and then he started to laugh, and I thought he would never stop. Finally, "You think like a Mongol. Do you really believe that we two—with no resources at all—can do what the great explorers have not been able to accomplish in many years?"

"Why not?"

Again came that grin.

"Clark, I'll join up with you. Remember just one thing, that a Mongol is not a Chinese; when we do a thing we do it straight with no hidden meanings. That's that, and we will talk about it no more. We are friends. And we will go to Tibet."

We shook hands on it.

Then Dorje said, "You say you want to go into Tibet, which, as you must know, is forbidden, not only by the Tibetans and lamas but by the Chinese. And while in Tibet you wish to find Amne Machin." He sat for a long while thinking this over—then: "This might be done by going from Lanchow to Labrang, a great Tibetan monastery some days south of here. My brother Minchur is in Lanchow, just back from the Gobi, and can supply a letter to Huang Suling, the Tibetan general commanding Nationalist forces of local tribesmen. I think it will be impossible to enter Tibet by trying a point farther north, say at Sining, as Governor Ma Pu-fang, the Moslem Tungan chief, will never permit it. But we shall see about that too."

With that Dorje left for his own quarters, and I undressed and got into my cot where I shivered from the cold all night. Next morning, I made known my true plans to the priests, and was immediately told such a journey was not possible either officially or in disguise. Hundreds of men had come to Lanchow with this idea, they said, and not one had ever gotten into inner Tibet, though a few such as Rock had penetrated a short way after leaving Labrang.

At noon, Dorje (who had lost none of his enthusiasm after sleeping on my proposal) and I were joined in my room for tiffin by his brother Prince Minchur. Tiffin was of black bread and tea; there was no butter, no sugar and cream. Minchur was a steely-eyed, small man with a straight, very tight mouth, and he wore a long black Chinese overcoat reaching nearly to the ground, and a Cossack fur cap of lamb.

He now politely said that entry into Tibet through Labrang—in spite of what Dorje had suggested—would be absolutely impossible. West of Labrang were only wild tribes, the worst of which were undoubtedly the Ngoloks, the same who had stopped Dr. Rock on his own expedition over 25 years before, and who would kill us on sight.

On Wednesday I talked with Judge Allman, who had just flown in by plane. He was an ex-advisor on China to the United States government, at present a sort of Civil Air Transport "representative." This meeting was in the New Village, near Lanchow, at the house of the Swedish business man, Mr. Gustav E. Söderbom, who was then CAT agent for Lanchow, and whose brother George was Sven Hedin's right-hand man in Mongolia and Sinkiang.

Gustav never knew during my stay in Lanchow that during the war I had once saved his brother, George from a secret night firing squad of General Tai Li's, the dread chief of Chinese Nationalist Intelligence and all subversive operations behind the Japanese lines in occupied China. Tai Li never penetrated north China east of the Yellow River Bend, whereas I had agents working into Mongolia, Manchuria, Korea, and in every north China province, and so was in many respects stronger than the Nationalist chief himself. At any rate I now watched Söderbom closely, and especially Allman, for although the latter was an American, sometimes, if they have resided long among the Chinese, Americans are your worst enemies, for at heart many are more Chinese than the Chinese themselves and will warn their friends against any strange compatriot.

However, both Söderbom and Allman agreed to send letters of introduction to Ma Pu-fang who was in Sining, west of us in north Tibet.

My one and only chance then to get into Tibet, they believed, would be to try Sining, as in their opinion Labrang was definitely out. Söderbom said he had been half a lifetime working this far west across China, even though he, together with George, was undoubtedly the best-informed foreigner on Mongolia and these northwest parts. And so it amused him that I, an American stranger, should barge into Lanchow and expect to go into Tibet, and, furthermore, to have Ma Pu-fang finance my expedition.

As a result of their discussion I threw out Dorje's original idea of a try through Labrang and concentrated on Sining and Ma Pu-fang, the terrible chief of a good section of those little-known ten million Chinese Moslems, some of whom had left Sinkiang and entered north Tibet under his father's Tungan banner, a banner now loyal to the Nationalists. Ma Pu-fang had about a million infantrymen in north China, fighting the Communists.

Both Allman and Söderbom then dispatched letters of introduction to Governor Ma Pu-fang in Chinghai; together with an outline of my own plan, which proposed that I organize and lead an expedition for him into Tibet and that he furnish the necessary authorization and field assistance. Allman then returned to Hong Kong, with a warning that I'd better hurry up, as China was doomed. After presenting ourselves personally before a very grim six-foot-four Moslem officer representing Ma Pu-fang in Lanchow, and whose headquarters were behind a row of stone lions and Tungan guards with bayonets fixed on their rifles, we returned to the mission and sat tight.

We began studying the Tibetan situation, and the German Fathers helped us in every way they possibly could, offering advice and supplying us with much material to study. The brazier burning charcoal—a convenience which I could sparingly afford only once daily early in the morning—we would sit in our heaviest clothes (and I had even fewer than Dorje) with the blankets thrown around us, and study the records of past expeditions into Tibet and particularly the approaches from the north and the northeast where we now were poised. These records were old books published in Europe many years ago, being well-thumbed curly-cornered volumes. Stacks of dusty papers were also brought to us by the Fathers, these written in every European language, but mostly in Chinese characters by the older priests.

The French Lazarists Huc and Gabet, whose immortal journey in a great trading caravan from Peking to Lhasa is known in most languages, reached the Forbidden City (Peking) in 1846 and left to us a priceless record describing mainly, however, the Chang Tang lying west and the southern parts of Tibet.

Then there were the Russians: Semenov had penetrated the Tien Shans, marking the frontier between Siberia and Turkestan (Sinkiang), in 1857; Severzov journeyed to north Tibet in 1864; Prjevalsky, more of a naturalist, explored in north Tibet and the Tsaidam Swamp was discovered by him in 1883-1885. Kozlov reached Koko Nor, only 170 miles west of Lanchow, in 1907.

Other explorers about and inside Tibet were Baron Richthofen (Nan Shan—border of Mongolia and Tibet); Lt. Colonel (later Sir Francis) Younghusband commanding the Lhasa Punitive Expedition, during which the present trade treaty with India was obtained, this in 1904; Dr. Sven Hedin early in the century traveled through the north, south, and west of Tibet—mainly in the western regions of the Chang Tang, his target Lhasa—which he never reached.

Now nearly all these great explorers worked on the edges of Tibet, and generally only on the fringes of the northeast regions. As for the interior here, excepting for one or two trade routes, very little work had been accomplished, as the fanatical Moslem and Buddhist rulers did not want foreigners exploring anywhere in Tibet, which they considered the "heartland" of the Eurasian continent.

One day Dorje said, "The Polar regions are far better known and mapped than Tibet. This whole northeast quarter is extremely dangerous due to a heavy tribal population, and has been almost invariably circumvented by the oldtime explorers. Many explorers have lost their lives in there, and some are known, and some are not."

I lay down my book and crossed over to the table where he was drawing a map.

"You see, Clark, explorers have kept mainly to the main caravan routes, or like Hedin worked in the sparsely inhabited west, or in the south centering on Lhasa—the prize all of them wanted. But here in the northeast shadow area of Tibet is supposed to exist that fantastic mountain called Amne Machin, and it is evidently guarded by wild tribes almost totally unknown even here in China, or so say the Chinese and Mongols. But, where is it exactly!"

I took a chair alongside and waited, puffing on my pipe.

"Lieutenant Wilhelm von Filchner's German General Staff expedition of 1908, is our most reliable and up-to-date source of information on the practical approaches to this mystery mountain. He had not seen the peak, or heard of it from the natives, but I estimate he passed about 150 miles west of where my brother believes it to lie."

Many of the older German priests in Lanchow remembered von Filchner. They showed us photographs of him, a big hawk-faced man, wearing a long Chinese gown in absolute tatters and patches—always the condition of his clothes after one of his excursions into the interior. Von Filchner used to cuss so badly at times that the Fathers would not allow him inside their mission. Then he would apparently change overnight after a good rest, and be as gay and cheerful as an angel, and then would be permitted inside their walls again.

The black-robed Fathers were excited about our scheme, though very pessimistic about eventual success, for no American explorer other than Rockhill had ever been successful (according to them) in reaching any point in true inner Tibet off the beaten track. But they were of the greatest assistance in helping us; including the loan of von Filchner's precious German army instruments and one of his priceless maps. After nearly 300 years off and on at Lanchow, none of their priests had themselves been fortunate enough to break very far through the savage tribes and pierce the wild interior. Evidently many of these good missionaries—all of whom spoke Chinese and many of them Tibetan and Mongolian—had tried over the years, and all had failed.

"Do not be naïve," they warned us smiling and waggling their forefingers under our noses. "We hope you realize by now the great dangers attendant in Tibet. We do not wish our friends from Mongolia and America to die. Northeast Tibet is very dangerous. Even the great Sven Hedin stayed well west and north of it!"

The premonitions of the Lanchow savants were well grounded in past personal experiences, experiences involving capture, torture, death.

Thus two weeks passed in strenuous and exciting work. Lacking a stove, our workroom (my room), a dank stone-and-plaster cell, was often 15° Centigrade below zero. We ate barley soup and sausages, soggy gray potatoes and string beans, topping off with "coffee" made from burnt barley. We walked in the city, buying old maps, soap, inexpensive gifts for the Tibetans, and warm underwear, closing our eyes against the swirling dust storms, peering at the ancient walls and forts erected against the invading tribal hordes of inner Asia, watching the muddy flood of the icy Yellow River flow near the city. We did not dare to hope that one day we would actually stand in central Tibet with our horses' feet in its headwaters.

One day Dorje said, "You know, certain lamaist priests called *bomboms* can cause rain to fall on alternate squares as on a checkerboard. They have great magic power and can also predict the things to come. Yesterday I talked to a bombom and he raised his 'thunderbolt,' drank from his cup made out of a human skull and told his beads. He said I would reach a mountain called 'Amne Machin' and the weather would be clear."

"Maybe he heard a rumor," I suggested, alarmed, "this town is full of agents from a hundred countries and tribal regions."

"Maybe he did. And maybe he did not. Anything is possible here." He was certainly correct in that last, for that night word came by an officer that Governor Ma wished us to proceed at once to his headquarters in Sining.

It was on a Saturday, March 5th, 1949, in freezing weather before dawn that we said goodbye to our loyal friends Bishop Buddenbrock and Father Senge, and after leaving a note for our friend Mr. Gustav E. Söderbom set out on the dirt road to High Tartary in a westbound rattletrap Chinese postal truck.

These postal trucks were regular American machines left over from the war, having high board sides, and equipped with double sets of springs. They carried not only mail, but freight and passengers. The crew consisted usually of a driver, mechanic, ticket collector, and a general factotum whose duty was to put gasoline and oil in the right places, keep water in the radiator, change tires, and the like. Sometimes there were soldiers aboard to guard the truck and cargo, and kick off any non-paying hitchhikers. These Chinese postal trucks, and the postal system itself, were the only things in China said to be run on the level without graft. I personally know otherwise, but I wish to leave at least one Chinese Santa Claus in which doting missionaries can believe, and so will say no more.

The driver of this junk-heap said this was the first truck out in a week, his predecessor having been stopped on the road by a band of renegade Moslem riders who had cut the throats of the crew and the 23 passengers, robbing them and the cargo afterwards. Mud villages flew past, strangely robed people in wide-winged fur hats rode by on shaggy ponies—Mongols, Moslem Turkomen, Tibetans—all wearing thick sheepskin wrap-around robes and curly-toed boots, the men carrying rifles slung across their backs. Many of their saddles were very high and covered with rich carpets and even silver and coral decorations.

The frozen dirt road led across barren mountains and hills and quite often along the north bank of the yellowish ice-bound Sining River. Sometimes we got out and pushed, and once we had to walk on frozen feet about a mile by trail above the river, to lighten the load in the truck so that it could proceed in its ruts up and over a mountain. Aboard once more, sitting here and there on the cargo, mostly matts of rice and merchandise, and our faces, hands and feet freezing, we set out on the final leg.

After some 120 miles of hard jolting among local Moslem passengers and polite Chinese businessmen packed around us like sardines, and half-suffocated by garlic fumes (the curse of China), baggage, and the cages of Mongolian singing larks heaped around us, we hailed the stone battlements of the mighty walls of Sining—China's last great city, glowing with the light of the setting sun through a dry crystal atmosphere. We were already actually in north geographical Tibet!

Through the dusky, narrow streets of this scented (and in some streets stinking), bustling outpost of 60,000 Tibetans, Mongols, Chinese, Tungans, Taranchi, Turki, Ouizhurs, Quergares, Hussacks (or Khasaks), Salars, Afridis and Afghans, majestically moved caravans of the giant taffy-colored two-humped Bactrian camels and inky-black yaks, richly laden and tinkling with bells. This was the seat of the Chinghai Provincial Government of all-powerful General Ma Pu-fang whom we had been summoned to see.

Dorje's small carpet-bag and my suitcase deposited on the ground, we hopped down, and were immediately escorted by twenty heavily armed Moslem Tungan soldiers to the hostel, a red-lacquered seraglio with double-decked Turkish balconies opening on a square court decorated with potted paper flowers (a winter custom). There we met a smiling subordinate in a black robe who immediately led us to the Headquarters of the Governor.

After walking briskly through the mixed crowd already described, we turned off a cobbled street into a high-walled Chinese style *yamen,* guarded by grim-faced Moslem soldiers with bayonets fixed on rifles held horizontal to the ground. All these troops were uniformed in long black padded overcoats, and crossed with bandoliers of ammunition. We marched under a huge Chinese gate, one gorgeously tiled roof stacked above the other, and beyond a pair of stone lions saw several very impressive buildings with fluted tile roofs and up-sweeping corners, the windows covered with taut glazed paper. More guards had to be passed, for the military control was very strict and complicated, with much signing in at small desks, clicking of heels, saluting with guns and sabers, examination for concealed weapons, and the like. I noticed at this time, as I returned each salute by these soldiers under arms, that Dorje did likewise, and in an astonishingly smart military manner. This many-sided character and I were marched up to a very large building and halted. I had heard many times that Ma Pu-fang was a fierce man, who thought nothing of shooting down whole regiments of captured Communist troops, and I was prepared for anything.

Finally we were brought into a very large room furnished, in the Chinese manner, with classical scrolls of flowers, pheasants, gods and philosophers hanging on the walls. An orderly stiffly seated us in dragon-carved teak chairs and handed us cups of hot tea and a box of cigarettes. The Governor then entered alone, and the guards stood back at attention.

His bearing was most impressive, his long beard was silky black, his manners perfect and warmly cordial. As he took his seat close to us, I judged this Tungan governor to be about 50 years of age. His fierce eyes, quite at variance with the faint smile, never for an instant left mine as I talked through Dorje. I knew this ruler, and his powerful father before him, had barred all explorers from going into Tibet.

Ma Pu-fang speaking in Chinese, politely inquired:

"Did the honorable Mr. Clarka have a good trip to Sining?"

"Yes, the trip was delightful."

"Chinghai is not too cold?"

"No colder than in Lanchow."

And so it went for about fifteen minutes. We then got down to brass tacks, as the Governor had much business to attend to in regard to the war in China where his armies were fighting. In fact his armies were the only Nationalist ones left intact.

I restated my purpose and my wish for his support. Further, I contended that such an expedition as I proposed might show him whether in case of defeat by Lin Pao, the best of the Communist generals (then very much on his neck), part of his great northwest Chinese armies of a million infantry could retreat across the mountain passes into west and south Chinghai (geographically and ethnologically north and northeast Tibet), and even into the inner Tibetan provinces of U and Tsang, and carry on their anti-Communist campaign there. He could become the bulwark against Red invasion of India. Scientists could investigate flood control, map the sources of the Yellow River, and study food possibilities among the Tibetan herds, and political officers could negotiate for treaties.

Dorje calmly smoked his cigarette and put all this into the flowery and official Chinese reserved for conversation with great men. Dorje would watch me and listen intently to a sentence at a time, then raise his hand and interpret, never letting me go beyond a stretch of fifteen or twenty words. This was not only to express to Ma Pu-fang my exact ideas, but also to show that ruler that he, Dorje, was not saying anything on his own responsibility, for should Ma be offended, it could well mean the Mongol prince's neck.

If I put the right ideas and words into Dorje's ears, I knew that Ma would receive them precisely correct at the other end, but even with this marvelous interpreting, it was going to take a bit of doing. When I had finished, I knew the Governor would either permit me to enter Tibet and foot the bill himself, or would take us out and have us shot in the courtyard. Here, just about word for word, is what I said in that big room ringed with guards holding cocked guns at shooting position:

"Excellency, I have recently been a free-lance observer at the Arab League in Cairo, Egypt. This is a sort of congress composed of various Moslem nations in Africa, Egypt, Arabia, and the Near East. In six months I learned much. I believe wholeheartedly that the entire Moslem belt extending half across the world, from the Pacific Ocean off Manchuria to the Atlantic across Asia and north Africa, must become the area for an eventual counterattack by the Moslems themselves against militant world totalitarian Communism. That is, if you wish to preserve your culture and your political freedom in any degree at all. Turkey must become the western hinge of this attack on Russia and her allies, and Ma Pu-fang—potentially stronger in a strategic sense than all the Arab League nations combined, with Turkey thrown in for good measure—must become the eastern hinge of this mighty wing of unbroken Moslems in their three hundred millions, who maintain contact with the twenty million suppressed Mohammedans within the Soviet bloc itself. The North Polar regions must, if war is declared by Russia, become the third pivot for attack. World War III can only be diverted if we recognize our potentialities in this interlocking continental scheme, and prepare to execute it now. World War III, then, if it should come, could truly be known as the 'War of the Triangle,'—Western Europe, Arctic (U. S. Air Army), Moslem Central Asia, and Africa."

Ma Pu-fang dropped his cigarette, but calmly reached out for another. He did not actually smoke this cigarette, for being orthodox Moslem he neither smoked or drank, but he held it out of politeness. I lit it for him before one of the soldiers could reach his side.

"Mr. Clark has a very steady hand," he observed quietly to Dorje, "I should rather think he would not be afraid to die before a firing squad."

Thus he had his little joke, and smiled faintly when I answered "No," through Dorje.

I had never seen a face like his; absolutely still, the eyes set at a metal-edged angle, never leaving mine. We continued our talk on how the Moslems themselves could regain their Red-infiltrated or lost lands, and the strategy and tactics to accomplish all this I am not going into detail about, but the end of it was unexpectedly sudden.

Governor Ma Pu-fang was a man who asked no congress or parliament to ratify anything important, for he was not only dictator, but

virtual and absolute law over life and death in all this part of
Central Asia. Also he was evidently a man of quick decision; for he
informed Dorje and me, on the spot, that we were to remain in
Sining as the guests of the government. Also he had decided to adopt
and expedite all my plans without reservation. He would personally
order the commissioning, equipping, furnishing, of a corps of scientists, and supply and finance up to any amount this expedition into
South Chinghai towards Lhasa.

When we stood up and shook hands, China had officially entered
the field of Tibetan and Amne Machin exploration, aligning her
ancient name alongside those of England, India, France, America,
Germany, and Russia. But much effort, of a kind new to exploration
and explorers, faced me before this unprecedented Asian-backed
expedition could materialize.

We returned to our quarters under guard and made ourselves
comfortable in the most luxurious suite in the city—long red-lacquered sitting room and bedrooms, all with real glass windows and
stoves as well as the Chinese brass charcoal burners. The room was
in old Chinese wallpaper, the furniture in the style of that country.

From this base I now undertook a short mission of extreme importance—a personal call on the Tibetan Panchen Lama, the 12-year-
old "living Buddha" whom some ten million followers in China,
Tibet, the northern hill states of India, Manchuria, Siberia, Inner
and Outer Mongolia, and Ladakh (or Little Tibet), all directly
honor and worship as the incarnate god of Tibet and lamaism; specifically, he is the Pope of the Ge-Luk-pa, Yellow Hat Sect (Reform
Church).

His Holiness is known also as the Tashi Lama, Reincarnation of
Öpame, Buddha of Boundless Light, Spiritual Godhead of Chenrezi,
the Protector of Tibet and Buddhism. At the great cloister city of
Kumbum, twenty miles south of Sining, His Holiness Tham-je
Khen-pei (as his secretary wrote it out for me) received Dorje and
me in formal audience in the flower-filled heavenly throne room.
Besides being real, and of paper, many of the flowers were made of
rare metals and jewels; emeralds, diamonds, jade, rubies, pearls,
their stems being of gold. Probably not since the days of Harun-al-
Rashid had such a garden bloomed. Above the throne was the sacred
baldaquin, umbrella of Heaven, and, flanking it, were gigantic Tibetan guards in red and yellow togas, their jeweled hands resting on

sword hilts. Behind us were massive doors of shining red lacquer fitted with massive brass (or gilded) plates and ring-bolts. Many of the attendants backed out, prostrating themselves in the doorway before the bolts were shot.

During the audience pigeons with whistles concealed in their tail feathers flew about in a potted garden court, providing an eerie musical background to our conversations. These were carried on in relays of English, Chinese (which the Panchen—or Tashi—is not supposed to understand, but does), and high Tibetan court language through interpreters: thus no earthly vibrations from me to the living Buddha could possibly contaminate His spiritual purity, the Light of the Real.

His Holiness, with considerable assistance from his advisors, dictated a letter in the Tibetan adaptation of Sanskrit to all Tibetans (there are about 3,000,000 of them), ordering that they assist and not obstruct our work in the Forbidden Land, which is not called "Tibet" by Tibetans, but Bod (or Bhöd) and inhabited by Bhōt-ias (possibly Europeans got the name "Tibet" from the Chinese, who call it To-bhöt). Advisors said that fast-mounted messengers would be sent far and wide throughout the northeast areas of Tibet. Radio transmitters would beam out this order: thus the High Lama of the Chokang Cathedral in medieval Lhasa, center of lamaism, would know of His Holiness' desires. The Tibetan *Kashak* (Cabinet) and the *Lönchen* (Prime Minister) would be advised, as would be the *Tsongdu* (National Assembly). The Dalai Lama, enthroned at the Potala, would be contacted. Though I suspected much of this was polite talk, still I treasured this ally, for never before in history had a Panchen Lama cooperated with an explorer during the planning stage of an expedition. Sven Hedin had once befriended a Panchen Lama, but only after he had forced a way into Tibet under protest of the Tibetans, and this could scarcely be called "cooperation."

At any rate, the Panchen suggested we go into the court outside and have our picture taken together, with me standing beside him, as this photograph could be useful when I later traveled among the chiefs and lamas. This we did. As I left the palace, hundreds of lamas, *geshe* (Doctors of Divinity), *gelongs* (priests), dignitaries and monks of all degrees were all about the temple buildings, prostrating themselves endlessly before their golden, black, red, and white idols, to the western mind (as explained to me by Dorje) almost incomprehensible symbols. Gautama smiled gigantically from *padmasana* (lotus posture) on all who would renounce the anguish of worldly existence and its material manifestations and bathe themselves in the wondrous light of His divine wisdom and will.

In the wooden floors the lamas had worn grooves from rising and falling flat before the beloved Buddhas. The small undying flames of many lovely silver, copper, brass and gold-plated butter-lamps—some reaching to my chest—flickered and danced above the prostrated human forms, adding a rancid odor to dank temple air but dispersing very little of the deepening shadows of the massive banner-hung rooms. According to local authorities Kumbum was probably established in 1516, 140 years after the death of Tsong Kapa (or Tsong Ka-pa) founder of the Yellow Church. Tsong Kapa, the Man from the Land of Onions, Am-do province (today northeast Tibet) was born in the year 1358, and later founded the monasteries of Gan-den and Se-ra, which today (together with Dre-pung) are the most important in Tibet. I was escorted by the seemingly six-and-a-half foot *Chötrimpa* or Overseer, in full canonicals—a yellow-fringed Grecian type helmet, cloaked in both dark and light red gowns and togas having armored shoulders exaggeratedly wide, and carrying an enormous square-hafted golden mace of authority—and seated with a *mantram* (blessing) in my American station wagon.

That night back in Sining (Hsi-ning), Ma Pu-fang held a gay Arabian-night's party in my honor. At the Moslem Governor's palace, in the Chinese style government yamen, before 300 guests representing not only the Chinese but most of the races of central Asia, the most beautiful dancing girls of High Tartary displayed their silk-screened charms. Some were from Kucha, said to be the greatest beauties and coquettes of Asia, formerly sent as tribute to the emperors of China and to those rulers of much of the known world, the Khans of Mongolia. One *houri* in diaphanous gold and blue (the color of Eternity) I pictured as Roxelana, Alexander's queen, and not without reason, for she was magnificent whirling in the same symbolic dance, perhaps that of the Seven Veils of Maya.

Even Prince Dorje forgot his books to polish his pince-nez carefully and scrutinize these sleek girls, especially the lovely, golden-bodied Persian-looking one whose self-control over the various parts of her joyous anatomy seemed to hypnotize the dry Mongol savant.

Musicians played intricate oriental strains possibly, my friend

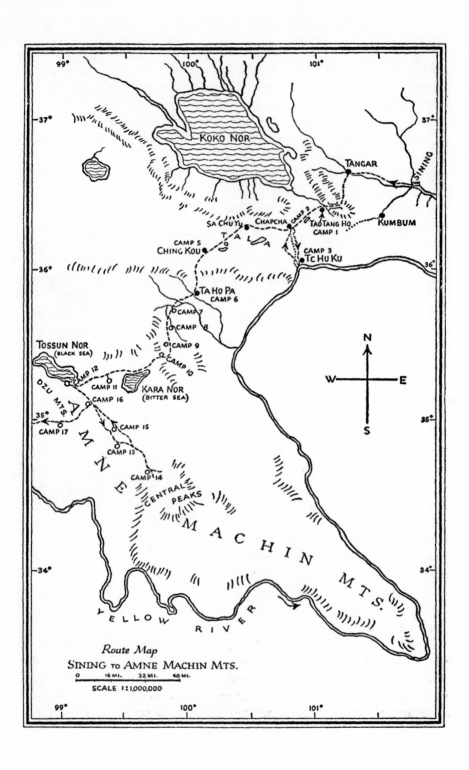

Route Map
SINING TO AMNE MACHIN MTS.

SCALE 1:1,000,000

thought, from ancient Persia and Samarkand, and others from Arabia and even Babylonia, from Mongolia and the ancient Chinese kingdom of Wei. Poets whose cultural roots lay (so it was suggested) in Byzantium and Egypt and the Great Mogul's Delhi Court, recited such unknown odes as *Beautiful Flower and Full Moon, Good Friends, Young Lovers Are Like the Mandarin Birds,* and (at my request, which pleased the governor), from Omar Khayyám. Rose-scented Khotan wines were served in small cups and, using chopsticks, we feasted on Kansu grapes, candied Bokhara melons, and then, with our hands, ate rare dishes in Moslem style—jellylike sheep tendons, heaps of specially bred black-skinned chickens, fat de-sexed pigeons strung on skewers, juicy, buttered yak steaks broiled over charcoal, unleavened bread, gazelle *shashlik* prepared on ramrods, ending the meal with the customary Chinese bowl of rice. Governor Ma leaned over saying that the best shashlik is prepared on the steppes from horse meat salted and tenderized by carrying it on a horse's back under the saddle.

"If only I could go into Tibet with you!" he smiled.

Soon our preparations were complete. Men and animals stood ready. There were wagonloads of saddlery and tons of animal feed. Our soldiers had been equipped with the best European .30-caliber rifles, and these in the main were loaded with 180-grain bullets, though a few had heavy 220-grain ammunition. Since I must go in disguise to escape possible assassins' bullets, bootmakers had fitted me out with Tibetan felt boots of various elegant patterns, and tailors had devised Chinese padded winter uniforms for wearing under practical Tibetan sheepskins and Bengal-lancer type robes trimmed with gold- and silver-woven bands. The robes had sleeves that hung eighteen inches below my fingertips. Rooflike Tibetan red-fox hats were my headgear, as well as an Astrakhan cap of black unborn lamb. A dagger, with damaskeened blade, the haft of ivory inlaid with gold—fine Lhasa work—and Mauser sidearm fairly describes my costumes.

Our last medical injections were completed.

Then, quite suddenly, I hit a snag and all my careful and intricate plans over the weeks of uncertainty seemed doomed for the ashcan. The exploration was off. Apparently chiefs professing all the faiths of Asia were approaching Governor Ma Pu-fang with protests at accepting a foreigner (and an American at that!) as leader of an expedition into Tibet. Evidently my political work had not even been started. The horses were unsaddled . . . the men sent to their barracks.

Many years before, members of Dr. Sven Hedin's great Central Asiatic Expedition had been imprisoned on reaching Sinkiang, stopped cold in Hami, the capital of Chinese Turkestan. To get started again and avoid a duplication of such misfortune in Tibet, my political arrangements had to be more thorough. I therefore got busy and concluded arrangements with strategically located semi-independent "ruby" Mongols—princes of the first class, chiefs of the Khoshoit, Khalka, Torgut and Charos federations—who through their *chanse* (secretariate), controlled important *Hoshun* (Leagues and Banners) and *Sumon* (Arrows) about which according to Sir Charles Bell, England's great Tibetan scholar and former righthand man in Lhasa, almost nothing is known.

Among my new friends was the powerful and personally beautiful six-foot Princess Chöd-Jab, cousin of Dorje, war and political leader of the North Banner of the Torgut Khanate, and senator in the Chinese Legislative Yuan. Centuries earlier her Torguts, perhaps numbering 400,000 under Aguk Khar, migrated to Russia and settled along the Volga to form the south front against Islam, whose expanding empire based on Constantinople threatened not only Russia but western Europe. The Great Mogul of India may (according to local legend) have come through lineal descent from her own Banner. Her connections with kings, kinglets, lamas, dictators and generals were apparently enormous. At any rate, in this part of Asia, her power and prestige were not to be ignored by any government agency let alone a would-be explorer.

Certain Turko *Aksakals* (White Beards) were also called upon for support: to which they agreed, though obviously puzzled that Ma Pu-fang, ruler (in a practical sense) of east Islam, had trusted a Christian as the leader of his Tibetan expedition. I also negotiated with wily citizens among the Sarts, townspeople of Turkestan who had migrated to the Moslem-conquered sedentary regions of north Chinghai. The headmen among these sat on *kangs* spread with Khotan rugs and pulled thoughtfully on small metal hubblebubbles, softly smiling their allegiance. No one in this part of Asia ever gives an outright no, so of course I never quite knew where I stood. I gathered from Dorje that this was not a flower garden where one

could easily pick flowers, but a very complex situation in which he
and Solomon Ma, our new friend, were very much involved. Solomon Ma was a young English-speaking Tungan, a trusted confidant
of the governor himself. Without him, certainly, there would not
have been the ghost of a chance for this journey of ours.

One morning—while thus winding up our affairs at this crossroads
of Asia—the *imams* (Moslem priests), a few of whom had been to
Holy Mecca in far Arabia, held in Dorje's and my honor an unprecedented breakfast at which a hundred of the foremost Moslem
military officers, politicians, and dignitaries of the church were commanded by the governor to appear. After ablutions, a High Church
feast was held at a splendid Chinese-style mosque, with its towering
blue, uniquely-interlocking wooden blocks fitted under fluted porcelain eaves, and its bowers of golden flowers supported by enormous
shiny red pillars. Blue pigeons rustled and flew over and settled in
the vast stone-flagged court around our carpets; green-robed *muez-
zins* called from the minarets for the faithful to witness the glory of
Allah, God the Compassionate, the Merciful.

During our *tête-à-tête* over fragrant teacups in which tiny blossoms opened, I was told that these imams and the other high church-
men were nearly all Tungan, of the same fierce giant race as General
Ma Pu-fang (who, on his mother's side, I understood, is partly Chinese). Evidence was said to have been presented by a Moslem
anthropologist that the Tungans may be descendants of the Medes,
an ancient Aryan race of Persia which had reached its glory in
600 B.C. only to be conquered by Cyprus in the reign of Astyages,
successor of Belshazzar. Tall men, one or two in dyed beards (as I
recall), smiling yet grave, their heads crowned with white or Nile-
green turbans, they blessed our expedition to Amne Machin, speaking softly in what Dorje called *mulla*, designed for international
intrigue in the Yuan Dynasty of the Mongol Kublai Khan.

Next, the Chinese civic leaders of Sining, not to be outdone,
donned their black silken gowns and gave a feast with classical
music in the beautiful Confucius Temple with its green dragon
curled watchfully on crisp glazed tiles forming the fluted roof. Nor
did I forget to pay my respects to the Tibetan abbot of the Sining
lamaist temple. Later the city elders trooped me over to the pagodas
of the City Temple to have our fate forecast by the immense red-
robed god "Chang Huang Yeh." The bearded god had received his

plaque of office from the Son of Heaven on his Dragon Throne in the Forbidden City in Peking. Amid the prayer-smokes, curling incense, and the beating of gongs and drums, I was gravely told, not without smiles, that I must be very cautious . . . or, the "God of Death" would stand at my elbow. Now while all this may seem incredible to modern 20th Century Americans and Europeans, it must be remembered that time in this corner of the world had gone back a thousand years, and that while in Rome I must do as the Romans do.

Stronger political fences now seemed raised at my back, and not without apprehension I checked them off: Tibetan (Panchen Lama); Moslem (Church); Chinese (Central Government); Northwest Political Headquarters (Ma Pu-fang); Mongol (Hutuktus—explained as living Buddha followers of the "ghost" of Bogdo Gegen, formerly in Urga and worshiped throughout the four Khanates of Mongolia; and also the followers of the late Yolros Lama, spiritual ruler of Inner Mongolia seated at Bater Halak Sume's Temple of the Larks); the lords of the Chinghai Leagues and Banners; and finally all the available headmen and princes of the scattered minorities.

My order was completed and sealed with my old OSS red Chinese chop, to move the expedition out of base and into Tibet.

On April 5, with a thumping of hooves and screeching of stallions, the first sections of what was probably the greatest civilian expedition of exploration * ever to leave for inner Tibet, traversed the hills out of the narrow valley of Kumbum Lamasery, twenty miles south of Sining, blessed by the mitered abbot of its 2,800 Tibetan, Mongolian, and other inmates who in the prayer-halls were said to be invoking for us the transcendental aid of Dröma, Goddess of Mercy, Queen of Heaven. Our ears tuned to the bee-like hum of countless spinning *chörlos* (prayer-wheels), we rode past red, white-and-black-banded temples some of which had roofs of sheet gold (probably plated) flashing in the rising sun.

Everywhere overhead gleamed tall golden spires and columns called *gyepi*, hammered with animal and various symbolic images. Our progression was at first flanked by white and gold *chörtens*—towering sarcophagus memorials, stupas containing the ashes of lamas beheaded by an invading Chinese army—now dedicated to the

---

* I do not include the Younghusband expedition against Lhasa, as this constituted an official *military* invasion of Tibet.

five material elements: earth, water, air, fire, and ether. Our way was heralded by foghorn-like blasts from silver-copper horns, some of which appeared to be twelve feet or more in length. On my high Turki saddle was draped a blue spiderweb-silk *hadak* (or *katak,* or *kattak* according to the lama's vernacular). a ceremonial scarf symbolic of the rainbow, blessed and sent as a reverent farewell by the Panchen Lama, who watched from his palace window on a hillside. I was mounted on Black Moon of Alashan, a Mongolian stallion from Black Gobi loaned me by Marshal Ma-yuan, Governor Ma's son commanding the reputed million troops of the Chinese field armies fighting desperately against the Communists around Sian and other strategic parts of north and northwest China.

The two governors of central and south Chinghai rode gravely with me in the role of Chinese-Moslem emissaries on skittish blooded Torgut stallions of the *Khara Shar* breed, a liver-roan and a flaming sorrel. Their robes were of Kashmiri velvet, sky blue and ox-blood red, gold-trimmed; their filigreed cavalry sabers and automatic Belgian sidearms were worked in various designs. Together these two officers, Colonel Ma Sheng-lung and Captain Tan Chen-te, mainly by sheer personal force, controlled for Governor Ma and China an area the size of Colorado. They were Tungans, fierce and clever men without the knowledge of fear, whose followers deliberately sought death "that they might 'live'."

As these two men are very important to the record of my journey in search of Amne Machin—a record of semi-starvation, incredible loyalties and disloyalties, some hardship, many disappointments and troubles, and perhaps a few successes—I must describe them in detail. They soon proved themselves to be my strongest and most loyal friends and (for a time) my bitterest adversaries. Even on that first day, though old comrades, the two governors engaged in a game of slashing each other with whips of plaited wild-yak leather, while their frightened stallions plunged and raced through the caravan, until one of the shouting combatants was thrown from his horse as it reared up and fell backwards.

While riding to the tune of creaking saddles through the *obo-* and temple-studded hills west of Kumbum I studied this pair out of the corner of my eye. Colonel Ma's black Moslem skullcap was worn like a navy sailor's, cocked over one narrow, baleful, dark-brown eye. The other one (for a few days) had a black patch on it. About forty, he was thick-set, not six feet tall, sausage-necked in the way that Prussian officers are supposed to be but seldom are, shave-headed, beet-red-faced; his hoarse voice was already heard bellowing orders, directing the line of march, sending out scouts to watch for possible Tibetan snipers out after a rifle, scolding half-playfully, slashing at tardy soldiers with a brass-tipped whip. He showed his teeth—flashing golden choppers that would do credit to a horse—in frequent fierce smiles; whenever he dismounted to tend to the call of nature he leapt back on his horse and into the high Mongol velvet-covered saddle without even using its silver-plated stirrups; in jest he called himself "Sultan of Tibet."

The other, his running partner, was not so obvious; he ran less to the physical and more to the psychological. Also about forty, Tan Chen-te was a tall thin man, almost an ascetic, who smiled frequently—not to show off his flashing white teeth but, I suspected, to throw you off your guard; suave in a worldly manner, inflexible in determination, quick as a steel whip when his temper was roused, which was to prove often. Abdul, one of the younger officers, whispered to Dorje that Tan could cut a man's head off in battle with a single stroke. Whether such a loyal remark was justified I had no way of knowing.

As the long column bucketed along I sized up our personal bodyguard: it consisted of dashing, weather-beaten, and considerably scarfaced fighting *hui hui*, (Moslem soldiers-of-fortune), for the most part dressed like dandies in fur caps, red robes, and either Tibetan or polished black Cossack boots: fifty hand-picked Salar and Tungan guerrilla cavalrymen mostly from Shengwha and Hochou, each of whom bore at least one wound fighting Communists. One of them, Habibu, was said to have had nineteen gunshot and sword wounds. I suggested he might have been hit at long range by a shotgun, and this fellow lost no time showing a few of his more dramatic wounds. There were among them apparently a few Afridis and Sharaunis (who called themselves Tungan), outlaws probably—too hot for even their own tribes to handle—blood enemies of the old British Raj on Khyber Pass, enemies of the Afghan kings. In addition to these so-called Sining Moslems, were twenty swaggering Tibetan fighting scouts, fanatical Buddhists claiming to be deliberately seeking liberation to *Nirvana,* Heaven, through a speedy death; none under six feet. They were armed with businesslike European rifles, German or Belgian automatic battle-pistols (a few of the magazines holding fifty shots), short Tibetan daggers suspended on long chains and also the broadswords of the Tibetans.

As the miles increased between Governor Ma Pu-fang and me, I feared my control over these men would decrease in exact proportion.

On this first leg of our journey we traveled light, our basic transport consisting now of eighty yaks (Tibetan oxen), seventy saddle horses bred for work at extreme altitudes, and a herd of remounts, pack-mules, and a few camels. Much later, wagons drawn by oxen would be added. Even pack-sheep. Of necessity, we were considered for all practical outward purposes, a military attacking party; as a guerrilla lieutenant colonel behind the Japanese lines in the late war, I already saw a few minor faults in the order-of-march which could probably be streamlined. At the moment, however, I did not antagonize Ma and Tan by any such ideas. At times I never quite knew whether I was guest or leader. Among our caravaners in a separate supporting group were blacksmiths and a veterinary, a medical doctor and his helper, a geologist of sorts, a topographer, a biologist and botanist, a horse-buyer, a law court, a professor of languages and acting surveyor, a meteorologist, a section of professional trackers (who knew the trail code-signs), game hunters, an army imam, political and military strategists, an epizootic scientist, intelligence operators, machine-gunners for our Japanese pieces. Habitual smokers of opium, which comes in part from the secret government poppy fields in west Szechwan, and of *hashish*, or *charas*, which is produced in Chinese Turkestan, had been weeded out at my suggestion.

Such was the caravan that maneuvered over the weeks to come in a long sinuous column of men and animals, bobbing across broad yellowish, dismal Tibetan upland plateaus, working over boundless screes, making its way through sandy deserts, bogging down in wide sterile gray mud flats, finally to emerge and plunge into an icy riddle of mountain ranges. The shadows of the caravan grew long, and so after a ride of ten hours through the freezing cold of late winter, the bugle called a halt, and we drew up to form a defensible encampment, for strangers were reported near.

Eight tents, black yak-hair ones and blue-and-white "flower tents" with formalized good-luck designs stamped on their sides soon

glowed through the dusk like jack-o'-lanterns on the shadowy plateau. We selected our campsite with an eye to defense, as well as
to pasturage (poor as it was), water, and yak dung for fuel. The
drivers tethered their tired but (at this stage) mildly contented and
cud-chewing yaks in sections of twenty to squares of lines pegged flat
on the plain. As the ground was frozen, most of the wooden pegs
merely broke off as we pounded them with stones, and iron ones
were brought out. Dung fires were set for cooking, warmth, and
watching. Circular barricades of grain bags and assorted packs were
stacked for protection against possible assault in the darkness. Sentries posted to the night-watch patrolled our periphery. Later I
went out and instructed them to hide behind rocks and bushes or
keep low in hollows and not to expose our position so readily.
Reconnaissance scouts on fresh horses ranged a mile or so beyond.

Such precautions were evidently necessary: the intelligence
branch of rather dirty-faced Tibetan Tangut * scouts had allegedly
reported to Colonel Ma earlier on the march that an entire Moslem
cavalry regiment screening ahead had not long before lost all its
horses; they were afoot, every man jack of them, and over 200 were
estimated dead. Another cavalry detachment riding far to the south
had been caught in a narrow defile by a large force of Tibetan
tribesmen out raiding, and massacred to the last man—all but the
commanding colonel, a friend of Ma Sheng-lung's, who had been
suspended by leather thongs tied to his arms and thrown in the
Yellow River, raised by the thongs for a quick gasp of air each
time he was about to die . . . finally released only after a two-hour
torture. Now or later, I had no way of personally cross-checking
such troop movements, numbers of men or casualties involved, or
even dates, and though probably greatly exaggerated for one reason
or another, I report them in this instance only for what they might
be worth—if only to show that Chinese control of the region was
not as secure as I had been led to believe in Sining and Lanchow.
Tibetans were no doubt, however, closely watching all troop movements southward due to fear of a general retreat into Tibet should
the Communists eventually prevail over Ma Pu-fang. I suspected
these two detachments had nothing to do with us, but had been on a
mission of their own at some earlier time, and Colonel Ma and

---

* Tangut—the Mongolian name for Tibetans, now locally applied to a tribe living
around Koko Nor, west of Sining.

Captain Tan were using this story as a means for impressing Dorje and me that we were not on a picnic. In fact, at this time, I had every reason to believe we were considered more enemy than friend, and only tolerated because of fear of Ma Pu-fang.

Colonel Ma explained that Tibetans will carefully slit open a living man's abdomen, and put their hand inside in order to squeeze his heart. And after the Tibetans would come the Ngoloks (or Golaks) . . . devils incarnate. Even now, early in the game, I wondered just how much Colonel Ma really hoped for a successful ending to this journey, which to his soldier's mind must seem a useless thing with great events such as war at hand.

Except for the noise of what they called wild dogs far out on the flat, we heard nothing. Ma thought the raiders were waiting for us to get cornered in a pocket, and it was his intention to steer clear of all such places. Instead of using heavy screens of troops to protect the caravan, for (if the reports were true) even Ma Pu-fang might suddenly decide we were paying too high a price for exploration and Amne Machin, I decided to convince them we must rely upon trickery and guile, fast and slow marches, twists and turns and back-tracking; camping away from age-old traditional caravan stops and circulating false rumors among the tribes as to our strength and routes. In this, both Tan and Ma eventually agreed. I decided that a few basic necessary adjustments in strategy had become obvious. A messenger had arrived, and not all was as well in Kumbum and Sining as it had seemed when we left. I had to return, therefore, and build political fences *ahead* of us, as well as patch up those *behind*.

By order of the governor, Tan was placed in command. Colonel Ma would stay with him and help the caravan through what they believed to be a dangerous pass region, and then join us. Under cover of darkness, I detached myself and rode back toward Kumbum a few degrees north of east. Tibetan tribesmen were undoubtedly hovering all about camp; through their light screen I crept forward with my two companions—Prince Dorje and Solomon Ma, the six-foot, bespectacled Tungan confidant of the governor who was the expedition's political liaison officer—keeping low in the bottoms of gullies, dismounting twice to scout a way past the camp fires, but finally breaking clear and passing beyond the tribesmen. This I had done behind Japanese lines for OSS over a nineteen-month period, and so found it old routine. By a more circuitous route we three would later intercept the expedition at Fort Ta Ho Pa. It is of course one of the rules of guerrillas never to follow the same route twice running. Fort Ta Ho Pa lay far south of the Sun and Moon Mountains, just below Tangar (Hwangyuan), also Tenkar, which lies thirty miles west of Sining. Colonel Ma would pick us up somewhere in the Sun and Moon Mountains and lead us to Ta Ho Pa.

To make a fast cold journey short, we safely reached Kumbum's holy residence, and there the aged retinue of cardinals and prelates attending the divine Panchen Lama received us coldly, though outwardly with smiles. Yes, they insisted, they had done all they could, but after all they had little power, they had helped us and if we had failed it was not the fault of Kumbum. By power alone we could not get into Tibet, that much I knew. We had to have the Panchen Lama's support, however limited. There was only one way to get it. . . .

During our audience, Dorje and I turned the conversation into new channels, as it was rapidly developing into a heated (though smiling) argument between the lamas and Solomon Ma. Now it is said the way to power and glory, to friendship and riches in Tibet lies always through religion. If I had forgotten that before, I knew it now, and it is never too late to reform. Through interpreters I began to talk about the ancient Mon Nordic Sanskrit scriptures pertaining to Shâkti and Shâkta, which I learned something of during a spot of war service in India.

Of the entire court apparently only two lamas, venerable men in silken red-and-purple *gyasoks* (gowns), had heard of these profoundly sacred theories and doctrine based on the old Vedantic philosophy of the *Shâkta Tantrashastra,* dealing with will or power, ideas, nature and the creation of life, matter and worlds without end through the illusion of time, and through *Ātmanic* (Soul) revelation.

The two old lamas became quite enthused, and spread the good news. Such abstract knowledge, I was learning, is often essential when trying to provoke even a reasonably good impression among the lamaists. And so, bluntly to approach personal business without first discoursing on abstractions would constitute a breach of good manners, making me *persona non grata* . . . and that is exactly what had happened on the first visit, though I was too stupid to know it.

I watched the Panchen Lama's face. His personal charm, rare in one so young, was not diminished by brocade vestments stiff with gold threads and rich silken togas of yellow, purple, and vermilion. He (or the interpreters at any rate) began to speak less guardedly, and soon the cat came bounding out of the bag. The Panchen Lama finally waved everybody out of the throne room except his *guru* (spiritual advisor) and a Tibetan colonel acting as official interpreter, and asked if he might, through me, request Ma Pu-fang to place him—the Panchen Lama!—at the head of a Moslem army so that he could invade Lhasa. Once beyond the Turquoise Bridge there, he would install himself at the Potala on the Dalai Lama's "temporal" throne, as well as retain his own "religious" throne at Tashi-Lhünpo, or Shigatse—the Rome of lamaism.

Since this is part of the story of Amne Machin I must explain that it is difficult for a Dalai Lama to live to be over eighteen years of age, for the law reads that on coming into his majority, he will exercise full ruling powers. The regents, being usually men of the world (pigtailed men) and not living gods (shave-heads), sometimes object to this; and the Dalai Lama, bound to the Wheel of Life like any human being, is usually called by the heavenly powers to present himself on earth in another incarnation. More precisely, a court poisoner is produced; aconite is used on ordinary lamas and politicians, but a secret drug at present unknown is said to be reserved for the living Buddha. The Dalai Lama's title may come from one given a predecessor by a Mongol chief, this being Dalai Lama Vjradhara "All Embracing Lama, Holder of the Thunderbolt." And while no layman would dare seize the throne for himself, the Panchen Lama's court apparently did dare.

The reason is that the Panchen is considered by them to be spiritually superior to the Dalai Lama. Also he has other claims based on history. In 1252 Kublai Khan gave sovereign powers over Tibet to a Sa-kya-pa lama named Pak-pa. He was to rule the provinces of U and Tsang (in the south), Kam (in the southeast), and Am-do (in the northeast). This dynasty ruled under twenty-one lamas successfully for seventy years (1270-1340). Now, the Dalai Lama, so they say, is temporal monarch of Tibet, and as such he is the Godhead *Gyaawarinpoche,* "The Great Gem of Majesty." However, *Öpome* is the spiritual father of Chenrezi, and it is from this legendary protector of Tibet that the Panchen Lama is believed to be reincarnated. Spiritually, then, the Panchen Lama is the holy of holies, ranking in this theological kingdom, in some quarters at least, even above the Dalai Lama.

Be that as it may, since it mattered not to me which of the pair was on the throne, or whether they ruled jointly, I answered:

"I will approach Governor Ma for you, *if* you will make true arrangements with the Tibetans between here and Amne Machin peak!" *

By nightfall our mission to the Panchen Lama and to Governor Ma was completed. It seemed that Ma Pu-fang was already familiar with Kumbum's ambitions for transferring the court to south Tibet, and he only smiled but annotated no further. Anyway I breathed easier. Prince Dorje, Solomon Ma, and I—torpid with the cold—again left Sining, this time by station wagon, waving to serious-faced Secretary General Ma-chi the Deputy Governor; and charming Mr. Gow, the right-hand man of the governor in his Chinese Legislative Yuan; both of whom came to see us off for what they probably hoped would be the last time. They even then must have sensed Nationalist defeat in China, and the collapse of Ma Pu-fang's armies in Inner Mongolia, Turkestan, the north China provinces and Tibet, and hinted that should we fail again no part of the Moslem armies could be saved from slaughter at the hands of the victorious Communists under Mao Tse-tung's ablest general—Lin Pao. With us also rode the Bishop of Chinghai, my delightful German friend, the Very Reverend Msgr. Hieronymus Haberstroh, who said,

"You, my friend, are very fortunate. We do not understand your success with Ma Pu-fang. Do you work for him?"

Thirty miles west of Sining the chauffeur turned in at a gate of the city wall of Tangar. At Magistrate Wong Wei-chung's invitation we established quarters in the offices of his government yamen, saying goodbye to the Bishop who wished me all good fortunes of the road. Here with the aid of army orderlies we changed to the Tibetan disguises. These, of course did not deceive anyone at close range, but were intended at least to make me less conspicuous to Tibetans looking us over from a distance.

---

* The Moslems did not support the Panchen and invade Lhasa, though it was not long before he was brought into south Tibet by the Communists where he and the Dalai Lama now rule under the Communists.

From the poplar forest in the valley below the city walls could be heard faintly the sweet calls of the so-called giant lark, *melano-croryphoides* (the name diligently furnished by Prince Dorje). To-morrow we would enter the forbidden land of Tibet. At Tangar meteorological observations were begun, for later correcting meas-urements of Amne Machin.

That night Dorje, a true Mongol, half-humorously arranged for our three horoscopes to be cast. Now I am not superstitious but the result of this little play did not ease my apprehensions of what lay in store for us, and I somehow felt in my bones that it truly forecast endless troubles. When the fortune-teller had finished his séance he rose to his feet hurriedly, and in a fluster grabbed up his holy books, charts, and other paraphernalia, and ran from our presence. Dorje followed, but the priest, apparently shaking with fright (more probably religious abhorrence), would not utter a word nor would he take any pay.

That last really got me to worrying.

2

Living Gods and a Massacre

BUNDLED in fur robes, we left Tangar at 10 A.M. heading for the nearest Moslem fort, Tao Tang Ho, still by station wagon. The road made us clinch our teeth, for it was rough as a washboard, leading along a frozen narrow riverine valley which headed on a southward strike. Tall poplar trees, stripped to the skin of every leaf, lined the fields and the icy river bed. The steeply rising hills and grim, stark, rock-walled canyons on both sides were of tilted sedimentary formations laid down in bands, and shattered by folding and weather and possibly by extrusive abutments of basaltic structures thrust up from below.

On rather high wind-blasted mountain slopes of yellow scree, Solomon Ma apprehensively pointed out in sheltered places only short grass, starvation fodder for our animals, old last year's ground cover soughing dismally in the wind. Here and there, clad in sheepskin robes, were rifle- and musket-armed *Chang-pas,* nomads from the Chang Tang (or Chang-t'ang) plateau in central Tibet—wildlooking and shaggy-haired. Above the river banks were the *Rong-pas,* valley agriculturists, distinguished by their coral-embellished pigtails.

There were also a few Mongols dejectedly cutting sod, which they were piling in twenty-foot circles, four feet high, and burning. Reversing Genghis Khan's war order to turn the world into pasture lands, the Chinese government had ordered the nomadic Mongols to destroy permanent sod forage lands and plant barley, and so forever push back the frontiers of agricultural China. Unfortunately they were only creating a dust-bowl. In this way also they destroyed the Mongols.

Dzos, a hybrid resulting from the Tibetan yak cross-bred with the Chinese "yellow cow," humbly packed burdens in moaning caravan files, or plowed patiently on the sunny side of the steep, rocky hillsides. Mud villages of a yellowish-orange clay surrounded by high mud walls went past, as well as innumerable bullet-pocked block-houses manned by Moslems.

Colonel Ma, by riding hard through the mountains, now joined us. Hopping into the car, bellowing that Tan was safe, that he himself was starved and freezing, he was soon directing us to the mud house of a Tibetan taxpayer where he, Colonel Ma, big-heart-edly invited us in to eat. The meal was of *tsamba,* ground and parched or roasted barley flour, kneaded with *tsula,* dried skimmed milk, to which was added a dash of *mör* (yak butter), and tea and sugar—brown crystal sugar imported usually by yak caravan from Szechwan Province. Solomon warned that I absolutely must learn such Tibetan words if I expected to eat when alone, as we were going to live off Tibetan food; so the reader has two choices: he may either slide his eyes over these foreign words, or he can learn them and enjoy their peculiar sound if he pronounces them. Any-way, you can't fit them into English; you can't call yak butter, butter, it's *mör,* just *mör,* including the yak hairs and green rot. Likewise roasted barley flour is not flour, it's *tsamba,* a dusty mix-ture of milled barley, husk scrapings, and sometimes alkali, sand, and mice droppings, in other words it's just—*tsamba.*

Our host hurried to eat this food first, to assure us—as custom dictates, apparently at least among Moslem soldiery—that his food was not poisoned. I dribbled a little tea into my bowl, dusted it with tsamba, stuck my finger in hopefully and came up with some-thing adhering to it that I wouldn't feed to a dog. All present but I and the taxpayer howled with glee. Prince Dorje, however, in his best classroom manner, first dampened the tsamba, a handful of it, with tea; then pressed the mess with his fingers against the side of his silver-engraved birch bowl, called a *purba,* thus efficiently pro-ducing a brown elongated sausage-shaped affair. This he popped between his jaws uncooked. Tsamba constitutes the Tibetan staff of life. A damned poor crutch for Amne Machin!

While the others watched from the corners of their eyes I mixed up a batch of tsamba, and as it turned out a little soupy, I diverted attention while pouring some of it down a crack by pointing out a camel caravan thumping by softly in the trail outside.

The Tibetan glanced across: "Honorable sir, an early caravan bound for Lhasa and Gya Khar (India)," he remarked indifferently though I nearly dropped my tsamba at the casualness of this remarkable statement which might just as well have been "Oh, they are only on their way to the moon."

"And how long will their journey take?"

"Four to five months if they get through safely." And then with a smile he added: "But of course few early caravans do."

"Is it the distance or the bullets?"

"Both," he answered.

About bullets I already knew. But for the first time I fully realized the tremendous size of Tibet and the task before us; four to five months traveling would carry this caravan over a distance a quarter of the way between New York and San Francisco; and about a third of the way to Lhasa in this southern direction we hoped somewhere to find Amne Machin. Strange, when you are suddenly confronted with distances, how men calculate them in different parts of the world. In this land only three main measurements are generally used—*kosatsa,* or voice-carrying distance, *tsapo,* or half-march, *shasa,* one march or daily stage.

Thanking our bowing host and continuing on our way for a tsapo, so smiling Colonel Ma instructed me, our car was soon climbing the *niha* or pass, leading out of the canyoned valley and up over the barren, rocky Sun and Moon Mountains. To the Tibetan— I was emphatically assured—*niha* means pass, *la* means the climb to the pass, *terh* means the descent from the pass after crossing over it. This detailed distinction has not to my knowledge been recorded in books of travel: heretofore explorers have called a pass *la* and let it go at that. I realized then the advantage (or disadvantage!) of having a professor of languages along on the expedition. Dorje assured me that not one native Tibetan taught Tibetan in the universities of Europe or America, and that the experts who did so knew only "classical" Lhasa dialect which was really only borrowed from the Province of U, and was mainly philosophical and religious in scope. Not being a scholar I wouldn't know, and of course the brother of the Dalai Lama had not yet made his residence in Berkeley, California.

At the stone *obo,* or votive sacrificial cairn raised to placate pre-Buddhistic *nei-ri,* mountain spirits, we stopped and in a cold wind took an aneroid reading—3,520 meters (10,725 feet).

Not geographically—for the Kansu frontier marked by the Nan Shan range lay still farther north by a hundred miles at our backs—

but certainly ethnologically, this bare, rocky range of hills comprising the Sun and Moon Mountains, extending on our right hand into the southeast corner of Koko Nor, lying not many miles northwest of us, is the extreme northern dividing line between China and Tibet for this particular sector. So it was in historical times, and so it is today. Many battles over the years have been fought out here; and, as yet, the feared *Gyami*, Chinese, have not gained a foothold for colonization in Tibet south of this point of the *Gya Lam*, China Road, leading to Lhasa.

We descended from the very cold Sun and Moon Mountains, and at 2:30 reached Fort Tao Tang Ho on a plain four or five miles beyond, a flat nest of bullet-riddled adobes surrounded by a high, thick wall of hammered clay. Inside we rested on *kangs*, shelves of wood and mud plaster, heated underneath by smoldering yak-dung fires and insulated with felts, bear pelts and *shudens* (mattresses).

Ma Ching, the commandante, plunged into an explanation of his own troubles: first, his concubine—a Tibetan girl—had vanished with vital information about us; last night three of his men had been shot at by snipers. The fate of the Lhasa camel caravan we had already seen north of the mountains was certain: it had passed by the post, and must now be surrounded by robbers. We certainly could get no farther south today in such troubled times.

I changed the subject to a conversation less gloomy, and Dorje learned that in June the spawning fish run in untold numbers up the nearby Tao Tang River out of Koko Nor, which lay northwest of us some 50 horse *li* (a Chinghai horse *li* equals half an English mile), and that yaks and camels are driven in to trample them to death. Tons of fish are thus collected and dried in the sun and wind, to be used in winter as army food. There are three kinds which, according to our professor were *schizopygopsis, leptocephalus, gracilis.* Our German missionary friends had supplied Prince Dorje with a paper on the matter; and henceforth the expedition was to hear much about the delicious finny inhabitants of both the salt and the fresh water seas, lakes and rivers of Tibet. He planned to use these fish to help feed the expedition. Also such a detailed report would (in Dorje's opinion) reveal one of the world's last untouched food supplies, food supplies to help offset a fast-growing global population.

"By the Blest Prophet!" cried Colonel Ma, striking the kang

with a ham-like fist; "I call fish 'yu'! Just 'yu'! Why the fuss! To me fish are just fish!"

"Dear colonel, never mind this monosyllabic 'yu'," advised Prince Dorje with a grin. "Times are changing in Asia, for better or worse, who knows? And fish along with the times."

Dinner was brought in and we crowded around the yak dung coals gleaming blue and red in the big brass brazier. We ate round, flat unleavened bread stuffed with mutton fat (*bao tze*) and sugar, the combined dish called *tong-jo*. It was delicious, and supplied energy for warming our blood. Next we were handed braised gazelle meat on skewers. We had no sooner wiped our greasy faces off with hot steaming towels when another course followed; broiled azure-eared pheasants originally having a brown and red plumage. Dessert was broiled fish and rice.

Content with the food and the coals and the company, I settled back on the kang and lit my pipe. As long as I didn't have to eat tsamba as a steady diet I would make out all right.

Addressing himself to Colonel Ma, Prince Dorje enquired with his devastating Mongol dignity, "Honorable associate, would you care for some *schizopygopsis?*" At the same time passing over a skeleton.

"Bring more 'yu'!" howled Ma Sheng-lung, banging his dagger against the brazier. "By the Lord God! The Merciful Lord God! A Mongol amongst us! Bring 'yu'! And without any fancy names attached to it!"

That night, the wind howling mournfully around the wall in consort with wolves creeping in close to look over our horses, we slept warmly on our kangs. At reveille we hustled into sheepskin robes and left the fort at the late hour of 7 A.M., necessitated by our scouts reporting a lurking pack of Tibetans nearby, riders who high-tailed it toward Koko Nor only after being approached by a section of Ma Ching's cavalry. One of these Moslems came back dragging a man's head on a rope. Whether they had killed a Tibetan or had found a head left behind by the Tibetans, I did not know and did not ask. It was plain already that things occurred in this part of the world not suspected by missionaries living in Tangar, Sining and Lanchow.

Our destination, still by station wagon, was Fort Chapcha, lying south a single stage. The temperature on the plain was cold at —12°

Centigrade, turning our hands and faces blue in the cutting wind. Oddly enough, we were finding that the nights turned bitter cold, but that on windless mornings, which were usually sunny, we were often quite hot in our heavy robes. Steep uphill gradients set us to climbing on foot over a rough gravel-topped military road now abandoned, which led southward to Fort Chapcha. Scouting ahead with the safety snapped off my rifle I cautiously peered over the top of a hill.

Right in front of me a man's corpse was sprawled on its back, and it was without a head. Scattered on down the hill were other dead men, also camels and horses. I waved for the party behind to come up. We walked well spread out through the remains of the caravan we had seen while comfortably eating in the valley north of the Sun and Moon Mountains. Several men, stripped to the skin, and mutilated, were lying over the slope. Blood was around them, and in at least one instance, guts of a man and a camel scattered together in a tangle. Clothing, arms, and cargo had been looted.

Colonel Ma whistled in surprise that the attack had happened so close to Tao Tang Ho. He pointed out that the caravaners must have put up a fight, otherwise the camels would merely have been driven off by the raiders—probably the main body of those seen by Ma Ching's scouts that morning. Such raiders really hesitate to kill, because this tends to reduce the number of caravans which would otherwise follow, and so cuts into their revenue. Raiding is a business and a science, and most caravans are allowed to pass unmolested, as a come-on to other merchants. So early in the year, however, the raiders are short of supplies after a long winter, and they strike more readily then. Needless to say we were worried, wondering if Ma Ching might not be right and that we couldn't make our way through to the fort.

I asked why the heads of three had been cut off, and the colonel answered offhand with a grim chuckle, probably so that the children of the raiders would have footballs to play with. At the time I had not realized the considerable amount of irregular warfare going on between the Tibetan tribes and the Sining Moslems (either now during the Communist civil war in China, or over the years preceding it). The reason for my ignorance was that these fights and battles were never to my knowledge—but for Dr. Rock's report—reported in detail to the outside world, and not only distance, but the strictest official censorship had been laid on for many years. The Chinese government did not hesitate to brand as a liar any traveler who dared suggest such troubles existed in their own Tibetan backyard.

In spite of this tragedy we decided to try and break through to Chapcha. All of us were either professional combat soldiers, or had served as such in the past—and this included Dorje. By scouting ahead of the car at three or four bad places where ambushes might be set, we lost several hours. Some Tibetans approached on horseback, but on seeing the light machine-gun mounted atop the station wagon, they withdrew a bit where they merely stood and watched us pass. Since we could carry only a negligible amount of cargo, often the chief consideration, and were well armed, no doubt the price they must pay was considered too high.

By midafternoon we reached Fort Chapcha, and were warmly greeted by black-uniformed Magistrate Chin Shian-sho, who controlled as best he could the (at the moment) turbulent district of Kung Ho Hsien. This commandante graciously fed us on finger-burning boiled mutton off which we cut juicy pieces with our daggers. We dipped the meat into a dish of red-peppers mortared with oil.

After eating, and to entertain our host—who, like most Moslem officers of Chinghai, appeared very congenial—we told of our experiences that day, as he had already voiced a fear that an attack might be attempted this very night. All morning, Colonel Ma and Dorje explained, we had come through rolling grass hills bright in a crystal atmosphere. At Ka Hai Tan, a blue lake, we saw from a distance an encampment of some score of unknown Drök-pas (nomads), having 30 massive black yak-hair *chari* (tents). A banner standard on a pole had been seen with Colonel Ma's binoculars to have a yak-tail streamer surmounted with a skull which may have been human.

The commandante thought it might be a certain robber, a renegade Tibetan responsible for the killing of Moslem troops. Colonel Ma described the scene of the caravan's massacre and included such details as the golden eagles and black vultures that had crouched over the corpses, flying off only when threatened with stones. Tibetans do not annoy such useful scavengers—which also might be incarnated humans, using as a temporary abode the material bodies of birds.

Here, at Fort Chapcha, we had reached a point under the very edge of the massive Tibetan inner escarpment called the Tala. This barren, frozen rim of rock to the south held the promise of discovery; and by its very look we knew it would extract a price from us. It extended approximately east and west and was only a few hundred yards across a gully from our square, battlemented Mohammedan outpost.

On the north side of the fort were Rong-pas, settled Tibetans, warmly dressed in sheepskin robes with the fur side in, and shod with black leather boots; people occasionally seen at work cultivating their fallow fields in the small rocky *rongs* (valleys). This was possible due to the soil thawing by day, though the winter was far from over. Some of these men used wooden plows dragged quite often by a team comprised of a yak and camel hitched together in tandem. Their massive, decked houses, which were surprisingly numerous, were of pounded clay, having open courtyards in the center and high mud walls with loopholes for shooting. These last appeared to be sometimes manned. The doors were guarded by chained mastiffs that seemed to roar rather than bark like ordinary dogs. Some of them had black coats as thick as a lion's mane. Chin warned us always to be on guard, as being trained to attack men on sight, they were more dangerous than a wild wolf. He said these dogs were a larger breed than that of south Tibet.

Within the fort's high walls Chin—responsible, so he assured Dorje, for our safety here—quartered us in his inner offices. Skirmishes had been averaging two or three a week. Even so close to Sining the situation apparently was touch and go. The Sining military telephone wire had been cut over a month before and was not yet repaired. Moslem soldiers were sniped at by Tibetan malcontents whenever they showed themselves, and it was said that many men had been lost trying to get that wire up. Two entire patrols had been wiped out only the week before. I doubted the high casualty figures mentioned (and will not repeat them), as at present only forty-eight troops were stationed here: these I saw were hard and bitter-faced, fur-robed, armed with new .30-caliber Skoda rifles fitted with bifurcated points (hinged prongs for steadying aim), and extremely well mounted on Mongol and Turki horses.

We passed the night quietly, and next morning the six-foot-three *dzongpön,* the smiling Tibetan commander hereabouts (with a scar running from ear to chin), together with four or five hundred of his followers, all in beautiful sheep- and wolf-lined *chupas* (robes), and fox hats, came to pay their respects, so they said, and at Chin's suggestion greeted us *outside* the fort on the parade ground. They dismounted and on seeing Chin's two machine-guns on the wall leveled down at them, politely stacked their bifurcated rifles. Sitting cross-legged on yellow Lhasa carpets our tall, lank callers gravely and proudly greeted us and pointed out the barren fields and the many fortress-houses lining the rong.

We all made elaborately polite and formal small-talk, so essential here: the Tibetans were certainly very charming when they wanted to be. One retainer of the dzongpön explained which fields were *rongpa* and which were *lama-ishing*. These latter, so indicated his star-sapphire-jeweled hand, were marked with prayer-flags and set aside by the families for the support of sons residing in the nearby *gompa* (lamasery). The dzongpön pointed out that the Tibetan of all classes—there is no caste system as in Hindu India—does not believe himself to be a soulless creature; he whole-heartedly believes in a deep spiritual life and while on earth is ever struggling to free himself from matter and return to God; he is proud of his church, of whatever sect it might be, and does not consider his priesthood to be parasitic as do so many enlightened modern people. I had to agree that without this hope of an existence better than that of a refined animal, life would indeed become a bore scarcely worth the game of feeding yourself, clothing yourself, housing yourself, and tending your vanity. The Moslems pretended they were shocked that I should agree. Much of the dislike of the Tibetan for the encroaching Chinese stems from this feeling of inner superiority: few Chinese really have any religious feelings and the Tibetans are aware of this streak of cynicism in their would-be conquerors. Apparently this feeling does not apply to the Sining Moslems whom they respect and fear.

Before leaving, the dzongpön—who was said to have killed many men in combat—smilingly pointed out the tiny green sprouts showing along the margin of the parade ground, saying: "Di yakpore" ("This is good"), and with a broad smile glancing toward the snow-edged mountains jutting far beyond the Tala. He explained gently that natural feed would soon be available for our caravan animals, that spring was fast mounting the sides of the highest mountains. "Your journey to Amne Machin God will be prosperous!"

Having looked us over the Tibetans soon after rode away, and we returned to the fort.

That night, with a small telescope, Solomon and I showed the moon to the garrison and their amazement was complete when they recognized mountains not unlike those about the fort itself. Curiously, the legs of this government-branded instrument were painted in bright colored bands. I idly asked Solomon Ma what this signified, if anything, for—as I knew after five trips to China—few things are done in this quarter of the Orient without having significance attached to them. He smilingly explained, after some moments' hesitation, that the bands signified China's plan for conquest: that red was the Chinese color, white the Moslem color, black the Tibetan color, yellow the Manchu color, blue the Mongol color—all of which practically added up to all of China's neighbors.

It is here, in central Asia, according to one faction in the German school of geopolitics, that humanity's fate ultimately rests. He who actually and objectively controls—as did the terrible and efficient Mongol Khans—its vast spaces, its energetic fighting peoples, its short lines of land communications (and now air) to all parts of the Eurasian continent, controls psychologically and to a certain extent militarily, the Asian half of that continent.

Surprisingly, our scientists estimated that among the basic foundation stones of this inherent Mongol power for war is grass, strong grass converted into excellent animal flesh—among the finest in the world. I was taking grass samples and seeds, hoping to transfer its power to the pastures of America and Europe now desperately engaged in building a way of life bedded solidly in "security," and doing it mainly—from our mid-Asian angle of view—ostrich fashion. Strange thoughts for an explorer on the way to Amne Machin, but necessary ones important to his getting there.

Next morning, under paling stars, with wild geese on the wing hissing and honking a hymn to the sun, we inspected an unruly, shaggy band of riding horses of several colors, brought in for our possible service. Some excellent dark ones, blacks and bays, not easily visible at night, were chosen and ordered shod. Others such as whites, buckskins, and pintos were cut out and discarded. We bought a few mares and seventeen stallions (as geldings are unknown here). Colonel Ma judged we must have at least twenty others. These could possibly only be obtained close by from the lamasery and from our old friend, the dzongpön.

We mounted and when the fort gates were unbolted and swung back, galloped out and were soon riding across the benched, gray highlands stretching northward ten li to the 31-year-old gompa of Jashi Tinchlo. From this cluster of stone and plaster temples a few lamas and their hundred or so followers of the Yellow Church presided benignly over the *de* (district).

As we rode up the last steep bench above the rong and approached the lamasery we heard a din of clashing cymbals, the sounds of drums accompanied by chanting, the blasts from bassoons and conches, and saw that a mystic ceremony of some sort was going on in the courtyard. Apparently Chin Shian-sho had already been invited. We sat our saddles and watched from a distance. A score of lamas seated under a yellow pavilion were dressed in costly garbs of yellow, blood-red, and royal purple, the upper halves of their bodies encased in gold-embroidered armor vestments, while yellow, fringed Greek helmets crowned their shaved heads.

Police overseers were preserving order among a crowd of seemingly frightened lay monks and Tibetans by cracking rawhide whips at them. Yells of pain (and excitement) came from the dense mob. In teams there appeared in the center of the court whirling devil dancers in enormous masks of the sacred *saba* stags; red, bull-headed Chenrezi with three eyes; horrible half-human half-devil things; dancing skeletons; and other demonic figures having tiny human bodies and monstrous, diabolical faces depicting passion, hate, greed, fear, stupidity. Here in a kind of measured dancing frenzy were many of the lamaist pantheon. Gorgeous brocade robes flashing all the rainbow's colors cloaked these fearful dancers; jewels glowed in prismatic colors. Weird other-world music, rising and falling in cadence, filled the cold, brittle air.

Dorje said the original significance of this devil dance is lost in early Shamanistic "black bones *pön*" and Buddhistic teachings, and is known today to only a very few of the highest initiate lamas. The spirits, or will, of these symbolic gods and devils are believed to manifest themselves in the priestly dancers, turning them into *gurtums*—actual gods and devils themselves—whose profoundly frightening ballets reveal that birth and death belong only to life, balancing the reciprocal conditions of each other, being the poles of the whole phenomenon of life. The *lingam,* symbol of generation, counterpart of death, signifying the correlation of generation and death, is cast out of enlightened man who thus annuls death, and so lives as a free-will of god and not a phenomenon. At last the dancing skeletons ran in a wide circle around the court, leaping wildly among the apparently terrified people not a few of whom seemed amused and even laughed aloud in joy, and cast out the lingam (a piece of refuse), ending the mystic ceremony. The overseers laid out left and right with their whistling whips, beating the crowd into submission and a semblance of order.

In the meantime I looked elsewhere about me: the lamasery of Jashi Tinchlo was one of several Tibetan cubical-style "modernistic" buildings and stone courts—very impressive with potted flowers of silk, paper, and metals such as copper and gold-plate, sheer-walled, multi-windowed, and boldly banded horizontally—the top half bright red, the lower half white. Gyepi spires rose gleaming in golden columns from the roofs. Red-lacquered masts perhaps forty feet tall were set around the wide court, and from these flowed scalloped pantalooned silken prayer-flags and yak tails, snapping benedictions in the wind. Two or three gazelles walked about, approaching and licking the salt off our calloused hands.

As the dance ended in a crashing bedlam of orchestration, we were met and dismounted by the bowing, smiling *chötrimpa,* chief overseer, in flowing red gowns and carrying a square-hilted mace. He presented to us the *chandzo,* treasurer; the *chinyer,* steward; the *lob-pön,* high professor of doctrine; the *ky-nyer,* sacristan. I had seen the ancient Pali shaft near Delhi and asked the lob-pön if lamaism knew Pali books. He answered, "Yes," having served in the sacred Blue Library in Lhasa, from the *Tri-pitaka* ("The Three Baskets of the Law"), the Pali canon, among the most transcendental texts of Buddhism, jealously guarded by oral symbol-codes.

With appropriate ecclesiastical pomp the living Buddha Kan Chan, fingering his rosary of 108 beads of human bones and amber, honored each of us in turn by tinkling the silver *tri-pus* (bell), thus bringing Moslem and Christian to the notice of heaven, and ordering that a temple sheep be sacrificed. Not too long after, we feasted on the blest sheep in the living Buddha's yellow-lacquered, flower-painted, and elegantly appointed private chambers. This suite would have been a masterpiece in any museum in the world. My place was at the back of the richly carpeted dais, the conventional place of honor. The living Buddha placed himself below me at my feet: such treatment seemed an indication of Tibetan good-will. I asked if the Panchen Lama had sent word of our coming.

"Yes, my star-mounting lord," replied Kan Chan (according to Dorje's rendition) with a slight inclination of his shaven head. "His Holiness sent word of your blessed coming to peaceful Jashi Tinchlo."

"The Court couriers ride fast," I noted, surprised at this ready answer.

"Great lord, no messenger came to Jashi Tinchlo," the lama answered, smiling gently.

"What is all this mystery? If no courier arrived, and you are isolated from the lay people today, and you do not possess a radio, then how did you know?"

"There are other forces in the sky and on the earth, Precious Lord," Kan Chan answered softly.

At this point Colonel Ma interrupted and let it be known in a bellowing voice, that Kan Chan was to send out lamas over the Tala with instructions to the Drök-pas that we were not to be molested. And that failing to do so, Fort Chapcha would send troops and burn his lamasery, and hang by their thumbs all of its priests including the living Buddha. Further, Colonel Ma demanded horses. Right now!

"At present the lamasery has but a single horse," quietly said the living Buddha, "and you shall be shown it when you leave."

At Kan Chan's invitation we and the lamas visited the main temple where long silver-copper horns were being blown for the gods. Swathing the massive pillars and hanging from the flower-painted ceilings were certainly thousands of silken prayer-banners —green, blue, red, and yellow. Wafer-thin drums of a three-foot diameter, and held overhead on a long handle, were beaten with swan-necked drumsticks knobbed with leather pads. Apparently the chanting priests, sitting in rows, predicted the fall of China and Ma Pu-fang, for they chanted to Chenrezi, the Protector of Tibet, anti-Communist dirges and scriptures they believed to be harmful to the Red conquest of the Buddhist inner domain.

Tibetans believe the power of prayer to be so great that whole armies of invaders can be halted by it, especially if emitted from the presence of the Panchen Lama. On the altars were any number of butter images, lotus blossoms, all brightly tinted; later they would be destroyed, though works of art. To honor us, other figurine *chopas* of tsamba and butter were hurriedly fashioned by the lamas in Colonel Ma's and my image, and after being painted in pastels, placed on the precious altars amid silver and bronze incense burners smoking with lotus perfume.

Day was fleeing and we must now hurry to see the dzongpön who lived not far away. When we left the temples, the lama brethren, softly singing and bowing graciously, stuffed into our woolen saddlebags sausages of blest aromatic fat, grass and flour. This grass is called *ko-do,* sometimes *shan-do,* a kind of alfalfa having a mild curry flavor. Mutton ribs known as *sho-chua-yang-jo,* literally "hand-grabbed-mutton," were stuffed on top.

The way was pointed out to the corral where the horse was kept. We then mounted and rode across to the corral; here was the most savage dog we had yet seen. Like some monstrous, moth-eaten, four-legged, frothing gorilla, it had black patches of wool hanging from its shoulders nearly to the ground. It was as big as any Saint Bernard. The enormous iron chain fastened to its iron collar seemed ready to snap at any second from the terrific lunges and weight of the maddened beast. The brute was chained to the partly-devoured carcass of a horse, which it actually dragged along the ground towards us. When the dog had devoured this half-ton of meat, it would be chained to a fresh carcass, perhaps that of a yak as many of these skeletons were scattered about. Its roars of rage set our horses shying by him fast. Other than that, the corral was empty.

"There is your horse, colonel!" I called back to the infuriated Ma Sheng-lung.

It was a further three li's ride to the walled house where the dzongpön had his lair. The chief himself bowed us into a room luxuriant with carpets and walls painted with multi-hued chained tigers and golden Buddhas. All about, in contrast to priceless antiques, and rare musical instruments and illuminated manuscripts, were stacked rifles, binoculars, swords, bugles, loaded leather bandoliers studded with Lhasa silver work, pistols, poniards. From low, pearl-inlaid teak and ebony tables about which we were seated cross-legged, we gaily ate a feast with mutton as the entree; this included clotted *kumiss,* fermented mare's milk sprinkled with brown sugar. To the dzongpön we now presented gold valued at perhaps $5,000.

Our disappointment was keen on receiving from him only eight horses, not enough with what we already had, to continue up on the Tala toward Tan's column which would meet us at Fort Ta Ho Pa still far in the south. That evening in a stiff, cold wind we rode with a rattle of bits back toward Fort Chapcha, using the pale light from an early moon to guide our way down the steep sides of the gravelly benches leading into the rong. Many covies of partridges crying "chu-kar," and called *ka la chia,* and bands of thousands of pigeons were watering with a rustle of feathers in the fast-freezing stream at the bottom of the valley.

Our escort shouted Chinese Moslem war sagas, and then sang compelling soft Tibetan love songs into their long sleeves. The charger I was riding liked these songs, jerking on his bridle to free his checked head for a hard gallop. After an hour our horses began to curvet around their saddle pommels and to whinny; we were soon after challenged by the sentries manning the battlements for the night's vigil. The gates creaked open, then slammed shut and were bolted behind our thumping, steaming cavalcade. In a few minutes we were bedded down on our warm kangs, for we were freezing.

Burrowing into my quilts and furs I tried to sleep, but could not. Where were we to find more horses? Would Moslem gold and outlandish threats of burning the lamasery keep our feet on the road to Amne Machin? Would such tactics stop the flow of blood said already to have been spilled as payment to the mountain god . . . ?

3

Over the Tala

STILL searching for more top-grade high-altitude-bred horses, and wishing to extend our map and ascertain the Tibetan Order-of-Battle for this strategic region, so that we could advance with knowledge of the situation in our rear, we left Fort Chapcha next morning under a grilled sky, striking east for the Yellow River. In the party were Colonel Ma, Commandante Chin, Solomon Ma, Prince Dorje and myself; and due to the presence of marauding elements and what was believed to be a dissident *öret* Mongol band from Inner Mongolia, an escort of 17 hui hui riflemen and a machine-gunner were included.

Beyond the fort we probed eastward, using normal leapfrog tactics to reconnoiter, riding 3½ hours through a winding gully bounded on the right especially by crumbling, water-eroded earthen cliffs of from half a mile to a mile apart. We cautiously approached five flat, squarish, round-cornered Tibetan fortress-houses topped with wind-snapping prayer-flags invoking the favors of nei-ri spirits and ghosts. While resting in one of these houses I tasted my first *chang,* a mild barley brew, and ate *momo,* a puffy partially-cooked dough stuffed with fatty mutton.

Just beyond, we found perched on a windy, dusty pass several *zih-das* (shrines) with painted devils seated inside, and a tall Mongol obo. Both were explained as survivals of the old Shamanistic religion of "Black Pön," about which almost nothing is known. The obo consisted of thousands of votive stones racked up and held tightly by a square log rail-fence, out of which sprouted fanwise hundreds of poles and sticks holding tattered yellow prayer streamers marked in paint with Sanskrit:—"Om Mani Padme Hum" ("Oh, the Jewel in the Lotus, Amen").

Since "Om" is a sacred syllable, the Word of God, and possibly also the name of an early Aryan Vedic guru in north India, about 1000 B.C., the syllable might actually mean, "Om, the God," or "Om, the guru" . . . so we were told by a mendicant lama crouching at the obo. Also, according to the Chandogya Upanishad the Udgitha (Loud Chant) is identified with the sacred syllable "Om." "The Rig is speech. The Saman is breath. The Udgitha is this syllable 'Om.'" Other travelers have translated "Om" into "Oh." While I have no wish to appear contrary or to quarrel with precedence, Prince Dorje's shocked silence over my timidity decides me to point out that "Oh" is decidedly incorrect. Among the prayer-flags were also rammed a hundred and eight fire-arrows notched and feathered, these of as large a size as were said to have been used in the Mongol sieges. Since they were some ten feet long I doubted it, and suspect they were used only as religious objects.

Cold and hungry, Dorje and I killed two butter-fat pigeons and three Mandarin ducks along the low banks of the Aë Hai (Mongol) River. After broiling the birds and eating, we followed the Aë Hai for 30 li down a twisting desert valley. Once we had a start, thinking robbers were waiting for us, when a few camels, *lo tuo* (Tungan) loomed up. They had racks of boat-like ribs due to a lean winter, and were browsing on a few low, thorny bushes rooted precariously in yellow sands. These shaggy camels were the two-humped *Camelus bactrianus*, exceedingly different from the famed Arabian one-humped variety, *Camelus dromedarius*. New wounds were pointed out on them, indicating they probably belonged to raiders.

Our scouts were not long in locating an encampment of Mongols who, showing themselves friendly, allowed us to ride past into the east. We came upon a natural hot-water spring smelling possibly of sulfur. It was marked by a *mani*, a pile of fitted black stones carved in Sanskrit. This was the work of Mongol magicians called *shanag*, "black hats." Some of those among us had a presentiment of close danger. We dismounted from our horses and took cover among the dunes. The click of rifle bolts came from our men.

Suddenly two Mongols ran out of a round felt *yurt* seen from around the side of a dune, grabbing up the chains of their mastiffs, who were now sounding off and lunging as if hoping to tear us asunder. One of them broke loose, bounding toward us, but was shot by Abdulla, one of the itchy-fingered guard. We approached in a fan and found that the Mongols had camped on the spring, hidden from sight by a dune, in order to worship the earth spirits. I was told no orthodox lamaist Tibetan or Mongol will dig into the earth or disturb it in any way, but choose springs when they wish to converse with the earth spirits. While Ma Pu-fang was very likely one of the world's richest men, his miners were Moslems, and their gold was secured in placers in order partially to placate the Buddhists. The lamas will receive placer gold as fees, and use it as we have seen, for common building material much as the ancient Incas did.

An old Mongol held aside the red-lacquered wooden door of his yurt, one of seven, and bade us enter and rest. We seated ourselves on frayed Urga rugs and warmed our hands at his fire.

The sulfur spring, believed the Mongols, was about halfway to the Yellow River. And so we did not tarry long after rounding up the Mongol horses, and bathing in the hot spring (our first bath since Sining), though the wind no doubt livened our departure considerably. A collection of partly ruined mud *dzongs*, Tibetan forts, were next seen through binoculars on the south rim of the gorge. Keeping our distance Solomon plotted them on the map. No riders came out and I began to take confidence in the gold left with the dzongpön. Just as we were congratulating ourselves, a troop of perhaps a hundred light cavalry rode at a dead run out of one of the forts, and slid down the face of the dirt cliff, heading straight for us. We jerked our horses' heads into the east, and set spurs. Bullets began whining past, accompanied by the crack of rifles some three hundred yards to the rear. We plunged into the sandy river bottom and finally left our pursuers. All three of the Mongol horses were lost.

A few miles beyond, at the Mohammedan town of Tchu Ku, which Dorje pronounced in a sort of sneeze, we were greeted by its more than a hundred citizens who had been warned of our approach by a look-out in a mud tower. Already, a crowd of fifty children in little sheepskin robes were lined up on both sides of the single, dusty, poplar-lined lane waving Chinese flags. We were led behind the yamen wall, and into a dinner being set in the headquarters. The proud villagers were all smiles and bows. Outside, as we ate (and we were starved), a clamorous celebration with firecrackers was going on, called "Appeasing of the Mongol Father."

In olden times, our hosts explained, Chinese imperial soldiers had come to Tchu Ku from Lanchow, and when they marched out not a single Mongol man, woman, or child remained alive. Three hundred and twenty-one posts had been set up, after the village was burned, and on each of the posts was impaled a human head. To the accursed spot came a tribe of Tibetans who settled there. Today, their descendants, and the Moslems who had followed much later, were observing the 400-year-old annual propitiating ceremonies honoring the ghosts of the Mongols.

"Bring out your horses! Or you may be celebrating your own funerals!" bellowed Colonel Ma's voice.

"The horses are on the banks of the Yellow River, just beyond," said the headmen, pointing east. "For a price they are yours. That is, for a *fat price* they are yours. We are forty-eight men strong, and every man has a good rifle!"

"Have it your own way," roared Colonel Ma, clapping each headman on his back, and smiling broadly.

Groaning from an excellent meal of "hand-grabbed-mutton," exclaiming as local connoisseurs do while swabbing our faces with steaming towels, and wondering aloud for all to hear if we could possibly manage to get back upon our saddles, we were craftily led out with deceptive words into still another dinner at the house of the local magnate, a patriarchal Moslem named Shih Ting-fu (his Chinese name), and a friend of socialite Ma Sheng-lung's.

"Old friend! You must hear the coin jingling in our saddlebags!" shouted Ma Sheng-lung with his usual heartiness.

"Ah, I hear only the angels singing your praises! May you enter the Province of Allah!" Shih Ting-fu greeted us, stroking his white beard, and symbolically pouring purification water over our hands.

"And may God make you fruitful of many sons," we answered with many bows.

"Why not!" he exclaimed, "I am only eighty-one!"

After more *sho-chua-yang-jo* we just managed to bow our way out with many smiles and speeches, and praise God, to mount our rested horses. Incidentally, this Chinghai mutton—of any age—has no "mutton" flavor whatever; this astonishing fact is due no doubt to the grasses of the country, for when some of the local breeds of sheep have been taken to Russia by Mongols, it is said the meat becomes "strong." The change of grass is believed to be the answer.

We practically purred in contentment, hiccuping politely, as custom dictates, into our bulky sleeves: we rode, gently so as not unduly to jolt ourselves, across bare fields toward the Yellow River. After a few miles we found its steep banks at the bottom of a high dirt

mountain rising in crumbling clay cliffs on the opposite side., The
river flowed musically, like rich, yellow yak cream, over rapids lined
with burl oak, willow clumps, and spiked brambles that tore our
robes. According to Dorje the river's elevation at this point was
2,548 meters (7,764 feet), and as distances go here was not far north
of the point reached west of the Yellow River in Tibet by Doctor
Joseph F. Rock on his great expedition to find "Amnyi Machen."
From a mountain called Shachü Yimkar, Dr. Rock observed three
"peaks" which for twenty years he maintained were "more than
28,000 feet" high.* In this region, while yet about fifty miles away,
he was halted by Ngoloks and turned back toward his base at Radja
Gomba on the Yellow River.

We found the Moslems' horses and with the guides' assistance cut
out twenty of the best. *Whang ya*, flocks of big "yellow duck" bobbed
on the rough water of this stretch of the upper Yellow River; they
were boldly painted—orange of body, red belly, pearly white wing
edges, black tail, black neck-ring, green wing tips and a whitewashed
head. Colonel Ma, obviously a crack shot, nailed one at nearly a
hundred yards; whereupon many of us leapt into our saddles and
raced yelling to see who would perform *tsai*, the cutting of any
animal's throat before it dies. Otherwise the meat would not be considered clean and rendered fit for Moslem consumption. Though my
horse was fast I was nosed out by three of the Moslems, who laughingly recovered the duck and stretched out its neck that I might have
the honor of performing the tsai ceremony.

That night we put up at a farmer's house. Our horses safely cor-
ralled and a guard set over them, we went inside and were soon
being fed salted pretzels some foot in diameter called *san-tse*. Pleased
over the horses we celebrated until 2 A.M., entertained by the dancing and music of our hosts. Their songs seemed basically Arabic and
were intriguing to listen to.

We finally got to sleep, curling up anywhere on the kangs and
floor in our robes; but were up at the first flush of light, cinching
each other tightly in silken sashes, buckling on looped ammunition
belts, dagger and pistol and (in Tan's and Ma's instance) swords;
beating off the watchdogs and mounting our horses impatiently

---

* See "Seeking the Mountains of Mystery," *National Geographic Magazine*, February 1930, page 185. Rock's spelling is probably correct, though I have used that common in present-day maps (Amne Machin).

champing their bits in the bitter cold. About three inches of snow had fallen. The woman of the house, who, like all Moslem women in this part of Tibet, wore a green hood fastened at the throat, came crawling on hands and knees before Commandante Chin—elegant in soft sheepskins, whose high, black, spurred Cossack boots she kissed reverently, and begged for some favor, apparently without luck, poor soul. I rode over and handed down a few silver coins, which though irritating to the great man, pleased our hostess:

"May you speedily ascend to the harems of Paradise!"

We rode north across the fields of fresh-fallen snow. All about were flocks of pigeons, called by the Tungans, *ke-tze,* tumbling happily in the variable breezes of early morning. After an hour the jovial Colonel Ma reined in to still another "friend's" house and a hot breakfast of many courses began coming on in a matter of minutes. I could never get over the speed with which such feasts were arranged. This hospitable custom is modestly called *min chia,* life rice.

Amid much merriment and horseplay with their whips, our three magistrates left us to hunt wild boars, while they rode off to hold court and settle a murder case. I noted my friends were not strong enough to go against local custom. They contented themselves with a visit to the nearby lama temple to arrange for the "blood price." The slayer was a Mohammedan whose village must pay the dead Tibetan's heirs. Not to pay the blood price would certainly start a feud whereby the price would be taken in blood by the Tibetan's family. Court was held in the temple and this decision was handed down: "Guilty, payment of $3,000." This though the defendant's evidence showed the Tibetan had been knifed only in self-defense after attacking the Mohammedan. Reason for the verdict?—politics! There were more Tibetans settled in the immediate region than Moslems! Anyway, guilt was unimportant: the price was the main thing—and as the Tibetan was poor, and the Moslem's friends rich, he was stuck—and on this score there was no dispute among the principals of the court; it was—as Dorje eventually learned—settled at the price stipulated above. The Moslem magistrates' personal squeeze was $2,000, the government's $1,000. Our host smilingly whispered that all *hsien* magistrates squeeze so hard that sky and earth meet, since the officials scratch so deeply that a great pile of earth is thrown up behind them.

While the boar hunt was being organized I noticed, dangling from smoke-blackened log rafters in the ceiling overhead, long strings of dried fish, *chin yu* (gold fish); good to eat I found upon sampling. Also there was a kind known as "dogfish," these being up to 1½ feet long, and definitely not good to eat. Dogfish is fed to horses for indigestion, and an excellent idea, Solomon Ma, Dorje and I agreed. Both kinds are taken from the Yellow River.

The boar hunt got under way, and during our scattered ride through the snowy thickets we jumped a small herd and also either saw other kinds of game or their tracks: *whang yang* (Tungan: gazelle); *lāng* (wolf); *hu li* (red fox); *lu* (deer); *yang* (bighorn sheep); *sheh chih* (musk-deer). The tracks of wapiti were also reported.

In another thicket a pair of hunters jumped three boars, killing two and wounding the third. This boar was soon brought to bay by a pack of local dogs. It stood under an earthen cliff, backed against the steepest part, its fangs curled out in a long, ugly snout of a head. Though the dogs stayed back in a half circle, the boar clacked its tusks furiously. Now I had killed pigs before, in Borneo, Mexico, Malaya, Kwangtung Province (south China), and in one or two other places. I knew better than to dismount, yet the men indicated the honor was mine. But I just couldn't shoot that boar from the saddle. I jumped down to the ground, and had no sooner landed than the boar grunted and rushed through the dogs, heading straight for me. I barely managed to throw my left leg over where I could get a quick snap shot off with my rifle. The result was that he was only creased by the bullet, which plowed along his right side. That turned the pig aside, however, and a second shot from one of the bystanders dropped it just far enough in front of me so that I could stretch out my rifle from a kneeling position and touch his tusks with the sight. I judged he stood about four feet at the shoulder and was a beauty of his kind. The tusks were chopped out by a farmer who came up, and we started back to the house. Moslems do not eat pork, nor would they touch it so that Dorje and I might eat it.

The farmers saw us off, clasping their hands together and bowing: "Thank you, honored sirs! That last boar has wounded four of our people!"

Not to be outdone in politeness, our men shouted back: "Praise be to Allah! The beasts are dead! All our hands are clean!"

Midafternoon had come. The party now assembled, and with the new horses herded together in our midst, we set off on a short cut to Fort Chapcha, circling the Tibetan strongholds. After four hours of cold, snowy riding with ice forming and crackling under the pacing horses' hooves, we luckily came upon an encampment of Moslems who offered to sell three horses. Here all the best gaited-horses are trained in pacing, or in a fast single-foot or amble; they seldom trot or walk. Our own buyers, and the sellers, each selected a man to represent them. These two held hands under a cloth, not with each other however, but with a third man whose job it was to transmit to each by finger codes, whatever offers and refusals they wish to convey. In this manner we acquired the three horses.

All our recently purchased horses—for the most part small-headed, light-footed, barrel-shaped and frisky—were probably the result of crosses in former times between Turkish, Arab, European, and Mongolian strains. Conquering Mongols have brought back many of the finest breeds to build up their own tough stocks. Ogadai alone once sent 20,000 matched white horses from conquered Russia and east Europe, to Genghis Khan as a personal gift. Colonel Ma bought with his hard-won court squeeze what might have been a fancy white African barb, a stallion said to have been trained by a prince of the Khara Shar Torguts, for war-charging. He could run and wheel like the wind. Ma playfully called him "Death Wind." Most horses, however, are known simply as "the big Sining black," or "Babar's short-legged roan," or "the red," and are not necessarily named.

Safely back at the fort Solomon and I hunted *yeh chih,* a fast flying bird. The evening was overcast with silver-edged clouds moving along in an orange sky, which brought the birds whirring into the open just before sundown. We killed five of these magnificent cock pheasants, having a very dark-red plumage but without the customary white neck-ring of the lowland Chinese variety known to millions of American sportsmen through transplanting as the "Chinaman," or more elegantly as the "ring-neck pheasant."

That night we sewed missing buttons on our wool-padded uniforms worn for warmth under the robes, and packed ammunition, instruments, and camp gear, as we planned to head south over the Tala before dawn. The Moslems banked on the cold keeping the Tibetans in their shelters till late; we could slip out and get a head-start on them. Two sections would go as small parties would attract less attention. I would lead off with the advance party, and do the scouting. Colonel Ma would follow with the more important pack train and extra horses, and a group of Tibetan mercenaries and Moslems. If the advance party was jumped by raiders, we were to kill a horse for food and if necessary others for barricades, send back a scout and await either Colonel Ma or a detachment of reenforcements from the fort which had been strengthened by new troops coming in.

It seemed I had barely shut my eyes when reveille sounded. The night was pitch dark, cold as the proverbial Tibetan bitch wolf, and hours before dawn. I figured there must be a mistake and was just tucking in for a last minute bit of shut-eye when Hassan, the chief scout, rousted me out. Hassan only had a single eye, the other having been knocked out by a bullet, but with that single eye nothing escaped him. There was not much I could do about it, as he simply walked off with my bed covers tucked under his arm. Without any breakfast and in a breathtaking, freezing temperature of $-28°$ Centigrade, we were presently clip-clopping out of Fort Chapcha.

My twenty-five-man group was escorted across the gulch and up to the tableland of the bitterly cold and gusty Tala, by Chin's troop of mounted-infantry. The stars looked cold in the blue-black sky and I concentrated my gaze on my horse's black ears, furry and warm-looking. As he sweated, little icicles formed on them. Our destination was Sa Chu Yu, the first apparently of three stages to Fort Ta Ho Pa, the last possible refuge north of the Amne Machin Range. Fort Ta Ho Pa was also our rendezvous with the main Kumbum column, and our hub base for the gathering from all directions of still more recruits, caravan animals and provisions, gear and treaties, for the long march on the Amne Machin peaks. We would now depart from the military road leading south and take a short cut known to the Moslems.

Sa Chu Yu was 60 li (30 miles) over rough terrain estimated at six hours of riding at a pace; on top of the Tala we struck west from the fort to throw off a possible Tibetan scout already sighted on our left flank, and then after an hour bent a bit left into the southwest. On the bone-dry, dusty Tala we moved across alluvial flats of wind-lashed sand and gravel. Dodging west again to keep out of ambush we broached at right angles a series of long, rolling north-and-south sand swells about 500 feet high. With daylight flashing in an apple-green sky we quickly saw that the Tala here was dotted thickly with Tibetan black charis.

We pulled up short. These tents were vast roomy spider-like affairs, held rigid by exterior poles propped under taut stays in turn secured by boulders lying on the ground. Sheep were scattered far and wide; horses with gangling foals cropped new tender grass growing short and thin between the spears of old clumps growing on knobs of hard, wind-carved sand. These nomadic Drök-pas seemed like migratory fowls, coming and going with the seasons, following eternally the game herds and the grass. Later they would strike their black camps and head south as grass enriched the drafty *drö* uplands, the worldly-heaven in their eyes.

We sheered sharply away from that camp, but later enquired the way from an old man engaged in solitary meditation and spinning a prayer-wheel clockwise. After directing us to continue on a new course to dodge "bandits" the aged rustic smiled:

"Please go slowly," he said in the polite departing phrase of the country, meaning to go so that accident will not befall you, and so that you can visit us in our tents where you may rest and take food. Dorje said he would rather walk into a tiger's den.

Along the way several of the lyre-horned *whang yang* gazelles winked signals with their white rumps and flanks and disappeared in little yellow puffs of dust.

After three hours Commandante Chin Shian-sho and his escort left us with a parting yell, as he was not anxious to overextend himself and be cut off from the fort. The column rambled along with an occasional clank of arms through a hollow region of coffin loneliness, a wind-corrugated, yellow sand desert of seemingly endless large and small dunes and crumbling cliffs, many of them hundreds of feet overhead. Here and there, sheltered in the labyrinth of the dunes, were forests, strange lilliputian weather-twisted dwarf conifers only a foot or two in height. These evergreen trees, which so fascinated Solomon and Dorje, had five-inch spokes for needles that pierced the tender hocks of our horses causing them to dance.

Crouching in abject terror in a gully were three Tibetan *a-ni,* nuns, whom the men thought might be robber scouts lying in hiding. These shave-headed woebegone females in the rags of penitents, called pitifully on Dröma, Goddess of Mercy, to save them from rape. The men calmed their wailings, assuring them somewhat sourly we were much too cold and tired to be lovers and were not avenging devils or robbers either. We learned they were on pilgrimage to some shrine, and gave them food and water, for they had strayed and seemed in a bad way. When their lament became one of thanksgiving I added a few *trangkas* (Lhasa silver coins).

Blinded from sand, our ears and mouths full of grit, we finally broke loose from the dunes and rode into the watery oasis of Narda. Close by was the caravansarai of Sa Chu Yu. This wide, barren valley was locally considered rich rong cultivation though its elevation was registered at 2,880 meters (8,775 feet), and its only crop in late summer being a scraggy barley. Narda was heavily settled, being dotted with big square-walled clay houses over whose doorways, churning with a whirr in the wind, were twin prayer-mills. Each revolution of the blades brought another benediction upon the owners of the houses. Tibetans believe that all such automatic devices as waterwheel prayer-mills, wind-driven mills, prayer-barrels and hand-propelled prayer-wheels, have a very special appeal to the gods.

Quite suddenly, without warning, out jumped a lurking wolf. It was a giant of its kind, very tall and thin, and began snarling and loping toward us. Tibetan wolves are quite often bold due to seldom being shot at, either on religious grounds or because the average man hesitates to waste expensive ammunition on them (in most regions the standard price for a rifle shell of any caliber was one Chinese silver dollar). This wolf was sand-colored and hard to see. Sliding off my saddle to the ground I fired a quick shot with the Japanese saddle carbine I sometimes carried, but missed. The wolf skidded to a stop and backed away in astonishment, turned and streaked past, jack-knifing through a herd of milling camels, scattering them in all directions. Apparently the wolf was angry, for in passing he made a pass at ripping out the guts of a camel. The second shot dropped him.

Camp was pitched inside a walled court acrid-smelling from ammonia contained in the urine of camels and other animals, but the *nepo* (landlord) soon had our party bedded down on clean straw. The horses stood about in pairs licking each other's necks for the salt which must have been sweated out of them in the rapid crossing of the desert. Soon night shadows slid across the valley, causing us to draw in closer to the watchfire around which we lay on sheepskins and saddle blankets thrown down on the straw. Later we would sleep inside the house and row of rooms within the wall. I lit my pipe and in the fading light read a few pages from Dorje's copy of James Joyce's *Ulysses*.

About midnight I awoke from a brittle cold of −21° C.; our baggage train had not come in, and I could picture that old buzzard Colonel Ma camping comfortably with all our extra blankets to keep him warm and our food supply to keep him in a happy frame of mind. Henceforth, whenever possible, I would stay with the baggage —and to hell with scouting ahead and such heroics. I lost no time going into the main house and taking a place on one of the fire-heated kangs.

4

Death in the Gomei Desert

DAWN came with a low howl and swish of winds, flashing in a vivid horse-tail sorrel-red sky. We threw off our extra sheepskins and going outside climbed a ladder to the top of the mud wall: by the clear high-elevation lights reflecting from the tropopause, we searched the sand dunes, but there was no sign of Colonel Ma and his pack outfit coming over the desert. Scouts later reported he had not camped at some other house in the valley of Narda. One of the hunters sent out into the desert returned dragging a blue heron; it was six feet from wing tip to wing tip, four feet from toes to beak. At breakfast this bird tasted like a boiled saddle blanket, but bespectacled Solomon Ma happily prepared the skin for his ornithological collection saying it was unfamiliar to him.

A Tangut scout was sent out on our back trail, and when he failed to report by midafternoon, a pair of Moslems were dispatched to investigate. Following his tracks they found the Tangut about two miles north, lying face-down in the sand, shot neatly through the side of the head, and stone dead. His rifle had been taken, and his horse. The tracks of a single horseman were followed for a few miles, when the wind rose and blotted them out.

A look-out on the wall called down that a caravan was coming over the dunes. Our elation turned to disappointment when we saw that this train was not Colonel Ma's, but a strange caravan of nearly a thousand neck-craning camels, smelling water in the oasis and roaring their joy. They picked up their long gangly legs and kicked sand before them in a quickened pace. The caravan's master, Mohammed Ali, a giant of a man, settled down his caravan by sections of a hundred long feed-lines of camels.

Soon Mohammed Ali donned a white Moslem cap something like a cook's, and a ground-sweeping gown, and courteously called on us. He had a wonderful Tungan hawk's face, lacerated by scars, winds, desert suns, and human passions. He was headed for the Tsaidam

Swamps in the far west, where in the fall he would collect a cargo of Mongol salt and carry it into China. A section of 200 of his prime woolly camels—whom he took us to inspect—were *café-au-lait* in color. They were obviously the pride and joy of his life.

He explained that the camels would go on summer pasture, for Tibetan camels are worked in winter. He pointed out that many were weeping as their foot-pads were tender from working on icy ground. He called a driver over, and had him get out a zither-looking instrument and sing to them, thus quieting the beasts and apparently making them more content. Walking down the feed-lines of crunching camels feeding on Tibetan *ney* (winter barley), Mohammed Ali explained in a low, excited voice that 180 Ngoloks, only the season before, had captured his great Kham caravan of 500 animals and all its cargo south of Amne Machin, killing seventeen of his gunmen. He warned us not to return to Sining by the same route we were taking, as ambuscades would surely be awaiting us, either Ngolok or some other Tibetan tribe. He feared for the safety of Colonel Ma. So saying, he was soon reading to us from his *Koran*.

Like not a few High Tartary Moslems, Mohammed Ali could read Arabic but not speak it; he translated aloud into mulla, the so-called mystic language already mentioned in Sining, and said by the Moslems to be used throughout a broad band some thousand miles long (as far east as Shanghai, as far west as Moscow). All the Moslems—ours and those belonging to the camel train—devotedly gathered and spread their saddle carpets, and facing Mecca in the west, prayed for our joint deliverance (according to Solomon—) . . . "In the Name of God, the Merciful, the Loving Kind."

At last Colonel Ma and his dusty troops, herding their plodding and fatigued train, arrived, led in at dusk by Tanguts sent out to find them. In the night just past, the colonel's camp in the desert had been raided by six Tibetans, who ran off three of our best saddle horses. The colonel had spent hours tracking them, but lost the tracks of the thieves when they led into a labyrinth of windy sand dunes. Reunited, soldiers' songs and copper pots boiling with meat and aromatic herbs became the order of the night. As darkness approached the tatter-gowned careworn *nemo* (landlady) of the caravansarai came into a room which had been cleared for me, and silently emptied the rank of six bronze cups placed along the dusty altar of the "House Goddess," Dörge-pamo—the "Pig-faced Goddess" —and reverently refilled them with fresh water.

Dorje and I lazily watched her fingers shape a bit of butter and tsamba into a *torma*-offering for the altar. The nemo prostrated herself several times, full length upon the earthen floor, before the Goddess. When she saw us lying on the kang she explained that a *terang-gunchi* spirit had left its child's footprint in the dust on the altar, and hence her prayers that all of us might be protected while in her house.

Our difficult problem of calculating time for guards, marches, etc., was finally decided upon, and we adopted the Tibetan system. As explained to me it is calculated thusly: *torang,* just before dawn; *tse shar* "peak-shining time" (sunrise); *nyima,* morning; *nyin gung,* noon; *sa rip,* dusk; *gongmo,* night; *nam che,* midnight. It was completely useless to point at your watch and say, "Be here in two hours." The Tibetan will smile, nod his head in agreement, and privately wonder if the spirits have bored holes in your head. Just tell him we will be leaving at *"tse shar"* and all mystery will fade, and your caravan will be on its way at sunrise. The Sining Moslem soldiery were familiar with all such Tibetan practices.

Inside the adobe house, with some fifty bedmates scattered around, I slept warmly on the heated kang, and then it was suddenly torang time, pre-dawn, the guard bellowing in our ears to get up: outside I sniffed the sharply cold air, glancing up at the enormous stars casting a brilliant light over the *sarai.* The men grumbled and moved stiffly in their frozen sheepskin robes as they slapped saddles on the horses, a few of whom bucked and squealed in protest; and like wooden men lifted packs off the ground with grunts, to hold them against the pack-horses for trimming and lashing. Colonel Ma had acquired not only men but some yaks, and this slower yak train now started off ahead, its bells clunking and receding in the frozen night.

An orderly broke off a handful of tea leaves—probably a concession to me as I was shivering—from a hollow cake resembling a large bird's nest, but curiously called "human head tea," and chucked it into a pot of boiling water. Our breakfast, a rarity on the trail, was of this same tea and *yung-ma,* a woody "horse turnip," one of the few north Tibetan vegetables at this season. The horses stood around the dying fire watching us. Most men saved a bite of turnip for their horses.

At 5 A.M. with a light baggage *ula* (train) of twelve horses and mules and eight yaks, we rode out through the gate and into the the black night cloaking the desert. We were muffled in thick furs and skins, our hands protected by long sleeves of sheepskin which were warmer than gloves. But still we shook with cold in the stillness of that crackling air, an air so cold that when a man spat you could hear a sharp *pfttt* as it froze before hitting the ground.

The moon shone over the dunes in the west, but it was not long before the sun's earliest rays began filtering through the sky, finally to burst overhead like the glow of slag and melt the clouds folded along the eastern dunes. Our destination was Ching Kou, 60 trail li through "empty" desert according to Narda's Rong-pas. That is, they slyly warned, empty of everything but robbers.

We soon pressed along the shaggy flanks of the yak train plodding along heads down, men and animals trying to protect themselves from the cold by crowding close together. The Tibetan drivers were hunched on their high, wooden yak-saddles, shivering in the depths of thick sheepskins. The only sound came from their long whips curling over the yaks and ending in a terrific crack.

Our party totaled about fifty rifles, three Japanese Nambu machine-guns and some miscellaneous weapons. Steering by compass first west a half hour then south of west, we noisily broke through an ice-sheathed marsh, and entered a sand-dune desert extending three marches north-and-south, two east-and-west. We must attempt to cross in a single march; neither of the two Tanguts sent out had located water. Owing to possible robbers, our Order-of-March was important. And Colonel Ma formed us thus:

In the great, yellow dunes ahead of the column he laid down a scouting point approximately three hundred yards out. And, when practical, ranging outside this point and in parallel wings on each side of the main column were files of two or three flankers. Ma or I rode at the head of the column, thus accelerating and directing the scouting point to left or right by sound signals or movements of the arm. Behind came the machine-gunner carrying his gun at the ready across the saddle. He was followed by a pair of mules packing two or more machine-guns lashed one on each side, together with ammunition cases. Following in a flexing queue were the troops and others who drove the baggage and extra animals along in the center. At the rear followed four guards armed with a small Japanese mortar, Skoda rifles, Chinese copies of American Tommy guns and Chinese potato-masher hand grenades. These latter rode in a fan formation whenever possible, to guard against attack on our rear and flanks. All guns were loaded, with shells in the chambers, safeties on. When Tibetans strike they often do so with the speed of lightning.

The desert as we entered its wind-shifting dunes—some as long as two to three city blocks and proportionately high—was silent. The wind stopped and a breeze began stirring out of the east, on our rear left side. The frozen sand was crusty underfoot, crunching under our hooves, little swirls of loose sand dancing over it. Above tipped a dome of red and blue sky, an inverted teacup lined with eggshell blue bottom and sides, its rim smeared with red. Steam spouted from our nostrils. As the horses gradually warmed they straightened out their kinks, bouncing up and down friskily. Riding over frozen sand seemed like sitting on air. Fifty pairs of sharp eyes peered out of weather-beaten faces, watching for the slightest movement out in the dunes.

Saddle leather creaked, horses mouthed steel bits, iron and silver stirrups clicked against boot heels, spurs and metal saddle orna· ments. Rifles thudded against men's bony hips. The swishing cut of whips on horseflesh. These were the only sounds during the first hour. And then there burst overhead a flare of light striking the tallest sandy crests—*tse shar* "peak-shining time," and the whole desert awoke as long points of light slid spinning among the long dunes.

Large, flat, squat partridges like huge wobbling beetles, scampered away from the marching column. Blue-gray in the body and slashed with brown and cream under short, hooked wings, they were probably a high-elevation cousin of the Indian chukar. When they burst flying out of hollows they sounded exactly like whirring mechanical machines, sometimes startling men and animals.

A *yeh tu* (rabbit) scampered off a knoll; except for its rather long tail it seemed exactly like our western jackrabbit. A hunting pair of *yeh ying* (eagles) flashed by in front of me with a wind-strumming sound. Crumbling animal tracks and hot, steaming droppings of *kulans* indicated we had jumped a herd of wild asses feeding on the few bushes scattered about. The kulan is called *kyang* by the Ti-betans, and *yeh ma* by the Tungans. A wolf howled on scenting us downwind, then remained quiet, watching from a ridge where some one spotted his ears sticking up. A pair of the hu li red foxes (from which our caps were made) bounced along the steep side of a very large dune. And so, the Gomei Desert was not "empty" after all, as the Narda people had insisted.

As we marched the breeze stiffened to a wind, and soon a blizzard struck, swirling sand against our faces, blinding our eyes and choking our lungs: both medium and great sand dunes were hidden in a ghostly pall. It was too cold for snow. A dog whined.

Suddenly—without warning—a rifle-shot rang out. It came from a high-crested dune on our left. I pulled up and saw that the machine-gunner just behind was slipping off his saddle headfirst into the sand, his horse rearing on its hind feet and attempting to strike at the body with its forefeet. The mules carrying the other two machine-guns pulled back squealing on their leadropes, and plunged off into the storm. I realized we were boxed between two long flanking dunes. The robbers, raiders, horse thieves or whatever they might be, commanded the heights only a hundred yards out on each side, and if we attempted to dig in, we would very likely be in for it. Our scout, only a single man at this point and no flankers, had been allowed to pass, and the column was under the sights of who knew how many robbers, or how well armed they were.

It had already been explained by someone at Chapcha that raiders will sometimes make a show of strength, though poorly armed, hoping thereby to frighten off guards and so seize stock, particularly stock packing cargo.

But there was only one order in such a situation, and Ma and I gave it at about the same time:

"Charge!"

Following us the entire column wheeled its horses to the left, and digging in spurs, plunged up the fairly steep, sandy hill. The crack of rifles came down from the ridge. A horse to the rear stumbled and fell. Some riders were cursing and lashing their mounts, others were silent. One fellow was firing his rifle with a single hand as if he held a pistol. Most had drawn the Chinese Mausers with which they were armed, and the rapid crack from these filled the hollow with a din and served to keep the attackers' heads down. A rider or two was thrown as horses took bullets in brisket or head. Colonel Ma was bellowing and had his saber out. Up, up—we went in the clinging sand. Ma, with me two lengths behind, reached the crest, but off to one side, and we began firing our pistols into some men who were lying along the rim.

The colonel leapt off his saddle and closed at a run with the sword, bringing the blade down on the nearest Tibetan's head, a fellow who ran to meet him. The attackers now turned their attention to us; a few dropping their rifles, mostly single-shot types and now empty, and drawing their broadswords from silver scabbards—the Tibetan's favorite weapon at close quarters, stood up in full sight. About forty men ran back and disappeared behind a dune. The Moslems charged raggedly over the crest and leaping from their mounts, closed with a yell and began efficiently slicing down those remaining. They were exceedingly efficient too, as General Ma Pu-fang, certainly one of Asia's most experienced battle swordsmen, had himself taught the Tungan cavalry the art—as I had seen at the military academy near Sining. Five Tibetans lay dead, and were judged robbers. And over the slope of the dune were scattered our own casualties:—two men and eight horses killed; some of both wounded. Fortunately, there had been no other robbers on the opposite ridge, for had there been we would doubtless have been caught in a serious cross-fire.

While the Moslems shot the wounded horses, looted the fallen, and found some Tibetan horses in a hollow just behind, the colonel sent a single Tangut to follow the robbers' tracks back to their camp, with orders to then rejoin us by picking up our own trail later. Apparently this was old stuff to these men, for they took it in their stride as if nothing unusual had happened.

We collected our dead and buried them at the foot of the dune. The bugle sounded the Chinese Moslem version of taps, and we swung into the saddles of our own horses and the remounts, and headed back on course. An hour later Ma intercepted a single running horse track and we followed it through the dunes to a pair of black tents, cleverly concealed in a sand gully. Before the occupants could flee, the others galloped in and surrounded the encampment. Some thirty Tibetans came running out, holding their rifles. One of our Tibetans shouted an order, and they threw down their guns, sticking out their tongues and showing their open palms. This (as later explained) was so we could see for ourselves they spoke no evil against us, and held no weapons.

I heard the click of rifle bolts and figured Colonel Ma might be going to shoot them down.

"Wait!" I called, spurring forward, "We will question them!"

The chief among the Tibetans stepped forward; I dismounted. He was a tall man, wearing a black cone-shaped hat with fur ear-flaps sticking out from his head. Solomon came up and this man told us that he and his people were friends: "Chuden-ja!" ("Please sit down!") he shouted to prove it.

Colonel Ma walked over to a mud-wall corral filled with horses. He vaulted over the fence and headed off one of the milling horses, and a moment later was running his hands along its sides.

"The flanks are hot," he said returning to our midst. "Who is the owner?"

A big, surly fellow was indicated by a woman who had appeared. The colonel strode up to him and pulled the rifle forward on its sling over the man's shoulder, and smelled the end of the barrel. Ma's hand darted downward, and when it came up it held an automatic spitting flame. The Tibetan's knees buckled and he slumped down into a sprawl on the ground.

During the powwow it was learned that the tribe occupied all this section of the desert: and its name was said to be the same as that uncharted space, "Gomei." The Duchu tribe ranged in the southern regions; they were the real "robbers," old Black Hat assured us vehemently. Sometimes the two tribes go to war against each other, mainly over hunting rights, though sometimes to capture new wives, or—and here he grinned widely—just for sport when life got a bit dull around camp.

Continuing, he coolly sketched a map in the sand, explaining that in this desolate desert are three fishless seas: in the north is Ta Lien Hai of the "golden sands"; in the south is Gunga Nor; and quite near us, as we could verify easily from the nearest crest, was Undur Nor. At present wild fowl covered the surface of Undur Nor.

"It is good to hear the honking of geese flying north," smilingly pointed out Black Hat glancing into the sky where many geese flew in V formations.

Black Hat energetically whirled his prayer-wheel and darted his eyes between Colonel Ma's and mine, and from time to time fervently chanted "Om Mani Padme Hum," fingering all the while his bone rosary. It seemed enough Moslem justice had been done that day, and we two—between the hard eyes of the colonel—exchanged hadaks as befitting pönpos, and, satisfied I was impractical beyond all his expectations, Ma then ordered the column to mount and round up the Tibetan horses as indemnity. The scouts went ahead and we followed through yet other miles and miles of desert. Snow-flakes began falling, snowflakes as dry and big as duck-down.

Spurs were occasionally touched to flanks and we moved swiftly into the endless dunes. After some thirty miles of twisting and turning through the sand, with not a drop of water anywhere, only a dry skiff of snow on the dunes, we approached a steep, possibly 1,000-foot-high bank of frozen sand and gravel. Spurring to the top of this we found ourselves on a narrow, flat plateau extending in a tongue out into the wilderness of sand. It was duly entered on the map as being 3,000 meters (9,141 feet) in elevation. The time was mid-afternoon, or a little later. With a few men I rode on ahead of the others.

While riding along the tongue we came to a stubbled field of ney. Apparently the direct line through the desert, and off the trail, was going to pay off: an hour later we rode up to a long, clay fortress-wall enclosing about half a city block. We banged on the doors with our rifle stocks, and were admitted by a Moslem criss-crossed with bandoliers: this was Ching Kou, our destination. Along the far wall were mud houses, with corrals taking up most of the other space. Thankfully we swung down from saddles, for we were cramped. The late winter temperature was proving variable in this inner region: during the day the mercury had ranged from a comparatively hot 58° C. to a freezing —35° C. The wind now shifted around from the east and howled in dismally from the west, the prevailing direction in the afternoons, blowing strong and kicking up a dust storm. This dust was gritty on our teeth, it burned our eyes and made them bloodshot.

Dusk brought hoof-beats along the outside wall. We and some soldiers stationed here turned to and swung open the gates, some of us covering our heads with blankets and squinting our smarting eyes against the wind and its dust. We drove in the bellowing train —yaks, horses, mules and men, all red-eyed and half-blinded—and in a mêlée of yells and cracking whips unloaded the fagged, puffing animals, fed them straw and barley, and turned them into the adobe corrals.

A black and starless night fell on Ching Kou, ringed by a few early wolves who howled at long intervals. We staggered out of the storm into our candle-lit room of packed earth, and squatted gladly around a pyre of hot blue yak-dung coals in a brazier. Colonel Ma said two of the wounded men would remain here, and seven new men would join us. Prince Dorje scratched together a bed of straws alongside and stretched out with a groan. Solomon Ma, Colonel Ma and I soon followed his example, grateful for this warm sanctuary. Soon Dorje was telling of his life among the little-known fighting tribes with whom he had had business during World War II as an agent for the Chinese Nationalists:—Uranhai, Ouizhur, Tatar, Uzbek, Taranchi, Khasak, Kalmuk, Quergare. . . .

As he believed some of these raided into Chinghai we must be on the alert for them; at any rate he told that the Uranhai are Buddhist, of Turko extraction and oriental in appearance; that the Ouizhurs are Mohammedan, of Turko extraction but European in looks; while the Kalmuk is lamaist, Mongol-blooded and of an oriental feature. Actually, the name "Kalmuk," he explained is Russian and Turkish, and usually describes only a remnant left of the Torgut horde sent against the Turks of Constantinople. When the Torguts left Russia—and though they had served loyally under the Russian Crown—imperial Cossacks treacherously cut off this remnant from the tribe escaping back into Gobi, and under the Slav heel have all but disappeared from the Volga.

After a time, when we were beginning to doze, Prince Dorje continued:

"I know very well a charming princess of the Ouizhurs. Her eyes are as cat-green as Clark's. She is Moslem and personally leads her troops into battle. Recently the princess raided the Soviet gold mines in the Republic of Tannu Tuva which lies between Siberia and Outer Mongolia. She is said to have a salon in Paris under a cover name, one in Cairo, still another in Peking. She is probably worth in gold bullion, $5,000,000."

I sensed that our little group had grown much closer since the desert and the skirmish, and was glad. I lit my pipe off a coal, and bent my ear for I was as bored as the rest of them.

"Where exactly do these Ouizhurs range?" quietly asked Solomon Ma, always in pursuit of facts. "As political agent I should like to consider a treaty with this worthy tribe."

"Yes! Where! My *Mongo* friend!" roared Colonel Ma, suddenly ceasing to doze on his pile of straw, and slapping his knees in high glee. "By the Sacred Footprint! She must be unmarried . . . and I, who am allowed four wives, have but one! We must go raiding with this one!"

"For pleasure? Or for profit?" enquired Solomon Ma in a business-like manner.

"I always mix the two unless I'm around Sining!" snorted the colonel.

"Is it legal to raid the Soviet Republics?" I cut in.

"What legality!" shouted Colonel Ma, "Do not be tiresome, my friend! It is a sacred duty! Allah will never forgive us if we do not consider it. . . . I personally will pass such laws! To raid the atheistic Soviet Urussu dogs is a short cut to Paradise!"

"If I planned holy war against the Soviets' gold mines," I continued undeterred, fixing Prince Dorje, Solomon and Colonel Ma, with a calculating eye, "I would of course expect command over this woman's troops and 51 per cent of the treasure."

"It simply can't be done," answered Prince Dorje, "I am planning it myself. Of course I might part with the 1 per cent."

"How much cavalry has this princess got?" asked Solomon, squirming nearer the coals, and taking out his notebook.

"Of course, this beautiful princess—and she's *a dead shot*—might claim the ancient tribal right to take to the royal couch any new man entering into formal treaty relations with her Banner," here Dorje leaned forward with studied indifference to toast a bit of yak liver over the coals.

Three voices—Tungan and American—came as one: "Well, what of it! It would only be polite!"

Bellowed the colonel, diplomatically for once, "I have always held the *Mongos* in the highest esteem. Take us in with you! Only troubles lie in the south. And what sensible man cares about looking for mountains anyway? Plenty of mountains everywhere, and one mountain is just like every other mountain!"

Solomon Ma quietly adjusted his glasses on his nose; "There is duty to consider. Perhaps the shortage of oxygen in these high regions of the Tala is responsible for this unseeming outburst of enthusiasm. If we fail to find Amne Machin, the sacred mountain of north Tibet, Governor Ma Pu-fang will certainly cut off all our heads."

We unanimously agreed when the colonel spoke up sternly:

"By the Prophet! Remember Amne Machin. . . ."

Long after midnight we were called out by a guard into the dust storm. The Tangut who had been sent across the desert on the tracks of the robbers, had just come in, and he was exhausted. Warming his hands at the coals inside one of the barracks, the scout reported that the tracks had led to the main Gomei encampment, far away near the middle of the desert. The taking of Black Hat's thirty-two horses didn't prey overmuch on my conscience after that. We finally got some sleep.

5

Action at Fort Ta Ho Pa

OUR ENERGIES fixed on the idea of Amne Machin once more, and wondering where exactly on the official Chinese map it might be, we broke the Ching Kou encampment at 4 A.M. Two or three wolves still howled. The air was perishingly cold, the cloudy night inky black, and we shivered like the dogs—the wind cutting sideways into our faces with an edge. The dust was bothersome. The sound of the wind along the wall had an uncanny whistle, and sounded more predatory than the wolves. We climbed into the saddles and even the horses whinnied and backed away and shied in protest at facing it. Ma noted that not even the *ying* (night hawks) were hunting.

Solomon said that this day we must ride a hard 110 li (55 miles) across mountains and in freezing, rarefied elevations. There was no safe place to camp between Ching Kou and Fort Ta Ho Pa; scouts sent out in the night had reported that Tibetans were swarming everywhere in the regions ahead. With stiff, cold-numbed knees we eased into our high carpet-covered saddles, picked up reins and lead-ropes and jerked the stubborn heads of the caravan into the wind. After a bitter hour's ride due west, we turned left 45 degrees, into the southwest, and holding fairly steady eventually strung out along the rocky bottom of a wide-spanned alluvial river valley called locally the Huku River Gorge. The spelling of this name, like all local names (few of which I have been able to find on any map) is as Dorje spelled it in English for me. I use it not because geographers will necessarily be interested, but for the possible guidance of any traveler who might attempt a penetration of the little-known regions south—from this inner (westward) direction.

The way was paved with slippery ice; when the wind tore aside the clouds and the starlight filtered in, I saw two riders and their horses sprawl flat. Climbing out of the gorge, and keeping under the steep lip of the windy rim, we moved forward until we broke out on top:—

All about, revealed in the first cold dawn light, were hundreds of squatting spider-like black hair tents. We halted and studied the situation: for miles south these tents were scattered across an entire plain. The whole countryside was covered with flocks of sheep, and thousands of yaks. We called a conclave and it was decided we were in jeopardy. At any moment we might be discovered. Colonel Ma bustled around on his horse, saying we had better turn around and head back for Ching Kou. I was scared stiff that this was it, that the search for Amne Machin would somehow, if we returned to Ching Kou, be called off. It would take only a single unfavorable report on me to General Ma to accomplish this—of that I was becoming daily ever more certain.

"To hell with that," I interrupted through Dorje, "You follow me!"

I headed straight down the middle of that plain. When some hundred yards out, I glanced back. No one had budged. Cutting in close to a sprawling black tent, I was suddenly charged by a pack of fierce shaggy dogs who began setting up a racket. The others behind now had no choice but to follow, and I could hear them begin to move along in a trot. Tibetans began running out of the nearest tents, shouting and releasing other dogs. These dogs were trained for the killing of humans as well as wolves, and I knew we were in for it.

I broke into a gallop, riding through a knot of Tibetans, scattering them to left and right. A dog leapt at my horse's head and bit him in the throat, another sank its fangs just at the base of his tail; I glanced down and saw that another dog had ripped away the top half of my left boot. It was useless to try and beat off these dogs with my whip. Colonel Ma plunged alongside and showed me how to twirl the whip on its foot-long bone handle. The dogs apparently are momentarily distracted watching the whip cut circles over the rider's head. At this very moment a quick gallop carried me safely away.

I yelled at Dorje: "Tell Ma Sheng-lung to tell these Tibetans we are an advance force of five thousand Moslem cavalry, and to get back into their tents!"

The Tibetans, taken by complete surprise, did exactly that, and the column rode right down that plain with its hundreds of black charis, and not a single shot was fired at it.

On the far side we skidded down into the Huku River Gorge; at several places in its frozen river bed, the tent nomads had lost about forty horses during this and other nights. A few the night before had been driven by a wolf pack over thin ice, through which the horses had broken, and became trapped. At first, tracks and blood told the grim story, and then the carcasses of three horses were seen scattered over the ice. It was a lesson never to leave our horses unguarded.

Ma turned left into a steep-walled corridor, following a trail. Sticking to this narrow, rocky, precipitous way, we passed by on the left side three *möndangs* (prayer-walls). To pass them in any other manner or direction would go against the religious formula prescribed for travelers. Should we be seen violating this rule, or should our tracks indicate we had done so, we might be subjected to a swift retaliation after the Tibetans had discovered our ruse. These sacred walls were constructed of thousands of slate slabs, many inscribed with Tibetan scriptures. We rode alongside a shoulder-high obo decorated with wild yak and bighorn sheep skulls. From the horns eerily fluttered prayer-flags.

A scout signaled caution. The canyon was narrow and, unable to turn aside or hide, we reluctantly passed a mixed caravan train of possibly a thousand yaks, horses and mules. It was convoyed by four strongly armed mounted parties of Tibetans, riding toward us through the slot. We put on a bold front and kept straight at them. The riders were hunched high over the withers of their mounts, due to very short stirrups: both yaks and mules were ridden. As we scraped by I stared unbelievingly—many of the Tibetans wore painted leather masks for breaking the force of the wind; these masks had terrifying faces, and were also intended to frighten away ghosts and devils. While the last band watched us, we stopped for our Tibetans to murmur prayers at the next obo, and, following their example, most of us added votive stones for luck.

Soon another band of riders came along; these Tibetans, and ourselves, instantly shouted "Aros!" ("Hello!") upon seeing each other appear around a corner in a cliff. This is a kind of desperate life-insurance universally practiced. These Tibetan itinerants wore short sheepskin chupas with wide hems of black or colored cloth just above the knee. The sleeves, out of which, regardless of the biting cold, bare right arms and shoulders were showing, were often long enough to dangle near the ground even when they were mounted. Usually, however, the end of the sleeve is tucked neatly under the sash at the rider's back.

There are no pockets in Tibet. Chupas are hiked up high and cinched tightly at the waist, leaving a very baggy midriff all the way around. Into this is loaded every conceivable item: pipe and tobacco, dice for fortune-telling, spinning-wool, charms, medicinals, dried raw meat, a hunk of brick tea, a tsamba bowl, leather pokes of tsamba, other bags of butter and salt, a chunk of animal sinew from which strong threads are pulled for sewing, needles, lead and powder pouches, a statue of Buddha, horseshoes and nails, extra clothes, coins, sacred books or scriptures, hobbles, a coil of hair rope, perhaps even a puppy or two.

Into the male Tibetan's leather-looped cartridge belt, surprisingly often fully loaded, or his sash, is thrust crosswise a silver scabbard containing a steel broadsword, the haft of which is studded with red corals and blue turquoises. On their heads, which many tribes usually shave but for a scalplock of long hair sometimes braided into a pigtail, are wide-flanged fox hats sometimes having crowns of red silk or silver-mesh threads; or again, sheepskin caps with ear-flaps; or white, peaked felt dunce-caps; or even gold-thread crowned hats with leopard fur trimming. Heavy boots are of black yak leather; lightweight slightly curve-toed boots are soled with soft leather and have cloth tops of pattern-dyed woven wool and string tie-tops. Across the bulky shoulders is slung a rifle or musket, the bifurcated prongs for steadying aim being of polished horn embossed with etched silver, others are of wood or lyre-shaped antelope or gazelle horns. Drök-pa Tibetans are crack shots, and seldom miss.

On their chests, suspended by a cord around the neck, are sacred square silver-and-turquoise shrines containing a Buddha or folded scriptures. Silken bandoliers slung cross-wise over the shoulder, hold packets of sacred *hadaks* (scarves) sometimes perfumed with musk taken from the indigenous musk-deer, said to be worth $35 an ounce. Rings and bracelets are often enormous—gold, silver, amber—sometimes enriched with precious or semi-precious stones mainly from India, and jade from Burma and China. Rosaries are wrapped around the wrist, their beads varying from colored stones and fragmented meteorites to elephant and other ivory and carved animal and human bones. Jewelry set with rubies and sapphires is sometimes seen. The men have a circular four-inch silver pendant ear-ring hanging from the left ear. Rank is denoted by a jeweled comb set in a twisted topknot on the head. Bone- and horn-hafted and steel-bladed daggers of brass, silver or even gold inlay, and turquoise-and-leather flint-and-steel kits hang down from sash or cartridge belt. All this is the traditional costume of Tibet as we were seeing it.

With the last Tibetan party that passed in the gap—and they appeared captivated with curiosity over us—we traded cloth for a sheep's stomach filled with ten "new" *catties* of greenish-yellow yak butter. (A "new" cattie equals 18 ounces.) Travelers to Tibet, almost without exception, speak of Tibetan butter as being "rancid." The butter contained in temple lamps is indeed often rancid, and some of it smells like hell. But I, personally, have never *tasted* rancid butter in northeast Tibet. This butter, like all other butter we eventually obtained, tasted fresh and mild, its flavor not unlike Roquefort cheese. This mör we would use in our brick tea, as butter is never used on bread.

The canyon narrowed down to only a few hundred feet across. Colonel Ma feared ambush. Through these barren mountains cut only by this single defile, he now fixed bayonets—an index of the wary Colonel's information from the scouts out skirmishing. I was shown a few bones of what were said to be the remains of some 150 Moslem troops who were rather recently ambushed trying to re-inforce Ma Pu-fang's Jyekundo garrison considerably north of Lhasa. Though armed with three machine-guns and a mortar they were pinned down and mopped up to the last man. Is it any wonder these Moslems rode with guns drawn, bayonets fixed and ready for instant use?

Breaking clear of this canyon finally, we stood somewhat relieved at the edge of a boggy valley, and near a conical stone obo thirty feet in height, the largest yet seen. A stranger dodged behind it, and two of the guard ran forward and rounded him up. He might have been a Tibetan scout. He told us the valley was known to his people as the "Huku" Valley. So that the fellow would not sound a warn-ing, he was bound with rope. Colonel Ma thought it might be better if his companions found him later after the "birds had flown."

Through binoculars from the top of the obo was spotted a Ti-betan encampment scattered across the far end of the valley. We decided to keep out of sight, for rest we must. A spring flowed nearby and our horses went to it, and also to lick the salt off the frozen grass. Marmots, yellowish rodents measuring a couple of feet in length, much valued for their fur, were popping up out of burrows, indicating the winter period of hibernation was ending. Their piercing whistles split the air. Our elevation was 3,280 meters (9,994 feet) and I realized we were (in relation to Sining and Lanchow) steadily climbing ever higher into the highlands from which was hoped would rise Amne Machin: our ears occasionally popped from the lessening air pressure.

Banks of clouds tore by, revealing the blue sky, and the sun came out: bleak stone mountains ringed the valley, their needle-sharp peaks scintillating with icy points three to four thousand feet above, while below broad snow-fields serenely reflected beams of light into the purple shadows puddled under cliffs and in the slits of ravines.

Keeping the obo between us and the far Tibetans, we tossed out the tea kettle, a copper pot holding 20 gallons of water. Lacking stones, for these had all been gathered to erect the obo over two hundred yards away, our men swiftly cut cubes of sod which they placed in three pillars. On this wobbly structure they balanced the copper pot, and then shoved a heap of dry, fairly smokeless yak dung under it. Flint and steel was applied. To keep our fire going, a yak skin bag with the hair still on was energetically flopped up and down as a bellows, worked by a man sitting up close to the embers. These bellows were necessary owing to less oxygen in the rarefied air, and, being non-rigid, were exceedingly tricky to use. Surprisingly, not all of the soldiers could manage to squirt sufficient air through its tin nozzle. They were not alone: try as I might, time after time, day after day, week after week, I could never get the hang of that damned contraption—I might as well have used a potato sack for a bellows.

The first duty after dismounting and unsaddling, or loosening the girths, and slipping the headstalls and bits so that the horses could feed, was to gather in the skirts of our chupas as much semi-dry yak dung as we could find. Fearing the Tibetans would see our smoke, we used only the dryest dung. Actually, if this fuel is too dry it contains no great heat, if too green it will not burn at high elevations. Mule and horse dung is second best as it burns too fast. No man is ashamed of this humble chore; Colonel Ma gathered it, and Solomon Ma and Prince Dorje, and I, also gathered it, daily.

In spite of the nearness of Tibetans, I simply couldn't resist letting fly a hunk at Colonel Ma as he bent over to salvage a rich find of yak droppings. So successful was my aim and so surprisingly loud was Ma Sheng-lung's yelp of dismay, that in a flash every man, stiff and tired though he was from cold and saddle, dropped everything and joined in with a howl and a strong arm against his nearest neighbor. Somebody knocked the tea kettle off the fire; the horses started stampeding; the battle ceasing only when the great Colonel Ma got a load of green stuff smack in the puss.

"Praise the Lord!" roared Colonel Ma, unlimbering his sword and slashing at the flying *argol* aimed at him.

"It serves the bloody bounder right!" cried our savant, Prince Dorje, taking off for the obo; "The old hound let me have it right in the ear!"

We soon settled down to making a new pot of tea and keeping an eye peeled for the Tibetans. A bone-freezing wind began pouring off the northernmost rock pinnacles and cradled glaciers overhead. The sun turned weak, the air became pea-soup, the temperature fell 10 degrees below freezing; and the sky was becoming obliterated by streaks of clouds hanging like hanks of hair from the tallest peaks. A storm was gathering and this was no place to camp. We bolted huge cold chunks of meat cut from a yak's carcass the night before, and boiled at Ching Kou, and tamped it down with lumps of tsamba and bowls of hot tea:—a sumptuous feast for hungry men.

The hot copper pot was dunked in the river to cool off, and we rounded up the scattered horses on the run. Slapping saddles on, we rode fast for 4½ hours that afternoon until we struck the outlying ridges of what Dorje believed to be the Semenov Range. Dorje had no particular prejudice against old Russian explorers and their findings, also he admired von Filchner who had marked these mountains the Semenovs. If my reportage on the region seems not standardized, this view of Dorje's may well be responsible. My main objective in writing this account is not to furnish material for the scholastic splitting of hairs, but to serve, at least in part, for directing the footsteps of some more competent and better equipped explorer, to those great mountains seen from a distance only by Pereira, Rock, Reynolds, the Hump pilots, and for all I know a few others.

Just beyond, in the south, lay Fort Ta Ho Pa. The captured possible scout had said this outpost had been raided by a well-known renegade, and razed and burned. But Ma didn't believe him: Tan Chen-te would be waiting there with the Kumbum column. In any event, our way back was cut off by the Tibetans on the plain above the Huku Gorge, and there was only one way to go, and that way was straight ahead across the Semenovs.

A light snow began falling. We trudged uphill on a trail with each thump of our hearts seemingly measuring only a couple of inches gained on the steep slope. The narrow trail of the rising *la* brought us an hour later to Chunlong Niha pass, which Dorje's aneroid measured at 3,900 meters (11,883 feet). Here a sudden squall of snow and cold caught us flatfooted: in a few minutes we were turned into a ghost caravan sheeted in white. We hurried on down the south side, slipping and sliding mainly on the seats of our pants 200 feet down the steeply descending *terh*. The yaks proved sure-footed, but some of the horses fell sprawling. Grabbing their leadropes we led them down, picking the less-slippery spots. Hitting bottom in a high valley we mounted and, blinded by wind and snow, worked along slowly. Six horses were down at one place, including a pack animal with a broken leg, and two were shot, their cargo being shifted to other mounts.

At last we reached the lower south slope of the range, where the caravan slid down steep gravel banks to a sand and stone plain. The storm lifted and all about were standing thousands of yaks: mostly jet black, some brown or even cream colored, and a few scattered white ones. Colonel Ma spotted a mark or brand and thought they belonged to the Tibetan said to have raided against the Moslems, and if he hadn't burned out Fort Ta Ho Pa we would try to choose from these herds the best animals, and offer to pay *nela,* a unique Tibetan form of rent and insurance.

We rounded up the last stragglers and made off for the fort, whose battlements presently loomed up miles away. Fort Ta Ho Pa was a sprawling, square-shaped, clay citadel, perched on a hillside near the sharp lip of a deep tree-lined canyon. In our binoculars we saw the Chinese flag, a many-pointed white star-burst on a blue field, flying from a mast in a tower, and knew the scout had lied. And if the fort was not burned out, Tan would be waiting for us!

Approaching Dorje, Solomon and I couldn't believe at first that the green patches on the far side of the deep canyon were trees. They were, though, the last we were to see for a long time. They proved to be tamarisks, several being giants with a three-foot diameter, having a dark-green foliage and red bark. The Mongols call them "Modo 'en Khan" ("King of Trees"). Though actually twisted, gnarled, and wind-torn, they seemed incredibly luxurious and stately.

Riding across the wide panorama of plain fringed with fairly tall stone mountains from eleven to seventeen thousand feet high, we espied innumerable herds of gazelles. Ma Sheng-lung and I cut left from the caravan hoping for a shot. As we approached one of these herds of some thousand gazelles, they suddenly raised their heads as one, quickly strung along together like beads on a string, and scampered off, easily swinging away and crossing over in front of the column to our right. We rejoined the caravan to help herd it along, for the pack beasts in particular seemed to be nearly dead with fatigue.

As we approached Fort Ta Ho Pa we were met by Tan Chen-te, and our Kumbum men, who all came out to cheer us in. At last we drove the column through the gate. Within the walls, I was assigned to a small dirt-floored room, where I immediately began to work out paper plans. The wind rose steadily in velocity, and it was not long before the freshly papered Chinese-style windows were blown out. Dust and sand blinded me so that I finally had to put away my work. I then went out on a tour of inspection.

Fort Ta Ho Pa's thick outer walls encompassed administrative offices, if you could call them that—storerooms, dung-fuel piles, a stack of straw, corrals, kitchen, blacksmithing shop, barracks, and a few more odds and ends—all scrambled together in one disorderly mixup of running soldiers, steaming pots, yelping dogs, wind and dust, men's voices bellowing orders, horses' squealing and kicking, and smells. In one of the storage rooms was found plenty of mutton stacked up, five tons of it, all handily hewn into chunks and frozen solid. With scores of men to feed here and on the expedition, this was a cardinal item and our chief concern. At first I was worried about seeing any number of rats about the room, but since no one else seemed to think anything was unusual about rats chewing away on our mutton, I tried to forget such things as typhus.

The magistrate here, actually sub-governor of south Chinghai, proved to be our own friend Captain Tan Chen-te, who, I hoped, would greatly simplify expediting our movement toward Amne

Machin. Tan controlled the district of Ta Ho Pa, measuring east-and-west two horse stages, north-and-south five stages.

Tan obviously ruled with a liberal hand for a despotic Chinese Moslem; his fort (so we learned in a roundabout manner, as he was evasive when questioned) had been taken in battle on at least two occasions and most of the garrison massacred, no doubt an excellent reason for a soft policy. Just in back of the fort was an abandoned airfield, built but not used in World War II.

With these tribes we would now negotiate for some sort of treaty which would indirectly facilitate Ma Pu-fang's partial military (not political) withdrawal from Red China, and permit the eventual establishment of a new base for fighting the Communists; and a treaty of peace which would get Dorje and me within striking range of Amne Machin. Unique in Tibetan history, I believe—certainly not often—is this arrangement where a traveler has acted as emissary (however unofficial) to a government in order to carry out his own work of discovery. Be that as it may, we would also attempt a volunteer mobilization for the procurement of Buddhist troops and secret agents; we would obtain subsistence for men and fodder for animals; and we would secure yaks, horses and mules; equipment, clothing, rifles, ammunition, saddles—and every other single item we might conceivably need. But, especially, we would secure arrangements, treaties of alliance, between Moslem and Tibetan, this being absolutely necessary to my plan for passing through the territories south and southwest of Ta Ho Pa in search of Amne Machin and an approach to it.

We had a terrific job to do in Fort Ta Ho Pa, and realizing time was short due to the unfavorable situation in China proper, I demanded action. But I didn't get it. A deep pessimism had fallen over the expedition; no one believed we could go any farther, and action, preparation, carried on at white heat, was all that would save us from bogging down in a complete funk. Everybody was worried about the war back home and their families. This search for a mountain range, and its penetration if found, seemed utterly useless to them. Food, Dorje soon learned, was a first drastic problem: a hard winter had left the tribes lean in reserves, reserves already drawn upon for the war in China.

We tackled that job. In the deep canyon-valley just outside the fort, ran a turbulent western tributary of the upper Yellow River, the sweet, rocky Ta Hua, filled with fish up to a foot in length. When dried they should prove good to eat. So far, so good. . . .

Moslem fishermen, who had never before caught a fish in their lives, were sent out. Their success was phenomenal: leave it to these resourceful fellows to find "God's way"—with dynamite and hand grenades.

Northward, as we knew, the plains swarmed with gazelles; these we must begin hunting. In the following days Dorje, Ma Sheng-lung, Solomon, Tan and I, usually by staying out all day in snowstorms, hailstorms and wind, brought this scheme to fruition. It was hard hunting, requiring endless perseverance, care, and patience; the gazelles were wary and the plain's spaces without appreciable cover. But a considerable reserve in gazelle meat was eventually drying in the sun and wind.

Further, in the mountains were *yang*, bighorn sheep said to be of two kinds. One was identified from an old skin as the so-called Chinese "stone sheep," the other possibly being the Marco Polo variation called the blue sheep. *Kyang* (wild ass) meat proved on tasting too strong for the prejudiced palate of either Moslem or Tibetan—though I found it good enough for a hungry man—and so no more were hunted. The objective was not to deplete the valley's fine game herds, but to fill our lank bellies, and try to find Amne Machin. The *sheh chih* musk-deer were reported roving in bands of hundreds. *Dre-mo*, the big Tibetan bears, were fairly plentiful, but again not eaten, this time (by the Tibetans at any rate) on religious grounds. Dorje found that the three kinds of bears so far reported in Tibet are undoubtedly all one and the same bear; a parallel might be the comparison between our own cinnamon and black bears. The Moslems pointed out that quite frequently, when wounded, these bears will charge a hunter. The naturalist and explorer, Schäfer, has secured photographs of these bears actually in the act of charging, this on an expedition halted at Jyekundo by the Sining Moslems.

But to return to that first night of our arrival:

I was dead tired and ached in every joint from the cold and over ten hours spent in a hard saddle. The seat of my pants felt as if a yak had planted all four feet there. However, before sleeping that night, we worked out general logistics, strengths, routes, treaties, full requirements for a three months' forced march to Amne Machin and return. This included exploring the headwaters of the Yellow River and the little-known regions lying between Amne Machin and the transcontinental Kun Lun Range. It was evident that a much stronger armed escort than originally planned in Sining must be recruited among the tribes.

In the midst of all this, at midnight, scouts banged their guns on the gates with news that a small party of Moslem officials had just been murdered only two miles away; these officials had been ordered up from Tangar to take Tan's place at the fort, and to try and secure our rear. Tan himself had been ordered that very afternoon, by radio from Governor Ma Pu-fang, to go all the way through to the interior with us.

In addition to this disturbing news of the killings, Tan Chen-te revealed he had recently sent thirteen men to the distant Fort Chakar, southwest of Amne Machin Range—officials who were to gather remounts and food for us, to be used in the Yellow River headwaters region after we had found Amne Machin and that all but one of these officers had been massacred from ambush. At 1 A.M., an hour after we heard of the nearby killings, the guards opened the gates; a strange sight greeted them.

A horse with a man on its back was standing there. A single survivor had been tortured, his eyes gouged out, his tongue, ears and nose cut off; his belly was filled with stones (*mani* stones consigning him to heaven) and his body mounted on a horse, tied in upright position and now driven back to Fort Ta Ho Pa as a grim warning that Tibetans must be consulted on such serious matters as the movements of Moslems and foreign strangers.

These two tragedies warned us to be on the alert. The very thought of such tough and reckless killers about made Colonel Ma jump: though late at night, even the tired troops were called out in the freezing air, and their firearms stripped, cleaned and reloaded. Four machine-gunners were mounted on the walls, in addition to the regular guards.

A guard with a Belgian automatic pistol in his hand, sat on our treasure chests of gold and silver. The gold bars were long, square-molded ones, and could be hacked off to any weight and value. The dollars were new Yuan Shih-K'ai, having more actual silver content than the United States dollar. These were preferred above all other silver coins by Tibetans. It was costly—this Moslem backed expedition—probably exceeding U.S. $100,000 if one had to purchase stock, arms, supplies, feed, provisions, services and all the rest on his own; believed by the Tungans and Dorje to be the greatest sum ever put into Tibet for the purpose of exploration. After midnight and before dawn I grabbed a few hours of sleep.

At daybreak I was up. Patrols were dispatched for gathering intelligence among the tribes, especially the Order-of-Battle. Tan's Tibetan agents were also sent out to glean whatever they could from the tribal conclaves. The quartermaster's agents were hurried out under escort to scour the countryside for riding and pack animal stock, provisions and gear.

By afternoon, stately *pönpos* (lords), carrying black Lhasa terriers resembling pekingese, began to ride in with their retinues and armed retainers to "pay their respects." More likely, as Solomon suggested in jest, they were sizing us up and measuring our throats. Long-haired, pigtailed and wild looking were the pönpos of the Wangshetihai tribe. Other chiefs were grim-faced, heavily-armed horsemen of the Shabrang and the Achuchu. Their chupas and gyasoks were of finest sheepskins, faced with rich brocaded silks and gold thread and trimmed with the furs of the white Tibetan snow-leopard, red fox, marmot, wolf, or ermine.

A few had firearms chased in Lhasa gold and silver; their high saddles sometimes plated with silver and inlaid with semi-precious stones; their prayer-wheels fashioned of leather, gold and silver, ivory or bone. Each carried on his sometimes massive, always bare, chest, a large silver-and-turquoise-inlaid *gao,* shrine-coffin, in which reposed holy scriptures or a precious terra-cotta Buddha.

Sausage-necked, bellowing Colonel Ma, and suave Captain Tan proclaimed that court was being held in the fort: a clan of the Naja tribe demanded satisfaction in silver or blood from a Shabrang headman, who, they claimed, had engaged a bombom "Black Bones" lama to kill a certain Naja by witchcraft. "Bombom" is the way it is pronounced in this part of Tibet, and he is a follower of the sect variously called Bon or Pön. Some of these men are not real lamas but are quite often called such. The accused lama, a "notorious" and much-feared bombom, was called before the court to give testimony as to the means of the killing. This lama was over 6 feet tall and very impressive in fur robes as he lectured on the subject of his powers over the forces of darkness. He endlessly spun his prayer-wheel, occasionally dangerously close to the purpling face of Colonel Ma and the smiling one of Captain Tan.

Yes, my lords, if it was anybody's business, he had taken a wild yak bull's horn, put it in a scripture paper, some special wood and a piece of cloth torn from the alleged victim's clothing, and in red ink he had written upon these objects the man's name and age; he then placed the fatal horn, anointed with oil, in the ground together with salt and garlic, and on the first, second, and seventh days thereafter, prayed and made incantations over it. At the end of this time the horn was dug out, and he, the "never failing" bombom, and his happy client, found it filled with blood; the victim lay paralyzed in his tent and died soon after.

The court's verdict was an instantaneous "guilty," the sentence was that the bombom banish himself from the hsien of Ta Ho Pa for thirty days, and that the guilty Shabrang headman who had hired him pay over the sum of $1,000 "blood money" to the Naja tribe, and another $1,000 for court "expenses."

As the bombom was leaving the fort, I sent Solomon Ma out to hire him; after all, a bombom of his ability might come in handy on the road to Amne Machin.

6

Snowbound

OUR preparations for decampment toward Amne Machin well advanced, Dorje surprisingly informed us that: "When traveling, Mongols say, you will circle to the right and arrive at your point of departure after a day's ride over the steppes, unless you have a left-handed man along."

"Don't worry," I advised, a little too quickly and without doubt a little too smugly, "we have oil compasses."

"May the mercy of the Lord descend on him at once! Prince Dorje is right!" boomed Colonel Ma, halting his pacing up and down the parapet under the battlements of the wall, "I too prefer to pair off a left-handed guide with a right-handed one!"

"But, the compasses are—" I began all over again.

"Compasses! Extremely unreliable in the highly magnetized mountains of Tibet!"

At this point Ma Sheng-lung looked aghast: "In the Name of the Lord, the Compassionate, the Merciful! Last night my number-one cook, Abdulla, and that scoundrel Habibur, the left-handed guide, deserted us!"

"This is very serious . . ." put in Captain Tan with a silky smile, spreading his fine hands as if to quiet stormy waters. He summoned an orderly and barked orders that the *hsien* be searched for a left-handed guide; that business attended to, they returned to their testing of a 25-caliber machine-gun, mounted on the top of the wall. I knew the piece fired perfectly, even in sub-zero weather, but they had hatched (in my opinion) a very precarious idea. Our treaty negotiations had bogged down. Hundreds of armed Tibetans of many tribes now swarmed around the fort. Tribesmen were everywhere, and becoming too full of swagger to suit Colonel Ma. And three of our men had vanished, apparently into thin air. Nearly a hundred black charis lay under the gun's sights.

Colonel Ma yanked back the bolt and pressed the trigger. The gun chattered. I saw he had not fired into the Tibetans but over their heads. He took his hands away from the gun and the smoke-tracers streaming over the Tibetan encampment stopped. It would be an understatement of fact to say a silence fell.

Then the Tibetans began running behind bag and saddle barricades, the women screaming in terror or anger, you couldn't tell which.

More Tibetans began gathering, some in knots, and presently most of them hurried into the charis. We left the wall by a ladder, smiling a little, and by nightfall the chiefs entered the fort with a treaty painted on rice paper . . . a guarantee which no amount of argument, negotiations, bribes and haggling had been able to produce.

New Tibetan recruits brought the roster up to full strength; this Buddhist contingent had its own priest and its own *nampa* (medico).

One of the Tibetans in our command died during the night. This in spite of the energetic ministrations of the nampa. Being a stubborn medico he tried to bring the dead man back to life. Lying full length on the corpse, he pried open the mouth, seized the tongue between his teeth and began to shake and breathe *mantras*. But it was no use, metaphysics would not work, the case was judged hopeless, the patient had evidently lived an evil life.

Early next morning the corpse was placed on a sizable mountain not far away, and near an obo. This particular monument consisted of tiers of mani stones some of which were inscribed with scriptures and surmounted by yellow prayer-flags; the man's saddle, gun, and other personal possessions were bound to the central mast of the obo, for he had been some sort of minor chief. The corpse was then turned over on its face and hacked into small pieces so that birds and other scavengers could more easily dispose of it—a typical, in fact almost universal, service for the lamaist dead.

At lamaseries there is found a caste, or more properly I suppose, simply outcasts called *ragyaba*, who trim the flesh off a corpse and feed it to pariah dogs and vultures that apparently answer by name. The skeleton is pounded to bits, mixed with tsamba, and fed to temple swine and dogs. Our bombom of the yak-horn incident explained to Dorje that this mortifies the flesh, shows its unimportance, exalts the spirit now released. Man's body, part of the flux of nature, has evolved from the dust of the stars, and to the dust of stars it returns. And that never-dying, never-born "thing-in-itself" which animated this dust and gave it consciousness is now set free, either to suffer new reincarnations in this "earthly hell," or to join the ordered vortex of eternal power. I doubted if this particular man had had any other hope in his mind than just obtaining for himself a slightly better and less hard incarnation than the one just finished.

Special exorcism rites were held that afternoon, as death by witchcraft was suspected by his tribe, and prayers demanded by many of our Tibetan contingent were intoned by a wandering Red lama of the old "Unreformed" sect of Black Bones. These rites of what were called the Bardo Thödol were to cast out spirits from the dead man's Vedic *ātman* (soul), and to protect it from the *namshi* (Shamanistic human and animal spirits) while on its devious search on the *bardo* plane for rebirth in an earthly manifestation—the body of a man or animal, or even a plant—in which to reincarnate according to the law of retribution. The lamas pointed out that the body of man, of course, is no more important than that of a flea or an ox; it is the evolved spirit that counts—the joining of the soul with that conscious *will* behind the atom and the worlds! All life must fulfil the inevitable chain of material transmigrations from single atom, through evolution of species, towards supermundane consciousness, and realization of Nirvana; or, as the case might be, if earned, release forever from all phenomenal existence in any form through rebirth, and so escape to the Ultimate Reality—*Dewajang*. Almost nothing is known of the ancient Shamanistic religion as practiced by the people of Tibet in the outlying regions, so different from the more orthodox Red and Yellow Churches. That, and the fact that it is another link in the story of our search for Amne Machin, is why I include it here. If you are to have all the facts, you might as well have these too, however indirect.

Hectic, busy preparations for our venture continued. Our spirits had improved. Copper cooking pots were purchased. Tsamba, the main food other than meat, for we had no foreign food of any kind except Chinese tea, was brought in on horses and put into leather bags. These tough bags would protect the flour from dampness; nor, was I assured, would they split under hard usage on the pack racks. Dried peas for horses were obtained by the ton, and packed in long, sausage-shaped woven-wool cord bags. Eight thousand eight hundred pounds of barley were stomped down tight into hide pouches. A sizable herd of sheep was slaughtered and boiled in kettles, and then laced in leather where it froze solid. Extra sheepskin robes were cut and sewn by nimble-fingered male Naja tailors; ropes of horsehair were twisted, braided and knotted; saddlery repaired; new wooden saddle racks constructed for yaks; rugs rolled and secured with leather thongs; raincoats of pressed sheep and camel felt were purchased by the stack, as were native boots and saddle blankets.

All our horses were being shod according to the prevailing custom of having only the two front hooves fitted with "cold" iron shoes. We bought tsula, dried skimmed yaks' milk, and mör, rich yak butter packed in sheep stomachs which are transparent as cellophane. In the canyon below were obtained thirty-eight large pheasants called *ma chi* (horse chicken), some measuring 2½ feet in length, a blue-gray bird with red legs, a bone-colored beak, finely penciled red eye-rings, a white head, a silky peacock-tail. These and about 50 brown-and-white gazelles were added to our growing larder; and of course, the fish, now dried.

While hunting, mirages due to refraction made gazelles tall as giraffes one moment, and suddenly telescoped them into gnats the next. In hunting these we learned that the gazelles would gather together then string out at a dead run as we approached. But as the distance increased between quarry and hunter, they did not seem to move forward at all, so great was the range—sometimes 500 to 1,000 yards. However, they almost invariably ran back in a wide loop until parallel with our line of approach, and then would cut in behind us and cross over our tracks; for this reason our hunters dropped out of the saddles, their horses remaining with the approaching column of hunters.

These dropped hunters would hide flat in the bottoms of hollows and as the gazelles cut back over our tracks, would quite often rise up and commence firing. This favorite tactic, more than any other, placed our soldiers close enough for an occasional shot at the extremely wily animals. Like soldiers the world over, these Moslems too, were practically useless for real hunting. A good trained shot does not necessarily guarantee a good hunter. Some men can hit a target, but not a moving animal or bird (much less hunt it successfully); while many men who are excellent game shots (whether they are hunters or not), are indifferent target shots.

A few times, however, I hunted alone for sport, digging into the mouths of the yard-wide marmot burrows to escape from snow and wind, and to hide. At such times I rested in these rodent holes, content and warm enough—once reading Dorje's copy of Plutarch's *Lives*—before continuing with my stalking, and always approaching the herd upwind. These were among the happiest hours of my life.

My request for the permanent Ta Ho Pa five-man radio team, to accompany us, was granted by Governor Ma Pu-fang. The expedition could keep in direct touch with its benefactor, though later he would be stationed at least 250 miles east and a bit north in Lanchow commanding the northwest Chinese armies.

The weather worried me, and the meteorologist was a pessimistic character. But as this soldier pointed out, the days were nearly always windy and dusty, invariably so in the afternoons; the temperature in the early mornings was often now −22° C. During the day it was sunny and warm one hour, cloudy and freezing the next. When snow fell it sometimes started off gently in big snowflakes, but almost invariably ended up driving like needles nearly horizontal to the ground, filling hollows and holes, into which our horses stumbled.

I began worrying about the prevailing visibility, which was at times exceedingly low around the surrounding mountains, and about our chances for observations on Amne Machin Peak should we ever locate that mythical tower. I could see only trouble. Clouds nearly always strung out from the peaks, or were lying around them. Also at times there were plumes, spindrift of loose snow not frozen into a solid pack. Everywhere lay miles-long streaks of wind-patterned, hard-packed snow sometimes reflecting an intense light; we learned that snow-glasses cut down refraction and glare sufficiently to measure four peaks with possibly a fair degree of accuracy. One of these to the southwest in a mountain range marked on one of the Chinese maps as "Wa Hung Shan," rose to 16,870 feet. Due west, and close by, another was 14,430 feet. Southward still another peak measured at 12,860 feet. We used the broad plain north of the fort for laying down our exaggeratedly long base-lines of a thousand yards. The craggy mountain a few degrees west of south from the fort, rising beyond the river gulch, was called Tsasura, "Sickle Rock," 14,752 feet and Tan said we would pass near it in heading for Amne Machin.

At the fort Dorje invariably was to be found over his books. At this time he obtained definite evidence of what was believed to be a secret Tibetan "White" Church. The Red and Yellow Churches, and even some sects of Pön, the pre-Buddhistic Shamanism, are more or less known, especially the two former, about which a great deal is known to western scholars, but there exist still other smaller sects apparently little known and possibly unknown.

For example: west of us was said to be a temple monastery of women priestesses, or *a-ni*, devoted to the meditation, adoration, and service of a cruel goddess of a type similar to the pagan Greek Fury. The female head-lama's followers hunt down male travelers and carry them off to the lamasery. Terrible (and interesting) tales were told; here their earthly existence is believed to end in sacrifice to the bloodthirsty deity. However, Sheja, a Shabrang headman, whispered that the fate of the victims is quite often something of a highly different nature. One of his own men who had escaped had told him so. Our scientific staff under the stern eye of Dorje, however, did not take this version too seriously as Sheja was considered something of a wag, and as usual, was probably just having a good time watching our consternation. In fact half the expedition, far from being appalled, wanted to investigate right away.

Since such information was difficult for us to come by, I should add that one day while still in Sining, Dorje and I visited Bishop Haberstroh and were introduced to a priest, Father Oberle, a jolly German ethnologist who had just come from Kuei-te on the Yellow River. We discussed Tibetan customs, as a knowledge of them might considerably aid our movement forward; and he told us about an affair of magic which he had just documented. It concerned a mendicant "Black" Pön lama, who had recently contracted to save barley crops from destruction by storm. Something went wrong, for he promptly lost part of the guaranteed crops to a hailstorm. Consequently he found himself being sued for damages in the Kuei-te court by the angry farmers.

This suggested another story; this one, as I recall, was about a Red lama who was hired to locate a "black charm" believed to be the cause of sickness in a rich man's family. After chanting the appropriate prayers the lama went through certain rites which he would not explain, and then smilingly placed two of Father Oberle's assistants at each end of a heavy table. Only their fingertips touched the top. The table rose off the ground and moved through the air across the field, and landed a considerable distance away. Here, under it, the lama dug and uncovered the "black charm." It proved to be comprised of certain scriptures, and had been put there by another lama retained by someone to do injury to the rich man's family.

One night in Fort Ta Ho Pa, before leaving, eight small gold nuggets were brought in to the dinner table by Magistrate Tan's six-year old son. That Tan had a son here was news to me, but here he was. I understood he had picked them out of a gravel bank inside the fort. Colonel Ma immediately hushed up the matter, being assisted by Tan who appeared to be thunderstruck. Evidently they feared more desertions and delays on the very eve of our departure. Apparently unknown to any great extent in the outside world, there are today as many gold rushes going on in Chinghai, as formerly went on in Alaska. But more on this later.

We decided on a farewell celebration and party. By noon next day a chief of the Naja tribe brought in ten girls, silver-bedecked and fur-clad. A few were pretty enough and all were vivacious. In their ears dangled turquoises; on their fingers they had star-sapphires and red stones (possibly rubies). They wore beautiful long black robes lined with soft lambs' wool, burgundy-red shirts with Chinese collars, red-fox hats; while two long tails or trains hung down almost to the floor, heavy with turquoises and corals and studded with silver bowls four to six inches in diameter of hammered designs. To our soldiers' courting, these dancing and singing girls' words said very loudly and very emphatically, "no-no-not-that!" while their smiles through milk-white teeth said, "maybe-maybe-take-it-easy!" but surely their long, thin, heavy-lashed brown eyes said, "don't-be-afraid 'yes-yes'!"

"I say, old boy, is this not a dangerous procedure?" enquired Prince Dorje in his meticulous Oxford accent, looking altogether pious, precious, stuffy, wise, and shocked. "Our men are very hot-blooded, you know. Better call it off. Fighting may break out over these wenches."

"If there are any casualties we can always get others."

"Dear fellow, don't smirk at me. I am not a prig, but, for the official government record what do we call this . . . this operation?" persisted Dorje.

"Why don't you stick it under 'Agriculture—Investigation of wild ney'."

"Come, come, that would never get by our governor, you know."

"How about 'Morale Operation'."

He fixed me with a censorious stare: "I am glad, Clark old boy, that you are calling it 'morale,' and not 'moral'!"

Our elated Moslem Chinese janizaries and mercenary Tibetans—decked out in their best furs and red Lhasa robes and boots and pistols and daggers and silver or golden chains and silk sashes, danced and sang—returning with a fine clanking gusto the tremulous song of the melting houris. After a couple of preliminary hours of warming up, our Salar and Tungan sons of Islam seemed already resurrected with one foot in Paradise. Their skill and passion in both song and dance—with plenty of lowbrow whooping, cat-calling, stomping, clapping, ogling—was scarcely of this unhappy earth. Colonel Ma pointed out that there was not one shrinking violet among the lot.

"They are all great lovers!" he bellowed unabashed for all to hear. "By Allah's smallest toe! If they are not, they will speedily land in the guardhouse!"

Being the guest of honor on this gala night, I was led sedately by the Naja pönpos, grave lordly Buddhasatvas, minor gods, to the big chair standing at one end of the hall. The tamarisk walls were solidly lined with hundreds of people, male and female. Heads stuck in through every window. With mincing steps a girl would walk to the center of the hall, and when the music—a wooden tom-tom and a pair of fantastic fiddles—started, she would begin to dance, using both skill and charm, and with an exaggerated coyness sing a love song into the fluffy white cuff of her long sleeve. All songs were sung into the sleeve, but whether symbolic of modesty, or to cut down volume, I could not ascertain. When the girl finished, one of our Tibetan or Moslem bravos—and without any personal invitation—would cavort out to the center as if shot from a catapult (sometimes there was a collision), and gallantly dance and sing a hot answer to the girl. To repeat the words of a song, or to fluff his lines, was absolutely forbidden, and if the dancer-singer-suitor couldn't remember a new song, then it was just too bad for him: he was declared socially a yak, and hauled off bodily, with apologies from Tan of course, to the guardhouse.

But assuming all goes well: after the steaming suitor finishes his heartfelt rendition—and under Colonel Ma's buzzard's eye it had better be heartfelt—the girl laughingly brings forth a cup of *ara* (fermented re-re-re-fermented chang) to the man she "loves" or wishes to honor, though not necessarily the dancer; in most cases that night, myself, who in turn must first toss off the ara, then rise —if I could—and dance before her in the difficult, stilted and dignified classical Tibetan style. For this job I borrowed Colonel Ma's black fan, though most of the dancers used the cuff of their long sleeve.

After I had returned my first such dance, Prince Dorje, possibly a bit mellowed, for ara cannot be refused if offered, strolled over grinning from ear to ear, and tried to get a raise out of me: "I say! Never suspected you were the Don Juan type."

"Calm yourself, honorable colleague. Back to your cobwebs. These girls are only trying to get a fat price for their barley."

There were either ten girls with a lot of barley on hand, or else they secretly really did "love" me, not a totally improbable supposition I was beginning to feel after ten stiff drinks of ara. The giant Najas yelled, howled wolf calls, and fired their guns off far into the wintry night. Sometimes they forgot they were inside government headquarters and fired their guns off through the roof anyway; but Captain Tan, always the host and diplomat, only smiled and said, "My roof is your roof" as he dusted himself off.

For all the world these Najas with their shaved heads, many with big hooked Roman noses, and scalplocks decorated with insignia of rank, gems and furs, were like Indian chiefs on the warpath. Couriers from among the tribes rode far and wide into the night, carrying news of our departure to the pönpos, and, we hoped, news that the Moslems and the foreigner were not such bad fellows after all.

By 3 A.M. all was quiet except for the chants of our departing guests—"Om Mani Padme Hum!" spoken in a fast, melodious, hypnotic cadence. The guards still vigilant, however, the gates of the fort were securely barred from the inside. Snow was gently falling.

While a poetic ending to our celebration, this last fact caused alarm. Delays might see our treaty canceled, many of our men scattered back to the tribes, our departure blocked, anything. . . .

We decided to risk the snowstorm. By morning the expedition must pull out. Even before dawn lamas and pönpos were sending in messengers saying our caravan could pass through their lands. And so after nearly a week of hectic days of preparation at Fort Ta Ho

Pa, from which Dorje and Solomon Ma had snatched success out of failure, our scouting cavalcade started off in a storm, but even so, not without high spirits, for we three at least were tingling with expectation.

We had scarcely cleared the fort when a last-minute warning from the pönpos came in. Scores of independent chiefs and robber bands, would consider us fair prey, and the chiefs insisted that their treaties could not hold them responsible. As the treaty-chiefs could not go *bow* (bond) for our security, we must ever be alert and on guard against attack. Only Dröma could help us now!

Thus warned, my own advance detachment, and part of the main column, rode out of Fort Ta Ho Pa and slid on its hooves down into the deep, steep-walled canyon. It was very cold. An explosion on the slope across the way, was said to be caused by a tamarisk bursting from the cold. Carefully we forded the icy Ta Hua River, and set a meandering course on a westward trail out of the canyon and through the gullies and flats folded under the white wing of Tsasura. Almost immediately we encountered a bit of nuisance at a group of black tents, with scattered yaks ruminating among lichens. Several Tibetans of a tribe not known to me leapt on their horses and started at a run for a point well back of the head of the column. They undoubtedly were not raiding, but simply young bucks making a nuisance of themselves, or else driving us away from their yaks. At any rate some of our own yaks took to their heels and were scattered beyond control of our herders. I touched my spurs to him and rammed the big bay horse I was riding that day, smack into the main group. One fellow let out an angry shout and swung his rifle's butt against my horse's head. A quick shot came from just behind. The Tibetan leaped down from his saddle, and Hassan, the chief scout, reined alongside, his pistol in hand. Startled by this quick show of impatience the Tibetan who was not hurt, remounted and he and his friends raced back to their tents. By noon we reached a point west of Tsasura.

Bivouac was made just short of a pass and at the head of a spring. We were in a grassy vale with plenty of dead grass for feed. And also camp would be sheltered from the cold wind, though at the moment partly enveloped in a damp fog. This camp was designated on our route chart as "Camp 7," it being my own seventh camp since Tangar. A scout had reported that grass was scarce beyond the pass, due to the high elevation of the country, hence our short ride of only a *tsapo* (half-march).

In this camp we awaited Colonel Ma and Captain Tan, who were escorting a Tibetan trader's caravan headed for Lhasa. This splendid train of hundreds of animals had arrived at the fort during the night. By orders of Ma Pu-fang we must let it join us and give convoy-protection against Tibetans and especially Ngoloks, to a safer region south of Amne Machin Range. Although our pace would now be slower than originally calculated, the added rifles increased our chances for getting through. I have not emphasized the great concern of the Governor and his two magistrates over the security of our expedition; the situation at that time south of Fort Ta Ho Pa was considered by them to be very, very dangerous. The whole country was roused over the expectation of Communist victory in China proper. But for the imminent fall of China's remaining northern armies under Ma Pu-fang—who was now carrying practically the full load of fighting as the Nationalists were beginning to flee to Formosa—the expedition would have been canceled even at this late hour.

An expedition under these circumstances to this even normally fairly dangerous region must eliminate as many blind spots in its master plan as possible. This requires not only political expediency but proper physical organization to give it any chance at all for success.* Since I would like the reader to accompany Dorje and me and our friends in spirit, and actually live through our problems, trials and tribulations, our failures and successes, he must be given all of the pertinent facts so that he can obtain a full picture and best judge for himself. In the radio order-of-the-day from Governor Ma, the following assignments were made and the senior members of the

---

* For those who have not been west of the Yellow River and north of the Himalayas, and particularly in northeast Tibet, these estimates of danger are to be supported in Rock's report and those of von Filchner, the many Russians, Pereira, the various French explorers, etc. Like many armchair and other experts I too was skeptical until actually in the field itself and saw the conditions prevailing at least in those hectic war years. As time passes the scholars, surveyors, and other technicians and scientists will be able to enter with little or no danger, but that is not to say that the stray traveler today is not beset by trouble, uncertainty and even a certain amount of danger. Many men to date have lost their lives and others have been robbed and set afoot without clothing and food. The story of Brooks Dolan coming to Sining to ask aid and release of Schäfer in Jyekundo, is only one of many tales of hardship. No one man can ever really conquer Tibet, all he can do is add his bit to the sum total, and that is all I hope to do.

expedition (at least all but Dorje and I) charged with certain responsibilities on pain of the customary reduction in rank, fines, imprisonment, and even death.

> Leonard Francis Clark, Colonel, leader.
> Tsedan Dorje, Prince, secretary, scientific.
> Ma Hsien-jui (Solomon Ma), liaison, political.
> Ma Sheng-lung, Colonel, security, intelligence.
> Tan Chen-te, Captain, transportation, recruitment, camp-gear, blacksmithing, veterinary, provisions (man and animal), messing, legal.
> Pao Chang-ching, Lieutenant, radio, courier communications.
> Abdul (Ma Wei-shan), scouting, gunnery.
> Tujeh, Chief, Tibetan armed escort, yak drivers.

Our caravan now officially included an absolute minimum of 80 yaks, though at the moment it was 210; 70 saddle horses accustomed to rarefied altitudes and extreme cold, though at present it was 117; a miscellaneous herd of pack mules totaling 56 (and later, camels and oxen). Added to the Lhasa party, our combined forces were said to number about 800 animals, 120 rifles.

During our march to Camp 7, the full panorama of much of this splendid caravan moving by sections on its mission of finding the mountains of mystery and among them perhaps the world's highest mountain, was a thrilling sight; swinging along under shining ever-changing skies and clouds; marching across the roof of the world, wending in and out and up and over and down—lake-dotted steppes, passes, glaciers, tundra, stony deserts, the beds of rushing riverine torrents, mountains, swamps. . . .

And so, that first grand march set our style for weeks to come, and as I will not describe other marches minutely, I will do so here as closely as memory and my few notes on the subject will permit—for in all Tibetan popular exploration literature there is not to my knowledge a really detailed account of such an expedition's orgnization and daily operations.

Scouts ranged ahead and flankers moved to left and right, while behind and in the middle followed the lumbering yak sections piled high with cargo. Sections of yaks, each of 20 animals, were under at least four armed Tibetan drivers. These herders rode saddle-yaks, though sometimes they walked on foot. The yak sections stayed anywhere from a hundred yards to a quarter of a mile apart as a rule, and trotted along characteristically on a broad front side by side, for yaks do not walk in single-file except along narrow paths in defiles or on steep slopes in a trail.

In urging forward their lumbering, humped, bison-like beasts, the drivers used long, yak-leather whips, with wooden handles having a swivel, and stones flung with unerring accuracy from slings, aided by whistling and a startling duck-quack kind of call. Often, when moving over easy country, the drivers spun wool thread on a twirling bobbin.

Leader and main guard usually moved out last. This was for protection against attack on the rear of the usually fairly widely scattered caravan and against its vulnerable flanks, which from this position could best be covered visually. This rear party rode with an alert eye to quick rallying at any possible threatened point of attack by either raiders or cattle and horse thieves. Riders from it were perpetually being detached to trot along the caravan's line-of-march to check up, perhaps issuing orders, stopping to make baggage and cargo adjustments, snaking out bogged-down animals, bringing in strays—for pack mules and horses were never linked together—and directing the movements of scouts if in bad or narrow terrain, selecting campsites and tending to anything else necessary.

Generally, in establishing a camp, a stretch of dry, level ground was selected whenever possible, and usually, as at Camp 7, it was an old site having clean glacial water with plenty of yak dung scattered nearby. Later, when using back trails or none at all or when under threat of attack, we could not be so particular: sometimes in regions estimated to be hostile we could not even light a fire, and sometimes we were forced to drink salt sea water—finally getting so we would not vomit it up. As the bellowing yak sections entered the selected camp area, each separate group was immediately turned aside and held together in a milling herd by its yelling drivers now on foot. Out of a seeming chaos of yaks, galloping horses, shouting men and even an occasional gunshot, order gradually came: each Tibetan yak-group formed a nucleus by stacking its food bags, saddlery and gear in separate spots whose position had been marked previously for defense of the camp as a whole.

Yak dung was quickly gathered, and fires were lit within the barricades. Rifles and ammunition belts were stacked inside. The yaks were then turned out to graze, still saddled with their wooden pack-racks and straw pads—as these served to keep their backs warm. On a winter expedition (Tan once explained) these are never removed except for repair, or when doctoring galls.

Preliminary to the establishment of camp a fast advance party with mules and pack horses, which are much speedier than yaks, had pressed forward the last few minutes and caught up with the screening scouts. The men of this detachment erected officers' tents, collected dung, stacked incoming saddles, blankets and bridles, rifles, chests, saddle-bags, bedding, gear, food bags—neatly, so that everything could be found later at each officer's proper tent door, thus cutting down time that otherwise might be lost in aimless searching.

When the main, rear guard rode in, food and tea were usually served piping hot in the mess tent, which was warmly carpeted with bear pelts, saddle rugs, and the like. The night watch was told off, and mounted scouts were sent out to rove; foot sentinels were posted on the periphery as well as inside camp. Raiders will enter a camp in the disguise of caravan members, and raise havoc, not hesitating to commit murder while stampeding stock. Change of sentinels and scouts was nearly always hourly, this to insure against guards falling asleep. A single sleepy guard has been known to cause disaster to an entire column of soldiers. Dogs were sent out to watch for the scouts of raiders, and to drive off wolves, bears, and leopards attracted to the stock.

At sundown the horses were driven in, blanketed for warmth, and a sufficient number resaddled for use in night fighting should that emergency arise. They were hobbled and picketed to ropes staked down in the middle of the tent area. By using hobbles, raiders could not as readily stampede all the lines at once. Dr. Rock used chain and padlock hobbles, but ours were mainly of leather. Yaks were then bunched near the barricades; each section of twenty being snubbed close up by its wooden nose-plug to pegged lines set in squares, although hollow squarish U's were more often used. The yaks' heads were turned toward the inner part of the U, where the animals would eat such forage as their drivers could collect for them, if any. In lean times, the pack mattresses were emptied of straw.

Horses and mules were then fed by nose-bags, barley and peas being sparingly ladled out in measured rations of about a quart and a half to each, this being a minimum allowance if the animal were to keep any part of its strength. They should have been fed much more under these conditions. Listening to the crunching of grain that first night beyond Fort Ta Ho Pa, I realized, and not without anguish, that each 100 horses and mules consumed over 35 gallons of feed each night. This was the absolute minimum for effective work in high altitudes and freezing cold. All such feed must be carried on the backs of the caravan, as it was not known whether more could be had in the spaces ahead.

That night it was *cold*—the shivering cooks soon got their fires going with sack bellows, clamorously tossing out small and huge copper pots, setting water and meat to boiling. Most such cooks are for some reason the dirtiest fellows in camp. In order to control amebic dysentery, typhoid, and other possible diseases, the cook situation was tackled by my seeing to it that before a meal was prepared, they had washed their hands in Chinese soap brought along for that purpose. Even on this first night a cook was caught neglecting this order: he was courtmartialed on the spot and fined $10. We never had a repeat; in fact the cooks were so anxious for sanitation they used to stand around to catch Dorje's or my eye, then show us the bar of soap!

The blacksmith and his sooty helpers clanked and hammered away, throwing down snorting, kicking horses to reset faulty and "thrown" shoes, busily paring hooves both over-long and split, working in a shower of sparks at their bellows. The Salar veterinary dashed around with his needles, patches, and salves. The radio masts were erected, and though 60 feet high, were in position in exactly eight minutes; the generator was started, and sparks began flying to the accompaniment of static squeals and a "hot" Confucian fist sending out *dit-dah-dits*. At first radio service was not too good, but whenever an exchange of messages broke down, the operator, Lieutenant Pao Chang-ching—our only Chinese officer—found himself fined $5. Thereafter, that is after three failures, it was good for the soul to see the improvement brought about: although the radio crew was often up half the night (due to high elevation problems), weeks went by before a single message failed to get through to Sining and Lanchow. The gods must surely be with us, as our gelong happily pointed out when hitting me for a raise—a raise which he didn't get.

To save the weight of cots, we slept on the ground, a universal custom here among these Moslem and Tibetan soldiery. That first night I watched Hassan, now promoted from the dangerous job of chief outrider to be my bodyguard, orderly, and "taster," an even more dangerous assignment due to the ever-present possibility of an *amok* suicide among one of our Moslems, or a spy and assassin among our Tibetans. First, Hassan made up my bed; he spread out a white felt Turkestan carpet on the frozen ground, over that went robes of bear and wolf, topped off by a pair of Chinese quilts—red silk and white linen stuffed fatly with inner camel-hair—and finally capped with a sheepskin robe and a moisture-proof raincoat of Lhasa red wool which was flung over the whole pile to keep off any dampness precipitating from the tent walls. Wind was driving snow and ice through the tent as easily as needles could be thrust through my hand. The pillow was my saddle (the uncomfortable Mongol saddle had been replaced by an old American cavalry saddle which I had purchased for thirty dollars from a Sining missionary) covered with a sheepskin robe, woolly side out.

With darkness upon us Dorje and I summoned Abdul (his Chinese name being Ma Wei-shan), to our tent. This twenty-six-year-old Salar was personal bodyguard to Marshal Ma-yuan, China's supreme field commander in the northwest against the Communists. He was loaned to me by the Marshal, who believed him to be the deadliest gunman in China, and that's saying quite a lot. I wanted to take Abdul's measure, for he was typical of the expedition's Moslems, men who could at least match up to an Afridi or a Waziri; the same Afridi and Waziri who recently descended Khyber Pass into India and killed perhaps a million or so Indians.

It was said that Abdul had been in Afghanistan and Persia (and likely fought there); under Ma Pu-fang he was a sergeant in the Peace Preservation Corps of Chinghai; by profession he was actually an expert guerrilla strategist, who would have rated a captaincy in any European army. He could draw up and was capable of executing a plan of battle, and personally lead a cavalry force of 300 men into battle. There are quite a few majors throughout the world who would like to be able to do just that. He, like many of our other fighting non-commissioned officers, and their men, often spurned a tent while on the march through Tibet. Very often, unless it was snowing or raining, Abdul simply crawled between a pair of sheepskin robes, which were cured and waterproofed by a local buttermilk process. He had fought against, and killed, according to Colonel Ma, Russians, Japanese, Mongols, Turks, Tibetans, Tungans, and Chinese bandits and Communists. Abdul—to my surprise—claimed that night that Tibetans were by far the smartest and most dangerous of all Asiatic soldiery including the Japanese.

Our Moslems preferred (he said), unless pinned down in the open by enemy fire, to mount and charge the flanks of the enemy's main position, terrain allowing. The main strength of the British army of occupation in India was usually stationed in the Moslem northwest posts, and especially in the Northwest Frontier Province, and here they learned a healthy respect for the Moslems. The British also rate the Gurkhas tops; the Gurkhas are Mongolian in race, and were, before British occupation, not only Tibetans in blood, but in allegiance as well. This yardstick is intended to give a definite idea of the actual effectiveness of our small expeditionary guard force, both Moslem and Buddhist. In addition, I had seen the Gurkha serve against the Burma Japanese Army, and as private citizen and United States Army officer, I had seen something of fighting in about half the provinces of China; therefore, my own experiences, too, would verify the opinions long held by the British concerning the Far East Moslem. Our Moslems nearly always followed up a victory by cutting the throats of the fallen. Few if any prisoners are ever taken in Tibet, by either side, except for questioning. Like most country-born central Asian Moslems, and completely unlike the Chinese, Abdul was both horse- and gun-wise, keeping these, his best friends, in top shape.

Abdul's pay was high—$30 (Chinese silver *yuan*) per month, and food and equipment; as well as robes of sheepskin, cloth and fur and wool. His arms were a Chinese copy of a German automatic sub-machine pistol, a bone and golden-hafted dagger, a new Skoda .30 caliber rifle inlaid with chased silver and having bifurcated resting-forks of polished buckhorn. Abdul was over six feet in his bare feet, lean and tough as whipcord, white-skinned, blue-eyed, handsome (except for a bad bayonet scar on his forehead) and gay; but, for all this he was very reserved and quiet. I don't want to give the impression his bearing was timid; it was extremely bold and dangerous-eyed, but perfectly disciplined and faultlessly mannered. Abdul did not wear a glove on his right hand—his gun hand. He did not drink. He was one of the finest singers I have ever heard: he could sing in Salar, Tibetan, Tungan, and Chinese. Colonel Ma swore by him and his kind, and though Abdul would in time, under the colonel's own tutelage, become a commissioned officer, he was perfectly content with his present lot. In short, he was a soldier. While traveling it was Abdul who nearly always led off the massed marching songs, so dear to the untamed hearts of these men of the inner steppes. That is the picture of Abdul, and that is the appropriate picture of his fifty comrades, our best bet for reaching Amne Machin.

Being apprehensive (because of my ignorance of the situation), and wishing to get a full view of the defense system should we ever be attacked, I asked Abdul by what tactics—exactly what tactics—did Tibetans usually strike a party such as ours. He lit his pipe, a queer-looking kind of aluminum Chinese water pipe: * after a few puffs, he began speaking (in effect):

"My Honorable Colonel Clark-ah, I have weathered five such attacks by Tibetans. . . ."

Briefly, the prime objective of Tibetan brigandage is to run off a caravan's or a military column's livestock, the second being to capture arms, supplies, and gear. To secure these four, raiders usually attack at dusk, or just before dawn. Diversions are sometimes made on the target-camp by a group of raiders pinning down the camp's guards, while a detached party rams in and drives off the animals should they be grazing, or stampedes them if picketed. If so far successful, the robbers rest content, for escape is now impossible for the caravan. Having secured the livestock, the attackers now go after the loot and especially the firearms and ammunition. A second attack might be launched at any moment of the following day, or on the second night; sometimes, however, days crawl by minute after minute until all fuel is exhausted, and the surrounded men become careless in their search for it. At that time the camp is usually attacked in a massed cavalry charge.

As many as a thousand horses and riflemen have been used; few caravans survive the bullets and swords. Abdul had seen Colonel Ma, with many of these same Moslems of ours, hold off as many as 500 Tibetans (probably an exaggeration) through charge after

---

* While there are many orthodox Moslems in Tibet, who neither use tobacco or alcohol, our own men for the most part were not averse to taking them in moderate quantities.

charge; Abdul claimed that the colonel was the best guerrilla fighter in the northwest. That was why he personally covered Ma Pu-fang's south flank backed against Tibet. His very name insured a considerable margin of safety for us. Then Abdul added:

"But even Colonel Ma can't help us against the Ngoloks!"

Dorje changed the subject: "Now, how about our scouts? And our own internal and external security systems?"

By this time the hubblebubble had to be refired. In a cloud of smoke Abdul answered that should a camp sentinel or a roving scout report, by visual or sound signal, anything suspicious out in the dark, our lights—candle and butter-lamps inside the tents—must be instantly extinguished. Campfires would be screened, or doused with water, or lacking that, packed with snow or earth. All tents must be immediately emptied, as these are the first to receive gunfire. Positions would be taken up near piles of gear and among the animals on the picket lines. Firearms were kept stacked at hand, and loaded at all times; inspections were made daily—fines, whippings, and punishment duly levied if all was not in order. Reports were already going out by Tujeh's agents among the Tibetans that we were in top shape, and so the likelihood of our being overrun, he hoped, was further cut down.

An ordinary Tibetan Drök-pa, tent-dweller clan chief, encamped a few miles away to the east, possessed over 500 good horses, 10,000 sheep, 3,000 yaks. And yet this man and his followers were continually raiding. They did it for two reasons: first, sport; second, gain. No caravan was safe, not even troops in strength. Nor was it really safe for us to move anywhere in this area of Tibet. Ninety-five percent of all male tribal Tibetans in this region go out on raids. Top horses are valued at $150 (yuan), and up; therefore, this comparatively "poor" Drök-pa's horse herd alone, which was rated good, had a cash value in north Tibet, Turkestan, or west China, of $75,000 (U. S.) as the current rate of exchange in Lanchow was $1 (silver yuan) for $1 (U. S.)!

At Fort Ta Ho Pa—in spite of Colonel Ma's and Captain Tan's wishes—not a single Tibetan had been "pressed" into service of the expedition, though I had wrangled for days with them about this, finally being forced to get a special order from the Governor to obtain my ends. Likewise not a single Tibetan animal had been confiscated for our use. All this was extremely unusual in Moslem vs Tibetan relations, in fact, unique. So far as I ever knew, we paid silver dollars or gold for services of men, animals, equipment, skins, clothing, feed and provisions, and for all of the many other items obtained. Some payments were made outright, some on a type of rental system having to do with tax collection. Had we not done so, we would not have moved many miles toward the mountains of mystery, for the whole region is in the hands of the tribes, who can, if they will, harass and eventually even destroy any Chinese force (less than field-army strength) based on Sining and Lanchow and attacking Tibet. Hence diplomacy, tribal alliances, false rumors, treaties with religious groups, fostering of internal discord between hostile tribes and lamaseries, treasure, and guile were the chief mainstays upon which Tan Chen-te relied finally to move us forward toward Amne Machin through the unruly federations.

"Honorable Commander . . . be prepared! . . . tread softly! . . . go far!" added Abdul to all his information, blowing the plug of ashes out of his hubblebubble (if you could call it that), and rising to inspect the change of guard.

After he had left Dorje and I felt much better about our being pocketed under Tsasura. In fact I was beginning to feel we were quite safe. Why, a weasel couldn't possibly get into this camp! Evidently nothing would come of my uncomfortable hunch which had prompted the interview, and I put it down to nerves. I had been working too hard. I read a few pages from Dorje's copy of Cunninghame Graham's *Mogreb-El-Acksa,* blew out the candle and snuggled down into my furs.

I must have dozed off, for about two hours after Abdul's departure, I heard the blast of a rifle. I scrambled out of bed, grabbed my pistol from off the saddle-pillow, and took a header through the open door-flaps of the tent.

Outside I realized I was standing in my underwear, and it was freezing. The night was pitch dark except for a sheen of starlight reflecting off the tents. Then there came a pair of quick shots some hundred yards east of camp. Several horses were snorting alongside me, and pulling back on their picket-ropes. I took a few steps and saw that three of them were lying on the ground, kicking their hooves out, as if dying. Abdul ran by and I collared him.

"What's up?"

"Plenty!" and that was all I saw or got out of him, for he was off like a streak in the direction of the shots.

I felt like an ass standing there in my longjohns, but this seemed no time to dress. A gang of men were dousing the main campfire, chucking handfuls of mud on it. I joined them and saw there was no panic—just an air of urgency. By this time the whole camp was in an uproar: sergeants were barking orders; animals were snorting on the picket lines; some of the yaks were trying to stampede; troops were running every which way to their posts, cocking rifles as they went. I managed to seize one of them by his robe-tail and he turned out to be the chief cook, holding a meat cleaver.

"Shabrangs!" he said softly, pulling loose and taking a stand among the frightened horses.

Prince Dorje came hurrying along in his shirt-tail, a big book tucked under his arm.

"What are you going to do—shoot them with the book?"

"Oh! I thought I had my pistol!" And he was off like a shot to his post inside one of the barricades.

Next I saw Abdul striding along a picket line quieting the horses. He explained that four Shabrangs had crept into camp, hamstrung three horses out of pure cussedness, and led out six of our best saddle horses including my black stallion—Black Moon of Alashan.

"The sons-of-bitches!"

When the alarm was given by a guard firing his rifle, it was too late. Tracks in the beam of a flashlight showed they had moved cautiously out to the edge of camp. Then the Shabrangs had evidently jumped on our horses and vanished into the night. They had done no shooting, had made no noise, and had left behind them only losses for us to report. Dorje came along, having found the barricade too cold to suit him.

"Commander—may I make a suggestion?" enquired Abdul standing at attention.

"Please do."

"You are standing in your underwear, sir. It is over twenty degrees *below* freezing."

I got back to my tent, pulled on boots and got into a sheepskin robe and for the rest of the night we kept watch. Nor did Colonel Ma's party arrive. At dawn, snow was falling rather heavily, as it had during much of the night, and by midmorning was over a foot deep in our hollow below the pass. The tracks of the four raiders were deeply covered, and the losses seemed sure.

I wanted to get back the black horse, but when I broached the subject to Abdul, he informed me that Tan had ordered no pursuits were to be made after casual stock thieves or raiders.

"*Casual!*"

"Yes, sir."

"Who is running this expedition? Tan, or me!—"

"You are, sir. But Tan Chen-te is commander of Fort Ta Ho Pa and governor of the hsien."

I went back to my tent and ordered Hassan to saddle the bay stallion. I was going to get back the black horse if it was the last thing I ever did. Riding through camp I called to Solomon Ma that I was going only as far as the head of the spring, and would be back in an hour. The tracks had led out of camp on the east side; the bay and I clattered along through the snow for three miles. We reached the top of a hog's-back ridge, and there—in full view, less than five hundred yards away—stood about eighty horses: our six among them. Ma-yuan's horse tossed his head, and I spurred the bay toward them. In a few minutes I had the band rounded up and started toward camp. Four Tibetans appeared on the top of a hill and began shooting at from four to five hundred yards, their bullets kicking up spurts of ice, none very close. They could not pursue apparently as all their camp horses were in the band.

Led by the six horses, the whole bunch kicked up their heels and headed for camp. As the horses ran through the tent area, I thought the men would throw a fit in their delight. Abdul started to open his mouth, took in my grin, and smiled instead.

"Count the horses!" I called out, "You will find our own six head, plus three for those hamstrung, and the others will be impounded against a court decision."

Exhausted from the all but sleepless night and the cold ride, I took a short nap, but soon wakened in something of a nightmare, actually smothering for lack of air. This was due, I finally realized, to the fairly high elevation, and in some alarm I sat upright breathing deeply for two or three minutes. The heart pumps fast at such times and appears even to skip a beat occasionally; heart seizure is said to be common even among the acclimated Tibetans. Later on our jour-

1. *The old city wall of Sining, the main forward base from which the expedition moved into Tibet from the north.* 2. *Mongol burial chortens discovered west of Koko Nor, Chinghai Province, China. These Mongols use the Tibetan type of tomb.*

3. *A group of Mongol yurts in the Tsaidam Swamp area, showing prayer flags flying from the masts.*   4. *Mongols of the Khoshoit tribe in native costume, settled in the extensive salt-lake region southwest of Koko Nor, the "Blue Sea."*

5. Tibetan girls who entertained the expedition with song and dance at Fort Ta Ho Po: note their fox hats and silver finery. 6. Temple of the Panchen lama at Tsaidam, showing the head lama who entertained the expedition. On the right is a Tibetan obo and on the left a prayer furnace. Mongol lamaseries are modeled on those of Tibet and sometimes show strong Chinese influence.

7. *On its way to Amne Machin the expedition traversed deserts whose great sand dunes resemble those in Arabia and in Sinkiang Province.* 8. *One of the many sturdy Tibetan scouts upon whose watchfulness and loyalty the expedition depended for much of its success: his dress is admirably adapted to all kinds of weather.* 9. *A wealthy Tibetan trader whose well-stocked and well-managed caravans link Turkestan, China, and India to Tibet.* 10. *A Moslem caravan driver, one of the many who were met by the expedition on its way into and out of the dangerous Amne Machin country of Tibet.*

11. *Explorer Leonard Clark, relaxing in conversation with a famous Pönpo
(priest) in Fort Chakar. The boy on the right is a typical Ngolok youth.*
12. *Chutsu Tsereng, called "Ti Jen" or "The Secretary," a valued member of
the expedition and a famous soldier of fortune. Behind him stretches the western fringe of Amne Machin.   13. Soldiers resting and testing equipment.
It was possible to use ox carts for transportation in the Tsaidam Swamp area.*

14. *A group of Tibetan caravan yaks, showing method of snubbing them to the restraining rope when in camp: they are indispensable for travel on the roof of the world.* 15. *In desert areas in the Tsaidam Swamp region camels were used.*

ney, in much higher regions, several animals were to die of what Solomon thought to be dilated hearts.

By early afternoon the storm abated a little, but still there was no sign of the follow-up party, and its Lhasa caravan. We were, however, now in possession of all the expedition's baggage. Our yaks and horses and mules all stood sleeping peacefully, as their pasturage was covered by snow. Two or three warm fires, burning low over the snowy camp area, lent a note of cheeriness, but how long this would last was anybody's guess: such fuel as had not been gathered on arrival now lay buried under two feet of snow. What little remained was already being conserved. Unless something happened soon, we could neither cook nor keep from freezing.

In the dusk of evening, with a dancing campfire shine on them, the wet horses stood at their picket lines, heads hanging low, shaggy manes dripping, eyes half-closed as if dreaming of green pastures. Sometimes they shivered and cowered at the swirling gusts of wind driving down from the peak of Tsasura. A top crust was already setting on the surface of the snow; if it got much thicker and harder we couldn't move back, let alone forward. Tents sagged dismally and perishable gear had to be dug out of drifted snow banks.

A single foot courier, apparently chosen for his ability to sneak past robber look-outs, was dispatched on the back trail; if Ma Shenglung was still at the fort, the scout had a message for him describing the condition of forage and fuel. This was written in Arabic, so that should the scout fall into robbers' hands, it could not be read. In this urgent message was a demand to build a fire under himself and get started.

During a lull in the storm, the Lhasa caravan came plugging in, announced in the distance by a rattling and banging of impedimenta, animal grunts, whinnies, the clunking of wooden clappers, and the tinkling of bronze bells. The men characteristically screamed at their yaks and mules, sounding like a band of banshees. Hundreds of flank-steaming animals were unloaded and staked out. Tents were pitched alongside. But to our astonishment neither Colonel Ma nor Captain Tan came in with it, nor any member of their own escort.

The caravan's master, a Lhasa dignitary and apparently part-time trader belonging to the Dalai Lama, called on us. By candlelight in my white tent, he predicted on his amber rosary that Colonel Ma would not arrive on the morrow either. Solomon was not long in learning that a new batch of dancing girls had arrived soon after our departure; I didn't need a rosary to foretell further delay!

Next morning everything was heavily weighted under an ever-deepening snow. We found ourselves pinned down by rampant winds. Inside the flapping tents, which were warmed now only by a candle for each, it was —38° C.! Still no Colonel Ma. Though not usually given to cursing, I let off a volley that seared the *djinns*. And very little fuel remained for heating our food. Dorje and Solomon were equally furious. There was only one decision, and I made it: as soon as the weather calmed down we would leave without them. A second messenger was dispatched northward to the fort informing our heroes of the decision.

They were also informed, and I could visualize the consternation on their faces as they read the order, that they and their forces in Ta Ho Pa, were now assigned and relegated to the ashcan as "a reinforcement and relief party," and were "detached" from the "main *attacking* party." *

---

* *Basic Roster (42 men) working out of Fort Ta Ho Pa:*

OF MAGISTRATE TAN CHEN-TE'S FORCE (6):

Ishmael (Yang Shu-jung)	Tungan	Moslem
Rabibu (Ma Chen-ming)	"	"
Rogomane (Ma Yi-shing)	"	"
Mohammed (Ma Yu-lung)	"	"
Peng Ke-tsing	Chinese	No religion
Ali (Ma Teng-hai)	Salar	Moslem

OF COLONEL MA SHENG-LUNG'S FORCE (6):

Abdul (Ma Wei-shan)	Salar	Moslem
Rabibu (Ma Chin-ching)	Tungan	"
Mosul (Han Mo-su)	"	"
Ma Liang	"	"
Chaharashambe (Hang Cheng-lu)	"	"
Hogurushe	"	"

OF CHUTSU TSERENG'S FORCE (6):

Chutsu Tsereng	Tu Jen	Lamaist
Bomba	Tibetan	"
Wang Shiu	"	"
Itan	"	"
Liang Wei-chung	Chinese	Confucian
Yang Kuei-chung	"	"

TIBETAN HEADMEN OVER DRIVERS AND RIFLEMEN (24 men):

Shabrang Tribe (14) — (Lamaists)

Chujeh	Urdan	Lashitsai
Obo	Sashu	Tsaikuanerja
Chemkurja	Guru	Danku
Huardamu	Danqu	Kunglo
Ibo	Shikuter	

This was a serious matter. No greater punishment could be meted out for insubordination to these proud Sining Moslems, committed before Chinghai to conquer Amne Machin—that God of north Tibet whose conquest would add so much to the face of Ma Pu-fang, and perhaps actually allow China to withdraw her last army into Tibet for carrying on the war against Communism.

Achuchu Tribe (10) — (*Lamaists*)

Gomba	Imba	Dambaserden
Huamba	Ramba	Kuru
Durdn	Dergja	
Gura	Durku	

7

The Mirror in the Sky

IN ORDER accurately to measure Amne Machin Peak, boiling-point recordings for establishing altitudes at key points were made from Camp 7, southward through the wide blank regions. Further, altimeter readings with aneroid barometers were regularly registered, to be later corrected against Lanchow and Sining meteorologists' data, and used finally for establishing accurate barometric variations due to changes in weather. Comparisons were also being made by radio against current government station recordings in those base cities, which were, by previous arrangement, sending their observations to us by coded radio signals. Dorje assured me all this was not as easy as it sounds.

Sometimes, radio exchanges, according to the crew, were being jammed by powerful Soviet radio-monitoring stations, as Siberia undoubtedly had evaluated the expedition and its Ta Ho Pa crew as purely military and political in scope. This apprehension of the Intelligence Division of the Soviet War Staff, can be better understood when it is realized that Ma Pu-fang was the only general on the entire mainland of Asia who at the moment stood in the path of Communist domination of the continent. The few Americans in Korean fringes, the French in Indochina, and the British in Malaya, were, according to the Moslems, considered diversions by the Reds. They calculated this by intercepts of their own, and by breaking one of the Red Army codes used in Sinkiang.*

At this camp, while awaiting a break in the blizzard, the expedition (so said the Moslems) also pioneered the first real medical work undertaken in Tibet proper. These medicines had originally been given to the Chinese Nationalist government by the United Nations

---

* During World War II I pioneered and commanded U.S. espionage and guerrilla activities in the region occupied (in N. China) by the Communist Eighth Route Army, and the (central China) war zone under the Communist New Fourth Army. These were the only two field armies then used by the Chinese Communists. As a result of operating radio nets behind the lines, I decided the Moslems knew what they were talking about in Tibet.

Health Organization, and forwarded to Ma Pu-fang. As a result of such humanitarian work, hundreds of injections of penicillin—to mention a single instance—were eventually given (or left in Tibet) by our medics for venereal diseases, the curse of the country. Hundreds of smallpox vaccinations were also accomplished. However, medicines, the Chinese Moslems believed, must be considered a military and political weapon, but as interest in this insidious aspect will undoubtedly be found latent in the American public, I will not go into details. Also I will enter in this record no information of a military or political nature not absolutely necessary for explaining in very general terms the circumstances leading up to and sustaining this expedition into Tibet. The aiding of man to a better life, and not the destruction of his freedom, is, after all, our American idea.

Prince Dorje, together with our Tungan so-called doctor for assistant, started off this dual program by breaking the seals on a wooden case marked with the Chinese characters for "smallpox." To his not altogether mild distress he found it necessary first to capture and then to disarm his first batch of intended victims. These were seven openly sneering, sword-and-musket-carrying Wangshetihai men-at-arms whom fate sent swaggering into camp openly to inspect us and our guns and gear. It took several Moslem guards to subdue these tough-fibered fellows, for they fought with tooth and toenail.

Our men, who did not escape altogether unscathed, held on grimly to each terrified patient as he received Dorje's needle scratch. In the meanwhile, my Mongol friend's shins suffered from their boot heels and he was bitten on the hand, while as for the faint-hearted medico—a Shanghai-trained Moslem—he gave up in fine oriental disgust. But in the end, science and Dorje's Mongolian zeal won out, and the seven bucks were released and booted homeward cursing for all they were worth. They swore a grim vengeance, and unlike the Moslems I did not take it as a joke. In fact I doubted the advisability of this clinic and its health-improving program as a practical means for penetrating the marble quarries of the tribal Tibetan heart, but Solomon Ma (always the politician) hoped we would continue the good work.

By 7:30 P.M. the caravan began loading, taking care with balancing the packs as no cinches are used on mules or pack horses. We must at all costs attempt escape from our unfavorable situation, and travel somehow over the storm-bound mountains under cover of night, in search for grass beyond the pass. Our gelong and bombom who were proving real pillars of moral strength, would precede the first section, divining the safest way with their magic wands. Without at least the gelong's guidance, our Tibetans would likely have refused to move out on such a march without Colonel Ma and the others. This baggage train would slip out under cover of night, while a second party of us would remain in camp until just before dawn, making a normal racket and setting fires in order to throw off any robbers who might be watching.

Clouds began coming in, blocking out the stars; at 8 o'clock the mercury stood at −13° C., indicating for the cargo caravan a comparatively mild night on the pass, unless of course, the wind should come up again. Chujeh, though at first fearful, finally seconded this nocturnal trek to foil the tribesmen, as the few thieves out would likely not suspect a move, knowing the party in Fort Ta Ho Pa was not yet joined with us. However, the Lhasa caravan would wait for Colonel Ma, as their unhappy master deemed our move too hazardous and the date inauspicious.

It was a fine, thrilling sight to watch our own string of yaks, mules, and horses, quietly slip off with lead bells silenced. Later we followed them through day-and-night binoculars: especially distinct were the jet-black yaks, with their long side-fringes trailing in the snow, steering along the steep, rocky sides of the mountain soaring above camp, the yaks moving slowly, steadily, imperturbable as tanks, zigzagging up, and ever up, aiming at a patch of stars over the frosty-white notch of the pass.

The rear guard broke the last of camp at 5:30 A.M., with the temperature standing at −15° C., and rode westward up the right-hand side of the valley, following carefully in the tracks of the caravan. Back and forth through the snow these zigzagged, ever aiming ultimately at the pass, appearing alternately now over our left shoulder, now dead ahead. The rising *la* was proving snowy and precipitous. A fresh wind in the higher elevations struck hard as we rounded a jutting cliff corner, and moved against us with almost the persistence of a movable concrete wall. Through this hard wall of air we were presently trying to walk dismounted. At times the force was so great I for one was actually afraid of being blown into the depths below, for the narrow trail was icy and slippery. We crawled up part way on hands and knees for about half a mile, scrambling and leading our alarmed, occasionally plunging and even falling horses.

At last, at 4,120 meters (12,554 feet) we reached the lowest point in the notch of the pass. Standing here cross-checking Dorje's instruments I could hardly catch my breath between the icy blasts. Gleaming like a freshly fractured diamond on our left, rose the ice tower of Sho Tsasura, "Small Sickle." Cautiously, taking care not to fall, we slid off the icy pass in the old tracks leading steeply downhill, working against a blizzard of wind filled with flying particles of dry ice. A few hundred feet lower snow began pelting our eyes with a sharp sideswipe. A bunch of frightened horses slid down a steep slant, starting a small avalanche, piling up in a mess of stones, snow, and ice. We worked a way down to them and pulled out all but six. Three were hopelessly buried, and three with broken legs were shot. Covered with snow, and freezing, we regained the yaks' trail, following it for about a quarter of a mile down to a bench. Our horses, even here in a partly sheltered ravine, could hardly face the sting of the in-rushing wind and its cargo of driven crystals sweeping off Tsasura Peak. My feet no longer ached with cold and I feared they were freezing. My hands were bluish-purple, and were hard with the cold. But there was no stopping to thaw out in such a place. A fire could not have been lit in any event. A ring of ice slowly caked the inside of my fox cap, its flaps tied under my chin. This ice was formed from the steam blowing out in gasps from between my teeth. From the set faces about me, the others too were silently suffering their cuts, bruises, and frostbites.

To the west, looming under high rolling black storm clouds, was the gigantic diamond of Ta Tsasura, "Large Sickle," part of the vertebrae in the backbone of the mighty Ugutu Range. At 9 o'clock we turned south, and to our delight found gazelles feeding quietly over sheltered meadow slopes. Such serenity after the noisy fury of the heights was startling.

Over this calm region we rode across the points of outlying ridges of a range on our left called Na-Shan-Ma-Tien Shan, and then turned down a rocky gulch to follow the banks of a river iced tight. By 11 A.M. we pitched Camp 8, after crossing the stream—called by one of our Tibetans, the "Rockti" River. The site was on the flat, wind-blasted, ice-stiffened west bank. The wind was sweeping away most of the snow, and we were satisfied with the grazing revealed so early in the approaching spring season at an altitude of 3,810 meters (11,609 feet). Our yaks were found feeding just around a low hill. A few were limping from the sharp stones which had cut their feet on the steep descent. The drivers, however, were fairly demoralized. Tujeh reported he had been forced to give the customary number of lashes to three of them. These had been stripped of their robes and staked to pegs. I told Tujeh to whip no more of the men, but to arrest such personnel if necessary and hold them for trial by court.

Tujeh was full of an air of bravado, and began a noisy harangue that brought many of the men gathering. I started to walk away, but he seized me by the arm and whirled me around. Without necessarily intending to, but being tired and disgusted, I came back with a hard lash with my own whip, straight across his face.

"The next time you touch me," I told him quietly through Solomon, "I'll have you shot." Whether I really meant it or not is aside from the point, but that ended the palaver, and that ended Tujeh's insubordination, at least for the moment.

The skies were soon swept clear, flashing a dark green, but the air was cold and blustery, the tents rocking, their weather sides dented. To start fires with stiff fingers, it was necessary to lie under a robe in order to strike a spark on the side of a piece of dry yak dung, then hold it in the wind which acted as a bellows. Several attempts were made before the men were successful with flint and steel; matches were useless. While thawing out over the fires, soon dangerously scattering coals and ashes, we saw in the east and west the wild, ragged escarpments and snow peaks of the so-called Ugutu system (a Mongolian name). Triangulations by transit-theodolite were made by Dorje on five of the loftiest, a couple of these unnamed peaks showing higher than 15,000 feet, about the height of Mount Blanc (due west lay a peak of 15,580 feet, in the southwest another of 15,900 feet, in the southeast a small one of 14,150 feet, etc., while northwest lay the same peak measured at Ta Ho Pa as being 16,870 plus feet).

For easy accessibility in case of trouble, Hassan, too tightly I thought, bound my carbine, pistol, and ammunition belts to my front tent pole, using buckskin cords. I showed him how to bind these arms to the pole by using only my riding whip: this method required only a flick of the hand to undo, and was easier, since there were no frozen knots to untie with cold-numbed fingers. By midafternoon the air warmed inside the tents to $-10°$ C., but with a hard shivering west wind standing in.

More than anything else, success would hinge on the human psychological angles and mental quirks peculiar to our followers. Some of them had brains that appeared to be atrophied; others displayed bizarre traits such as sheer stupidity or even brilliance; some moved along in their thinking at a good clip, others plodded; and some acted as if they had jingling bells in their skulls. One of the men, who had not made much of an impression at first, due to his quietness, now appeared head and shoulders above the crowd; he was effective, he was competent. He was called the "Secretary," and sometimes, the "Tu Jen" (*Tu*—"native," *Jen*—"person"). This man-at-arms was believed by the Tibetans to be pre-Tibetan, descended from "a very ancient race." A few of these probably unrecorded aborigines are said to survive in northeast Tibet at Ta Tung, Lo Tu and Hu Chou, west of Lanchow. The Secretary could speak and write Chinese, Tibetan, Arabic, and two Indian dialects, and spoke a few words of English; as a result his "face" was constantly being renewed with the honorific title of "Secretary."

He was the leader of a motley crew of crack mercenaries, Moslems, and Buddhists, some of whom were believed to have fought under him from Siberia to Lhasa, from Mongolia to Afghanistan. At any rate, in his travels (so said Colonel Ma) he had served as an officer under kings, warlords, lamas, chiefs, generals, and princes. The Secretary was one of those rare men with an inherent bent for personal freedom, who owe fealty only to themselves, for he was the citizen of no country, a non-tax-paying subject of no particular government unless it suited his well-patinaed purse. At present that purse was empty, hence he was following our own fortunes. He combined, with perfect balance, the qualities of intelligence, astuteness, common sense, and initiative: his formal education was said to have been acquired in Pakistan (this I doubted). He rode a magnificent white-dappled stallion, showing three black sword scars on its shoulders, claimed by one of his men to be captured from the King of Afghanistan's army; his red-leather, high-cantled saddle was of silver plate, engraved, and studded with turquoises, his tattered saddleblanket the remains of a brocaded robe, the horse's martingale embossed with jade Buddhas. A Russian-Turko Mussulman syce tended his mount, often swishing a red horsehair fly switch, though in winter there were no flies; and a Nepalese gun bearer, a Gurkha, rode at his side with a rifle—a Mannlicher, probably the world's finest 8 mm. sporting gun. The forty-year-old Secretary's Tibetan robes were scented with musk, which was just as well, as his last bath had been at Kumbum. In the Secretary, on that day, I found both ally and friend, and, frankly (for the moment), did not regret teaching the two magistrates a lesson in discipline.

Fresh food was a problem in these frozen Ugutu Mountains. What food we had Solomon wished to conserve, and so had sent men out hunting. In spite of their hard survival culture, the Achuchu riflemen complained that they were prejudiced against the eating of rabbit, kyang, wild chicken, birds, duck eggs, fish, bear, even domestic horse—which we were having for dinner, as one had been shot near camp. Now chicken, even domestic chicken, is considered by Tibetans to be especially filthy—like snake with us. They were finicky in what appeared to be a mystical sense, and preferred milk, gazelle, domesticated sheep, yak, marmot, and *dzo*. And they made no bones about it.

"For 'pigtail men' you are damned particular."

They wore pigtails, they were quick to point out, but had I noticed half the hair on their scalps had been shaved off? This I gathered meant they were "half lama."

And so we purchased, at their insistence, two sheep from a shepherd turned up by one of the hunters, at the stiff price of $9 each. The Achuchus tied the feet of these sheep, and while standing on the horns, plugged the animals' nostrils with their thumbs. Thus, they explained when I appeared on the scene, the sheep were "accidentally" done away with, and not killed outright: in this manner of death, no blame could attach itself to our pious lamaists for taking life, which is taboo because of their belief in reincarnation. Obviously, as any fool could see, the sheep had just died a natural death.

There are breeds of sheep in Tibet about which little is known to the outside world. At the sight of these *four-horned* sheep (two horns to a side!), some of the Moslems who, like myself, had not been here before thought sure they were seeing djinns.

With the wind screeching thinly around the tops of the tent poles, blowing furiously out of an icebox canyon nearby, I crawled into my bed shivering with cold. As I pulled my sheepskin robe over my head, I noticed it was frozen fairly stiff. No matter what we did to keep moisture out of our clothes, there was always at least enough to freeze and harden. If we tried to dry them over a fire, the raw sheepskins thawed and became wet; if we took them into our beds to keep them from freezing, we ourselves got cold and damp.

All night the wind raged, and it snowed. At 4 A.M. we were wakened by Hassan; it was time to hit the trail. I had insisted earlier on the men taking over my tent, and had crawled into Dorje's and Solomon Ma's small white one. Now in the darkness, shivering violently in the sub-zero wind raging around and under the tent, the candle tipping over in the gusty drafts, its sizzling hot tallow burning my frozen fingers, I felt more like some greasy soldier in the horde of Hulagu on the way to conquer Persia, than a 20th-century traveler. Little, irksome, personal quirks began to show, quirks not seen before or overlooked during the busy preparations: Solomon Ma, here, and anyplace, could never locate his spectacles (splendid ones, he kept insisting, from Shanghai), and he was blinder than a bat without them. He would fumble and stumble about the tent, sometimes planting his number 10 foot in my face, mumbling to himself, groaning like a bear with a sore nose, calling on god, scratching his head and—we hoped—his memory. He wore a greasy "hairdresser," a disgusting blue-cloth aviator's helmet sort of gadget, out of which his enormous red ears sailed, through loopholes like those in an elf's hat. Dorje, or I, in some desperation, always got out of a warm bed and found the confounded spectacles for him; sometimes they were in his bed, or under his bed, or in his breast pocket, or in a boot, or amongst the ammunition or his paper files, and at least once after we had searched for half an hour, and high and low, turning the whole tent upside down—right smack on his forehead.

"Praise be to the Lord of the Worlds!" he would cry in absolute disbelief.

The only time we were ever really baffled was that morning in Camp 8, when we found Solomon Ma's glasses pinned with a safety pin high in the *ceiling* of the tent. The cargo train had pulled out long before, but we were actually delayed an hour.

Prince Dorje and Solomon, in turn, that night (and particularly later) complained bitterly of my habit of waking at all hours of the night to make up records and reports. They would try anything, hatch all sorts of stratagems, to get the candle extinguished; even

blowing on it and then trying to blame the wind. Prince Dorje had
the unprincely habit of snoring. And if there was anything Solomon
Ma and I hated it was a snorer. He would lie on his back and snore
so loudly that once the guard came running, thinking the man was
being choked to death by a brigand who must have gotten into
camp. The only way you could stop the racket was to stick your
foot out in the freezing air and give his bed a shove; in that way he
usually turned over and shut up for awhile. In all fairness I must
say that Prince Dorje and Solomon Ma, being married men and
therefore used to all sorts of indignities and inconveniences, took
these minor privations in their stride; whereas, I, a bachelor, long-
ing for peace, order and privacy, became insufferably cantankerous.

The glasses found at last—and still pitch dark—we struck the
Rockti camp, somehow getting the last tents collapsed in the wind,
loading our accouterments and camp paraphernalia on the last of
the restless pack horses, and cleared out at the late hour of five.
The wind's acoustics were frightening to the animals, echoing among
the frozen crags; the temperature standing at twenty-four degrees
below freezing. If a man wears wind glasses at such times he may
even risk freezing his eyeballs.

While mounting the Sining black, there came to my mind a very
serious doubt as to the wisdom, even the good sense, of an exploring
career in this century. It was certainly the worst life in the world.
There was no money in the game, and with rare exceptions scarcely
ever any honor during the explorer's lifetime. Any sap, so long as
he could promote, could go on a hunt to Africa and reap the rewards
of being an expert in the field of exploration, but the few who actu-
traveled in *unknown* places, were never heard of, and if they were
it was usually because of bitter denunciation by the experts, none
of whom in the case of Tibet particularly had ever gotten north of
the Himalayas or west of Tangar. I knew; I had spent a good part
of twenty years in deserts, jungles, and waste regions. What was it
that made me do it! Simply some crazy driving idea that truth (however unscholarly) was still worth striving for, that an *idea* was still
worth pursuing—even if it was unprofitable in every practical sense
—and in the end would beat me down if I let it. Yet I could no more
fight against such outland traveling than an opium addict could lay
off opium, or a whoremonger lay off whores. I cussed at the horse

and felt better, though my freezing, whiskery chin felt as though novocaine had been needled into it.

Our heads pulled down into the collars of sheepskin chupas to protect our faces against the wind, we followed doggedly in the icy snow-skimmed tracks of the yaks. Our feet and knees were soon stiff, our hands so clumsy we could scarcely check the ice-stiffened reins as we guided the trembling horses over patches of slippery ground.

A compass bearing taken on a theoretical point marked with a penciled cross on the comparatively white blank of the map, was being followed; our direction was now pointing southward. It led us across snowy mountain slopes crusty underfoot with ice slicks. Beams of light began at last to crack through the thin lips of moving cloud banks clustered around the eastern peaks on our left. Gradually we worked a way around towering mountains that looked like heaps of sugar. Landscapes here seemed exaggerated; Solomon pointed out this probably was due to the clear atmosphere of the high altitudes, to lack of dust in the frozen ground, and to oxygen-starved blood which pounded through our veins. We of course were not mountaineers, and in any case were at the moment far from being acclimatized.

In an icy canyon where we slipped and floundered while bucking against occasional snowdrifts, the wind was turbulently trapped; it swirled this way and that, as if trying to escape the pressures piled on from the spaces above. An avalanche thundered into the canyon ahead, loosed by the crushing weight of incalculable tons of snow and ice, combined with the downward push of high elevation winds. The debris roared down, sending up cascades of ice splinters and showers of snow, echoing and reëchoing against the steep-slanted walls of rock a mile high on either hand. Two hours were lost picking our way through the wreckage of avalanches.

Beyond, in side gullies swept free of snow were standing a few herds of kyang, in my opinion the most beautiful of all Tibetan big game. The Venetian, Marco Polo, undoubtedly first recorded them, when in the 13th century he found wild ass hundreds of miles north of us in Chinese Turkestan, a region closed to European knowledge again till 1860 when British and Russian explorers came. It was as late as 1871, only 78 years ago, when Prjevalsky reached Lop-Nor for the first time since Marco Polo and saw kyangs. To my knowledge a detailed description for the public has not often been made.

The upper body of this Tibetan variety is yellow, belly and legs are white with a dark brown stripe marking the spine. In galloping, the head and neck bob backward and forward, somewhat like a hobbyhorse being rocked. The kyang's gait is rigid, something like that of a galloping giraffe; and seems momentarily about to get all mixed up and lock its legs together, and go down head over heels. I never tired of watching these creatures.

The men began unlimbering their rifles, but I told them not to shoot. Grumbling, they slid the weapons back into the scabbards. Kyang meat had already, at Fort Ta Ho Pa, proved to be too strong for their taste. Tibetan mercenary soldiers, probably to save cartridges, do not often kill the kyang, but Moslems wantonly blast into the herds and leave carcasses strewn all about without even bothering to take off the hides for leather.

Moving slowly ever upward into a storm sky, sometimes backsliding on ice, but always regaining by persistence and care what was lost, we at last reached at 9:35 A.M., what was called locally Dangnur Pass (I couldn't find it on a map), 4,380 meters (13,346 feet) high. A steady west wind pushed against us, its temperature —26° C. Curiously, the wind registered a velocity of 32 miles per hour; this was unusual for such a low temperature, for Tibetan winds, we were learning, usually slow down when touched by intense cold.

On Dangnur Pass we took shelter behind an obo, horses and men huddling together in the lee for warmth. Tujeh ordered three of the most tired horses fed with dried meat and tsamba, which seemed to revive them. Tibetans and Mongols feed fatty meat to their horses during such emergencies of cold, or when on a fast raid or hard journey. Mongol legend says they were able to cover great distances at high speed by the use of this feeding; hence the superiority of their cavalry over all others.

While most of the men busied themselves at keeping warm, I got out my binoculars and studied, point by point, the frozen horizon extending into central Tibet. It was very likely from somewhere in this region on the south faces of the Ugutu Range, or possibly farther west, that the famous English explorer, General George Pereira, had sighted during his Peking to Lhasa journey, the great snow-capped "Amnyi Machen" Range which he told Dr. Joseph Rock, (then leader of the National Geographic Society's expedition, who met Pereira at Tengyueh, in Yunan, during 1923) he had seen from a distance of more than 100 miles. Very likely, Pereira remarked, the "Amnyi Machen," when surveyed, might prove higher than Mount Everest. He also spoke of the turbulent Ngolok tribes and their queen, and of his own ambition to attempt a journey of exploration in their country. Before doing so however, General Pereira died on the cold and hostile Chino-Tibet frontier.* It was Pereira, then, who in 1921 started the legend of Amne Machin's being a contender for Mount Everest's title. Pereira was not only a gallant and brave man, but had made three important expeditions into Tibet and was therefore to be considered (in my opinion) a judge of mountains and their heights.

Death and misfortune, notoriety, misery and failure, have followed all the travelers (adventurers, flyers, explorers) who have since sought the mystery mountains out; Pereira, himself, (as we have seen), died in the field. More often than not, since World War II, when off-course "Hump" American flyers linking India and China, reported seeing an incredible mountain deep in northeast Tibet, it was being referred to as "The Thing." One of these pilots reported he had been "flying at an altitude of well over 29,000 feet" when he suddenly found himself looking *up* at the mammoth wall of a mountain that towered far above him. It was not until other pilots corroborated the official report of the first officer that skepticism began to waver. They all insisted they had seen an immense, uncharted pinnacle that seemed to be nearly 30,000 feet high. Such flyers (so far as can be determined) were subsequently either lost in Tibet after reporting the mountain by radio, or were invariably lost later during battle or in crashes. Thus, like the mysterious deaths of twenty of the finders of the tomb (in 1923) of Pharaoh Tut-ankh A-men in Egypt, all those who approach anywhere near Amne Machin, even at relatively great distances, seem doomed. Whether this doom is the result of "coincidence" or of supernatural fate (is there a difference?) is of no practical importance to the explorer: the records show that they *are* doomed. It is a sobering fact, and one you can't get away from: but more on this compendium of disaster later.

Carefully as I searched the whole region with glasses, no fantastic

---

* See Dr. Joseph F. Rock's "Seeking the Mountains of Mystery," *National Geographic Magazine*, February, 1930 (pages 134 and 140).

white tower thrust itself into the wind-scoured pale blue sky above the scores of white frozen peaks thrust up everywhere on a rather titanic scale to the south. I was terribly discouraged, but tried not to show it. After Dorje had hopefully cleaned off the lenses, which had become frosted by my breath, I climbed to the top of the obo and squatted on a pile of yak skulls.

As I turned the focusing-knob the blurred images of the far mountains became sharply defined and then crisped to a fine hair, looming up eight times their direct-vision size. I caught my breath against the wind, and slowly—mil by mil—studied the far-away, white crusty rim of the earth. . . .

Only serrated, shark-toothed ranges of ice-and-snow-covered mountains lay in the field of vision. Then suddenly, I detected a low isolated streak of cloud hanging in a pale blue patch of sky, and instantly *knew* that under it lay the great icy tilted reflecting mirror of Amne Machin, itself not directly visible from this distance through the lenses.

Immediately I spread a map on a clear patch of the snowy top of the obo, and spinning it for exact orientation with the compass, carefully penciled the spot indicated by the cloud and drew a line linking us to Amne Machin. It did exist . . . it was practically mine . . . of that I was sure. If the truth had not been revealed to me at that moment, we would likely have turned back to Fort Ta Ho Pa.

Under the obo, a ring of eager, sun-blackened faces turned up. These men thought we were trying to reach Amne Machin to locate atomic ores such as pitchblende, for we carried two small Geiger counters. In the face of such dangers and hardships, no other explanation was conceivable. They said that Russian Red Army troops were illegally guarding "secret" radioactive ores believed to have been uncovered in Turkestan (Sinkiang). I never at any time denied what they wished to believe. Only Ma Pu-fang recognized the timely worth of Amne Machin—a psychological value which he intended (there was no other explanation for his support) to exploit in the withdrawal of a defeated army, and perhaps the gathering around his Chinese standard of a still greater force, some of the Buddhists of Tibet.

"Can you see it—?" called Prince Dorje in a shout heard as a whisper in the whistling wind, forgetting to protect his face.

"It's there."

His smile, and a few rapid words reassured the others, and with lighter hearts and a vision of eventual quick return to Sining, the whole caravan started with a yell down off Dangnur Pass on foot, driving the yaks and horses ahead. In Tibet, one rides uphill, but walks downhill to save his animal.

Cautiously we felt our way down, in places toehold by toehold, sliding awkwardly in the trail-breaking animals' tracks. Sometimes we fell and hurt ourselves, for being stiff with the cold, we could not relax properly. The wind continued to blow with thin whistling sounds around cliffs, and humming over snow and ice fields swirling with ice-dust (frozen crystals), now gradually unfolding to view below us.

8

Hounded by the Ngoloks

HOURS LATER, and safely off the pass—though several complained of frostbitten hands and feet—we skirted an abyss and climbed to a frozen, barren hog's-back. A man up forward signaled a warning, crouching down as he did so: riding to a point under the crest we looked over and at once a concerned expression came over the faces about. In the distance a mile away, were several smokes—"Ngoloks!" someone whispered.

Hassan handed me the binoculars and after studying the smokes, I broke out laughing. Instead of trouble, salvation had appeared in the form of several hot springs. The steaming potholes were in a thawed-out morass and lay on the far side of a dusty, windy valley which was formed by an encircling black-stone range of breathtaking grandeur. It was slashed with gullies packed with frozen snow and ice, at the foot of which, lying in the "milk" of the glaciers we soon saw countless animal bones; these must be the remains of animals trapped for perhaps hundreds of years past in the crevasses on the mountain sides higher up.

One of the Naja scouts called out he had once heard of this strange graveyard and that the valley was called "Jeh Shi." As we approached we realized that several of the potholes were boiling and smelled like a duck farm. Dismounting hurriedly we ran to the water and were soon thawing our hands and feet. Thus the only permanent damage suffered on the pass was the freezing of three fingers of a single man, these amputated a week later.

As Camp 9 was being pitched nearby, I took a stroll to investigate the seepages. A 50-foot-wide river was found in a gulch below, collecting the minor feeder streams flowing from the scattered springs. Above this junction the river was capped with ice ten feet thick, and 200 yards below it was capped again; in between flowed tepid water, the home of darting minnows with prominent elbow-like pelvis fins. These strange fish swam away in all directions, trying to hide under the rocks.

In this place, on sudden impulse, I asked that a small tent be pitched over one of the cooler potholes having a convenient five-foot diameter, and after first testing the water's temperature with my finger. The men protested that I would surely die of pneumonia if I took a bath; better to wait until we returned to Tangar. But my exaggerated *salaaming* and approximate version of "Great is the Mercy of Our Lord," brought good-natured grins and the raising of the tent. Although it was cold in this animal graveyard I abandoned my vile sheepskins, pants, and boots. Only a quick plunge saved me from discomfort; in the tent a freezing wind was curling under the flapping edges of the bathhouse. The Tibetans and Moslems came crowding around to view this marvel of Tibet. Very few country Tibetans ever bathe from birth to death.

I lost no time squatting down up to my nose in the hot steaming water; when I soaped a foot it was necessary to hold it in the cold air. Luxuriating in the middle of soapsuds, my foot accidentally turned up a slate on which was beautifully chiseled, "Om Mani Padme Hum"; there was certainly no getting around the fact that Tibetans took their religion seriously. Two fantailed fishes of the type in the river were engraved below the scripture. One of the Tibetans snatched it up, exclaiming: "Ngolok!" This seemed rather improbable as we were undoubtedly too far north, even if they did possess craftsmen capable of such work.

I took this opportunity to sprinkle not only my discarded robes with DDT, but myself as well, before donning clean ones. A scout came up while I was pulling on soft-soled Tibetan boots, reporting that horse tracks had been found crossing our own on the other side of the hog's-back from which we had seen the springs. They must be Ngoloks, was the opinion of all, for they seemed to have these on the brain. Even so, after my bath, I felt in a downright festive mood.

I tried to interest Dorje in gin rummy but he sourly replied he had a temperature of 102°. Solomon Ma informed us he was in his sixth day of dysentery. He had eaten some raw Tibetan yak meat apparently not sufficiently frozen the fall before.

"You had better doctor us," suggested Dorje, "and then you can play solitaire afterwards."

I found Solomon Ma's glasses for him, hidden away in a bundle of bird skins, shoved him into the bathhouse, and handed him a paper-backed Chinese translation of Scheherazade's *Thousand and*

One Nights. Then I got into a pack and found Charles Bell's *Tibetan Dictionary*, which I handed to Dorje.

"My friend, you would make an excellent Chinese medico," he complained over his spectacles, "all they do is look wise and hand you a pinch of rhinoceros horn and seaweed powders."

Solomon darted into the tent, burrowing into his bed.

"How about a diagnosis!" he chattered.

"Okay," and I proceeded to diagnose.

"God the Lord!" gurgled Solomon Ma in an alarmed manner, "Take your riding crop out of my throat!"

"How about a diagnosis for you, Dorje?"

"Skip it. I'll read the dictionary."

"What about the Moslem doctor and his understudy?"

"Are you crazy!" they grumbled, "We prefer to die in peace."

In the early evening under a cloud-purpling sky, Mosul, a Tungan riding out on look-out duty, took a shot at some 450 yards at a lone yellow-gray wolf prowling around some of the yaks. As the Ngoloks had probably heard the shot, several men rode out to have a look around.

The wind strummed through the radio antenna, sparking with a message to Governor Ma. Dorje, apparently feeling better, called me in and read a paper previously translated by our Lhasa friends in Camp 7: it told of life in the holy city of Tashilunpo's "Gelukpa," ("Community of the Virtuous"), and we decided that such a terrifying ecclesiastical existence of resigned immurement, a life spent in a dark sealed underground cave from which the devoted, contemplating inmate is not released until death, was not for us in our present existence. Such transcendental faith in the quieting of the "will," that power which moves the Tibetan conception of the atom, and the necessary renunciation of all phenomenal existence, required a stronger man than any mere Mongol, Tungan, or American explorer.

Under a blue-black night sky, we all of us (Dorje and Solomon interpreting the more unobvious ideas) sat huddled together talking around the low-glowing watchfire. It was beastly cold; our fronts would warm a little, but our backs would freeze. From time to time we would shift around to toast the other side. We were ever conscious however of the glistening towers of eternally brooding animal traps of ice, leaning over us as if in expectation, and of the starlit snow fields floating overhead shining like mirrors of silver turned to the constellations wheeling toward the west.

Very softly Ishmael, a cut-throat said to have been released from the Sining jail to accompany us, said smiling:

"God our Lord, Praise be to Him. He made the day, and He made the night."

Enchanted by our unity with the awesome Tibetan mother-father spirit abroad in the glowing night; with the softly shadowed valley laced with winds and the steaming springs rising from the bosom of the earth; with the ageless living mountains and the little sounds and the smoke curling up as an offering from the campfires, we did not think of bed until midnight, when a pack of wolves began unaccountably to howl. At least one of us hoped they were real wolves smelling out the blood of a yak which had been killed and butchered for food. A few men stole off quietly in that direction.

We had acquired somewhere along the line of march, a wolf-hound named by the three of us Tsong Karpa because of his habit of contemplating when he should have been hounding back the wolves occasionally serenading one of the camps. This useless dog adopted me that night, and informed me quietly, sticking his cold nose inside my sheepskin sleeve, that he wished I wouldn't send him out into the night to draw off the pack; he would much prefer to sleep inside the doorway of my tent.

"Do you understand each other, Commander?" asked Ali, glancing across the coats, bright-eyed that a man and a dog were talking to each other.

"Why not?" I returned, getting up with Solomon and Dorje to head for our tent.

"With the Lord's permission many strange things happen in Tibet."

"Perhaps. But if, after all, as your Koran so wisely indicates, the illusion of all organized life and unorganized matter is merely the man-visible phenomenon, the realized idea of will, then—is this so strange?"

"Allah! Life is good, but death is the gateway to Paradise. We will follow you anywhere." I gathered from this they still had Ngoloks on their mind.

That night the wolves were real wolves, and the raiders did not show themselves though most thought they must be somewhere around. We broke Camp 9 at 5 A.M. in a low temperature of —28° C. Our elevation was 3,850 meters (11,731 feet), causing the men to puff as they loaded the yaks and horses. That day began clear, the old grass of the past summer brittle and crunchy underfoot; though cold, there was no wind, and for this we were thankful. The column, in single file, moved soundlessly (but for the squeaking peculiar to walking in that medium) across a cushion of snow, and, alert for trouble, trekked out of the shadowed vacuum of the valley, and headed into the river canyon.

The direction of march was west—our backs to the unseen but fast-rising sun. We worked along the river upstream. It was narrow in the fairly steep-walled canyon, and it became necessary to turn into the river: this highway was iced over to a depth of about ten feet, but was spongy, causing us to break through. Yaks and horses began falling into snow-covered crevasses, and a yak was lost, together with most of its load of straw. As the sun climbed higher, casting a good light into the gloom of the gulch, I shot three rabbits with the carbine favored for that day. They weighed about ten pounds each by our Chinese pole-scales; and had white snowshoes and a thick brown curly body with a four-inch scut. During the rest of the journey these rabbits swung pendulum fashion from a mule's pack, continually reminding us that good eating was in store for the night.

By midafternoon we reined in and camped on a small bench lying above the stream. An obo having sacred mani stones, proclaimed it to be one called the Djanchou. In these upper reaches of the canyon the stream was frozen tight except for a trickle in the bottom of its rocky bed. In the north rose a rock mountain of the same name, judged at 16,000 feet above sea level. The old Tibetan, sometimes called by us Chu-jeh, (different from Tujeh) our senior tailor, soon settled himself out of the biting wind in his barricade of sacked barley. He had deciphered the names on the stones. He now busied himself extending the sleeves of our shabby sheepskin chupas; after first assuring us that when he was finished there would be far less chance of frostbite, than with the tight wolf-fur gloves we had taken to wearing that day. The traveler in these parts is wise who tries to understand the humbler men among his companions, for on them more often than not, hinges failure or success.

We had many such men in our party, men of menial work, and a description of Chu-jeh—perhaps the most humble—will suffice as an evaluation of their general worth. At any hour, in all our camps, old Chu-jeh—who preferred to be called Chemkurja, his formal name—would patiently patch our robes, mend out goatskin socks, bind lashings or fix gun-slings, repair saddlery, make up leather bags from the raw hides and sinew brought in, cobble our worn boots, sew on frogs and buttons when we handed over our shirts. Without him we would have suffered even greater hardships; we would also have looked like a troupe of ragpickers.

This old man's brown parchment face was always breaking—at unexpected and distressing times—into the most wonderful smile; usually, when we were worn to a frazzle and colder than any corpse has a right to be. All the sunshine of his heart showed there for us to see and wonder at. That day in Djanchou canyon I came to know that life's suffering, coupled with meditations, had moved the old man head and shoulders above our younger, richer, shallower-minded, grasping, ambitious, fearful men. Chemkurja had been a lama. He was not an ignorant, dirty, old Tibetan oriental—as I had always thought—he was a philosopher built on profound lines who actually lived his convictions and homely preachings; above all he was not a clever dilettante satisfied with aimless surmising, he had arrived at a decision concerning the meaning of life—think of it!—his trade as a tailor was as good as another; he no longer struggled with his life, speaking as if it were something entirely different from "him": earthly frustrations had long departed, and peace had settled, he said, like gold in a torrent's bed. I had been in many countries, and yet had never heard a man on any continent, or of any race, say:

"Peace has come to me. Death of family, of friends, loss of possessions, failure or success—none of these calamities causes me any unhappiness now. All is the will of forces greater than man-the-ego. Knowing this, I am a free man. I am a very happy man!"

I liked old Chemkurja, our tailor, and from time to time when my rather feeble attempts at Tibetan lotus-eating turned too often into sour boiled mutton, I would invite him (and usually Solomon or Dorje to do the interpreting) to sit with me in my tent out of the cold and wind—a great honor for him, he always politely assured me—or I would sit in his barricade while he worked. Our legs tucked under in impromptu camp fashion, we would talk at his suggestion of "practical" things: such as "The Greater Wisdom," or perhaps of life on the other worlds. Of how life could have started there and here, or if the universe is running down, or if instead—as he believed—it was eternal "food" for itself, moving in endless forms from life to stone and back again.

"Lord," he would begin, without slowing his busy fingers, "Dogma is for the ignorant and the blind. Truth is for him who will listen to the 'dweller in the heart.' Is it not possible that life and man and all his vegetable and animal incarnations, could have started on other worlds; incalculable worlds in the nebulous Kingdom of Buddha, worlds and clusters of worlds without end, worlds forever and ever forming and dissolving out of 'idea'—?"

He would glance up and smile.

"It would seem incredible if out of billions of worlds this were not so, wise one," I would say, "All is born, dissolved, born again by the will of the Ultimate Reality."

"Lord, do you know the word, *iva?*"

"It is the Sanskrit symbol for what we of the west call 'relativity'." This much I knew from Dorje.

"And you, my Lord, knowing the word 'iva' would use this profound knowledge to go out among the ordered universes if you could? And try to set humanity's feet upon the stars?" he would say, fixing me with a sly darting glance. "Have you never, lying in your tent, heard the wind of the worlds calling to you?"

"It is impossible for our technocracy to do this now, wise one," I would answer with an air of wisdom I didn't feel, "Of course, rockets will one day. . . ."

"Lord, you would be disappointed," his smiling answer would come, as he put down his work; "On the other worlds, which you and I have always been a part of, you will find only this world, in its nebulous creative form perhaps, or in its solid fruitful form, or in its disintegrating form, at any rate completing its eternal cycle of recreating again and again through all eternity." I always wondered if I was getting the pure ideas of Chemkurja, or if Dorje's ideas were well salted throughout since in them I recognized points on which we two often argued. At any rate:

"And of life there?" I would ask.

"Why do you believe this?"

"Perhaps I don't. But by the law of averages life could have come through space to this planet."

"Lord, it is unimportant. Everything comes out of star dust. We are all tied, here and there, to names and forms. Life everywhere exists only as idea in the phenomenal brain of man the animal, existing in space and time—mere illusions. In other worlds you would only find life such as earth's life, in different forms no doubt, in different norms, on different planes of matter and comprehension, different names, but 'will' ever struggling to manifest itself in matter as here on earth, this earth, our mother-father, the manifested earth which like other earths binds our spirits to ever-evolving forms of atoms and resultant matter. To know this is to refute the will and to destroy the will to live. To know this cuts the bonds of will to phenomena, and sets free the intelligent will that can now join in eternal bliss the Ultimate Reality, *itself* now knowing."

And so the old tailor and I, together with Dorje (or Solomon) would talk. From time to time he would put down his work, rest his red-rimmed, rheumy, old eyes, perhaps rub them a bit, give his prayer-wheel a twirl or two, chanting in a low quick voice, "Om Mani Padme Hum!"

Again, the old man would speak of "less practical matters" such as hunting; of the habits of animals; of why some gods are hermaphrodite; of the ways of devils and the symbolism behind the seven-armed goddess; of a lama who can raise dead men to life again through vibrations transmitted to him from the sun; of benevolent gods and what they signify; of why symbolic or personal gods and idols are erected for the masses of men to worship; of why the image of man, together with a flower, a monkey, and a piece of dung, would be the ideal symbol for God—all equally a part of Him; of why snow-eaters go mad; of eggs and their philosophic aspect; of how a male and a female embryo can be told apart before birth; of a lama who has been mapping the moon for eighty years (most improbable); of tribal starvation; of the cosmic nature of war; of why a lama undergoes *kalimudrea,* self-induced death lasting as long as thirty days, without decomposition setting in, and then *willing* his own "resurrection."

Old Chemkurja had a stumpy little pipe fashioned by his own hands from gold and a human shinbone. The gold he had found in a lump somewhere; the shinbone was his dear uncle Kurja's. While we smoked sparingly of my limited stick of tobacco, the old fellow would contentedly sew and talk, while I stretched out on my back blowing smoke rings. Through Dorje's quick mind and flow of language, I never tired of probing the chasms and the shining peaks of this Tibetan brain—a brain electrically clear in the cold, brittle air of these regions so close to the stars.

A most profound and timely idea came from this fellow. I had idly asked the cause of war and human suffering, and if these could ever be regulated by man.

He said: "Lord, only the *ego* could think of such a thing. All is marked for destruction and recreation by the Divine Will. Nor is the answer so simple as religions would have us believe (here I suspected the fine hand of Dorje). War and human misery are not punishments issued by the Divine Power as rewards for evil committed by man on earth, but are the necessary result of the blind, groping First Cause Will's struggle to manifest itself through primitive forms evolved to the tool of reason, the human brain in phenomenal man, so as to attain *knowledge of Itself:* therefore, only when man is no longer man, but pure knowledge, God Himself, can war and suffering ever cease."

On the slopes around Camp 10 were a few extensive thickets of a reddish bush some three feet high. The grass appearing between these thickets was old, leached and pale, short and thin, brittle with frost. We were always concerned about grass; it was our life blood on the search for Amne Machin. This stuff could have little strength in it. It was almost useless for anything but fuel, and we were forced to use it instead of dung. It was twisted into knots, and fed to the fire along with twigs gathered from the thickets. Ill-favored as the place was, there was a reason for our people camping here, away from any possible place where yak dung might be located. Two scouts sent out in the night had reported that a strange band of horsemen had picked up our trail and were following it, apparently two smaller bands riding parallel on both sides. Kung-Lo, a Shabrang far-ranging scout, trotted into camp in the late afternoon: he had seen the glint of rifle barrels farther down the canyon. He believed we had definitely reached the northern edge of the fighting grounds of the Ngoloks—the guardians of holy Amne Machin. Due to camp being protected on two sides by high mountains, the Ngoloks could not swing around in front of us, but might attack from the lower end of the canyon under cover of night. Therefore a rather heavy guard was set on the back trail at a point three hundred yards from camp. Half an hour later the Ngoloks made contact with them, and the mountains rang with gunshots echoing among the cliffs.

A crisis was imminent, as the Ngoloks were probably trying for only a few horses, but even so a meeting was called in our tent. Abdul was there, Tujeh (not Chu-jeh the tailor), and Chutsu Tsereng—the Secretary. The latter spoke up:

"The vultures are gathering. They very often follow Ngoloks, you know." He pushed aside the door-flaps and pointed into the sky where a few birds were gliding. "Since Colonel Ma and Captain Tan are absent, it might be useful for you to learn about Ngoloks."

Darkness was creeping into the gulch; before the powwow began, soldiers were dispatched to relieve the others east of camp, a few besides going up the canyon and standing guard against possible encirclement, not so much of camp as of our animals. Cavalry in Ngolok regions sometimes have chain and padlock hobbles to discourage such raiders, but we had no such safety measures due mainly to our plan of grazing as much as possible off the country. When hobbles were used, these were mainly of leather, and so guards must be used. It was now 6:30, the temperature in the tent—8.5° C. Later, yaks, horses and mules were gathered and tethered, the riding animals roughly curried, blanketed, saddled and fed. Above the tents lay a smoke stratum between two cross breezes overhead, a welcome roof and protection against frost.

Tujeh, chief of this particular Tibetan contingent, began speaking. A summary of his harangue is that the Ngoloks, conservatively numbering, he believed, 20,000 cavalry,* habitually raided this far north of Amne Machin. The names of some of these clans which were mentioned are the Archung, Tsanggor, Kangsar, Kangren, Sertat, Butsang, Kangyin, Riman, Toba. The Ngoloks of such sub-tribes are organized under *khumbos,* whose followers have never known a conqueror for long. The khumbos command 500 families and up. The Secretary now cut in on Tujeh: he knew the Ngolok language.

Freedom—the Secretary explained at length, has ever been the keynote of the long unenlightened Ngolok history, including even

---

* Dr. Rock estimates 90,000 Ngoloks in all.

that black time suffered by Asia at the bloody hands of the Manchus. It was not known to me that this Chinese dynasty held extensive parts of the continent, including Siberia, Mongolia, Turkestan (Russian), India, Malaya, Afghanistan, Burma. But not an inch of Ngolok territory could be conquered by the Manchu generals, and these unruly Ngolok barbarians, alone, were the only nation of all east and central Asia to the borders of Europe, to remain free.

This information created an important problem for the expedition. The Secretary was now revealed as Governor Ma Pu-fang's personal key ambassador with the Ngoloks—who covered much of his south side; it was the Secretary who was sent to the tribes to recover some four or five thousand Chinese cavalry horses stolen by their warriors. But even the Secretary had no luck; nor had he ever been able while on any Ngolok mission, regardless of Moslem or Chinese gifts and promises of greater "prosperity and security," to retrieve any losses suffered by army units or merchants' caravans. He admitted all this with a wry smile: "Not even a copper pot," he added by way of emphasis.

A deputation of twenty Ngoloks (whom I remembered seeing in Sining), had recently visited Governor Ma about negotiating a treaty which they wanted, and an understanding with him was reached; the Ngoloks receiving rifles to seal their end of the alliance—but this accounted for only two of the clans. This divide-and-rule move was intended to secure Ma Pu-fang's position in that quarter, a turbulent one where fierce battles had first been fought on the Ganja Plain and in Song Chu Valley. Here the wild Ngura charged the Moslems with thirty-foot lances, killing many and all but routing them, and the tribes had won when the Amchoks began robbing the tents of their own allies. And though hundreds fell on both sides, and the Moslems ultimately held out and beheaded many, that northeast end of the Amne Machin Range still was held by the Ngoloks. Unfortunately for us these two reputedly pro-Moslem clans were on the eastern end of the Ngolok Confederation, and so were of no practical use.

The Ngoloks wore their hair long, and sometimes as a result, are locally called "Long-haired Ngoloks." They are spoken of also as "The Black Ngolok." They are a pastoral nation, a loose combination of tribes made up of clans living by their skill in the chase, by the natural increase of their herds, and by their courage and astuteness in raiding.

Tujeh mentioned hearing that the Mongols of central and south Chinghai were fast vanishing, being massacred by the Ngoloks. Among those mentioned were the Sokwo Arik tribe which had assisted Dr. Rock to reach his farthest west beyond the Yellow River. The southward-expanding Mongols, coming down out of Mongolia and Sinkiang, were apparently not giving the Ngoloks enough elbow room, and when the fierce and bloody Mongols, descendants of the terrible Khans, had approached within 100 miles, the inevitable happened—a reverse fate struck like lightning: the Ngolok horde rode over their yurts, killing them (according to my friends) by the thousands. To complicate the situation further, the Moslems had rather recently struck the Ngoloks on the far side of their west flank near the Yellow River—the side we were approaching—killing 700 families in a single surprise raid. The Ngolok clans here hated Moslems as a result, and I realized they might even try to wipe us out. Rock's great fear of the Ngoloks, I saw now, was more than justified.

The Ngoloks, continued Chutsu Tsereng, sucking calmly on his Chinese metal hubblebubble, torture and kill, they hold few if any prisoners for ransom. At this last, I cleared my throat as if in doubt.

"Specifically," he added, smiling, "they strangle their captives with rawhides, behead, drown, cut throats, slice bodies into small pieces," here he held up his thumb under my nose—"this size! They shoot, stone to death, burn and blind their victims." Then he took a puff, exhaled the smoke, and annotated: "They like to be free. They do not wish to be exploited for the good of China. They do not wish to become civilized Chinese. They will kill all of us . . ."

He resumed more or less in this vein, "Usually when they enter battle the Ngoloks do so on horseback, then dismount and attack on their bellies. They kill before you can see them. If we had been in the open they would probably have struck already by early morning, or just after sunset. But they are unpredictable, they even ambush from cover in broad daylight, or charge right out in the open. Here of course this isolated band of only a few men cannot cut in ahead of us. But day or night, it makes no difference. The Ngoloks attack silently or sometimes with cries to their gods. They vary their tactics. Since we beat them on the Yellow River and strung 156 heads on a rope at Labrang Monastery, they are more clever than even before. They now know the danger of 'characteristics,' and above all they will kill—with a finality and detail horrible to behold. During attack they execute a prearranged plan, they obey one leader during battle, for to do otherwise is not to receive a reprimand but a prolonged death by torture from their own comrades."

It seemed that Huang Suling, a Tibetan, the official Chinese general in charge at Labrang, the great lamasery of some five thousand monks, not far from Lanchow and east of the Yellow River, wisely married off his two sisters to a pair of rich Ngolok khumbos. As a result nearly all Ngolok trade at the moment flowed through Labrang, whose abbot lama is brother to Huang. Thus, for all practical purposes, this Tibetan general actually controls much of the northwest frontier of China proper, as a result of his Ngolok connections! The Secretary added that recently a surviving Mongol chief had sent his daughter to be bride to a Ngolok, and with her went 200 picked warhorses as dowry, valued at $30,000 (U.S.). We heard also that a Ngolok clan chieftainess famous for having 17 husbands, had recently died. Other explorers including Pereira, knew of this woman and referred to her as the "Queen of the Ngoloks"; this was very likely an overestimate of her rank, since these Moslems claimed she was merely a clan leader. Polyandry with the Ngoloks is not, however, as widely spread as among other Tibetans. When it is practiced, the number-one husband of the all-powerful bride usually arranges to confine the lesser husbands to his own brothers. The marriages of polyandry are the result of trying to protect property rights; also, unlike nearly all other Asian countries, the Tibetans have strict laws protecting the property rights of women—and quite often the women prefer, themselves, several husbands.

Of all the Tibetan tribes the Ngoloks possess the best horses, sheep, yaks, and goats; but they breed no mules, and possess only those which they capture. Recently they sold to Ma Pu-fang 10,000 cavalry remounts at the reputed fancy price of $1,000,000 (U.S.)— though originally these were for the most part his own horses or those of other factions loyal to the Nationalists. They eat boiled meat, but prefer it raw. They travel to Lhasa on pilgrimage to be rid of their multitudinous sins, but usually rob the other Tibetan tribes (many of whom are also robbers) en route. Formerly it was decreed by a Lhasa heirarchy to behead all Ngoloks bent on holy pilgrimage.

But this law backfired when the Ngoloks broke out and killed every lama they could find. In fact these soul-searching, belligerent rascals retaliated so bitterly with lead, fire and sword, that the pontiffs and lay lawgivers of Tibet speedily rescinded this law. In appearance, the Ngoloks are preeminently Tibetan; only later, seeing them face to face, we found they are actually even better looking than this generally handsome people, a few even resembling somewhat the ancient sculptured figures of the Aryan Mons of north India. They are teetotalers. And now they were believed to have a few bold lamas among them, who instruct the tribes in the ways of the spirit. It was in this scrap of information that I saw a first glimmer of possibilities . . . Dorje's and my *letter from the Panchen Lama!*

With night descending, the skirmish broke off (perhaps 20 rounds had been expended altogether), and the Ngoloks withdrew down the canyon to light fires and warm themselves: the air was cold at 10:15—19.5° below zero C.

A cold night's vigil was kept, but not a peep came from the camp below. From now on we could expect no more open attacks, though with allies and their mobility they might hound us—and attempt a surprise move (or so thought the Secretary).

Within our bit of extraterritorial ground in Ngolok country, we kept reasonably warm, all of us standing guard in hourly intervals.

At 3:30 A.M. we loaded up and spurred out of the gulch, using a twisting and turning tactic to throw off possible scouts near camp. There was a calm all about in the dark, for the wind had died. The men rode watchfully, Abdul's voice issuing orders. Whips curled over the yaks, lashing them into a trot. We crossed a pass and trotted at a quartering angle down long gravelly slopes. Again we began climbing, keeping to narrow terrain where we could not be flanked, and reached Djanchou Pass at 4,350 meters (13,254 feet). Here a wind was encountered

Our shivering horses, out of necessity, put their heads down and at places plowed through the crystal-hard snow, belly-deep in drifts, facing presently a hard-driven snowstorm. The Tibetan watch- and hunting-dogs left pink tracks across the sandpaper-rough snow, into which they were fortunately too light in weight to sink far. I noted drifting snow soon hid these marks of passing.

While descending from this pass, the wind suddenly hushed and we entered an airless, steep-walled valley. The column stumbled along downhill, moving as fast as possible—for the Ngoloks could not be far behind—falling and sliding until we at last hit bottom in a long gulch. A mile of rough rocky going, lashing the yaks into a trot, and we broke out of it, to ride across pleasant valleys linked together in a chain, through a gentle snowfall. This should blot out our tracks as well as conceal us from Ngoloks who might have reached the pass. It was not yet midday when the Secretary hailed turquoise-green Kara Nor (or as the Chinese spell it, "K'o-la Hu"), the "Bitter Sea."

Hundreds of orange-hued kyang—the beautiful kulan equines— were everywhere kicking up their heels in this windless region. A band of perhaps five hundred stood and watched us pass at three hundred yards. A red fox scampered nearby, disturbed in its stalking of a gaggle of snow geese. The snowfall slacked off gradually, and finally stopped altogether, as we rode along with soft snow-crunching squeaky sounds. Scouting, I cut off to the left of the caravan, riding presently along the rodent-pocked northern shore of the sea, the earth under the snow rotten with countless burrows into which my horse stumbled. Dismounted, we managed to struggle through deep muck, and reaching the beach followed the seashore littoral close up to an open ice lead.

The great sea, a white alabaster raft of thick ice flashing green in the thin air, was frozen over everywhere except for a single stretch of open water, twenty to thirty feet wide, just offshore, in which thousands of wild fowl, including swans, were feeding. These birds took off by the hundreds as we walked along the beach, circling and landing behind. Dorje later said the elevation was 4,080 meters (12,432 feet).

Thirsty, I swung out of the saddle—for I had mounted on reaching the firm beach—and the horse and I drank from the open lead. The water was bitter with saline salts. I was forced to vomit, but felt better after eating a handful of snow. I spotted a movement near the summit of a near hill and snatched my binoculars from its case on the saddle. Instead of Ngoloks I saw three bands of kyang and two herds of gazelles, grazing at the extreme heights of

13,000 feet on the hills above the sea. It was pleasant here after the wind and cold and storm-racket of Djanchou Pass. The temperature was only —3° C., with a light chorus of breezes stirring the air and snow crystals.

When the sun was approaching its zenith I joined the others. We soon stopped and loosened saddles and slipped bridles, and enjoyed a snack of frozen Ta Ho Pa sheep hearts handily boiled the night before; these were thawed out over a dung fire. Afterwards our Tibetans gathered under their *tanka,* a banner of dyed red and yellow yak tails. With singular charm in both manner and voices, they began praying, long and loudly, very high and very low in key, chanting from the 108 sacred texts of the *Tanjur.* Under our ge-long's direction they performed certain mystic rites.

They knew, for I had taken pains indirectly to let them know, of our cordial relationship with the Panchen Lama and his court—one reason for splendid service they had given and for our lack of internal dissensions.

We idly tossed scraps of meat into the air, where they were seized by hawks. The loony cry of a bird came from the direction of the sea. We sat on our saddles and watched the Tibetans. The astute Tu Jen, the Secretary, Chutsu Tsereng, who had become a strong personal ally and loyal friend, listened carefully, and then began with Dorje's help to interpret the rites:

Apparently the Tibetans prayed for the light of eternal bliss. They addressed their prayers to the Panchen Lama—living Buddha, omnipotent, omnipresent Creator and Savior. They prayed to the Dhyani Buddhas from whom the living God incarnates, among whom Amitabha Buddha, Lord of the West Paradise, is greatest; they bowed toward Kumbum in the northeast, to Öpame, Heavenly Buddha of Measureless Light; to Panchen Rimpoche, Precious Teacher . . . and chanted, "Oh, Lord, protect Your children from Yama, God of Infernal Regions, of whom the Ngoloks are favored sons . . . 'Om Mani Padme Hum!' "

Their prayers had ended none too soon. Riding over the crest of a ridge, less than 300 yards at our backs, came some fifty riders—charging with considerable noise—straight down upon our rather far-grazing animals:—a few rifles crackling. Chaos reigned among the horses and yaks—many beginning to stampede—a few running about crippled.

There was no panic among the expedition's men, just an absolute dumbfoundedness—and a stone immobility!

I let out a yell and jerking the nearest rifle out of one of the few saddle scabbards we had pulled the bead down on the Ngolok leader riding at a swerving gallop well in advance of the mass of horsemen. But I was not alone, and a scattering volley shot him out of his saddle. The rank and file of Moslems and Tibetans under Abdul and Tujeh suddenly came to life at their leaders' commands and leaped up, running all over the place, grabbing rifles, and throwing themselves down behind rocks and saddles—and opened up on their own. Once started they were cool enough, for all of them had been through this many times before.

Two Ngoloks and a horse with its rider pitched to the ground. But still the Ngoloks kept coming, the sharp tattoo of their horses' hooves louder and louder, yelling and shooting. Suddenly, at some seventy paces in front of us, they saw that their surprise had failed; they pulled up sharply, wheeled their mounts, and rode at a zigzagging run back over their fallen. Others stopped and pulled the wounded up behind them. One rider reined in at the side of the leader who was sitting up, and flung him into the saddle across his belly, lashed him there, and then drove the horse ahead of him over the hill. Probably the rescued one was only wounded. Three or four men who were dismounted, and afoot, were running back uphill. In a few moments the last of them vanished.

But they had left behind a fair mess of our temporary halting ground. A Tibetan lay sprawled on his face. A Moslem hit in the head by a lucky shot was dying. Another fellow had a scratch on his arm. Three Ngoloks, together with nine horses, lay on the slope, whether dead or wounded was anybody's guess. The Moslems rushed out and picked up four Chinese army rifles. When they returned I saw that the metal knife scabbard of one had a smear of blood on it, and guessed at least one Ngolok had had his throat slashed.

9

Establishment of the Black Sea Base

O̲U̲R̲ wounded were bandaged and injected with tet-
anus, to prevent blood-poisoning. Both of them
could ride. Two dead yaks, a mule and a horse were stripped of
their saddles and cargo packs, and these distributed among the caravan. Two other wounded animals were shot. The Moslem, hardly
cold, was hurriedly buried under a mound of stones, after first being undressed, washed and wrapped in a shroud of sheeting; the
other Moslems turning their faces toward Sining, then Mecca, and
praying in loud voices—Abdul acting as muezzin.

Exposed on the sea plain as we were, and undermanned, we decided to move on. The abandoned military road runs south of this
place paralleling the sea on its east side, but this was not judged
safe with Ngoloks in the area. Therefore we must go west on a
Tibetan trail. The gelong and bombom were leaping about, energetically chasing away with their prayer-ribbon wands any chance
devils loitering among men and animals. We mounted as soon as
possible, and keeping north, carefully circumventing the rodent-
pocked ground near the sea, hurried into the west. With the Bitter
Sea yet in sight, I rode off scouting with two Moslems: from a hill-
top we looked back and saw the Ngoloks in full sight—now apparently quite heavily reinforced. Even so, the Moslems referred to
them as only a small party out after horses or whatever they could
get. It was not such a band they feared, but some main raiding
party with hundreds of rifles and out for rifles and horses (of course)
but mainly hoping for a strike at some Moslem military column.

Trailing behind, the Ngoloks—perhaps thinking to cut off part
of our caravan—had circled pell-mell into the rodent-rotted grounds,
and there they were:—floundering, over two hundred dismounted
warriors, trying to extricate themselves from the mud.

The Moslems chuckled and turned aside to join the caravan. In
order to make up lost time, we took a short cut, but missed the
others, after intersecting what we thought would be the most likely

route. By throwing out a five-mile loop across the most likely country—for low hills were now everywhere—we picked up tracks which
indicated the caravan had turned left and hurried past some mud
flats into the south. A few yaks had broken through the deceptive
frozen crust and bogged: four of them had been abandoned (though
relieved of their packs).

And so we followed in this new direction, at a leisurely canter,
watching to the rear so we would not be cut off, and occasionally
nosing over ridges into short cuts, and even hunting a bit—killing
two antelopes (which are larger than gazelles) in a gully. Tying
them behind our saddles, we continued on the way. Once we were
jerked up short during a short cut by suddenly encountering more
of the treacherous melted rodent-rotted ground, into which the
hocks of the horses sank, causing them to founder and plunge about.
Dismounted, we led them across what seemed the more solid places.
We finally struggled out of the mud, thankful that no Ngoloks
had appeared.

After an hour, when we were mounted again, snow started falling.
Except for an occasional sign of the caravan's tracks, not yet completely covered by new snow, we would certainly have lost the way.
Half an hour later we did lose our way: all tracks on the frozen
ground were covered smoothly by from two to five inches of powdery snow. Our relative position we knew quite well, and my compass showed that the sea lay about eight miles east of us. Normally,
whether following big game, or my own or the enemy's troops, I
often leave the trail to study the country: I then do whatever a
bear, sheep, or a deer would do (and some bucks and rams will
back-track and watch you from a ridge), taking my direction from
the lay of the terrain most likely be picked as a route by whatever
or whomever I am following; in this instance, the caravan's guides.

But the caravan, itself, seemed to have become confused in the
storm, and to have wandered about and lost its own way. So we continued on over what I reckoned to be the correct pass, and dropped
down over the ridge, where, instead of finding our friends, we
merely descended into a new set of valley-flats, each about five miles
in diameter and hill-girded. At last, after fruitlessly throwing out
three long feelers and cutting for signs to pick up the trail, the two
Moslems gave up in disgust. At times the storm would lift and we

could see for miles, at other times our range of vision was reduced to less than a few hundred feet.

A cold spell had set in, and, our feet freezing, we sat down behind a boulder, where I smoked my pipe. Figuring that the caravan might show up on one of the plains below, I wasn't too worried. No Ngoloks were in sight. But there was no sign of it, either on the plains or on any of the low hills slashed with snow-marked gullies, which girt the flats. I knocked out my pipe ashes, and we mounted, jogging hopefully along a logical course southward across some hills and canyons for another five miles. We were now about fifteen miles southwest of the sea.

Standing there in a blinding snowstorm, we suddenly had a very bad fright. A horse neighed very close—less than 200 feet.

"Ngoloks!" whispered the two Moslems, unslinging their rifles.

At that moment I made out the indistinct shapes of horses and men just ahead. Standing very still, we watched them—and suddenly I realized it was our own column, actually doubling back on its own tracks!

The lead scout, Danku, a Shabrang whom I recognized by his robe, snatched his rifle off the cantle of his saddle, and leveled it at me. A warning shout went up from the caravan and we heard several rifle bolts click. I lost no time calling out who we were. Tujeh galloped alongside, with a wide grin on his flat face; exclaiming that it was miraculous that I had found them . . . that they were lost and didn't know where they were in relation to a campsite with water found earlier by one of the men. Dorje and I let Tujeh think as he pleased, mumbling something about "His Holiness," and that the Panchen Lama's scriptures were always carried with me wrapped in the hadak he had presented in Kumbum. This news was spread by relayed shouts downwind, and the Tibetans smiled knowingly.

It was evident from the caravan's exhausted condition that we must halt and rest, awaiting the storm's lifting. Dismounting reluctantly, I joked with the Moslems and flung horse blankets over them as they crouched freezing against the wet bellies of their horses —trained mounts, now hobbled and made to lie down as a wind- and snow-break. The yaks stood, all turned in one direction, their rumps toward the wind and caked with snow. After more than an hour the snowfall and its sharp drift abated somewhat and we began to make out objects a few hundred yards away. Somebody yelled and pointed out a rock landmark, which with binoculars I made out to be an old wind-wrecked obo.

By my compass and his own map already marked with the scout's waterhole, Tujeh set a new course through the softly falling snow-flakes, now gathering in an easy swirl around us. Urging the tired yaks forward, with freezing men and animals all pulling their heads down, we plowed forward behind the scout-guide. The wet mane of the black stallion kept whipping back across my face; scenting open water, he pranced up and down and back and forth through the streaming caravan, his dancing hooves throwing clods of packed snow all over the place.

As we were riding through the falling flakes, I observed, as I often did with pleasure, the way Prince Dorje sat his tall iron-gray mare. He had a private string of splendid mounts to choose from, but this mare was his favorite. Although a professor, a sedentary un-Mongol Mongolian who preferred a backyard to the wider ranges of the world itself, Dorje sat that pacing mare as only a Mongol could. I was no rider myself, but a fair judge of riders, having owned at one time the S-Bar-S Ranch in California. Of course he had ridden all his life, and the Mongolian gaits were instinctive with him, but that alone will not guarantee the seat that he had: such perfection could only come from generations of ancestral nomads, who consider it bad manners to walk even when exchanging greetings between one yurt-dweller to another, men and women who must ride even when calling on their next-door neighbor.

None of our professional cavalry Moslems, and they were hand-picked riders born to the saddle, could hold a candle to Dorje in the way he so easily, and apparently without effort, covered considerable distances in all kinds of weather, with no evidence of turning a single hair on the mare, or on himself. Two miles more and we came upon the campsite Danku's man had found, but the precious dung we hoped for was covered by snow—nine inches of it!

Now according to our Chinese general staff maps, there was supposed to be a Mongol town here. Actually, the Chinese practice, as we were learning all along, is to spot towns or stations on these maps where none perhaps has existed for a long time, and then not always correct the maps when the place ceases to exist. For example: nothing other than Tibetan Rong-pas' settlements—which are generally unmarked—exists anywhere on this particular Lhasa route south of

Fort Ta Ho Pa all the way to Jyekundo. And this in spite of the highly-detailed maps, Chinese and foreign, reading to the contrary. A cartographer or military strategist, working in London or Washington over his precious maps of northeast Tibet, would think the region to be almost completely explored, when in fact (according to the Moslems), it is sixty per cent unknown and unexplored off the main avenues of traffic. Specific details on this later.

We slid wearily to the ground, fairly done in and exhausted. We had ridden 60 li (30 miles) that freezing snow-blown day, driven off a band of rustlers, made an escape over frozen ground and crusty bogs of mud, gotten ourselves lost . . . and now, somewhere about, these rough-and-tumble Ngolok clansmen were very likely ranging in search of us. These malevolent fellows, I was assured, would be plotting a special revenge, and our heads would certainly be lopped off if they caught any stragglers.

But even if there was a decent chance for escape by turning tail and cutting back to Ta Ho Pa, I could not have done it—the latest radiograms from Governor Ma warned that we must not fail. Nationalist China was defeated and, even worse than this, the eastern hinge of world Islam was in great jeopardy! Eventual defeat in far east Asia by the Communist coalition must inevitably follow. To prevent this in full we must find Amne Machin—the token that would assist in allowing Ma Pu-fang to withdraw some of his Moslems into Buddhist Tibet.

Guards were dispatched to ring the area: camp was pitched on a rather wet, flat, alkaline floor comprising the bottom of a small, round valley formed in part by snowy round-shouldered rock mountains. Alongside our tents was a small lake whose amber-colored ice provided the only means for quenching thirst. We had reached a point southwest of Kara Nor, and this pond was certainly one of the sea mother's bitterest offspring. Our murky tea tasted like gall, but I for one found it warming and put down two cups of the steamy stuff—and managed to keep it down.

At Camp 11, our elevation was 4,060 meters (12,371 feet), only a little above our norm, which was puzzling, for we seemed to be getting into country basically no higher than that in the north. Amne Machin *couldn't possibly* rise out of such a low place in the Tala's plateau! Perhaps I was mistaken in thinking I had seen it reflected on the underside of that cloud observed south from Dang-nur Pass.

I rested awhile and then, feeling stronger, had a fresh horse saddled. The Scriptures tell us that Elijah was fed by ravens, but our motley crew had little to recommend itself to divine assistance, even if scavengers could survive in such a bleak country, which at this season they apparently could not for none were about. The best bet for finding food was on the rock-crested mountain standing to the south. It looked good for mountain sheep, though it was barren enough except for tall rock outcroppings, beetling cliffs, and needle pinnacles hundreds of feet high, its lower slopes spanned by wide patches of snow. From these fields of snow rose whirling plumes of crystals, indicating a high-elevation wind there. But cold and wind, and even approaching night, notwithstanding, the cooks wailed that but for the antelopes the larder was lean, and there were many hungry bellies to feed. There was very little tsamba left, and we were eating nothing but tea and meat. We had lost to thieves, rough trekking, wolves, sickness, bogs, and even to the cooks' pots, too many of the caravan animals. Of late the men had been forced to kill even a few weakening mules, horses, and yaks for meat. Even so, these were so emaciated and gristly—without an ounce of fat—that we gained little nourishment and strength from such fare. From this place onward, we couldn't afford, unless in final stages of starvation, to slaughter any more of them; unless, of course, they must be put out of their misery for one reason or another.

The hour was late: 3:35 before we got started on the hunt. A light snow was falling. Bomba, a silent wooden-faced Tibetan, our keenest hunter, and I, set out together. We rode across the valley and quartered up the side of the mountain, keeping out of the snow fields which he judged were crevassed. After a hard, slippery climb of perhaps 3,000 feet in a fairly stiff wind, we safely reached the icy summit on the mountain's west side. Here we tied together the reins of our gasping, steaming horses. Leaving them, and soon puffing from lack of sufficient oxygen, the pair of us scrambled on foot along the precipitous edge of a knife-narrow, yellowish stone ridge. Once I became dizzy from the high elevation and exertion, and rested, my heart pounding. It was cold at —23° C., and impossible to touch bare hands to the metal of our guns without "burning" off the skin. Crouching down, we cautiously peered over the rocky crest caked with ice. On the far side of an almost perpendicular-walled gully, and about 300 yards in front of our lofty perch, spread out a sight that few white hunters have seen in this day and age.

Bighorn sheep—over a thousand of them—were browsing on low bushes. Bomba's wooden face burst into a net of hilarious cracks, and he was all for blasting away on the instant. But I slowly placed my sheepskin sleeve over his rifle which had come out of Frederick the Great's arsenal; and gazed my fill for ten wonderful minutes. The sheep (which Bomba called *yang*) were gray and white in color, having a faint tinge of yellow. According to their tracks they had banded together and crossed over to this mountain from another range just north. Due to changing feed conditions and storms, they do not necessarily remain on the same mountains throughout the year, or so believed Bomba.

Finally I grinned at my companion. He grimly pulled his hands out from under his robe, where he had been thawing them out, unfolded the gazelle-horn prongs hinged to the end of the rifle barrel, and aimed at some point across the way. It was his moment of triumph and I held my breath—300 yards is a hell of a long shot. He took three or four sightings, squirmed around into a firmer seat for himself, and finally squeezed off the trigger. The old blunder-buss made a crashing noise in the thin air, and instantly after came the dull plop of lead hitting flesh at a fairly low velocity, then whistled sharply as it ricochetted off a stone. A gut shot!

The ram, tumbling down a short pitch, and the loud report of the gun sent the entire herd leaping up the side of the rocky canyon, and then streaming over into its bottom higher up where they flowed together like a river, broad here, narrow there, until they disappeared over a pass some mile and a half east. And there went our dinner. A life-long fear of crippling game had instinctively prevented me from trying a running-jumping shot at that range.

I looked at Bomba, and he looked at me:

"A piece of snow hit me in the eye," says he, backing it up with the appropriate gesture.

The ram had somehow gotten on its feet in the mêlée, and was moving off to the left in the opposite direction from that taken by the herd, trotting along the steep side of the canyon. We started down the precipitous slope on our side, and crossed the intervening canyon, floundering in the fairly deep snow trapped in the sharp wedge of its bottom here, and quickly took up the ram's tracks.

These we followed; half an hour later, a spot of clotted blood showed red in one of the footprints. Bomba was eager as a hound to find the wounded ram, and started to run as fast as he could manage through the rocks. I grabbed him and forced him to sit down. Now there are a lot of theories about hunting down wounded game, and while hunters may not all agree about this one, it sometimes works.

I wanted to give the ram a chance to "bed" down. At this elevation and in this intense cold, he might then stiffen, allowing us to work in close and jump him out at short range, and so get in another shot. Should we press forward too quickly, we would certainly lose this ram before nightfall. He was only gut shot, the type of blood clot confirming this, and with a new flurry of snow falling in his tracks, he would be lost. The wolves would get him if we didn't win our race against time. Sometimes the best way to win a race is to sit down. Twenty minutes later, our feet numb, we cautiously advanced again. Half an hour of scrambling among frozen-snow blocks and stones passed.

Then suddenly we jumped the ram from under a cliff across a gulch, standing above us like a statue, watching his back trail. Fortunately we had left the trail before reaching the gulch, and cut back over a ridge, figuring he would circle above in order to watch his tracks to see if he was being followed. Snapping my rifle hard against my shoulder, I fired. The ram rolled about 200 yards downhill, turning over once in midair. We climbed down a slope of loose detritus, and safely reached the bottom of the gulch; in a few minutes we were dressing out the carcass. It was fat! And the hide, being thick furred, similar to but heavier than deer skin, was in the best possible pelage.

This job warmed us somewhat—for we immediately plunged our hands into the warm guts—and found we still had an hour left before dark. The sky was a lustrous white, holding plenty of diffused light in spite of occasional snow flurries. And so we set out again, this time seeing a second herd and, after a hard half-hour's climbing killing an isolated ram lying on a cliff shelf, probably a three-year-old like the first. The wind sprang up, and snow began falling in earnest, darkness fast approaching.

We had to get off that mountain before night set in, as the temperature had fallen to —27° C. We could not possibly survive a night on the mountain without fire or shelter. Hurrying, I returned for the horses, and found them stomping on the summit impatiently; I led them back to each of the separated rams. But for the fact that these native horses were sure-footed, it would have been impossible in such rough country. In semi-darkness we loaded the rams in the saddles, and zigzagged a sliding retreat down the steep grade, bracing ourselves against the wind, cold and blustering, and smothered with driving snowflakes.

There had been two herds of bighorns, each herd numbering approximately a thousand sheep. Our two rams, killed for meat, would scarcely be missed, and the country was so "spooked" now, that Tibetans and Ngoloks would have a hard time getting any. This might seem ungenerous; but when they locate such herds—as proved by the hundreds if not thousands of old sheep skulls we had passed enroute—Tibetans practically eliminate them. Strangely, they have no conception of game preservation, which would insure never-ending bags; they are strictly short-range meat-hunters, taking little pleasure in the hunt itself. In such snow-bound country, that day, we might possibly have killed ten sheep out of the last herd, for Bomba was an excellent hunter as well as a reliable shot, but not being able to carry them off the mountain, we would—I explained to the puzzled Bomba—only be fattening the wolves, whose tracks were everywhere. He understood perfectly, however, when I reminded him of Ngoloks in the region, who might hear us shooting.

While heading on a circuitous route back to camp to avoid a series of steep slopes and cliffs, we saw, reflected through an electric-blue twilight in the far north, a titanic skyline, many peaks being over 15,000 feet high—undoubtedly the Doche Lun, or Chandia Mountains. These had never been explored, only reported to Chinese cartographers by Mongols a century or more ago. In sheltering side canyons—half-hidden in spume clouds and darkness—we surprised and jumped at close range hundreds of kyang and gazelles, grazing up to 14,500 feet! As night fell, we were only half-way down the mountain; fortunately, star-clusters began showing through torn holes in the clouds. We were frozen, dead-tired, and aching all over, as we had put in twelve hours that day in the saddle alone, even before beginning our eight-hour hunting trip. Four times it was necessary to stop and sit awhile and massage each other's feet, for the blood was sluggish and coagulating. We finally hit bottom on the valley floor, and shortly after 9 o'clock, Bomba and I limped into camp—dogs barking and guards challenging.

The men, seeing the fatty meat, were soon quarreling in amusement over various pieces as they broke out the pots and pans: with more fresh good meat in camp, all was jolly; the campfires' smoke smelled good, indicating fuel had been dug from under the drifts. From the copper pots soon came tantalizing odors. However, I could eat very little of the sheep meat, as I seemed to be suffocating for lack of sufficient air. I made grateful sounds to Hassan, for he appeared worried, and in one great ache I at last near midnight crawled into bed, and was soon submerged in a frozen oblivion.

By the morning's first flashing lights, we trekked out of the round valley which had hidden us so effectively from the Ngoloks, and began a 45-li ride. The caravan, lean, emaciated, hard-faced, settled to a smooth rhythm of march in spite of a stiff, quick snowfall on the first ridge, and the blasting of strong southeast winds. At times I was actually paralyzed by this cold air. But there was no sitting it out in camp. Our yaks and horses were hungry.

Najas sent out in the night had returned with valuable information. We spread the map out on the rocks, anchoring it with stones: our direction must be, first a short zig west, and then a long zag southwest, capped by an abrupt turn to a big spring flowing at the southeast corner of Tossun Nor (not to be confused with another sea of that name between Tsaidam Swamp and Koko Nor), the "Black Sea." Von Filchner calls this sea Tossan Nor; Rand Mc-Nally, Tosu nor; the Chinese T'o-so Hu or Ts'o-kuo. However it is spelled, I doubt if anyone, regardless of whatever authority he may follow, can confuse this sea with another. Dorje, by the way, says Tossun is correct, and that is why I use it here.

The column was waved on the course, for we dared not use the bugle in this region. For hours we jogged along, partly through an amethystine mist, and partly through cutting crystal ice which could only have been blown off some tremendous mountains on our left rear somewhere southeast, and then across a yellow-brown, windy and gritty sand-dune desert. All about were thousands of kyang and a few antelopes. Gazelles were everywhere, and superabundant.

Once, Abdul halted the column, saying he wanted to test his

machine-gun, which was now being carried across the saddle due to his fear of ambuscade. Inwardly I was filled with apprehension, but hated to make him lose face by ordering the column to continue. The gun was a businesslike .25-caliber Nambu, said to have been captured by Abdul in the Twelfth War Zone of Inner Mongolia. As I say, we pulled up, and to my astonishment, our otherwise chivalrous trooper took sight on a small herd of gazelles about 450 yards out in the desert. Before I could recover from surprise at his unexpected action, he had gotten off two or three quick bursts, which scattered the herd in all directions—without killing one. Though we needed the fresh meat, somehow I was relieved.

Later on, Solomon and I each killed a kyang after a long, patient foot-stalk through the dunes, mine being taken at 375 yards by a fantastically lucky shoulder shot. Then Solomon Ma's was killed at 125 paces after the band had turned and run smack into him while making a wide escape swing. Pacing off the distance I came up to my downed kyang, and its beauty came as a shock. It was a stallion weighing about 600 pounds before being dressed out. The body was a camel-brown with a flaming orange tinge, dark brown mane and black stripe down the spine; while belly and sides and muzzle were of a creamy white, as were the underjaws. The pair of kyangs provided us with some 400 pounds of dressed meat for our try at Amne Machin, which must lie in the direction of the blowing ice crystals just southeast of the desert. This was no time to be finicky about strong-tasting meat. There were no Drök-pas in this place from whom we could buy sheep or yaks.

Even so, there was some scattered grumbling among the men as they cut the meat. I called them together and told them I was through dry-nursing them, and it was time for a ventilation of the facts. They were supposed to be the best soldiers in Asia, and they were acting like a lot of spoiled babies. God help them if they ever had to fight the Communists from Tibet. After that they fell to, swiftly carving up the kyangs, saying piously (according to Solomon), to save their faces amongst themselves:

"A dreadful thing has happened to us! The heresy of our life! That tricky foreigner is a djinn! May the Twelfth Imam geld him when he enters Paradise by trickery! He performs *tsai* after his game is dead! He works us to the death! Look! All my white fingers are black bones! He feeds us with horse meat!"—so approximately they cried amongst themselves.

Others took up the refrain something like this:

"Praise be to the Merciful One! May this foreigner's hell-hound's teeth all fall out when he bites into this tough horse meat . . . this accursed horse flesh fit only for dogs!" Others stood around to uh-huh their recriminations.

By late afternoon we pulled up at the Black Sea (printed on the Chinese maps as not only T'o-so Hu and Ts'o-kuo, but as T'o-hsün-no-erh), where many honking geese rose out of the dry grass, their wings flashing in the setting sun. The geographical (not the political) center of Tibet was about on a line of 92° of longitude; it lay about 350 miles west of the Black Sea, somewhere in the eastern Chang Tang, the approximately 16,000-foot plateau reaching as far west as the Karakorums. Dorje, Solomon and I calculated we were now within practical striking range of Amne Machin itself. It is some-times called locally Grandfather of the Yellow River, and heads south and west of this mysterious range. As the Yellow River was bound up with Amne Machin, we intended to try and clear up some details of this also, as well as to measure the highest elevation in the Amne Machin Range. Furthermore, we would attempt penetration of that range farther east than any explorer had yet been. To my knowledge the last foreign traveler to have crossed the western Amne Machins was Major Tolstoy on an OSS mission during World War II.

I called Solomon and Tujeh over for information: the Tibetan said his people's name for the snow crests along the southern beach of the sea is "Dzu," meaning "Half-yak, half-cow," with wind-whetted points and sharp ridges running in a fairly broken range of from fifteen to sixteen thousand feet elevation. One of the peaks at one camp, and just south, was called Chi Shan by the Chinese Mos-lems and measured at a little more than 16,000 feet. All these peaks were visible only when the wind momentarily tore aside their cloud caps. Below, there was an indefinable, wild and primeval beauty in the broad alluvial valley lying east of Tossun Nor. The western, nar-row end, in which the sea lay, was veiled here and there by different snowstorms—white screens shimmering like showers of diamond dust in the glare of the slanted sunshine. The air was so clear it was like standing in the center of a glass ball. The elevation at the spring where Camp 12 was being pitched registered 4,040 meters (12,310 feet)—I was puzzled about this comparatively low elevation.

The whole wide mountain-encompassed valley extending east of the Black Sea and along the north flank of "Long Stone Mountain," the ridge just above camp comprising this segment of the Dzu Range, was an unspoiled Eden of a big-game paradise. I resolved to despoil it as little as possible. Game herds and flocks of migrating birds were everywhere in sight.

The pink-stone Dzu Mountains rising in shattered ruddy cliffs hundreds of feet high on the south edge of camp, were, so Tujeh reasoned, the actual western ridges of the main Amne Machin Range itself. Von Filchner who had crossed in about this region, marks his map at this point as the "Amne Matschin" and places the western parts of the range as extending far west of us. Dorje's and my excitement knew no bounds. From here, at this very spot on the Black Sea, we must attempt to ride out and find the mystery peaks.

But first we needed more food. After hunting among cliffs and over around snow fields among the peaks, one of the Moslems presently returned to camp dragging some kind of meat. It proved to be that of a male bear. The hunter was very excited; the bear had charged him after being wounded by a too-quickly aimed shot, which hit only its lower jaw. Hunger may have contributed to the beast's bad temper in charging. Fortunately Ali had killed it in the nick of time with a second shot. Other men went up for the rest of the meat; the Moslems could eat it if the Tibetans wouldn't, for Ali had cut the throat. This bear had apparently just come out of winter hibernation, for the meat was tough as Tibetan shoe leather.

Under a latticed sky that evening, a second bear showed up. This one, also a male, wandered near camp, ambling along black as coal and racked up nearly as big as a yak. He was neither fishing nor hunting geese; only poking around for lack of a lady friend, following our scent upwind, sitting on his broad ursuline bottom and wrinkling his nose at our strange smells, minding his own business. He approached within a hundred yards. Since it too, was lean, and as Ngoloks might be near, I asked the men not to shoot, though they were already collecting guns. One of the Moslems, a wild, thin, dry, leathery man, a former outlaw said to be a Momand run out of Khyber country, paid no attention—merely yelling something about an unbelieving *sahib:* and it was necessary, not so much for the bear's sake as my own face, to bounce a tent peg off the fellow's ribs.

In the night a new snowstorm descended, and a marrow-freezing wind poured thick with snow off the ice pack of the boreal-like Black Sea. We were hungry and the kyang meat proved palatable enough, if somewhat strong, dark in color, and (being too fresh) tough and also dry in texture.

Morning brought a clear sky. With a new skit of snow, excellent for tracking, Tibetan hunters hustled off. Afraid Ngoloks might find or stumble across us, I decided that before dawn the following day, we should aim at departure from our Tossun base, which in the night had been strongly established and barricaded to serve as our main pivot in the west. The men felt it would be nip and tuck getting into the foot of the peak (or peaks as reported by Dr. Rock), and out again. A small party would be the best bet, leaving behind the yaks, camp gear, tired horses and mules, and most of the personnel, and try going south of east and locating "The Thing."

I was worried that The Thing, or the mountain, might not even exist; after all, many had claimed to have seen it, usually from far distances, but no two photographs were comparable. Dr. Joseph Rock, stopped in the eastern regions north of the range by gathering Ngoloks in 1927, and while yet east perhaps 50 miles, had reported in the *National Geographic Magazine* that Amne Machin would go up to 28,000 feet (the exact words are: "I came to the conclusion that the Amnyi Machen towers more than 28,000 feet.")—this celebrated scientist had no instruments, however, and presumably made his calculations from a study of photographs; Moon Chin the airline manager, who claimed to have flown near it in 1948, put the mountain at 19,000 feet; Mr. Milton Reynolds announced in 1948 to the American press, that he and his aircraft crew estimated the height at 30,000 feet. Now it was also possible that none of these travelers had even seen the main peak, assuming it might be screened by other peaks or ranges.

A partial compendium of other previous expeditions showed that all had been unsuccessful at even seeing the mountain:—Schäfer, the great German naturalist, noted that eleven previous expeditions had been unsuccessful; he, himself, was held by the Moslems at Jyekundo. One French explorer, M. Dutreuil de Rhins, in the early 1890's was laced in a leather bag and tossed by Ngoloks into the Yellow River where he drowned. Wilhelm von Filchner was plundered. Dr. Migot, a Buddhist scholar, was robbed and set afoot naked. Mr. Harrison Forman was turned back when two men of his party were killed by bandits in 1934. And so it went.

Tibet is a large country—it is wide, and many mountains no doubt have never been viewed by any explorer. About airmen I wouldn't know. And it is possible, in fact highly probable, that some travelers had not located Amne Machin Peak at all, but some other great mountain. Ma Pu-fang's people said the Ngolok federation live all around the Amne Machin Range, as well as in it, and therefore it seemed highly improbable that any other travelers with the exceptions of General Pereira (from the north), and Dr. Rock (from the east), the Hump pilots (from the south), and Mr. Reynolds (possibly from the east), have even glimpsed it.

Our Tossun base was primarily established here, in the west, so as to remove it as far as practical from these main Ngolok strongholds. Other vital reasons existed too, which will be brought to light in their proper places in this report.

Frankly, our chances did not look good. A council was called at the campfire, the only warm spot in camp. On the haggard faces of the Tibetans and Moslems I noticed, for the first time, discouragement and fatigue, even some elements of worry and perhaps fright. It was not that these men were overmuch afraid to die—for all men must do that—it was, with the Moslems especially, the manner of death: the infamous Ngolok tortures, and they, as Moslems, could not endure the thought of improper burial. To say nothing of their speculations—though incomprehensible to the western mind—on the ghastly aspects of the supernatural with which Tibetan legend has cloaked the whole Amne Machin Range.

And this was only the beginning of our problems and of the obstacles with which we were faced.

10

Failure in the West

WHEN all the men were gathered around the fire, and were sitting cross-legged as was their custom, I explained through Solomon, step by step, why we had executed our strategic approach via the remote west. We had already taken care to use the Chinese intelligence agencies in Tibet, the various Moslem sources of information, our own agents among the tribes, our contacts with the Lhasa caravan (which was an agency of the Dalai Lama)—as a means for spreading news far and wide that Lhasa was our "true" destination. We had let news leak that Amne Machin was only a "cover."

So far we had only been bothered by incidental horse and cargo thieves; no concerted campaign for our destruction had, as yet, been the object of the Ngolok federation, for our deception had led them to believe we were by-passing Amne Machin, and heading for Lhasa via a short cut west of their sacred mountains. Their own intelligence system, which is undoubtedly extensive, must have reported we were Lhasa-bound. And so, safe and very nearly completely intact thus far, we had now arrived at a geographical point only a few compass degrees north, and supposedly northwest, of the main peaks —our secret objective. Thus, our geographical position at Tossun Nor, put us actually close enough to make an attempt on the target if we used our fastest horses.

Murmurs of protest came up from the circle of men.

Also—I added—the element of surprise was on our side.

Further—as they were professional soldiers—I wished them to grasp two essential lines of thought:

1. The Ngoloks were, as the Sining Moslems well knew—on the basis of their war record—the greatest cavalry existing on earth anywhere today, not excepting even the Soviet Cossack regiments. I had read a few reports in Sining, reports not available in Europe or the United States. The Ngoloks were believed by most Sining officials to limit their western range midway between Amne Machin Peak and

Tossun Nor. This estimate we knew now from scouts' reports coming in, was only partially correct: actually, the Ngolok range extends much farther west than Tossun Nor, westward by another hundred miles, even beyond the southern seas of Oring Nor and Tsaring Nor, and actually curved in a horn north again toward the Tsaidam Swamp: all of which actually placed our Black Sea base in a Ngolok pocket! Thus, to resume Sining's thought: an approach, however fast, from any other direction than west, aimed at Amne Machin Peak—directions such as the other explorers had attempted in the past—was unreasonable, and unlikely to succeed, in fact must end in failure. The explorers' failures had already proved this hypothesis. Even those soldiers; General Pereira, the Englishman, and Lieutenant von Filchner, the German (who, it is true, had tested the west), were not in sufficient strength, their intelligence was poor, their tactical mobility was nil. Now, learning from their mistakes, we could develop our situation. The men stirred uneasily.

2. The Ngolok war horses had *winter-ranged,* and were now, in the late winter, still being fed only on last year's old, yellowed, snow-leached grass, and so were not yet strong enough to be in top form. Measured against their situation, our own horses were being grain-fed, this in addition to our utilizing the leached stuff for filler. Thus, a fast penetration through the weakened thin side of the western elements of the Ngolok light cavalry, was entirely reasonable.

The troops stared at each other.

I continued: of course we carried no armament weight, such as would give us superiority, but our very lightness in this regard could be turned to a decisive asset due to our increased mobility. I explained when they demanded a practical example: My great grandfather (Charles League), scouting with Ormsby in Utah territory (now Nevada), and before being killed by Modoc Indians from the Pitt River—who with the Apaches were probably the best American native fighters—knew that this very mobility of Chief "Captain Jack's" raiders was the reason the Indians beat the heavy United States cavalry in practically every engagement. Now General Wood also was a relation of mine, and in charge of the northern half of California: and during this time the Indians are said to have killed some 4,000 pioneers. Down south, the fifty Apaches under Geronimo, had killed over 3,000 whites and all but defeated General Howard at the head of 10,000 heavy cavalry. They were brought to heel only by trickery and the offer of sanctuary. Now I explained, I intended to use this lesson of trickery, learned so bitterly in American pioneer days, to my own advantage here in Tibet.

The expedition, therefore, was electing to accept a calculated gamble that the Ngoloks would not be able to organize, gather together their forces, and carry out a smashing, concerted counter-thrust fast enough to block us off in the approach, or to cut us off from withdrawal and escape after our measurements had been made at the mountain. And so, barring ambush by localized western Ngolok clan units, we had—in my opinion—a reasonable chance of emerging alive with the desired measurements of the mountain *if we could find it. . . .*

Protests went up from the council:

"The cavalry dates you mention are old, *old!*"

I realized that either I or Dorje (through Solomon) must apply more coercion and act fast. "Listen! You know about Rommel, the German?"

"Yes!" The Sining Moslems knew quite a lot of German military history. I was learning, and admired them.

"When Rommel was a student in an American military academy, his favorite study was about an old American civil war general called Bedford Forest: it was this man's cavalry strategy and tactics, applied to north African tank warfare that immortalized the name of Rommel as a soldier."

"Commander! We die to live! We will follow you!"

I doubted it, but this, at any rate, was a fair approximation of our situation, problems and obstacles.

Preparations were initiated and carried out with efficiency by Solomon Ma, who, for this particular job, was appointed operations and logistics officer. Tibetans were sent into the grass to hunt geese, as they strongly objected to the eating of these game birds, but this was apparently considered by the gelong the lesser of two evils. Unfortunately they got only a few geese.

Camp hummed with activity: the blacksmith was clanging away at setting new shoes. The cooks were stuffing pots and pans together. Animal and man feed was hurriedly tamped into leather bags after being examined for mold and worms, and then lashed securely to prevent bursting.

With all going well, I took the opportunity to photograph two wolf cubs brought in by the goose hunters. I didn't think the mother would take them back with human scent on them, and so Hassan prepared a bed of yak wool for the orphans in our tent. The hunters, of course, had wanted to destroy them. Their names were "Pal" and "Rover"—so called after a pair of dogs I had once owned.

Itan, a Shabrang, reported that up in the Dzu Mountains he had seen the tracks of wapiti (possible ancestors of the American elk), bear, deer, wolf, musk-deer, yaks, bighorn sheep, various carnivorous cats including snow leopard, and he described an animal that might have been goral—a kind of goat. Whether ibex exist, he did not know.

Snow conditions at Amne Machin Peak were important. A storm might hide the peak from us or, almost worse, cut off the summit from sight. It is characteristic here that most high peaks are nearly always capped with a cloud. Comparatively little snow actually falls in inner Tibet, and is believed (together with rainfall) to total per annum less than ten inches. Blowing northwards out of the Indian Ocean, the monsoon winds dump their tropical downpours mostly on the slopes of the Himalayas, far south of us, and most of the rest on the Trans-Himalaya (or Hedin) mountain system paralleling the Himalayas and lying north of them. Similarly, from the north, the sub-Arctic winds are mostly dry, having already dumped their loads in Siberia and on the high Tien Shan Range, any remaining moisture being left on the mighty Kun Lun (or Kuenlun) Range which extends clear across most of Tibet, in an east-west direction from the Pamirs on the Afghan frontier to a point somewhere west of the Black Sea. As for localized conditions on Amne Machin Peak, our own prevailing winds, during the present transition period between winter and spring, came blowing in mainly from the west after crossing the high, dry, Chang Tang, and the Kun Luns. Any moisture remaining in these winds had already been dumped on the fifteen-thousand-foot-high plateau extending south of the Kun Luns all the way to Trans-Himalaya.

To continue this very important phase:—in summer, after the thaws, much of central Tibet is a great bog—or so our people had learned from nomadic Chang-pas—apparently alternated with highland deserts, and crossed in an east-west direction mainly by hills and minor mountain systems blocking off the whole region in basins. Central Tibet, then, appeared to us much like a shallow dish, or series of dishes, placed side by side, hence the hundreds of lakes also reported by the Drök-pas. Part of this vast Chang Tang is drained by continental rivers—the Yangtse, Mekong, Salween, flowing eastward and southward to China and the countries south; and by the Yellow River flowing off in a great bend around the Amne Machins and eventually toward the northeast between Inner Mongolia and China before turning south, then east, to the Pacific.

The sea's feeder stream here was constant and had a westward direction from the head of the underground outpouring on which we were camped, the current being timed at 6 seconds per yard of flow, average width being 80 feet to 100 feet, depth averaging 3 to 4 feet. It must be one of the main constant feeders of the Black Sea. From it we took sweet water.

A second short conference was called at the fire, to clean up loose operational details and to leave instructions. I proposed that our Amne Machin Peak "attack" detachment, with its high mobility and speed, extend its "peak expedition" for ten days, into the regions lying east of the main target. No one had ever been there, or, for that matter, had ever crossed anywhere the mighty two-hundred-mile-long Amne Machin Range at any point east of Amne Machin Peak. But the motion was voted down: Black Ngoloks, lack of animal feed, no knowledge of trails, even if these existed, not enough troops, not enough armament. . . .

We ordered hot tea, and tried another tack; countering with ideas of deception, quick route switches, rumors started amongst the tribes:—all designed to dodge Ngolok ambushes. I appealed to their sense of curiosity, of adventure—which Dorje claimed lurked at the bottom of every man's heart: I emphasized that the whole of Amne Machin Range was to us absolutely unknown, that we must take this heaven-sent opportunity, which might never again be repeated, to get astride the range and cover as much ground as possible . . . and that we might even find there food and shelter for Ma Pu-fang's army facing retreat already in North China, Mongolia, and Turkestan. But their supercilious eyes and drooping lids indicated that Amne Machin Range, east of Amne Machin Peak, could remain unexplored to us or anybody else as far as they were concerned.

There was more behind their reluctance than met the eye. It was here, in the Amne Machin Range, that the Chinese government intensely suspected—for what valid reason I could never learn—the existence of vast deposits of radioactive ores. A former central government intelligence agent, who knew me when I pioneered some of the United States intelligence and underground in China against Japan, had told me in Lanchow that it was due to the belief that Mr. Milton Reynolds' airplane was carrying Geiger-counters for detecting such ores that led to sabotage, and brought about the failure of his expedition in 1948 to Amne Machin. Failures and death have dogged Bill Odom, the pilot, and the other members of this expedition . . . that is, whenever the Chinese can get at them.

Needless to say, I, myself, was being watched during this expedition, for any such activities I might be planning in regard to locating these fabulous ores.

We had so little to go on; even the representatives of the well-informed princes and dukes of the Mongol Leagues and Banners in Sining, do not know (or say they do not know) this area of mystery, as their tribal "arrows" do not now have contact with any Ngolok tribes except in the east; in fact, as we knew now, the Mongols in any number do not even exist on the north, south and west approaches today, due to mass pogroms by the Ngoloks and other wild Tibetan tribes of the region.

And so, all who wonder at my limited objective—Amne Machin Peak—will now see why. The others felt there was already too much blind groping among unknown dangers, and all of Dorje's and my plans for penetrating east of the peak were defeated. Solomon, as Governor Ma's political officer, put the final kibosh on it, saying the orders were specific, that we were to stay out of the areas east of the peak, as the Tungans had no treaties with these clans (other than the two mentioned); and that the expedition would be wiped out if it proceeded there. He thought we would be very, *very* lucky, indeed, even to make the main peaks, let alone try anything farther east of them.

Therefore, our target was narrowed down, finally, and definitely, to the location and the measurement of the tallest Amne Machin Peak itself.*

There was still no sign of the belated Colonel Ma Sheng-lung and Captain Tan Chen-te and their force of fifty or more men, or of the

---

* Dr. Rock believed there were three great peaks, Amnyi Machen Peak being the lesser of these.

Lhasa caravan. I realized it was probably due to this factor that we had successfully reached our position on the Black Sea. So far we had come to the attention of only a few horse rustlers. The Ngoloks would be watching the rich Lhasa cargo caravan and the famous fighting colonel, never dreaming we were anything but an unimportant scouting detachment with camp baggage. However, the Ngoloks would certainly allow us no spare moments to waste in waiting further. Orders were therefore issued to proceed southeast, aiming at the central Amne Machin Range and whatever it might contain. The selected advance men of the attack party were, after a good rest, fairly content with the decision—indeed, at times they seemed actually eager for the try. Of course they were playing to the grandstand. But even so, as I have said, they were hand-picked down to the last man. So far, only two men had been summarily dismissed for laziness at Fort Ta Ho Pa, a lesson to all these other bold fellows who wished to escape a similar humiliation and to brave the regions of Amne Machin Peak, not for any hope of material gain but for the mere hell of it. Further, supplies—such as they were—had always been divided impartially in the American way among officers and men since my taking over, an unheard-of procedure that was paying off in loyalty.

Our problems seemed never-ending. There was no use depending on existing maps in our possession to reach Amne Machin Peak. Let me explain—The Chinese general staff map (Scale: 1:50,000) of China and her "dependencies" is mainly based on the old European maps drawn in Peking for the Emperor Ching-lung in the middle 1700's, being astronomically correct at only a few main China cities. The original of this map, so detailed as to show trees, trails and houses, was constructed in Peking by the old European friars, and copperplated in France for printing. It is important to know that the local Tibetan place-names given were mainly based on Manchu and Mongol names—bearing usually no relation whatsoever to present native names designating the same place.

Today the maps are very nearly impractical for tactical field use by the explorer. The reason is that the local people in Tibet do not recognize these places except by their own local names, which have been in constant use for hundreds, or even perhaps for thousands of years. In addition to this, the former tribes—now mainly migrated or wiped out of existence—in many outlying regions were misunderstood by the old Chinese and European cartographers. For these reasons, modern military maps should adopt universally this Moslem expedition's system of using only standard common Tibetan names. We found all these maps—American, British, Chinese. German, Russian—to be useless for detailed field work. The United States Air Force chart 435, dated Sept. 1947 and the very latest of all, actually shows in the center of the Chi Shih Shan Mo or Amne Machin Range, a peak measuring an exact 19,993 feet! A second peak, also of 19,993 feet, bears (on this aeronautical chart) some eighteen miles northeast of the first peak. This would seem fantastic in view of the Pereira, Rock, Hump pilots and Reynolds reports, and is made even more incredulous by two peaks of exactly the same height. These peaks are marked as lying between latitudes 35° and 35°30′, and between longitude 100° and 100°30′. Obviously the northern peak lies north of the Amne Machin Range and yet Dr. Rock while in the locality, saw no such arrangement in the peaks of the "Amnyi Machen." We were forced to draw our own maps for Governor Ma, maps on which he could depend in preparing an effective withdrawal from China, should that become necessary.

Our geologist of sorts found that a hole in the sod produced gas, perhaps petroleum. Ma Pu-fang already was operating the motorized sections of his armies largely on gasoline and lubricants pumped in part from wells located in north geographic Tibet between Sining and Lanchow. We had apparently already found tungsten, iron, copper, gold, and other minerals.

In studying the revealed crust of the earth's basic structure, which might be centered in Amne Machin Peak, we saw that the rose-tinted Dzu Mountains are also slashed with rocks of gray, pink, red, white, black—most of them of a brittle hardness. Outcroppings and dykes are thrust as high as 15,300 feet and more above sea level and laid out in long folded ridges, and these appear to be shattered saw-tooth projections; the strike of this ruddy water- and sand-scrubbed range, looming as high as three to four thousand feet above the level of the Black Sea, is roughly west to east. Caves are common, pitting the cliffs. On the lower slopes of these offshoots of the western Amne Machin, are finely shattered screes, patches of yellow grass, snow and ice, and long boulder slides. Though examined superficially, there is no evidence of plutonic activity.

Across our east end of the sea, and bearing northwest from camp, jutting like an anvil, was an isolated, snow- and ice-bound peak, gleaming white and blue in the sun's rays. Its height figured out at

15,410 feet, and is a point of the mountains called by our Chinese map Chi-Lo-Cha-Tung Shan. Beyond and northwest of it, lay a higher unnamed peak of more than 16,400 feet. Around the frosted inland sea towered everywhere gaunt, silent, stony mountains—snow- and ice-covered.

Flocks of seagulls dove by overhead, white with a small black head. Long-legged waders, nesting ducks, and bar-headed geese, small migrating birds of many kinds were thought to have come up out of India, Burma, and Malaya. Swans, pigeons, hawks, and eagles also contributed endless calls and a ruffling beauty to this Tibetan sea aviary in the skies.

The Secretary's scouts came in reporting seeing a peak south, a tremendous snow mountain a bit to the right of where the sun would rise on the morrow. Snow was blowing in from the western sea by midafternoon. We ran from our work into the shelter of the tents, where, cozy and fairly warm, we became musical. It was not long before I saw the men were getting an occasional tear in their eyes, and this was certainly no time to soften up; lying on a bear rug in the audience tent, Abdul was playing a guitar of some sort, and singing sentimental songs. Now love is a fine institution in the proper place, but the Black Sea was not the proper place; and this was certainly not the time. When Solomon and I remarked that love was highly overrated and occupied far too much of the world's time, that it was in the final analysis merely a means for propagating a doubtful species, Abdul roared with laughter and strummed all the faster, saying, "Love makes the whole world spin round!"

"Nonsense!" (as Solomon explained to me later) "What makes the world spin is the momentum gained when its original gases were exploded from the sun." We were about to continue philosophizing when one of the more stupid of the Moslems remarked that apparently what Solomon Ma and Clark-ah knew about love, could be chiseled on a stone and hidden in a flea's ear.

"And you are so damned dumb," I told him, "that when Allah blows the bugle, you will probably arrive at the Pearly Gates of the Celestial Harem with a poem in each hand, instead of the head of a Ngolok unbeliever, and Allah isn't going to like you much!"

"But . . . Commander!"

"Get your confounded rumps off those saddle rugs and get your guns cleaned!"

Later, when the snow abated, and in the lee of the buckling, noisily-drumming tents, they began testing machine-guns, automatic rifles, bolt-action rifles, Mauser type battle-pistols—necessary preparations for our ride of the morrow. Man and horse would both eat the same saved-back rations (tsamba), ours being supplemented with meat and tea. Packing for both cold and wet weather was going on everywhere, designed to keep our few provisions and gear as dry and compact as possible. For ready identification, labels in English and Chinese, were painted in black letters and characters, on each main bale and pack.

That night was declared a celebration in the form of a rare treat: —rice swimming in yak butter. The rice was difficult to boil at such an altitude, but plenty of work at the bellows, and numerous appeals to Allah did the trick, though not quite, I thought.

Seventeen men would be in the Amne Machin party; our names, origins, religions (this last a very important matter in central Asia) and assignments were:—

Chutsu Tsereng	Tu Jen	Buddhist	Guide
Abdul (Ma Wei-shan)	Salar	Moslem	Soldier
Bomba	Tibetan	Buddhist	Scout
Ali (Ma Teng-hai)	Salar	Moslem	Soldier
Yang Kuei-chung	Chinese		Soldier
Solomon Ma (Ma Hsien-hui)	Tungan	Moslem	Operations
Prince Tsedan Dorje	Mongol		Surveyor
Danku	Tibetan	Buddhist	Scout
Leonard Francis Clark	American	Christian	Leader
Kung Lo	Tibetan	Buddhist	Soldier
Mosul (Han Mo-su)	Tungan	Moslem	Soldier
Ismael (Yang Shu-jung)	Tungan	Moslem	Soldier
Peng Ke-tsing	Tungan	Moslem	Soldier
Rabibu (Ma Chin-ching)	Tungan	Moslem	Soldier
Wang Shiu	Tibetan	Buddhist	Soldier
Chaharashambe	Tungan	Moslem	Soldier
Rogomane (Ma Yi-shing)	Tungan	Moslem	Soldier

At 10:15 P.M., Solomon noted the thermometer registered —5° C. (23° F.). There was no appreciable wind, the stars were out, and a new moon shone. Elevation showed 3,908 meters (11,908 feet). The camp buzzed with activity. About the area Moslems spread their rain robes as prayer-rugs and faced Mecca; while in fast cadence from their barricades, the Tibetans chanted, "Om Mani Padme

Hum! Om Mani Padme Hum! Om Mani Padme Hum!" over and over, endlessly. Around midnight we got to bed.

The next day, Thursday, May 5, we were wakened by a guard.

"We are ready, Colonel Clark!" cried Solomon Ma, behind a candle, his usually dead-pan Tungan mask split by a grin from ear to ear. Dorje announced he had made out his will. I only just recalled he was married to a beautiful Chinese Peking lady and had a whole houseful of little semi-Tartars of whom he seemed inordinately fond. I suggested he stay at base and take over here, but he was having none of it. It was still dark, the temperature was $-11°$ C., the air blustery with variable wind directions, the Black Sea area registering a low pressure. Conditions as to weather looked favorable. Whether they would remain so in the central Amne Machins we could not judge.

Our horses were standing ready—saddled and packed. We mounted. Chutsu Tsereng (the Secretary) led off and we rode out of camp into the east keeping close to the base of the Dzu Mountains which lay south and on our right side. A scouting point was established by a rider a few hundred yards ahead; two flankers were sent out on our left about seventy yards. A man or two rode in the rear to whip up the laggard pack horses.

Dawn came soon after, and it was a bright one, presently showing our early morning line-of-march to be directly into the eye of the sun. This was judged bad for us should a trap be laid on—for with the sun at the back of a Ngolok ambuscade we would be cold meat for them. Therefore, partially to counteract this disadvantage, the scouting point began weaving back and forth in shallow zigzags.

The horses were kept at a walk to reduce chances of some Ngolok spotting us through movement. Our eyes ached from the sun's rays reflecting off the snow fields ahead. At 10 A.M. a single range, glass-like in frozen snow, very clear due to high elevation and lack of humidity (excellent for observations), rose on our northeast, and we swung south of it steadying on a weaving course a few degrees south of east. Our route was along a wide, flat, gravelly, snow-patched valley cut out (in part at least) by water-erosion from glaciers melting in the spring seasons. Potholes in the thin sod covered with ice sheeting and snow drifts were proving traps for the horses who fell and stumbled quite frequently.

Herds of wild ass and gazelles; eight bears, a single bull yak, and a few bighorn sheep were to be seen. We picked our way along care-

fully, gradually edging over toward the southeast and traversing into
the first northern folds of the Amne Machin Range. Scouts were sent
ahead to join the forward point. Still no sign of the Ngoloks. Silence
and distance were the dominating features of these massive mountains. Earth and exposed stone structures, when bare of snow and
ice, were a shining red, brown, black, yellow, pink.

A flight of white birds not unlike meadowlarks were crossing the
Amne Machins and heading north. Taking a cue from them our
ride became quietly musical for awhile. The "larks" (as Dorje called
them) fed on bugs that looked like small spiders crawling over the
snow fields. The scouts suddenly swung farther right directly into
the southeast and followed up a gently rising valley. This lay northwest of a pair of twin peaks, splendid mountains of bare rock, ribbed
and rubbled, red, brown, black, with long white snow stringers
reaching down their steep sides. Dorje took botanical and rock samples, while I did a little hunting along the side of the column thereby
identifying (from tracks or by seeing them) rabbits, rodents, musk-
deer, deer, eagles, wapiti, vultures, and a wolf. Then signs of human
beings were found. We scouted the area and approached carefully.
We passed fairly fresh yak dung piled up and packed tight in square
fuel walls three feet high. Tents had been pitched over them so that
fuel might be gathered from inside during storm. The walls marked
Ngolok camps judged to have been used only a few days before by
either guardians or pilgrims to the sacred mountain (or mountains).

We hurried on. Snow, wind, and sun burned our faces quite
badly. The men covered theirs whenever possible with scarfs. Snow
"glasses" had to be issued; our Tibetan types were convex-shaped
and of stiff black thread mesh, very effective in cutting down the
dangerous diffused glare which causes snow-blindness.

We crossed an ice-capped stream, wide and humped from repeated top floods and freezes. Three or four horses made a considerable racket when they fell sprawling and it became necessary to
carry sand and gravel for constructing a non-skid trail across. After
accomplishing this task we began to lead them over. Nothing is so
careful as a Tibetan horse walking on ice; even so, hooves broke
through the spongy upper crusts. But fortunately no legs were
broken.

At 3:50 P.M. we shot two young bighorn rams out of a herd of 300
or more, a beautiful sight as the great sheep ran scattering up the
mountain alongside. The men were delighted, though the shots

made me apprehensive that we might have been heard by Ngoloks. These sheep would weigh up light, only about 150 pounds; they were gray-brown and had very heavy coats, hard gums lined the top jaw, cutting teeth set like chisels into the lower. They are possibly the Blue Sheep or a local variation—probably no Marco Polos in here (at least I saw none, or any skulls).

We went over a pass marked by a stone obo decorated with big-horn sheep skulls. Below this we made a photograph of the two snow peaks standing off southeast some few miles. We estimated them at about 16,000 feet, not high (though higher than the Alps), but beautiful pyramids, crisp, clean buttresses of ridges girding them up . . . and a promise of others ahead.* Our route elevation inside the outer folds of the main range, for we were not well within the Amne Machin system itself, was 4,100 meters (12,493 feet) by aneroid barometer, surprisingly low.

We found and then rode into a wide canyon, high-walled and lined with pink stone cliffs, and hung higher up with glacier ice and snow. In this slot, we followed the bottom by walking on ice bridging a gushing, noisy stream, but as the horses were widely dispersed, no break-through occurred. The ice ended abruptly in rapid water, and we jumped off to find the depth belly-deep, and very swift and rocky. I spurred ahead, for the guides hesitated, and led the party down into the ever deepening and narrowing canyon; vocal warnings as to deep holes, rapid water, etc., were impossible to issue due to the echoing crash of water all around. All I could do was point out the dangers to the man behind, and he in turn relay them back, and so on back up the line.

Finally we rode out of the river's bed a mile beyond the range, which had been split by the canyon, and climbed to the side of a flanking hill on the right. The rubble here proved loose, the ground very wet. We finally broke out of this dangerous slide area into a comparatively wide alluvial valley, filled with herds of game. In addition to kyang there were gazelles (believed by Dorje to be possibly *Prodorcas gutturosa*). All about were mountain chains and peaks of considerable dimensions. The mirrored glare from one to the other (and though the sun was low) was so intense we could not stare long in trying to calculate even roughly their heights.

---

* I did not name these peaks, or any others seen in the Amne Machins. This I feel is a job for surveyor and geographer rather than the reconnaissance scout.

11

Amne Machin, God of the World

THE TIME was 5:15 P.M. when the new snow mountains and peaks came into view. As we progressed
down the valley others appeared in the north and still others showed
in the south—unnamed ranges possibly not before seen or approached by an explorer. Still later, a saw-toothed rocky range, with
crevasses holding snow and ice, stood high in the east.

The scouts ahead let out a yell and dug their heels into their
horses, presently grabbing a man mounted on a yak. I rode alongside and questioned him through one of our Tibetans knowing
Ngolok; he turned out to be an old Ngolok herder. The canyon and
valley he said were both called "Nien Dah" (meaning to me unknown). He was evidently surprised at seeing us riding out of the
canyon from the west. We took this as a sign that the famous Ngolok
reconnaissance screen must yet be unaware of our having worked in
so close. The scouts jumped four bears out of the eastern end of
Nien Dah soon after we released the old man; these were digging for
rodents whose burrows pocked the lower slopes of the mountains.
Tracks were scattered over the valley, and could possibly be some
kind of high-elevation type of goat-like antelope—goral and *serow*
(or *paran*) or even the hollow-horned *takin* of southeast Tibet. Dr.
Rock reported seeing animals west of the Yellow River and east of
Amne Machin Range, animals unknown to him.

We pitched Camp 13 at 3,980 meters (12,127 feet) on a flat in the
lower end of the gulch-like valley, and above a fairly large icy
stream flowing fast in an easterly direction. This was probably the
headwaters of the Cheb Chu, which flows east along the north side
of the Amne Machin Range and enters the Yellow River north of
Radja Gomba (Tieng-te La-chia-ssu). This marked the general direction of our road for the morrow. Large blue clouds formed in the
evening. If this sudden break (for the worse) in weather should per-
sist we would never get our observations at the mountain, even if
we could find it. Most of us felt in our bones that Amne Machin

peak did actually exist. Yet so far it had not been sighted by anyone in the present party, though the Secretary's scouts still insisted they had seen a tremendous peak from the Dzu Mountains. The lesser peaks about were soon hidden in fast-moving cloud caps.

At dusk the patrolling scouts were waved in; it was their decision we could raise the central Amne Machin tomorrow. Though the whole party was tired, for we had been in the saddle ten and three quarter hours and covered 80 *li* (about 40 miles) today, fresh scouts were to be changed every hour during the night due to the intense cold which was clamping down now that the sun was gone. The fresh tracks of horses ridden by Ngoloks—who do not shoe their mounts—had been found half-a-mile east just over the first ridge. Fires were doused early and no candles were lit in our pair of tents. I wrote notes by flashlight under a blanket. Winds scattered the dinner smoke hanging over the valley. Ngoloks could smell smoke miles away, a Tungan said, and we feared it might yet lead them to us. Solomon Ma suffered with a blood-flux type of dysentery. He had lost considerable weight since leaving Fort Ta Ho Pa and was actually a six-foot bag of bones. Everybody seemed a bit jittery. I wouldn't have minded a hot toddy myself. The night passed quietly, and we slept well.

Next morning (Friday, May 6) we left camp at 6:30, our aneroid altitude on the low ridge just above (at the east end of the valley), registered 12,792 feet; the temperature −2° C. (about 28.4° F.), with ice cracking in the river, which was from 50 to 300 feet wide at this point. Apparently when the midday sun strikes the river, a thaw begins, the released waters flowing down over the still-frozen parts of the ice-cap, causing top floods and the clattering telescoping of displaced layers of ice. At night it freezes tight again. I mention this as Dr. Rock has suggested that the upper Cheb Chu and its tributaries in the Amne Machin Range might be frozen tight the year round.

We now turned away from the river (which bent a bit northward) and kept to the right, and crossed over the ridge, heading *east*. I recalled that it was from a mountain called Shachü Yimkar, some fifty miles east of the central Amne Machins, that Dr. Rock had "beheld the majestic peaks of one of the grandest mountain ranges of all Asia." He had stood at an elevation of nearly 16,000 feet, yet in the distance rose still higher peaks—yet another 12,000 feet of snow and ice! Rock reported to the National Geographic Society that the dome

Drandel Rung Shukh is the highest, though the pyramid of Shen-rezig is a close second and even more imposing. The third in size was the central peak, and this is "Amnyi Machen." He came to the conclusion that the Amnyi Machen towers "more than 28,000 feet."

It was this sight I prepared myself to see, and approach at close range, any moment now.

At 8:35 A.M. (by my watch, which was correct due to radio signals received at the Black Sea base) we saw from a ridge while looking slightly to right of east a white mountain mass of rounded, upleading ridges, crowned with wide-flowing saddles and rounded domes. This was obviously the culminating point of the great central mountain mass toward which we had been approaching. . . .

Amne Machin Peak, itself . . . *it did exist!* I say "Amne Machin Peak," because that is the name spontaneously shouted out by the Tibetans with the party.

Surrounding this were sentinel peaks and mountains (chains of them in the north), all snowy, flashing white in the sun's rays. The amazing thing was that not a cloud was in the sky—all of the main peak was revealed—*otherwise we might have passed it by on our right side.*

Two and a half hours later, at 11 A.M. we saw four herds of kyang in a wide valley, varying some mile to two miles wide, off Amne Machin's northwest buttress. The herds must have totaled about 700 to 750 head (indicating that if Ngoloks were here they had only just moved in!)—Bomba, the Tibetan hunter, killed an ass for meat, galloping up to observe the tsai custom. All "dead" meat the Tibetans, Prince Dorje and I ate; all "live" (purified by letting blood) meat went to the Moslems. Of course all of us ate tsai meat.

At 12 o'clock we ran into three Ngolok warriors skinning a kyang just shot. These men were dressed in sheepskin robes, their shoulders bare and greased, and carried broadswords crosswise in sashes and had rifles (said by the Secretary to have been captured in battle); their hair was black and long, not shaved in the usual Tibetan scalp-lock style, and unbraided. Their handsome faces and fairly high-bridged noses were wind- and sun-burned a brownish red. These were not necessarily Mongolian in appearance (as some others are), but resembled North American Indians, even "dark Caucasian," perhaps of the Aryan type one sees in North India. They were truly amazing men:—the Ngoloks and the headshrinking Aguarunas in the upper-Amazon are by far the most virile-looking races I had yet run across. The Borneo Dyaks aren't bad, but the Ngoloks make even these look like a lot of sick Chinamen. Such was our first introduction to Ngoloks living within the Range: these two specimens smiled and at the same time roughly warned us to get the hell back into the west, and to lose no time about it, waving their rifles and swords under our seventeen noses to emphasize their demands.

Now courage is perhaps man's one valid excuse for existence, and I liked that. Theirs was a very brave gesture; our Moslems were not exactly fancy-pants characters either—in fact they were blood enemies of the Ngoloks and as tough-looking a bunch as you could collect anywhere—and were already itching to slit a Ngolok throat, fearing these to be enemy scouts reporting our movements. I demanded the pair of Ngoloks be left alone: A universal policy of toughness against this nation from all quarters (Chinese, Mongol, Tibetan, Moslem, and other peoples) was no doubt the best reason why they were so bloodthirsty, and anyway, short of outright war, I hated the idea of killing any of them in cold blood. There was much grumbling, but I won out and we headed east. The best argument with an angry Tungan scout (the last to be convinced) is to level your pistol at his head, and say—"Scram, you son-of-a-bitch!" Being intuitive he gets the idea perfectly.

At 12:40 we dismounted at the far end of the valley. Here Camp 14 was set up on a high gravel bench whose uncorrected altitude registered 3,950 (12,005 feet), which, surprisingly, was lower than even yesterday's camp. I couldn't figure it out. We were now above a river (on the west bank) called the "Gitong" by wild Ngoloks, several of whom were all about us. This river flowed into the glaciated "Niencha" River just north of this, our second camp since leaving the Black Sea; then the combined rivers flowed northeast, cutting through conglomerate strata obviously laid down by flood waters in a 100-yard-wide bed. I suspected the Niencha jogged a bit northward through the outer folds of the range and is a major tributary to the Cheb Chu.*

All about camp were Ngolok yak-hair tents. The warriors from

---

* Though he *did not see them*, Dr. Rock has marked three tributaries on his map as the (west to east) Yikokh, Domkokh, Yonkokh. I do not claim he may be wrong, but list the names supplied me by Ngoloks living on the spot. I do not know whether each Ngolok tribe has a different name or not. Again, they could be unmarked tributaries of the Rock tributaries of the Cheb Chu.

them walked with broadswords stuck through leather belts or sashes, and modern rifles were balanced in the hands of some. The swords, with silver and turquoise hilts, were said to be from Derge Monastery between Jyekundo and Tachienlu (Tatsienlu) which is on the west Szechwan border. Their dogs howled incessantly.

True to Chutsu Tsereng's scouts' prediction last night we are now actually beside the main Amne Machin Peak, which was in clear view of me at the moment. It was only by an effort of will that I could sit quietly and write in the logbook.

The actual base of the peak was only two miles due east, directly across the Gitong. The mighty mountain was a glorious sight that no explorer living or dead, had ever positively seen before, and certainly not from this side. Due north of camp was a peak called "Ilan," said Chutsu Tsereng, who was stubbornly conducting a rather one-sided conversation with an angry Ngolok "Long-hair" warrior. These fanatics were dangerous-looking, and I knew there would be no time to stall around. Rock has been criticized for not taking the bull by the horns and barging in closer instead of retreating. Seeing these Ngoloks, I knew why he got out of there, and that's just what I intended to do myself and lose no time about it.

While others unpacked equipment and finished making camp, we took our first instrument observations of Amne Machin Peak. This was done back in the valley, and the mountain was less than five miles away. We were on the south side which rises toward a mountain. Photographs were made. As the base lines had to be measured carefully by tape, all this took considerable time, for the distances were 1,000 meters (3,280 feet), on the more level ground bearing southeast to the peak. While obtaining these observations we waited four or five times for clouds to clear in order to get the peak's top dome clearly outlined on the horizontal hair of the theodolite telescope. There is plenty of room for reflection error in figuring measurements, and this can vary as much as 1,000 feet. To compensate for possible light refraction due to glare reflected off the dome, Dorje actually shot a little under the summit.

In laying down these extremely long base lines, including a double one totaling 2,000 meters, to give a check on total readings, we crossed ruts on the high south slope of the valley of what the Moslems took to be the oldest pilgrim-road to Lhasa. It is believed by them to have passed west of the peak, crossing the range somewhere at this point. Due to the Ngoloks spreading westward and raiding more than ever in recent years, the ancient route was seldom used; pilgrims choosing the safer far-western way from Koko Nor to Tsaidam and the eastern Chang Tang—far west of Oring and Tsaring seas.

Amne Machin Peak lay at a great distance *back of two big foundation piles* (or piers) on this western side, and appeared to be separated widely from the great upsweeping massif—though this seemed highly improbable—by canyons, more likely by a deep saddle-connection.

A reconnaissance toward the south of the peak should show this construction better. Amne Machin would undoubtedly be tough to climb in its higher elevations because of ice-covered surfaces and steep slopes, to say nothing of oxygen lack. A wide shallow rift, or glaciated valley, strikes at an upward slant straight eastward along Amne Machin's north flank, and this must be traversed to get a sight from that side (the north) by instruments, and especially to obtain photographs and sketches showing details. From the head of this rift one could also look perhaps into the regions beyond in the east and see if other peaks exist—peaks which might have been mistaken for this main one.

While waiting once for a line of white clouds to clear, several of the soldiers wearied of standing around and went off hunting, shooting a kyang stallion; Solomon and I called them in, fearing Ngoloks would drive us out as they threatened to do to Dr. Rock and Dr. Simpson west of the Yellow River when they sighted far away the central peaks in 1926. Having talked in Sining to the explorer-missionary, Dr. Plymer, who was a friend of Simpson (also a missionary and later killed near Labrang), I was familiar with some details of that great expedition. It very likely had reached its farthest toward the peaks at a point approximately fifty miles, some 15°, south of east of our position.

Amne Machin's mountain mass was covered over with snow and ice brushed smooth by high winds, from its base in the 15,000-foot level to its ridge or dome-like peak (which was the appearance it gave from our position in the northwest). While perhaps confusing, these directions and minute details will perhaps be useful to geographers, mountain-climbers, and other experts interested in the reconnaissance explorer's necessarily limited findings. Dorje's sights were

during one observation laid on the southward tip of the summit—
once the clouds were gone—as this appeared to be slightly higher
than the northern top on the "English saddle"-shaped crown or
dome. The whole mountain seemed to float in the blue air and not
to rest on the earth—a close observation made by Mosul. If such a
description can be fitted to a mountain—it was like a feather, not
just a heap of stones.

Only the thin, dark edges of stony ridges running upwards toward
the culminating peak were clear of snow and ice. This appeared
very thin in the lower regions, but deep at the summit. Possibly
the wind never ceases in these higher regions. Amne Machin Peak
is a great stone fortress of unknown antiquity, perhaps the pinnacle
of the earth's crust, built up on continents, with water-leveled mountain range upon mountain range laid down around its founda-
tions. . . .

Four other peaks standing near camp, two other points on the
Amne Machin massif itself, and a peak close by rising on "A/M's"
southwest skirt, also a peak bordering the rift on its north side, and
the easternmost head of the rift, were all calculated at the same time
by swinging the theodolite on its mounting and obtaining readings
from the same measured flat of the river's plain. All were carefully
measured by angles, the figures read and made by Prince Dorje, and
cross-checked by Solomon Ma and me (at Dorje's insistence), then
recorded in two record books and sketched by Dorje for details.

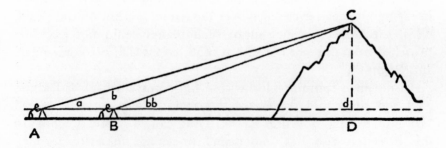

Dorje "drew" triangles *ABC* and *BCD*. Our purpose was to find
the height of Amne Machin above the plateau. Line *AB* was measured out, 1,000 meters by tape. Angles *a* and *b* were measured by
instruments. Knowing length of one side of triangle and size of
angles, he used trigonometric formula to get length of line *BC*,

which is also one side of triangle *BCD*. He computed angle *bb* and knew, since line *CD* was perpendicular, that angle *d* was a right angle (90°). He thus had one side and two angles of triangle *BCD* and could compute length of perpendicular. He added this to the height of the instrument stations above sea level (15,300 feet), obtained from Chinese military maps (said to have been drawn in World War II) which were double-checked by taking barometric pressure and the boiling point of water.

These observations were triangulations by theodolite sightings through a four-power scope of English make,* measured base lines, boiling point and altimeter readings, and the calculations of the Jyekundo military road engineers and surveyors who had worked in the west. At various points contacted on this abandoned road Dorje had already been checking his instruments against their surveys, and found we were consistently reading too low, due, he believed, to prevailing barometric pressures. The first observations were begun by him at 12:40 P.M., and continued till near dusk. A south wind prevailed at 20 miles per hour at the valley "OB" (observation) positions, sky averaging 1/3 clouds of stratocumulus formation.

The swiftness of our circuitous assault based on the Black Sea, and our final twisting dash to the foot of the peak had prevented any large bands of Ngoloks from reaching us as yet. A few warriors, however, had come into camp saying angrily they were of a clan called Kagurma. We and our men, particularly the Secretary, described airplanes to those willing to listen and they were emphatic in saying none had ever flown over the Amne Machin central peaks. This, I realized, did not mean such planes could not have approached from the south or east as reported by U.S. Air Force pilots and Reynolds.

An old man spinning clockwise a large prayer-wheel of leather, gold and silver said the sacred mountains about us were named "Djegardensheng" ("White Rock") lying east of Amne Machin. In this direction also lies "Gomtsun" (meaning unknown to me). "Toker Ibdjin Nowu" ("Place before the Precious Stone") to the south, and "Shunwhun Djegarang" ("Uncle of the God") on the west.

---

* Loaned by Chinghai Highway Bureau. This instrument was heavy duty, used by the engineers for road building, surveying of airfields, etc. Tripod of oak, brass head and fittings, retractable legs, plumb-line, conventional cone of brass, scope-4 power, scope picture hairlines (2 vertical, 1 horizontal).

To the southwest lies "Yev Serengajev" ("Father of the God Peak"). He pointed out (bowing in turn in the direction of each god) that none of these mighty peaks ever avalanches like others in Tibet. Through binoculars, however, I spotted a wide avalanche scar near the white, glimmering saddle-summit of Amne Machin. How could such a magnificent, beautiful mountain bring ill luck to any man! *

"Amnyi Rmachin" (Ngolok pronunciation), The Holy Mountain, means, according to these Kagurma Ngoloks, "Name of the Greatest God." Another said, "God of This World." Other translations have had it "Grandfather of the Peaks" or "Grandfather of the Yellow River." There is no Ngolok taboo in calling aloud the sacred name "Amnyi Rmachin."

The old man warned us about returning via the "Obo of the Doorkeeper," the pass we had taken leading into the sacred area, as an ambush might be lying in wait for our return to the west. I remembered this obo, decorated with sheep skulls and marking the pass near the two big peaks. He said we must sacrifice to the Spirit of "Amnyi Rmachin" and then leave quickly by a *new* route. For this useful advice we were more than grateful. But I was not yet ready to go. All evening the men came and argued about leaving while we were still able, saying there was a drastic feed shortage for the horses and nothing could be obtained from the Ngoloks unless it be "shindig!" ("poison weed!"); that there was no strength in the old grass alone; that the Ngoloks were surely organizing; and finally that they were afraid and had no wish to die over a quarrel about any "devil mountain!" In general I patiently told them:

"You have no choice but to stay. You are soldiers." I repeated this carelessly, feigning puzzlement with Moslems who have no wish to die and enter Paradise. "I will not leave before the work of measuring is done on the north and northeast sides. If you abandon me to die among these 'Long-hairs' you will have to answer to Ma Pu-fang. If you mutiny as you threaten and take me back a prisoner, I will charge you at my court martial with cowardice, and the result for you will be worse than if you were slowly burned by the Ngoloks. . . ."

I was really terribly sorry to have to do this, for I liked these men.

---

* Dr. Rock's map shows three peaks named, north to south—Drandel Rung Shukh, Amnye Machin, Shenrezig. It therefore would seem that the various Ngolok clans have their own names for them.

We had been through much together and they were my loyal friends. And I knew better than most from working as an American colonel in native disguises behind Japanese and Red Army lines, that no man, however good at bluffing, is consistently brave *all* the time, nor is he a coward *all* of the time; but that men, of all nations and races, are brave some of the time and cowardly at other times. Any fool can be brave over a short period of time, but most of these men, before assignment to this expedition, had been under pressure for months while fighting Communists. I had a motive for being here, while they had none. How could you expect an Asian soldier to grasp the "idea" behind Amne Machin, and how their beloved Ma Pu-fang could use that "idea" to strengthen their position, acquire allies, and so together fight the common enemy and ultimately recover their homes and the beloved ones many of them would leave behind? To them the venture now seemed impossible! Nothing at all plausible that a down-to-earth, practical, sensible man, could get his teeth into.

That night no one spoke to me. Only Prince Dorje; at first he tried to persuade me to change my mind, and failing that, declared his loyalty. His idea was that we had measured the mountain, now let's get out while we still had our skins. But I knew what kind of criticism would be heaped upon my head once I got clear of Tibet. It has never failed that many of the Tibetan armchair explorers and other experts such as mountaineers—though how they attain "expertness" has escaped me—have jumped feet-first into every traveler who returns without his guts being armorplated. Dr. Rock's figure of 28,000 feet had never been transferred to the maps, and yet he was the greatest of west China and east Tibetan explorers of our day. The same applied to Mr. Reynolds and the off-course Hump pilots. They were called liars and subject to insinuations of the most appalling type. Yet they, like Pereira, were honorable men doing the best reportage possible under very difficult circumstances. Instead of experts taking their findings and convictions in a grateful manner as aids to eventual clarification of the central mountain's true light, they were cruelly and unjustly punished. Thus we needed more facts; figures.

I explained we must climb east and look beyond the peak. Dorje finally won over Solomon Ma, who had been sulking not only from his illness but at our delay over returning, and together they began working on the Secretary, who was in anything but a pleasant mood. By midnight we settled on a compromise, the others obtained a promise from me that after the north and northeast sides of the mountain had been seen at close range, we would return to our base on the Black Sea with all possible haste.

Thus on May 7 (Sat.) we left camp at 7:45 A.M., with ten armed men, their new-found eagerness for adventure somewhat dampened by blasts of wind as it was freezing. We would attempt to take bearings, triangulate elevations, survey the general lay of the land about, photograph and sketch Amne Machin farther along its north slopes. We would try today to reach the head of the rift and see what lay east of the main peak.

Our direction was first north for nearly half an hour, across the Gitong River, then east for half an hour, and finally we steadied southeast up the broad floor of the rift. We climbed steadily in shallow loops up thinly glaciated slants (ice slicks), back and forth across patches of thin snow, and over pebbly meadows partly free of snow, and in and out of an eroded gutter cut by water set loose by daily recurring afternoon thaws. The horses stopped every few hundred yards to catch their breath in the rarefied air. Their shoulders and flanks soon became lathered. I could feel the heartbeats of the big stallion between my knees. A few times I got off and led him.

Alashan set a hard pace on the average, however, and it was often necessary to rein him in and wait for the others, who were plodding along, following not too enthusiastically in our muddy trail. And so I did the forward scouting, moving ahead, weaving in and out of the brush patching the slopes on the sides of the rift. Our party stopped periodically so that Dorje could obtain bearings on two pointed marginal peaks north of the valley-rift. One peak (from our angle of view) was crowned with a saddle summit, the south point being slightly higher. On this he took his sights from a pair of 1,000-meter base lines. Big wool-ball clouds began coming in, blanketing out approximately half the blue sky and capping several peaks. I was not feeling too good about this. At this time, 10 A.M., the temperature showed 6.5° C., thawing a little, and the ground muddy. The clouds did not however prevent photographing and measuring vertically three subsidiary points on the main Amne Machin mountain pass. At times there was an incredible calm among the holy mountains.

The encroaching base of Amne Machin was only two miles off our right-hand side, and quite often as close by as a mile—consisting of massive-ridged, deep-canyoned and sparsely glaciated white snowy peaks piled one above the other. From time to time we stopped to take measurements on still other mountains, diamond-like peaks and (from this distance) razor-sharp ridges, lying in the north on our left side. Also various points rising on the structural buttresses of Amne Machin, other than the central main peak which was hidden due to our being so close, were also surveyed and charted as to their positions in the greater mass, and had their elevations ascertained. Bigger clouds began streaming in from the northeast, the ground wind subsided to zero and a hushed calm seemed to descend over the region. Lightning flashed and thunder boomed in the higher crags.

At two encampments of Ngoloks, mastiffs were deliberately turned loose on us, but there was no shooting in spite of our apprehensions. The women ran out shouting at us, brandishing (of all things!) firebrands, running alongside to shoo us along and no doubt to check on our arms and the condition of our horses. Afoot here, a stranger would be as good as dead. Abdul whacked one old she-devil on her fanny with the end of his whip, and you would have thought she was a Sabine virgin being raped by an enemy legion. That leather-clad old wench was trying to put his horse's eyes out!

Our men bellowed we were an advance scouting party for a thousand Moslem cavalry following just behind, and to get the hell back to camp before they were beheaded. Rock's trip had been interrupted during a Ngolok-Sining Moslem war, many Tibetans who fell alive into enemy hands were hung up by their thumbs, disemboweled alive and their abdominal cavities then filled with hot stones; also the Moslems had slaughtered women and children as in the days of Genghis Khan, each rider having ten or fifteen human heads tied to his saddle. And of course the Ngoloks had been engaged in scores of other battles with the Moslems never reported in the outside world. And so this intelligence set them to lamenting, shaking their firebrands at us, and running back to report the news to their male betters who were hiding in the tents (we could see their boots under the uplifted flaps). Abdul cocked his machine-gun, carried across the saddle, saying these Ngoloks had their guns trained on us. We continued on our way, southeast, up the rift. At this time Abdul called out that we had better go back, that the Ngoloks would undoubtedly like my horse and rifle.

A strong wind pushed from behind, suddenly moving in from the west at 11:30. Still we were climbing, the horses exerting every ounce of strength, shivering now from cold and buffeted by icy blasts. Once we dismounted to knock off icicles and to stand against the surprisingly warm flanks of the horses to seek warmth and thaw our hands, as we could not handle our firearms.

At 1:45 P.M. the winds reversed and a stinging snow-blizzard hit us full in the face. The men wanted to return, but I kept on and after a time they followed. The horses shied away from the storm, shivering once in a while, and began walking sideways into it. We were finally stopped in a narrow canyon. Here occurred one of the worst things on the whole expedition into Tibet. The men began shouting angrily at me that we must return—at once—or perish. Prince Dorje and Solomon Ma wavered about going along with the others in abusing me.

Perhaps in my anxiety to get the *facts and details,* I had not realized the really end-of-the-rope condition we had reached that day: some of us claimed to be frozen on hands and feet, ears and noses. The animals were exhausted—four men and horses had already dropped out along the way and hidden from the Ngoloks. I was told these savages might be gathering in the storm. That was the picture—and a rather distressing one. I argued above the wind, and finally losing all patience began to curse them—slashing Abdul across his chest with my whip, for he had started this mutiny and was feeding it with loud talk. He made a noise like a shot stallion, and swung his machine-gun on me. There wasn't much time, but I spurred in, and knocking his horse off balance, struck the gun up and over his shoulder, where it fell into the snow. This time I raised in my stirrups and slashed at his head. He dismounted.

I made no move to draw my pistol. "For shame, Abdul! You call yourself my friend!"

He recovered his gun, wiped it off, and remounted. His face was now a greenish-white.

"We go?" the Secretary asked of me.

"The order is—*to stay!*"

We stayed. For the next twenty minutes we sat our horses. The snow fell thickly about, settling on our shoulders. The horses

stomped and neighed. But not one man spoke. Just stared straight
ahead over his horse's ears. And no one turned a hair. They were
praying, but what they were praying for, God alone knew.

And then all at once someone shouted the Tungan version for:
"Allah!" I saw it was one of the Tungans, Rogomane, fox cap askew,
staring into the sky.

I glanced up. The clouds were parting overhead. Parting in no
other place but just—overhead. It was fantastic, that torn piece of
blue sky. With a yell I set my horse to digging a way up the slope
alongside, to gain a point on the bench extending along the high
north river bank, and perhaps suitable for recording altitudes and
angles. The men followed with shouts. Their face was saved; Allah
had intervened. On top we dismounted and unpacked our gear;
several observations were obtained on points of the north face of
Amne Machin—a dazzlingly beautiful, white-clad lady.

"Praise God!" the men were calling out to each other, and to me,
in joyous voices. Funny about Moslems; one minute they are ready
to take you apart, and the next they are blessing you. Photographs
and sketches were made with stiff fingers of still other snow peaks
standing serene and gigantic in white mantles clear down to their
bases, their icy parapets gleaming now with the sun's rays shining
full upon them. We were very close to Amne Machin, for only a
narrow but deep river canyon in the head of the rift, now separated
us. Dorje swung the theodolite left on its swivel, into the southeast,
then left into the east, thus measuring two other great peaks. The
nearest stood a mile away, close by the rift, a mighty cone—a perfect
pyramid—Djegardensheng (White Rock). Still another giant lay
southeast of it—partly obscured by mist. This second cone might
be the Ngolok's Gomtsun. In measuring the 1,000-meter base lines
by tape, the soldiers ran as fast as stiff knees, the rarefied altitude,
heavy clothing, and the freshly-fallen new snow would let them: this
was our last job before clearing out. It was still freezing and our
hands lost skin whenever they came in touch with gun-metal or the
metal on the surveying instruments. It was impossible to work in
the bulky wolf-skin gloves.

With Dorje and Solomon in charge of the surveying, I sat on a
rock, lit my pipe and feasted my eyes on the sight before us:

Djegardensheng rising majestic as a marble breast in our eastern
quarter, Amne Machin dead south and only a mile away, both of

their snowy feet standing squarely on the south wall of the rift. A long, black, humped, whale-like ridge called by a glowering Ngolok bravo—one of several warriors who were gathering—Amnyi Rmachin's "Whipper," connected the northwest slopes of Djegardensheng with Amne Machin's northeast buttress. The Whipper formed the high south embankment of the upper rift. The river in the gorge just in front of us, thundering and crashing with muddy water, ice and rolling rocks, was called "Jegideh."

Dorje's chart numbers "1" and "2," the main north buttresses of Amne Machin, standing in an approximate east-west line, were steep shoulder piers of stone, plastered over thinly with ice and wind-packed snow. Behind them rose a long, straight east-west ridge, connecting the two. Farther beyond this, in the far south, was Amne Machin's main peak (unseen from this point, owing to our extreme nearness).

Big blue clouds rushed in, capping several peaks. We packed and turned our horses through a new storm, heading for camp through a few inches of snow and falling flakes, our route along the roaring river. Fortunately the new snow was very cold, dry and powdery— we moved fast. Altogether we had obtained the measurements of six new peaks this day, and several lower points on Amne Machin's mass. I was not a little satisfied with the work. Dorje had not had the time to work out the triangulations, however; and we did not know the height of even Amne Machin itself.

For a while we rode through snowflakes, but before reaching camp the storm turned to one of driving hail, the particles of dry ice stinging our faces till they actually hurt, with the paralyzing aching kind of hurt. And no matter which way you turned your head you got it. The snow and hail, though dry as gunpowder, were soon melting on the puffing horses, sliding and slipping downward—and so we were soon not only cold but wet as well, our teeth chattering and our voices turned into a kind of croaking whisper. Our heaviest sheepskins and yak-hair packed felt boots seemed as if made of tissue paper.

Added to my own misery was a bad tumble sustained when I galloped my horse too eagerly down the shale and conglomerate embankment of the Gitong River. I was going along with others to recover a gazelle shot from the rim. The stallion stumbled over an outcropping of stone, sending us both flying bottoms over tea-kettle.

Fortunately no bones were broken, though apparently all four legs of the tiring horse had locked.

Ngoloks were still milling around camp, and they and their dogs were setting up a racket. The Secretary said we were warned to go—at once. I suggested we take it easy. In spite of sheepskin sleeves and chupa, considerable skin was gone from my hands and wrists, knees and elbows, and I was frozen stiff as a board, or thought I was. The gazelle was butchered and cut into bits for shashlik, the pieces strung on ramrods, salted and peppered, then squatting around we held them out over the coals of a dung fire.

Once thawed out we became hungry and paid little attention to the Ngoloks except to carry our own weapons about with us. There were some fifty of the warriors gathered now, all armed with swords, daggers, rifles. After we had eaten, the Secretary left the fire and sat with me in my tent. In a low voice he explained that the hand of these Kagurmas was stayed only by intercession of a Yellow Hat lama, to whom he had already shown our letter from the Panchen Lama. Hearing this I had the lama brought to me. This man was evidently deeply distressed, torn between loyalties, and not feigning the shock he showed. He was our lifeboat, and I lost no time fitting the oars to him. This was best done over a cup of tea. He was seated on carpets, and candles were lit in the tent.

This Ngolok living Buddha of Amne Machin is Namug Kangser, a handsome 30-year-old scholar, recently sent among his tribesmen from Lhasa where he was ordained. He was visiting his family at the moment, in one of the hair tents nearby—about 300 feet from our encampment. I recalled hearing him at night; beating drums, chanting, singing, and reading scriptures. He said his own tent lamasery is called Dashtang Gompa and lies south-southeast half a day's ride. I called in Abdul and gave him orders; a few minutes later he returned and I handed the lama a hadak scarf folded around a gold bar. The bar was eight inches long, and hefty. He had just said he intended building a stone lamasery, the first in the Amne Machins, and that the Kagurmas were his friends. He was too much of a lama to show surprise, but his eyes betrayed feelings of gratitude.

It soon followed (according to Namug Kangser) that 40 living Buddhas exist today throughout the Ngolok regions. No head chief rules among these warrior people. There are 16 major chiefs (khumbos) and some lesser ones, also heads of clans or sub-tribes. There is no paramount tribal council for the clans, and the great confederation among these cannot be too binding as they raid even among themselves.

I found this lama, Namug Kangser, though rather young in years, most charming and not without wisdom. Kagurma legend says the Ngoloks came from the "east," from the direction of the rising sun, and "out of the sun." The Secretary had already related another legend about them coming out of India. But regardless of whence they might have hailed, the point is that today they control Amne Machin God, and hang on the northwest frontiers of Red China. I doctored Namug Kangser's ancient friend and guru, an old, old, lama whose eyes were in terrible shape from looking, he explained, on the sins of man. After this the two men, the old guru Shikutur, and his disciple Namug Kangser, seemed reconciled to our presence in the shadow of the gods: for, as they explained on leaving at midnight, all lives are in the hand of God, and their kharma will eventually work out to full enlightenment at the end of time. I liked this long-range point of view. On the other hand, there was the short-range view to consider also.

12

Pursued by the Guardians

IT WAS still about two hours before dawn when we turned out; the night was black, the wind cold and blustery. Lights soon appeared in the Ngolok tents all around. I should like to have spent more time here at Amne Machin, but it was impossible in the face of my promise. Also, danger—as the men pointed out—seemed very close. A stranger called to us from the darkness beyond the campfire; we breathed easier when the lama Namug Kangser's face was recognized in the light. The old lama was with him.

Ngoloks were soon crowding around, surly and taut. A burnt gazelle bone gave evidence before all, through these lamas' divination, of a lost pack-saddle of ours lying several li west in some brush. Two Tungan soldiers rode out skeptically with the younger lama for protection, and found that what they supposed had been stolen was exactly on the spot foretold. I do not wish to seem over-impressed with all this magical work, but since the pertinent facts of the journey should be told, I include this sort of information too.

In a few minutes after their return, while the others were saddling and packing, and thinking of some other traveler who might come here in the future, I gave yet other gifts to our friend, explaining that they were to be used in good works to counteract our sacrilege of entering the presence of the gods without some supernatural sign being first revealed through his own mediations. But all our haste was in vain—the best pack horse was not found in the roundup. The lama came again to the fore; and again, as a result of divination and prediction, the lost horse was located feeding in a canyon where it had strayed after breaking a hobble. The saddle and straw mat kept on for warmth were gone, however, so we traded flour (the last we had) for a Ngolok pack rack.

With Ngoloks gathering on all sides, apparently undecided, but definitely surly, Camp 14 was then swiftly struck; and alert for possible attack we rode hard into the west, following our inbound tracks. One of the pack horses was carrying chunks of ice for our water supply, as the Secretary explained we were deliberately heading for roundabout northern regions where deserts north of the Amne Machins were said to lie flanking it in the west. At 7 A.M., with the sun rising into a blue sky, we reconnoitered and reined sharply into the north up a long, broad valley rising gently to a flat pass, thus skirting wide the possible place of ambush at the "Keeper of the Obo" pass. To manage this we first had to cross the river ice below our old Camp 13, our first within the Amne Machins. We were cold, but after an accident on the ice during which a horse hurt its leg, we had to dismount and carry sand and gravel in the skirts of our robes, pouring a trail over the ice to give the horses surer footing; and in doing so we warmed up a bit. About 15 minutes were lost however, and as we rode beyond the river some of us kept a sharp watch to the rear.

It was just as well, for the last couple of men in the column signaled by low whistles that they had just seen some Ngolok horsemen coming over a ridge. A little later, hand signals told that some 500 cavalry were practically on top of us, and not much over 300 yards just behind. I called a halt. The ground here was in places soft and dry, and dust was being stirred under our hooves. There was no time for taking up effective positions of defense. If the stony ground on the opposite side of the river threw their leaders off for a time in the old Camp 13 gulch, we might be able to sneak away. Also the Ngoloks' minds could be made up that we were high-tailing it out on our old route, and if so they were probably not even watching the ground now but riding hard into the west.

Apparently we had slipped out of the Amne Machin Camp 14 just in time to escape a surprise late-dawn raid in force. Wang Shiu, a Tibetan scout, crept to the top of the point on the low ridge screening us, and signaled that the pursuit was riding past and toward the Keeper of the Obo pass. With that we began walking our horses slowly northward, keeping to the left (west) side of the miles-wide valley. Hundreds of kyangs were grazing in scattered herds throughout its full length as far as the eye could reach. I hoped fervently that no Ngolok eye saw these raise their heads to stare in our direction.

A few miles beyond, while galloping after four bears that were disappearing speedily up a side canyon full of rocks, my horse again took a somersault, throwing me hard down a slope strewn with boulders. Other than a good trouncing no damage seemed to have been done, though once more I was rather skinned up. The bears escaped having their picture taken, and I turned back to the column.

There was now considerable evidence scattered around, from tumbled-down walls along this side of the valley, of former mud-walled villages being here. These had been destroyed with the hope that the rong (valley farm lands) would revert back to grazing pasturage. The two lamas had discreetly mentioned this route, describing the ruins as landmarks. The Ngoloks had all but leveled the houses, as well as killing their Rong-pa occupants—unwelcome Tibetan squatters—the year before. Human bones, splintered and scattered by animals such as wolves, were at times on the ground in and about such settlements. Unfortunately all that remained was a desert since the sod had been cut out by the farmers and burned. The dust from this yellowish sand valley filled our eyes for hours on end. All day we trudged up that valley.

We pitched Camp 15 on the *la* just short of the *niha* of the pass, as it was too late in the day to cross over to the *terh*. A strong, dry, but freezing wind was blowing out of the northwest across it, and so, though we had hoped for protection near the foot of the western ridge, we were partly exposed. We were (by aneroid) at 4,090 meters (12,462 feet). Thrusting our hands into the wolf-skin gloves, for we dare not touch metal otherwise, five or six of us ran a final "OB" (observation) on Amne Machin Peak, now glowing with the fire of sunset an estimated 25 miles away in the southeast, a jewel set in a pale blue sky. Then Dorje shot the peak once again, as night glided in under rolling black clouds being drawn straight to the mountain like nails pulled to a magnet. The job was finished, and we packed the instruments. Final calculations—Dorje reminded me—would be complete only when field ones were compensated, after comparison with barometric pressures being recorded in Sining and Lanchow. However in our tent that night, bundled against the bitter cold, Dorje worked out preliminary figures from a few of all the several observations.

An hour, then two hours went by, and he was still hunched over the ammunition case serving as table, a candle for light. The box top was too small to hold all his notebooks, papers, and trigono-metric formula, and these were scattered about the floor and on his lap. The candle blew out twice and had to be relit by either Solo-mon or me. Solomon Ma's interest appeared mild and I suspected he felt that only the political phase of the mountain, as it might relate to Moslem influence over Tibetans who must support Ma Pu-fang's retreat, was important. It was my impression that Dorje was interested primarily in the figures as a mathematical problem, and probably didn't care one way or the other whether the moun-tain was as high as General Pereira, Dr. Rock, the Hump pilots and Mr. Reynolds had believed. The wind whistled now and then around the corners of the tent, but Dorje didn't seem to notice.

"How high is the old girl?" I finally asked as carelessly as I could, while lighting my pipe. I had climbed Orizaba in Mexico, seen the Peruvian and Ecuadorian Andes, the Alps, the Yunnan and Sikkim Himalayas, and a few other lesser ranges; but even so I was far from knowing anything about mountains; the snow-line levels in Tibet were unlike anything I had noted before. For example: the inner Tala peaks of Tibet do not have the low snow-lines seen in the Himalayas which are due chiefly to the heavy precipitation of the Indian monsoon. Here in inner northeast Tibet the air is unusually dry, with very little snowfall, and the snow-lines on the mountains are very high, and by comparison with other mountains only a very little of it. It was this, I felt, that possibly threw off experts in judg-ing Dr. Rock's photographs, which they believed showed peaks not so high as he calculated on the spot. For myself, not being an expert on mountains, I could only feel that the peak Dorje was estimating had seemed to be very high—how high, I couldn't even hazard a guess.

"I say, how high. . . ." I blew a puff of smoke into his face.

Dorje turned toward me, and carefully put his pencil into a drawing box. He was not smiling and his hand trembled ever so slightly, though this could have been from the cold. He tossed over a sheet of paper with several sets of calculations scribbled over it.*

"Higher than Mount Everest," he said quietly.

"Are you sure?" I finally managed to get out.

---

* See page xiv for original field calculations.

"Quite. I've checked all sets of figures twice," he answered.
"Alright. Now let's eat. I'm starved."

Later I wondered at myself for not thinking of some remark more
fitting to such an occasion. Actually, as a matter of fact, I was not
at all sure I would even tell now (at home) of the trip into Tibet,
much less mention our dash to Amne Machin Peak and the measurements obtained there. In the first place the geographers and
mountain experts would ask two preliminary questions—was Dorje
a professional surveyor? And was I a professional surveyor? Since
we were not, very probably only a great deal of wrangling, suspicion
of us, even hatred, could ever come of it. Later, we three just squatted with the others around the hole in which the campfire was
glowing, chewing on our ramrod-skewered gazelle meat, and staring
into the coals. As I recall, all the others with the possible exception
of Solomon and Dorje, were completely indifferent as to the reputed
height. As a matter of fact, few had even heard of Everest.

At 11 o'clock in pitch darkness, our gear was hauled over, con-
solidated and repacked for better distribution on three pack horses.
Our firearms were stripped and cleaned (but no oil was used due to
sand and cold), and reassembled for any eventualities, as we were
far from being safely away. Some men reported frostbite on their
hands. We got to work thawing these out. The trouble had apparently been caused by handling the guns during their cleaning, for
though they had been held over the fire first, they were still cold.
That night the horses appeared very tired, many lying down which
was a rarity in frozen Tibet. We had been driving them too fast,
and on poor feed. This had been cut down to the poor grass fodder,
fortified only with a little of our own tsamba, for they had consumed theirs; which we gladly gave up to them. Better to starve on
horseback than to starve afoot.

By midnight, with the work done and stars shining out of a black
sky, the Tibetans were moved to seek the solace of their gods in
space and in the heart through meditation and chanting. And the
Moslems too gave thanks to Allah by droning the poetically beautiful words in the first chapter of the Koran—the "Fatima." Later,
Abdul came and sat in my tent. I too had been unable to sleep due
to the intense cold. I was reading a book by the carefully shaded
candle-light, for Ngoloks had been reported fairly close by. I placed

a cartridge in my book for marker, put it down, and smiled at him. Dorje laid aside his own book.

"I am sorry—" Abdul began limply, "that you had to beat me yesterday. I have decided to kill you. But I cannot. I was not myself at the mountain in that storm. *I am not afraid to die!*" This last he cried out in anguish as if in pain, looking me straight in the eyes.

"Think no more of this matter, Abdul," I answered, putting my hand on his shoulder. "Amne Machin bewitched you. All men, Tibetans and others, know the power of this mountain."

"Praise the Lord! Master!—a djinn must have forced me to do it!" he cried out relieved.

"That reminds me. We do not mention the foolish doings of djinns in the official report," I answered gravely, stroking my bare chin (which always amused them), and picking up my book. "Salaam, Abdul—now go check the guard. Be sure the two gray-white horses are out of sight. Use only bays or blacks for the out-guards. All is well with us. Praise God."

We swiftly broke camp in a dusky dawn at 5:30, shivering in the wind. I have never in my life been colder. As soon as the animals were saddled and the packs lashed, they were driven northwest toward the pass. Herds of kyangs, unintentionally started up the valley the day before by our column, also picked up their feet and went slowly over the top with us. Some were only a little more than a hundred yards away; there must have been a thousand animals in that magnificent herd.

On the gray, icy, stony hills toeing in on the mile-wide pass, grew patches of *lieu-tso*, a kind of snow willow some two to three feet high: Tibetans call it *glong-ma*. It was the only high vegetation seen in the region of Amne Machin. We had used it for fuel during the night, having deliberately chosen our harsh open campsite where no dung existed, as Ngoloks would not be so apt to search in such a place. This had been fortunate, as a Ngolok patrol moving close by, checking apparently on possible sites, had passed within half a mile about midnight.

Well clear of the pass and beyond the game herd, at 7 A.M., we swung left, thus changing course into the west, riding across frozen mud flats spread over a wide valley. No hair tents were in sight and we hurried on as fast as possible. The mud had a deceptive crust on top, partly frozen, but as the sun rose higher, this thawed in places, and our horses sank to their hocks, skating around and even falling. I knew my compass was approximately correct, for the morning sun threw out long shadows dead ahead, and we followed them just off the cliff ramparts of a high pink-stone range (the same extending to the Black Sea) jagged and contorted into various shapes, keeping it on our left a few miles off. The ground became more solid and we moved fast in the single-footed gait peculiar to these horses. A few Ngoloks, probably hunters, were now seen off to the right (the north), but these we rode wide of.

Alert for possible ambush we passed safely by the wide maws of three rocky canyons anatomically named "Gi Dzu" ("Neck Joint of the Dzu"), "Ga Dzu" ("Back Joint"), and "Gna Dzu" ("Tail Joint")—all links of snow-covered Mount Dzurgan, the "Old Hybrid." In the north loomed snow fields flat against a rather large mountain called by the Tibetans "Jehsum" ("Tongue of the Old Hybrid"). All this is information of a vital sort. I have not attempted to hide the location of Amne Machin, but in every way in this record have tried to give full directions and particulars to any traveler who should attempt to reach the mountain.

While going ahead of the column, I turned the last jut of rocks standing south of the head of the spring—200 yards beyond which would lie our base near the bleak southeastern shore of Tossun Nor.

Only there wasn't any camp. . . .

I pulled my horse to a stop—stunned with disbelief. I rubbed my eyes, thinking the glare off the snow and ice must have been worse than I had realized. I took another look, a sharp one. Camp 12 was gone—vanished in thin air. The whole site at the spring was deserted. As the others rode around the rock pinnacle they reined in and stared, uncomprehending.

The first thing I did was unlimber my rifle; if raiders had overwhelmed our base recently, it must have fallen without the firing of a shot—surely we would have heard the sounds of battle in that walled valley. Even so, raiders might be lying in wait for us to return. The men dismounted and scattered, cocking their guns as they ran. I rode on across the head of the spring and turned right into the deserting camping grounds. The others in twos and threes began running forward to join me. The tents, all the caravan's men, our animal herds of horses and yaks—all were gone.

There was a sinking feeling in the pit of my stomach. I should have waited at Tsasura for the Ta Ho Pa reinforcements. In my enthusiasm to find Amne Machin, I had gone off half-cocked.

The Secretary and a Tungan joined me. "What do you make of it?" I asked them.

They never even answered, just stared around in disbelief.

"Maybe Amne Machin got them," I suggested.

"Don't joke about that!" snapped the Tungan, beginning an argument with the Secretary.

I dismounted and walked around, kneeling to feel the ashes in our old fireplaces. These were warm . . . but, no, underneath they were cold, the sun's rays had merely warmed the top crust: no possible fire since morning. Abdul rode up with the others and reported that there were no Ngoloks about. We stared at one another with mixed expressions. Someone laughed; others cursed; mostly we were silent.

All of us now began searching carefully for telltale signs of a fatal raid. But there were none; we could find no corpses in the spring alongside, there was no blood on the worn frozen turf, no empty cartridges indicating a fight, no carcasses of our animals. Desertion was emphatically ruled out. We sat down and scratched our heads and unshaved chins, feeling very much alone in Tibet, staring up at the red cliffs: from the looks of the melted ground freezing up around the campfires and the others' tracks, we finally decided that camp had been struck only a few hours before. Fresh dung which no longer steamed, confirmed this in the opinion of the Tibetans. If these deductions were correct, where in hell did the caravan go? And why had it gone? Had it been forced out, or had it really deserted? Scouts went out in pairs to try and pick up the departing trail, though as one of them pointed out, snow flurries and hail had obliterated most of the tracks by this time.

Dorje looped a leg over his saddle pommel and slid groaning to the ground. "I am afraid I have lost my collections and notes, all my specimens."

Two hours later a team of scouts came galloping in; and a more puzzled pair of trackers I never saw. Shouting above the afternoon wind which had risen belatedly with a vengeance, one of them—a wild-eyed fellow with a gold ring in his left ear and his face framed in long hair—reported that a large party of riders had surprised the base camp and gathering in everything and everybody, had vanished into the *east*.

I swung into my saddle, and beckoning the scouts to follow, turned the horse's head back into the east.

"Where are you going?" the others called out.

"To find the column and get it back, of course. Come on!"

After considerable delay and with all kinds of protests, they stiffly got on their horses, for we were tired, and not long after Bomba was picking up our friends' tracks which were leading east alright, keeping to the south side of the broad valley along the foot of the Dzu Mountains, and more or less in the tracks we ourselves had made going to the Amne Machin Peaks. Whenever Ngolok riders, probably game hunters, were spotted far out in the valley on our left, we simply moved behind boulders and waited for them to disappear, or rode along in the bottoms of slight depressions. An hour and a half later, the tracks abruptly turned to the right out of the valley and led off into a canyon, headed *south*.

The seventeen of us laid up for a bit in the canyon, for two Ngolok riders were seen on the far east rim above, until approaching dusk; then set out again—determined to charge into the Ngoloks who had apparently captured the caravan, and blast them into Nirvana. Without our caravan we were, in the opinion of the others, doomed to starvation and exposure, and should we fail to carry the assault at least it would be over quickly. We were walking our horses slowly, the scouts tracking on foot ahead, cutting down all rattles and other noises, when quite suddenly we rounded a cliff, and there it was—

A very large camp lay in the wide gulch just ahead—cleverly sited so as to be concealed well within one of the hostile-looking passes we had been so careful to skirt that morning, and which had been called "Gna Dzu" the "Tail Joint."

Besides black hair charis, there were our white tents and the blue flower ones; many yaks and horses were tethered, and men were everywhere. "Tail joint! Tail joint!" suddenly cried out Solomon Ma, apparently beside himself with anger; "That big fellow over there by the fire is Colonel Ma Sheng-lung! And I'm going to swing him by *his* 'tail joint'!"

I only then realized what had happened. "I wouldn't do that if I were you," I advised, not knowing whether to laugh or go blind with anger. And so at this point, two days' travel northwest of Amne Machin Peak, we at last found our base camp, where we were welcomed by our belated companions who said they had given us up for lost. But of course the human element, the psychological hitch, had to enter into our complicated affairs:

By this time Prince Dorje, Solomon Ma, and the other members of the Amne Machin party, were for the most part so angry they couldn't see straight. Some half our animals had broken down on the last twenty miles. It was obvious to them that Colonel Ma had deliberately let us ride past the canyon on our return from Amne Machin, purposely not intercepting us, knowing we would find the old deserted camp at the Black Sea. Standing there on the outskirts of his camp, I realized that Colonel Ma was now the great Poobah, and I was just the Poo. There was only one chance to recover the initiative, and this I decided to take.

Therefore I spurred up to the pompous looking Colonel Ma and the group of his grinning officers, all of them standing with an air of insolence before Ma's massive blue "flower" pavilion. The bugler began blowing his horn with a flourish; it was a Moslem victory march. Without glancing to either right or left, I rode on past them and dismounted at my own tent door, on the far side of the encampment. Solomon Ma and Dorje followed at my heels.

The suave Magistrate Tan Chen-te, smiling in a most graciously offensive manner, came swaggering over in a gorgeous robe and a sword, and in a wheedling voice tried to get me to come back and enter Ma Sheng-lung's audience tent, where "welcome festivities" had started . . . but without any luck. Perhaps I should say that after five trips to China, I understood a little the strong Chinese angle of the importance of face; also I understood the importance of single command on any expedition—military or exploration—especially one having the complex organization and aims of this one. Two leaders in the field are worse than two generals trying to command the same army, or two cooks presiding over the same soup pot.

That evening, as Tan Chen-te, now thoroughly rankled, and a new very tough-looking Moslem colonel bowed into my tent, I sensed danger in their narrowed eyes and curt manner. They lost little time in polite talk, before threatening me in no uncertain terms, with an "accident" if Colonel Ma continued to lose face because of my deliberate ignoring of him. The entire encampment, apparently were reveling secretly at the showdown, as every one of its members had suffered in one way or another because of his foolishness at Fort Ta Ho Pa. I heard them out, feigning indifference, and then answered politely through Solomon, "God is merciful. His ways indirect."

Solomon became very angry, saying they could kill him, all three of us, and go to hell while they were about it.

I fiddled around with some notepaper; I dawdled over a book—and all the time they were talking: finally I told Tan and his hard-looking Mauser-girded friend, that as a matter of fact, I had anticipated them. How—? Well, I had already sent back to Governor Ma Pu-fang, a report on their defection at Fort Ta Ho Pa, and that he had been forewarned of the possibility of such an "accident" befalling me. Further, if this unfortunate event occurred, I had already suggested to our superior that he bring both his magistrate-governors to Sining for court martial. I added, with a pretty good imitation of a yawn, that to insure of this message reaching him, I had dispatched two different Tibetan scouts unknown to the magistrates —Tibetan enemies, whom they could not intercept by warning troops on the radio, and that in short . . . their goose was cleaned, picked, and cooked. Dorje and Solomon kept very quiet.

I was bluffing, of course: but having played my bluff, I realized I was much too tired from the day's efforts to exploit our immediate gain. The pair seemed absolutely stunned. I kicked out a bear rug flat on the ground and stretched out with an apology, composed myself for sleep, and soon let fly a few false snores. My friends followed suit.

"God the All-seeing! May these fiends' bones turn to dust!" cried Tan Chen-te (according to Solomon later).

"Ahaya! May the Lord strike his tribe to ashes unto the fourth generation!" quietly remarked the new colonel; then after thinking it over, added—"To the very day of requital!"

Feeling as ornery as they, I snored a little louder. They rose abruptly and left the tent. I realized all of us had a bad case of nerves, myself included, and we were acting more like a bunch of damned fools than fully grown men who were supposed to have at least a yak's common sense. After nightfall Tan Chen-te returned, now in a far more cordial mood (which I matched), and smoothly and smilingly informed me (through Dorje) that the Ngoloks were having a hard time organizing a raid, due mainly to horse-feed shortage. Of course the spring grass was not yet out in these elevations, but in emergencies the Ngoloks chop dried kyang meat and feed it to their horses.

"All this is of no interest to me," I pointed out, "tell it to the expedition's commander."

"That is what I am doing at the moment," he protested with a smile.

"Then you have decided to follow your governor's wishes, is that it?" asked Solomon.

"The wise man has no other choice."

"Is this Ngolok matter serious so far west as this?"

"It is!" Tan said in a low voice, and in general added, "This meat feeding is effective, and some of the chiefs may attack . . . as already groups are gathering twenty miles east. Scouts report they will not be in sufficient strength to come against our 125 rifles and our machine-guns for three more days. They appear to be angry that you escaped them this morning . . . and yet they hesitate. We do not understand."

Before Tan left, I put forth the hope that next day the expedition would strike south, then west, for the Yellow River headwaters. We were saddled with finding a place for Ma Pu-fang's army. And I wished now to follow up on the Yellow River reconnaissance in order to determine its relationship to the Amne Machin Range. Tan requested an order in writing, which I wrote out. All such requests on my part were in English and Chinese, so that should trouble come, responsibility could be fixed, for I was told Governor Ma was not the man to overlook failure or avoidable loss.

I was now of course indirectly warned: when a Chinese Moslem army officer begins waving papers, you may take it as a signal that troubles lie ahead. As for this matter of squabbling, I decided to handle all internal disruptions myself, and not to radio a hint of our differences to the governor. Sining and Lanchow detractors could always be depended upon to pounce upon the doubtful wisdom of sending out this expedition, and might even bring about its recall in these troubled times. The Chinese, especially, surrounding the governor, were distrustful of me—being an American, and especially one who had served 24 months in China with the OSS and believed by them to be, at least in part, responsible for us maintaining a separate intelligence organization from Tai-li's (who tried every trick to take us over complete). Since we have supported them for so many years, and demanded they show nothing concrete in return, they feel for us at bottom, though rather good at hiding it, only the most arrogant contempt and deep-seated scorn.

Thus, at Camp 16 (as it was marked on the route map) was further widened the break with Colonel Ma, as if we hadn't enough troubles already. Stubborn to the last, he had alienated even his staunchest followers by giving twenty lashes each to four of his own men who had gone toward Amne Machin with me. They should never have left Camp 7 with me, he roared all over camp. It especially riled him to think that he and his "supporting party" had been forced to use a single common bowl for their tea, all the way from the fort, as their own gear was with us on the yak train.

The Secretary—Chutsu Tsereng, semi-independent as a freelance mercenary, mentioned, smiling, that Ma Sheng-lung, the "uncrowned Sultan of Moslem Tibet," was like a sheep's stomach that has been pricked after the sheep had been feeding on too much spring pasturage. "If you should be annihilated in a 'Tibetan ambush'," he politely added in a whisper, "I shall see to it that Governor Ma learns the truth."

"That would be a little late, my friend."

"But consider your next incarnation," suggested Chutsu Tsereng blandly with a faint smile, at the same time tempting me with a piece of gristle he was shaving off a yak rib carried around in his robe.

I asked if his *machen* (Tibetan cook) could not broil some liver on a ramrod and bring it into our tent; for due to the high elevations and hard rides, Solomon Ma and Dorje were lying apparently exhausted in their beds. They were also troubled with nausea, dizziness, and insomnia.

The Lhasa caravan which Colonel Ma had brought with him was encamped alongside our own bivouac. Its masters were two Lhasa men, Lobsang Chiempa and Sor Dörge. They were traveling to the lamaseries of Sera (Si-ra)—having 5,400 monks, and Drepöng (or Dre-pung)—having some 6,000, hoping, if all went well, to arrive in three or four months. That night they came to the tent. Dorje explained that unlike the Chinese, Tibetans understand each other fairly well regardless of their home province, and they call their language, Bodskad. There are, however, apparently, three main vernaculars spoken in the country—*ch'os-skad* (high court), *rje-sa* (gentry), and *P'al-skad* (rong-pa). The alphabet is one of 30 letters, pronounced in rising, medium, and lowering tones. Foreign-language authorities (they agreed) usually pronounce Tibetan in the accent of Sikkim or Ladakh, or of U and Tsang—the official language of Lhasa, but bearing little relation to the outland dialects. The Lhasans explained through Dorje—who was never too ill or done in to tackle something interesting—that arguments over "Tibetan pronunciation," and its conversion into Romanized English spelling, are very involved; as an example:—"Spyan-ras-gzigo" ("Great Passionate Lord") is pronounced "Shen-re-zi," while "Ting-nge-hzin Bsam-gtam Bardo" ("Ecstatic Equilibrium") is pronounced "Tin-ge-zin Samtam Bardo." The Tibetan language was first put in writing by Indian Buddhist monks in the mid 1600's working with a Tibetan layman named Thonmi.

Though Ngoloks were seen nearby, and driven off, storm prevented us from leaving next morning. A wind had risen in the very late hours of the night. By day it was necessary to pile all the various cargoes on the weather-side of the tents in order to anchor them down. Afterwards we crawled inside our tents and tried to keep warm while the wind blew outside. There was a lull at midday, then rather suddenly, at one o'clock a sand- and wind-storm blew with a whistle down from the north end of the canyon, bowling over some of the tents. Our teeth became gritty with dirt. Our faces and eyes were stung from the driving mixture of sand and hail. Outside, visibility dropped to practically zero; the yellow sky blotting out completely in a grayish fog of hail and dust. We leapt on the beating tents to hold them down as they were causing stampedes amongst the yaks and horses. In the meantime our stuff was being ransacked by gusts of icy wind, and sent flying and tumbling pell-mell all over the canyon—blankets, empty boxes, dung, coals, laundry. . . .

The Lhasa caravan even lost for a time its priceless Lhasa terriers and mascot ram—this last presented by the Panchen Lama. All this turmoil inspired me to send Colonel Ma's gift back to him; it was a golden toothpick presented in Fort Ta Ho Pa. A few minutes later a messenger from his tent arrived, with the pocketknife I had once given to him. And so like the storm our own feud continued. The Tibetans thankfully led in their precious talisman ram—without which, they insisted, they could not safely proceed toward Lhasa. It was a big sheep, its white wool trailing on the ground, its wide horns painted red, and its neck hung with red prayer-tassels and tinkling silver bells.

In the afternoon Colonel Ma's bodyguard was ordered to sing and console him. In his own quarter of the camp, he could still be heard roaring orders from time to time, but he did not enter my area. Further misadventures must certainly be kept down to a minimum. I had no idea where it would all lead to. Nevertheless, a showdown seemed long overdue, and rationalization was out as far as I was concerned. Though at heart I really liked Colonel Ma, and missed his good company, and even felt I was as much to blame as he was if not more so, still, as far as I was concerned he could go soak his head. The storm abated, no doubt due to the prayers of our indefatigable gelong and bombom who in their own barricade performed mystic rites and chewed on their cuds.

The day continued bitterly cold and blustery, delaying for the present at least any idea of our moving, in spite of the closer approach of three fairly strong Ngolok bands believed to be identified as Tsanggor, Riman, and Toba. That probably meant a fair portion of the Ngolok federation was gathering here in force. Our twenty-five exhausted animals used in the thrust toward Amne Machin, could really not face such a storm. Fresh snow was everywhere, and our ten tents bogged down.

The radio masts were flattened in the evening by a gust of wind, coming down with a rattle, but were soon rigged again. Snoring huskily, Prince Dorje and Solomon Ma were both feeling better after food and rest. I was burned from the snow glare and wind on the back trail, and most of my skin was coming off in patches due to this, combined with frostbite. I tried to ease my discomfort by shaving, but made little headway as the razor seemed made of barbed-wire.

The mountains above were reported to abound in game. Some of us went out (I personally had no luck), and three bighorn sheep, identified by the Moslems as the Chinese stone sheep, were obtained late in the evening, a welcome addition to our meager larder. Tibetans boil their meat, believing that roasted meat impedes their breathing when climbing in high altitudes. A feast was proclaimed, and the three fat sheep vanished at one sitting!

Early morning next day showed we were no longer weather bound, and so the combined trains were marshaled under a blue sky glinting with stars between the canyon rims, and began a 60-li ride westward, away from the hovering Ngoloks. Heading down the stone-strewn canyon, we went first west an hour, then steadied south of west, through drafty rongs. For 30 miles we passed through frosty mountains and hills enveloped in a cold wind that sent shivers through us in spite of heavy furs. We found a poor little stray wolf-whelp—apparently lost, and freezing under a bush where it had taken refuge. Though it tried to bite, I took it on my saddle, warming it inside my chupa, where eventually it napped between periods of shivering. As we moved into a grassy valley hundreds of kyang raised their heads and then moved indifferently over to the opposite side where they continued grazing. All day we had kept out of possible ambush by a careful choice of route: but still small bands of curious Ngoloks hung on our flanks. Camp 17 was pitched at an altitude of 4,330 meters (13,498 feet) at a place called "Ma's Curve," in memory of a trader killed by Ngoloks.

With camp settled, Prince Dorje and I returned the visit of the elegant Lhasans, one a trader the other a Tibetan diplomat and world-ranging ambassador at large who knew Delhi, Paris, London, Peking. Their ladies were with them, and draped in green-edged and black Cossack coats and riding boots. When riding, these ladies wore hats of black-fox fur, but in the tents their *partuks* (coiffures) were piled high and sometimes elaborately dressed with jade, pearls or coral, and the like. Around their slim waists, in holster and silver scabbard attached to a yak-hair girdle, were Chinese Mauser and poniard. Whenever the watch mastiffs growled at us, the ladies' long whips flicked warningly toward the beasts. Such ladies, Lhasan aristocrats, are addressed as "Chamkusho," meaning, "Your Lady Excellency." Both were stunning beauties.

Lobsang Chiempa, a familiar of the Panchen Lama and the Kumbum Court, was the diplomat; Prince Dorje had known him casually in Peking society: and he was a most delightful character. He spoke considerable English, Dorje warned me; but he pretended not to understand a word. He was undoubtedly a smoothy, a past master at intrigue. Most trade from these regions, he told us, went south into south Tibet and India, some diverting east into Chinese Szechwan. Their caravan would winter in Lhasa, and then go to

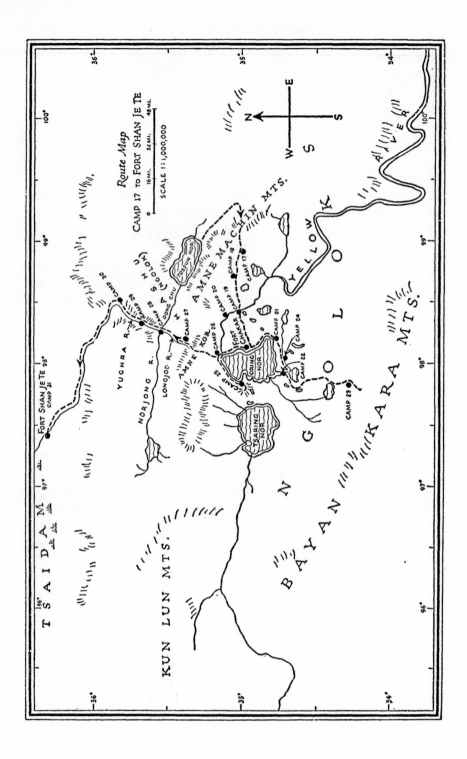

Route Map
CAMP 17 to FORT SHAN JE TE
SCALE 1 : 1,000,000

SCALE 1:1,000,000
0   16 MI.   32 MI.   48 MI.

N

W ── E
S

TSAIDAM

KUN LUN MTS.

FORT SHAN JE TE
CAMP 31

YUCHRA R.

NORJONG R.

LONGJOC R.

CAMP 30

CAMP 29

DONG CHU

(GOLOK) SU

TOSSUN NOR

AMNE MACHIN MTS.

CAMP 28

CAMP 27

CAMP 26

CAMP 20

CAMP 19

CAMP 18

CAMP 17

AMNE KOB.

FORT CHAKAR

CAMP 25

ORING NOR

CAMP 21

CAMP 24

CAMP 22

YELLOW

R I V E R

N G O L O

BAYAN KARA MTS.

TSARING NOR

CAMP 23

Tachienlu on the Chinese-Tibet frontier. They carried a rich cargo of goods from Sinkiang; carpets indirectly from Samarkand and possibly Persia, Arctic furs, tooled and dyed leathers, metals, drugs, gold ingots, silver coins and bars, silks, China tea, Siberian ivory (walrus and mammoth), incense. . . .

We were served with Tibetan churned tea, made from hot milk, soda, tea leaves and stems, and butter. Everything in their luxurious tents, which were blue and white, and in designs, seemed embellished with either silver or gold leaf. The tents were double lined with silk; furnishings were of rare aromatic woods. We sat on a robe of leopard skins, thrown over a single mattress divan. Their saddles were of tooled leather, covered with quilted red and green velvet. Their firearms were among the finest in European sporting models. Their horses were all matched blacks and bays. Even the black mules, for both riding and packing, were hung with red leather trappings, tinkling bells, and tassels of red gauds.

Our hosts said gravely they hoped our attempt on Amne Machin would not bring our combined caravan ill luck. They confessed their fears that the Ngoloks might raid us in retaliation. They were charming people, worldly, suave in manner, keen in taking care of their own interests, considerate in speech and action; by contrast they made our rough, tough Moslem and Buddhist, soldiery look even rougher and tougher than they were. And so we drank tea, scalding-hot, prepared by the smiling *nyerpa* (butler), in his silver-and-bamboo yard-long churn. The tea was served in jade bowls rimmed with old gold etched in Buddhist scriptures. We talked of the two great lamaist Buddhist collections of sacred books, or canons, known as the Kangyur (108 volumes), and the Tengyur (225 volumes)—the latter being a commentary on the former, which is pure orthodoxy. Neither, I gathered, has been fully translated into European languages.

Later that afternoon, in a clear air of −9° C., Dorje and I strolled about camp. It was the first time I had actually had the leisure or the inclination to examine in idle detail one of our own camps. Scattered over the valley were patches of snow, polka-dotted with yaks and their inky shadows, difficult to tell apart. A stream, iced halfway to its bed, was the source of water supply. Dung fires glowed red and blue among the tents. Feed was still last year's old grass, on which the yaks were almost entirely supported. That night we were feeding barley and tsamba to our considerably weakened horses; the mules (I believe) being allowed only such grain as they found in the horses' droppings.

Prayer-flags and a dyed yak-tail standard blew out stiff from staffs thrust into the turf before one of the tents. Belonging to the Lhasa caravan were several Lhasa lion-dogs decorated with silken collars and red wool tassels. There was a curious herd of pack sheep attached to us now, for carrying the lighter loads; ultimately they would be used for food.

Later, Colonel Ma Sheng-lung called at my tent; we were both coolly cordial. But the ice was broken. That night I agreed, to Tan's apparent joy, to break the stalemate, and accept Colonel Ma's half-heartedly offered dinner invitation, reasoning that he had suffered sufficiently for his brash face-making at my expense. Also I missed the old codger.

When I entered the audience tent the assembly of some fifty men more or less out of our two hundred (we were always dropping some off and picking others up) seemed startled and I could see that Tan had not informed them. Colonel Ma, wheezy with the emotion of gratitude (I don't think it was all an act), leapt up and seized my hand, and bowing low pressed it to his forehead; we both laughed and chided each other, and seemed better friends than ever before. This little play amused us, for each knew the other was rolling the dice for power and his own pet fixations; but we were practical too, and knew concessions must be made both ways. We were investing a dangerous region, one requiring full cooperation. At the far end of the tent we took our seats on a divan of wolf skins thrown over mattresses; two wings of guests formed left and right down the full length of each wall of the tent.

The brazier glowed brightly in the center, shining on the faces of the grinning Tungans and Buddhists, the Salars and others—all in their robes and side arms, and butter-lamps furnished further light. We took out our Tibetan daggers, for we had no other service but chopsticks which were useless with our kind of food. I saw that *hors d'oeuvres* were of hot boiled mutton ribs, main course was of hot boiled mutton ribs, dessert was of hot boiled mutton ribs.

But to us, hungry as we were, this seemed a feast fit for kings, especially when the cook raised the lid and we were permitted to glance into the steaming pot filled to the brim with a finger-scalding

rich bounty covered over with a special treat of rich-smelling antique butter. First we must wait before starting, hanging back and
following Ma Sheng-lung's lead, our host in his own tent. We settled
back as if we were not even hungry. We spoke of the cold weather
outside. Coyly, his eyes dancing joyfully, our host took out his gold
toothpick, the supreme touch of our expedition's elegance, and
daintily applied it to his molars. Finding no practical use for it as
yet, he feigned surprise. Pretending to be startled that we had not
eaten, and amazed at the lack of hospitality in his own tent, the
Colonel bellowed for the orderlies to rush in some yak bones, big
joints (from one which had died of exhaustion), and some stones for
cracking them so that we might get at the marrow. Our mouths
watered at the treat to come, our hands shook a bit in anticipation,
but we waited with outward indifference for Ma to stow the gold
toothpick. And when, in time, he did, we began to thrive.

"Allah is bountiful. . . ."

Again we were one party, a band of merry adventurers, with a
single heart, united, and we began to throb with energy and the
hope of enjoyment and great things yet to be done. The past was
forgotten, until Prince Dorje observed (after reading a note brought
in from the radio tent), as he chewed fastidiously on a succulent
piece of boiling hot fat, that now we had reached Amne Machin,
we must find a haven and somehow prepare it for the withdrawal
of an army from China, for the Reds were sweeping victorious, and
Sian had fallen.*. . Ma Pu-fang, our patron and commander, was
in retreat toward Lanchow!

Thoughtfully, we thrust our boots forward toward the glowing
brazier, for they squelched with water, and with the night cold
were already beginning to stiffen with ice. Dinner finished, the men
were dismissed, and we others went over my plans for covering the
Yellow River headwaters, and the region extending north to Tsaidam Swamp. I suspected the Amne Machins supplied little of the
water that made up the headwaters proper (though they undoubtedly added great volumes to the lower reaches in the gorges seen
400 miles below us by Dr. Rock, after the river had flowed east and
then twined north and northwest around the end of the range).
Also by extending our travels north of the headwaters to the Tsai-

---

* The key to the military situation for control of North China.

dam Swamp we would doubtless determine how far west the Amne Machins extended.

So, soon after our reconciliation, I found eager Moslem and Tibetan ears anxious to listen where before they had been half-deaf. Dorje told how we could make economical use of ground and assets to carry out our obligations, and so explore farther west into the outlying regions which might be able to support Ma Pu-fang's retreat into Tibet. The plan need commit but few extra men and animals, and of course some feed. This written plan started a somewhat feverish activity in Colonel Ma; heretofore, all the way from Kumbum to Fort Ta Ho Pa, he had been very cold and pessimistic about either reaching Amne Machin or the headwaters of the Yellow River. He frequently stated that the Chinese armies were hopelessly doomed. Now he was suddenly all cooperation, any opposition silenced under his glances and voice.

Later alone, I assured him the governor knew nothing of our old troubles, and his delight knew no bounds. Thus, from misunderstanding, bitterness, and plain human cussedness on the part of both of us was struck the spark that might just burn off the locks to that Tibet lying south of the Amne Machins.

13

Across the Yellow River

EARLY next morning at 5:15, the highly organized sections of our hundreds of animals—yaks, mules, horses—comprising the two combined caravans, unwound somewhat as a snail from its shell, meandering down through the star- and moon-lit boulders of the pass leading out of the valley. Over the top, and emerging beyond in the dawn's yellow glow, the yak caravan—trotting and widening on a broad front of marching horned phalanxes—flowed in black units of twenty bulls out over a flat plain reaching to a flaming sky. Before us lay a country immeasurably desolate.

Here in the west, south of the Amne Machin Range through which we had passed, was the loneliness of utter geographical space; the weird, gray, empty plain almost as broad and long as the sky itself, with hardly (at that-season) a spear of grass enriching it, and descriptively known to our people as the Ching Ping Nien, "Nude Plain." It was unbelievably sinister, littered with not a few yak and horse skeletons, carrion upon which vultures perched. Hogurushe, a Tungan, a gaunt, hawk-nosed desperado type, rode alongside Dorje and me saying:

"Ngoloks . . . this is a Mongol camp destroyed about a week ago."

As we marched west, hurrying along to the crack of whips, mountains appeared ahead, crudely drawn in charcoal smears and lying against a grayish plaque of earth and sky. Due to the tremendous flux of heat and cold in Tibetan temperatures, especially the day and night extremes, the larger stones of the plain had split and broken down into rubble, sand, and mud. Across this flat desolation we marched, and I realized we had moved into a kind of sanctuary. Here in the open our enemies could not attack. Long but thin columns of Ngolok horsemen were riding our flanks a mile or more beyond, seemingly furtive and suspicious, very swift, moving with single-mindedness. That they were not in attacking strength might be due to any number of reasons ranging from feed shortages to the possibility that our rumors among the Kagurma guardian Ngoloks of a thousand Moslem cavalry penetrating to the sacred Amne Machin Peaks was pinning down the main forces there. Like a gamester who hits a jackpot where he pulls the lever on a slot-machine, we were not too concerned analyzing how our good fortune came about. The fact that it existed was enough.

All day the yaks trotted along while the horses ambled after, sometimes their riders stopping to snake out an animal caught in a mud hole: three yaks and a pack horse being greatly weakened were lost in bogs and we could not delay long enough to butcher them and save the meat. Our compass course continued due west, following the swing of the sun, with a few southing jogs necessitated by ground contours which might conceivably have held Ngolok ambuscades. We scouted such places and hills as appeared from time to time, due to Ngoloks picked up with our glasses, and the tracks of their outriders being intercepted by our flankers. Once, Colonel Ma and I with a group of thirty mounted arms spurred up and rode over some low dangerous-looking hills on the right side, thus screening these off from the right flank of the caravan. Ngolok tracks were found here indicating a party had lain in ambush then cleared out on our approach. Kyang were scattered over the Nude Plain, but only a very few gazelles were seen. This was taken as a sign of the nearness of permanent nomadic Ngoloks; tracks where they had been hunting were reported, confirming Tan's evaluation. Ngoloks then (I realized) must lie to the west of us, as well as behind and on our flanks.

Crossing the Nude Plain, we worked and sweated our way up over a rocky, long, steep *la* toward a pass strewn with hundreds of skeletons—believed to be Mongol animals caught in an ambush while retreating west. Many vultures were here, so stuffed with meat they hardly were able to take off into the air. The pass was called Ma La Yi and Dorje recorded it at 4,430 meters (13,498 feet). Here in the far west, we were higher apparently, than even the passes of the west Amne Machin Range (at least those we had seen). Thus I realized that Amne Machin was not the "father" of the Yellow River, whose true source lay not only south of it, but far in the west. Beyond the pass we established Camp 18 in a round, sky-high valley, enriched in spite of the elevation with rather better feed than heretofore. The knots were shaken out of the horses' tails, their frisky ears rubbed, their feet examined—especially the frogs for stones and caked mud. The yaks, scenting feed, snuffed hungrily, hardly able to wait while being unloaded. Bomba killed three gazelles in a side valley. Barring further weakness in our animals, Colonel Ma calculated as scouts reported in that we would reach Huang Ho Yen tomorrow. These were the grazing meadows on the north bank of the upper Yellow River, said by a Tibetan—who claimed to have raided here—to be not many miles east of its source in the great sea called Oring Nor.

Our altitude now showed 4,375 meters (13,330 feet); incredibly windy, a balky sun peeping only partly out of a gray sky. It was still cloudy at 7 P.M., the approach of nightfall here in the open. I strolled, with icy grass crackling underfoot, through the noisy camp of probably some 450 animals, a clean-cut village of wind-rustling canvas, smoking fires, busy soldiers, yelling yak drivers, cursing mule-skinners, clanging blacksmiths, red-faced cooks, grunting men loading bags on barricades, herders watching over their charges, and still other caravaners bending hair ropes on tents. Wending my way past gaudy saddles piled in long, neat rows and bales of labeled trade goods, stacked rifles, ammunition cases, mules kicking friskily; mounted machine-guns; past our chanting priest and bombom calling upon the gods to bring a clear night so that the grass would not be covered with snow . . . it was a whole world, this nomadic camp, a world at peace with the greater world so big and round. And yet over it all hovered the fear, evidenced in a kind of tension, that tonight might be the night the Ngoloks would strike in force.

I knew then the answer to people back home, who after each journey to outlandish places down through the years, would ask with perplexed expressions on their faces as if they might be missing something; "You are not getting any younger, you know! *Why* don't you settle down? You have your security to think of. From what are you *escaping? What* can you see in such a life?"

My answer could be, but probably wouldn't be: "Raise your sights. We all have our own backyards. Mine is the world and its waste regions, and from these (in the sense you mean) I have no wish to 'escape.' Anyway all this incessant talk of security is foolish, there is no security for the individual anywhere; we all came from dust and that's where we are going back to, our only security as the Tibetans say being in Eternity and God. If we were not so damned foolish that's the security we would all be seeking, and to hell with the rest."

Ma Sheng-lung was feeling gay, and so a sociable dinner for our epicures was held in the blue flower-tent. The feast was of steamy yak, for one of the weakest pack animals had been expended, joints and chunks of meat; and wild duck, and tsamba, and strong buttered tea. It was decided here that our yaks and horses urgently needed resting. On the day's march, in order to reach feed, we had made a good 70 li (35 miles) instead of the planned 60 li, by moving along mostly at a steady pace for 12 hours. Due to the urgency of finding feed, this was deemed wiser than two slow, over-long marches.

Our personnel were in fine health; Abdul explained that the reason none of us had colds was that the musk of the *sheh chih* deer was sometimes sprinkled into our cooking pot! After dinner, in spite of this admission, he came for medicine.

"What's wrong with you?"

"Oh! Sir! I am not sick. I just want to take some 'foreigner' medicine now, in case I should become sick later on."

His face must have reflected my own, for it crinkled into a broad grin; and he left with many bows, and rather speedily.

The others' premonition of trouble persisted that night. At 10 P.M. Solomon Ma, Prince Dorje and I inspected camp on our last round: picket lines were staked taut, criss-crossing the ground around the tents; horses were haltered, saddled and ready for mounting in case of a surprise charge. Since no quarter from Ngoloks could be expected, the camp's standing orders issued by Colonel Ma were— should our scouts be surprised and overwhelmed, and not able to warn us in time for further organization—that our Moslem center would mount, and counter by charging directly into the point of heaviest Ngolok concentration, smashing into their cavalry with the objective of splitting or fragmenting it. Two other groups, Tibetan and Moslem, tented on the wings of the camp, would simultaneously mount and ride yelling in two directions, as if escaping in alarm, and then suddenly, they would wheel and ride back through the Ngolok flanks and rear, now supposedly shattered by our center thrust. Anyway it was a good theory, but sometimes, as I well knew from their endless stories, Moslem tactical theories didn't always pan out against Ngolok ones. That was one of the things which made life so interesting to them and kept them ready to meet their destiny at practically any moment—hence their devotion to their religion. At my suggestion, Ma Sheng-lung, in charge of security, ordered that no man was to dismount during the fight to commit tsai, the usual Moslem *coup de grâce,* but must keep on firing (particularly if the long Ngolok lances were used), and no looting was to take place; all loot to be divided afterwards, laurels distributed. And then, on his own accord, Colonel Ma added as an afterthought, any man who broke and ran, would be summarily executed.

"God grant thy wishes!" the troops had answered as one man. They knew the danger of panic created by the defection of even a single coward in this kind of open battle. Above all, since Ngoloks killed more Moslems by the lance than by rifle fire, they must remain cool, get inside the lances and use their swords as a final weapon. So much for that.

A full moon shone out from behind dark cloud banks, and its light, pooled with that from myriad suns greater than our own, brightly illuminated the wide camp. Eight sentries were posted on the surrounding ridges, silhouetted against the deep, ink-blue sky. These too we inspected, suggesting to each that he sit tight in a marmot hole and not expose himself. Their purpose was to spot Ngolok scouts creeping forward, and not to show off our guard system by walking up and down like ordinary soldiers.

Lowing yak sections (left out as long as possible so they could feed) were now being driven in and picketed close by the tents. The wind had died and, seemingly propped by tall pillars from our fires, smoke was lying over the valley in streaks, an effective roof against dew that might otherwise precipitate and freeze everything stiff. Our unlined tents were aglow, and campfires burned red and blue where unleavened Moslem bread baked in the ashes. The radio tent hummed, sparks flew off the antenna. Men gathering in knots about the fires were singing of their girls back home, and of our adventures in the wilds of Tibet. One such improvised epical song-poem was about a nymph seen by a night guard, apparently she was made of snow with stars for eyes and breezes for hands. Through it all tinkled the bells of the lead animals. When our inspection ended, our hearts were warm with peace.

We had but one regret that day: the last section of horses, which had been slowly breaking down, and our tiredest yaks, were only now just coming in under armed escort. The premonitions of trouble were justified if its locale was misplaced: nineteen animals had been driven off by the Ngoloks. The many survivors needed rest badly, most of the horses and yaks standing with their heads low to the ground. Consequently we decided to leave rather late the following day. I hated to do this, for we preferred to get the daily march finished before the strong afternoon winds came up. The governor of Bayan Kara, out toward the southeast Tibetan province of Kham (Chinese Sikang), would probably meet us tomorrow at the Yellow River. A scout had contacted one of his own. Apparently he had been ordered up from his district far north of Lhasa by Governor Ma Pu-fang to intercept us, and offer protection and feed.

We broke camp and rode slowly only from 8:45 A.M. to 12:15 P.M., sparing the caravan, moving gently in a meandering westerly direction, paying attention to the easiest ground. I judged we logged a few degrees of southing. Our way was over an old Ngolok trail picked for its gentleness, but here and there we departed from it, seeing Ngoloks ahead, and though the way was rougher moved safely past them. The caravan unwillingly faced a west wind cutting sharp under long, thin clouds, but mostly the ride was bright and sunny, if cold.

With some difficulty, continually stopping and starting, breathing laboriously, our weary, limping, half-starved train crossed over a low notched pass at 4,375 meters (13,331 feet), buffeted by high winds, and passing a high obo in the proper style, by keeping it on our right, lest the gods become angry and withhold their protection. This stone obo was decorated with the weather-beaten, gigantic skulls of wild yaks—whose wild protective spirits were invoked by our Tibetans reverently placing (usually) colored stones, perhaps for lack of flowers, on the cairn. I called the gelong over on a hunch, and he was soon scribbling in Tibetan Sanskrit a message to the gods which he placed in the obo. This pleased the Tibetans.

After a steep descent from the pass, during which animals sometimes stumbled because of rolling stones and sheets of ice, we crossed a broad plain and cautiously approached some sun-baked brick ruins.

These were all that remained of the Chinese Moslems' once important Fort Hwang Ho Yen. This former key to Ma Pu-fang's southern communications, reaching in a single line from Fort Ta Ho Pa to the frontiers of the central Tibetan provinces of U and

Tsang—Chinese targets marked for ultimate conquest—had (I only now learned) been abandoned the year before, due to repeated and very costly Ngolok raids. This was west of what I had supposed to be the Ngolok range. An island, in a nearby so-called sea (actually a lake) just south of the Yellow River, the last stand desperately defended by the Mussulmen, had also been lost after a series of battles. The Sining-to-Jyekundo military "road," built during World War II, the dream of outright Tibetan conquest, was now abandoned, definitely shelved for the time being, that is, until the Communists should take it up on the road to Lhasa, and the ultimate underground invasion of India.

A few Ngoloks were standing motionless on the pass behind. We rounded up the animals and continued west. While traveling through this geographical transition region, between Amne Machin Range and the whole vast sea area of the upper Yellow River basin, we suddenly came up against a gash in the plain and saw the pale-amber flood of the Yellow River itself! We were now close to its fabled source; the flow was judged to be 50 to 200 feet wide, flaring here, pinching up there, and we decided to cross over, as the feed looked better on the other side.

We probed for a fording place, and finally, after a few riders and their horses had plunged in deep, we located a shallow spot which proved somewhat deep, but passable, though the turgid water reached to our horses' backs. The current was fairly swift in the middle, bordered by a muddy ice-foot extending out from points of the banks. Some of us became wet to the waist, and exclaimed aloud with the icy cold.

"God's beard!" boomed Colonel Ma's voice half in jest as he clutched wildly at his mare's mane, "I am freezing!"

Dorje and Solomon timed the current and found that it flowed (in that month and year) at the rate of 0.2666 meters in one second, or 960 meters per hour. Strange, there are no Tibetan skin coracles used on the upper Yellow River. I was excited over the hardly practical (for me) possibility of one day running this mighty river from here to the point we had reached east of Fort Chapcha, as this approximately 500-mile stretch of the headwaters had not (to our knowledge) been explored except for Dr. Rock reaching from the north the deep gorges (10,200 feet above sea level) east of the Amne Machin Range; and von Filchner's following its course part way southeast while enroute from Sining to Sung-pan-ting and China. The river's elevation above sea level at this point of our intersection, about thirty miles below the Oring Nor outlet reported by our scouts, was 4,100 meters (12,493 feet). It was one of Ma Pu-fang's officers' hopes to study the entire terrain with an eye to possible eventual control of the Yellow River, China's "Sorrow." The only major flood-control work (other than traditional) on the Yellow River so far attempted, was being done on the dykes low down in China itself; I gathered the Moslem idea was to attack the problem of floods at their source. If practical (which I doubted) the lives and fortunes of millions of people could be directly involved in this pioneering survey. Also, by diverting inland seas into the river, the devastation of Communist-held north China could be insured.

We had advanced our position on the map only 40 li westward, yet many of the yak sections were hours coming in. Several animals were reported down, including a few of the precious pack horses. Uneasy forebodings prevailed. This sudden, new tendency towards gloom must be controlled. I envisioned no quick calamities; all those downed animal carriers were ordered slaughtered, butchered, and converted forthwith into chunks of boiled mule, yak, and horse meat. In a blasting cold the job was accomplished out on the plain, and the harvest of meat was packed away in leather bags, where it froze solid. No caravan animals were to be abandoned if possible, and nothing should be wasted. Tails and manes were saved and twisted into new ropes. Hides were dried and converted into bags, rawhide lashings, boot soles, saddle covers, stirrup leathers, bellows. The inner wool of the yak and sheep pelts was combed out, and used for making thread, the outer wool pressed into felt blankets and Tibetan-type raincoats with peaked caps. Many Tibetan domestic animals, including dogs, have a second coat of very fine, long hair, which is in demand on the Indian and Chinese markets.

On the Yellow River's banks we found fairly good fodder, some of it actually being new green grass, but with little strength of course, and only an inch or two high. We safely nursed the last of the flagging caravan across to the south bank. And then, as throughout all our journeying, set the guards.

Mirrored in full view, south of camp, was a blue ice-bound lake called Ah Shun Gunha. Going on foot, I trudged toward it, following a meandering stream that cut out of the Yellow River's right south bank and flowed downhill into this so-called sea. The Yellow River is actually tributary to Ah Shun Gunha, and not vice versa— an item for Ripley. Lying east was another body of water, just beyond a long, low ridge. West, and behind a high ridge was an even greater sea, salty Tou Long Ra, lying, as we were to see, in a bed of glittering saline encrustations and ice. The two eastern seas are of sweet water.

Returning to camp, I got out my fishing tackle—lines, leaders and hooks. As it was very improbable anyone had ever cast a fly in this part of Tibet, I decided to tie one and see what would happen. I plucked a few hairs out of a yak's ear, cut a hackle off a dead seagull, plucked a green thread off Colonel Ma's shirt, pulled a bit of blue yarn out of Dorje's frayed sweater sleeve; and after tying my fly got the gelong to spit on it for good luck. By this time the whole camp was following, quite wall-eyed. Obviously, fishing with a hook was unknown in Tibet, to say nothing of fly casting. There were no willows, but I found a fishing pole when I borrowed the flagstaff. I gave the fly a heave into the current, and *bang!* Down it went into the deeps, with a tremendous fish well-hooked!

The others (to say nothing of myself) were absolutely thunder-struck, standing about with their mouths hanging open, practically speechless. I horsed in the fish, for it was impossible to play it, and found I had caught some kind of a giant goldfish. The Moslems let out howls of glee and began ransacking camp for lines of their own. I loaned them fishhooks, and soon a number of eager beavers were at it. Colonel Ma made himself a fly out of the hairs plucked from a Tibetan head.

With it he landed himself a two-foot fish, to his amazement and delight. Some of the men baited their hooks with unleavened bread, and even they caught fish. After an hour we had thirty-odd fish lying on the snow patches along the bank for half a mile. They were a congenial carp-like type, without teeth, and were for the most part in length from eighteen inches to just over two feet; beauties with white bellies, tan-golden back with black speckles. They had a golden ring around each ebony eye. Surprisingly these fish some-times jumped at our flies, working practically like trout. Their flesh was a faint salmon-pink in color. I got hungry as I fished, contemplating dinner.

The Tibetans, however, were disgusted and would eat none of the catch, disdainfully calling them "yellow fish."

"What do you want, Lord Huardamu?" (our Tibetan politico), cried Dorje, who had joined in with a fly that looked like an old hat baited with yak liver, "Snails and champagne!"

That night we fared excellently and amid much joking, talk of hunting on the morrow, entries on the maps, highly improbable river dams, we dined on old yak meat most tender, and gazelle shash-lik sprinkled with salt from Tou Long Ra, and prepared over an iron brazier stuffed with coals. The dung smoke from them gave a surprisingly good flavor to the meat. Also there was fried goldfish cut into long strips and eaten elegantly with our rarely used chopsticks. And uncooked fingers of tsamba, and hard-boiled goose eggs dipped in rock salt, and finally churned tea most delicious to the palate.

Our tea was made thus: a big piece was broken off from a "brick" of tea about the size of a regular building brick only flatter, and dropped plump into boiling saline water; a pinch of soda was added, then a big gob of a couple of pounds of butter, and the whole mess churned in a nearly four-foot-long tube of bamboo bound with copper bands. The tea came out white and foamy with sticks floating on top. This type of China tea is overwhelmingly favored by all Tibetans, in spite of the debris. There were yellow pearls of the rich butter. We made a racket drinking the tea, for it was good, and needed aerating to keep it from scalding our mouths.

When we had finished this delicious meal, I felt as pleased as any one of the minor Bodhisattvas among our Tibetan contingent. Colonel Ma and I grinned at each other, and at last knew that our feud was really finished. Strange what a little sport and a decent meal will do toward establishing peace and good will. No scurvy had appeared among us; and this though we were without vegetables of any kind; no greens, no limes, no potatoes, nor any of the other foods considered antiscorbutic:—only fresh meats and fats. Even so, we were healthy and strong, though our diet, of necessity, was even more Spartan than that of the Drök-pa who had milk and other foods not available to us.

"God has made us brothers," I called over to Ma Sheng-lung, for all in the tent to hear (Solomon laughingly interpreting into two languages), "May you soon become *Padi-shah* of Tibet!"

His florid face beamed with surprise and delight and he cried out, "May the peace of our Lord be with thee forever and forever!" The big gold teeth shone. And turning quietly to the others, he said very calmly (according to Solomon), "Praise thou the Lord. We Moslems have a friend. May Allah strengthen thee for the work we have to do!"

He then reminded our followers that we had been charged with accomplishing great things. He defined our objectives, military and political, scientific, humanitarian. And he ended with:

"On our findings, will depend whether we will be able to withdraw any of our brave Moslems now fighting Mao Tse-tung (the Communist) alone in China. We are outnumbered five to one," and then he asked: "Other than this American, who is with thee?"

And they all answered as one man:

"Only God."

14

Camping in the Star Country

I TOOK LEAVE of Colonel Ma and his staff, now discussing plans for exploring the upper Yellow River,
and went through a gusty wind to my tent. I was cold and tired after
the short but hard day's march. Hassan had made my bed, and after
undressing I put on a pair of wolf-fur gloves to keep my hands
warm, and read a translation from Mila Repa (or Milarepa), Tibet's
ascetic poet. Unlike the saint, who lived in a cave in the dead of
winter, I continued shivering. I put Dorje's translation aside and
picked up a book by the French Tibetan scholar, Madame Alex-
andra David-Neel, who as a "beggar" reached Lhasa and apparently
(according to some chits by Dorje) obtained knowledge of *Tummo*—
the production of internal bodily heat. I had heard of a demonstra-
tion of Tummo at Kumbum, where a monk sat out naked in a
temperature of —28° all night, without ill effects—the explanation
given that he was concentrating on a flame, the visionary picture of
a flame, and by so doing was generating heat within his own body.
I put down the book and tried it myself, concentrating and medi-
tating on the inside of a furnace, but it was no use: I only shivered
more if that were possible. There was no getting around the fact
that I just wasn't the spiritual type, though many travelers in Tibet
seem to be. I began counting yaks. . . .

Consciousness returned with Hassan's bellowing voice:

"It is snowing!"

I rolled over and saw that he was holding aside the tent flaps for
me to see; it was snowing alright, and in the middle of May (according to my notebook the fourteenth), the ground already covered by
some five inches of powdery snow. The valley lay under a quilt of
white—our new grazing grounds had vanished. When the almost
certain afternoon winds came up, conditions on the trail would be
impossible. Before striking west for the shores of Oring Nor, one
of the most important of Tibet's seas, we must first wait for the snow
drifts to level off, drifts now being piled up by the wind. In the

meanwhile we could rest and loaf, find a little grazing in the pack-pads and in sheltered ravines. Outside the horses stood about with heads down, tails switching listlessly, now and then stamping and snorting their hunger. We must find new yaks and pack horses at Oring Nor, or else walk on our own feet back to Sining. And I doubted if there was time for that. With the burning of Hwang Ho Yen, Ma Pu-fang had sent Moslems either to establish or strengthen (I was, because of Moslem reluctance to divulge military secrets, never able to ascertain which) another base farther west, on the mideastern shore of Oring Nor. It was said to have stone-battle-mented walls, trenches and revetments; and was called Fort Chakar. There was a tradition that it had been a Mongol strong point in the past. If it had really been successfully built, it would be the only Chinese fort at present remaining for the seven hundred trail miles said to lie between Jyekundo and Fort Ta Ho Pa. Consequently we hoped that all was well at Chakar—if not, we might as well start walking from Oring north. This of course would eliminate any chance for finding a haven for the retreating forces.

Many people in Europe and America would doubtless consider our life at the top of the world one of extreme hardship and priva-tion; but everything seems comparative in this life, one man's hell being another's paradise. True, we had no plays to watch, not one new novel, no motion pictures, no art galleries, no cocktail parties; but I for one had found an immense inner peace and contentment. My momentary renunciation of worldly matters, however, could not have been the answer, for I still took pleasure in acquiring informa-tion on Tibet for my backer. It was the opinion of our officers that much of our scientific work was the first ever undertaken in this region. The census on the local Tibetan population and the animal herds, alone, was invaluable to the government which would soon have a defeated army to feed and mount—and they had no real friends (that is, any in a practical position to help) anywhere in the world.

I took pleasure in reviewing our reputed accomplishments. Geo-logical specimens would give Governor Ma an index to the wealth of the country claimed by him. Rock specimens sent by me to the U.S. Geologic Mission in Hong Kong, brought eventually back to Lanchow a report of possible new sources of tungsten, petroleum, gold, silver, coal, and other valuables. And there were many other fields of enquiry being covered by our variously trained troops: these ranged from language studies to medical work, botany and ethnology; natural history, flood control, estimates on the political situation, treaties, the mapping of the ever-changing trade routes and the main geographical features—and so our hardships (if such they were) seemed only a challenge to be overcome, and the best life that my own short time as a traveler to such remote places could possibly buy.

That morning, while waiting on the weather in the audience tent out of the moaning snow-filled wind, we pulled off our boots and toasted our shins alongside the brazier. I lit my pipe and a few others who smoked applied yak-dung coals to their queer metal hubble-bubbles. We eased back on divans built up thickly of bear skins, Turki rugs, and Chinese red and green quilts. Ma Sheng-lung grinned happily. He leaned near, and knowing what pleased me most, mentioned that no one had ever plumbed the depths of either of the two seas, Oring or Tsaring—undoubtedly among the least known of all the seas of the world.

"This honor shall be reserved for you, my friend!"

There had been a time in the past, when Colonel Ma would in-variably grimace in boredom and desperation at my eternal curiosity; but no longer was this invariably so (though to the end he, Tan and the others often evaded direct questions or else gave me incorrect answers). For him, however, especially since the moment I had mentioned that a sea of fish could for a time even feed a desperate army, he was reasonably cooperative and patient. Fishing had taught him something.

Close by Fort Chakar and just offshore, he continued, the depth was some 30 feet to a rocky bottom; and in the cold waters are seen fine, big, firm fish! Enough, indeed, to feed many armies. The ice freezes down to about 4 feet in thickness, and the ice-fields go out normally, in Oring, in the 5th Chinese month (June). He had not seen Tsaring farther west. However, both seas are of fresh water, he believed, being snow- and glacier-fed. Oring is so clearly transparent that its bottom can be seen through holes in the ice at great depths. Colonel Ma had heard from Drök-pa traders other news:—that on the high Chang Tang, extending west of the mountains lying be-yond the seas to the Karakorums in Ladakh (in northwest India), the lakes seemed to be receding through evaporation, leaving behind wind-stacked deposits of potash, soda, salt, borax. These thousands of lakes are nearly all salty. While in the east, among the mountains of the eastern Drö regions, where we now camped, and south of the Trans-Himalaya the lake waters (he called them seas) are usually fresh, having rivers draining them off into the Bay of Bengal (Brahmaputra) and even the Pacific Ocean.

I suggested we plan a report on the deposits of nitrate of potash, from which gunpowder could be manufactured. Ma Sheng-lung and his lounging officers became all ears and smiles. They had been saying that unless the United States supplied them, they could no longer fight the Communists; while I had been arguing that any Tungan army worth its salt could supply itself.

Later a party of local Ngolok chieftains came dashing in under a truce banner, accusing me of poisoning the Yellow River so their nation would perish. They knew of the journey to Amne Machin. To fight fire in Asia, one frequently uses fire; and so (through the Secretary) I pointed out to the Ngoloks—giants with hard, unfathomable eyes:

"Amne Machin is pleased. Otherwise we would have been driven out or have perished like all other strangers before us."

Having secured their attention, they sat at the fire, and I went on (still through the Secretary)—"The Ngoloks are meant to aid us, and China, against the Red 'Oros' ('Russians'), and if they do not, I swear on the Spirit of Amne Machin, that I will poison the Yellow River (Machu). And your tribes, all your herds, your whole nation, will certainly perish as you say."

Before leaving camp the leather-clad, bloodstained Ngoloks held a council, and came up with a promise of aid. And now Colonel Ma, after the gunpowder suggestion, was more enthused than ever to proceed and not return in partial disgrace to Sining. On such chance and thin threads hang the fate of travelers in this part of Tibet. The possibilities for converting enemies, or even natural obstacles, into assets, could not be overlooked in our rather desperate straits; this was mainly "idea"—a point of view, a psychological thing, that must be used like a velvet glove on the hand, and not a club in the fist, if I was ever to work out the general lay of these Amne Machin regions in the west. Otherwise, we too, as some other explorers in the past, would have to scatter and perhaps even continue in disguise, and work on the "outside" snatching whatever we could by our own lean resources. In short, to gain the last objectives, I could use, and did use, the very devil himself as an ally—the Ngoloks, "his favorite sons."

At 11:30 A.M. someone noticed the thermometer stood at 8° C. It was no longer freezing. We threw off our outer robes. The sun was emerging and was soon out hot, blazing white in a pale blue sky. Patches of grass slowly emerged from the higher wind-swept areas, especially on the exposed, rounded hillsides and along the tops of ridges leading down into the valley. Green grass, rather like a haze than the real article, showed finely everywhere, and our yaks, mules and horses raised their tired, heavy, weather-beaten heads and scattered slowly over the broad valley toward it.

The following incident, arising out of idle loafing, is one of those foolish sidelights on the human character of wanderers, and is set down (as best I can remember it) not only as a part of this record, but a warning to future travelers in Tibet. Among Asians such incidents could have serious consequences.

I had to shave; sunburned beyond belief, wind-cracked lips, and barbed whiskers with a motheaten appearance, were irritating to my physical well-being and peace of mind. Also I had to take this opportunity to get a bath, my first since the Jeh Shi potholes at Camp 9. Attending to this last urgent need, I folded the edges of a piece of canvas, and into it Hassan poured water scooped from the river and slightly heated in one of our copper cooking pots. The whole camp turned out, for the men had never before in the field seen a bathtub; Chinese, from whom much of the Tungan culture derives, bathe mostly with a towel dipped into a basin. Colonel Ma took one quick look at me all soaped up, and with a delighted howl, was soon constructing his own tub out of a felled tent. Twenty men held up the edges, while he wallowed and blew like a porpoise in a veritable swimming pool. The bath over, I went after the shave. Hassan brought steaming water, and as I shaved carefully, with not a few groans and twitches, he hovered about like a hen over a brood, voicing various fears, expostulations and advice which went something like this:

"Do not hack at your throat like that! Who knows God's purposes? You were meant to wear a beard!"

I knew better. Some of the Moslems of different tribes serving with us wore dignified beards, a few of these being long and black and silky, if somewhat weedy, but they were real beards, handy for stroking when stalling for time in a conversation; while under no circumstance can I claim a beard—only an outrageous growth having neither rhyme nor reason, sheer whiskers that would disgrace a goat. Finally I finished, and examined myself in the polished bottom of a pot held by Hassan: I was shocked at the emaciated, red-and-white-patched, beaten-up, sun-scarred wolf's face that glared evilly back at me. It is a shocking thing suddenly to see yourself as others must see you. Hassan's thin lips curled into a huge grin, half appalled, and I couldn't blame him. Maybe if I cut that wild crop of hair surmounting that idiot face!

Dorje, putting aside a geology report, elected himself barber: with a dark gleam in his narrow eye he clipped me about as close as the mane of his gray mare. After one look at my face and head in Hassan's mirror, I was overwhelmed with an urgent need for trimming the hair of a certain shaggy Torgut noble. But the wily "White Bones" would have none of it.

"It is not, Clark, old boy, that I don't trust you . . ."

I began, somewhat wildly, reaching for the old-style Chinese scissors, which my friend and colleague held both high in the air and clutched tightly.

"See here! I might add, old top," the busy prince rasped, "that you are far too impetuous a character to be masquerading as a barber . . . now, I say! Clark! That's not cricket! Ishmael! Ishmael! (Dorje's orderly) Help!"

"You're damned right it's not cricket!" I hissed, "Don't be a pantywaist!" By this time, to Hassan's great glee, I had my Torgut White Bones pinned down and was cinching a headlock on the royal crest; but he finally kicked out of it like a Tartar being boiled in oil, and his spurs split one of my boots. Dorje banged me in the eye, "Be a gentleman!" And I whapped him on the teeth so hard you would have thought we were rolling dice.

By this time the tent had partially collapsed, and we were outside. The entire encampment rose up with an unbelievable interest; yaks raised shaggy heads, horses pulled back on the ropes attached to headstalls, a mule kicked out at somebody. Ma Sheng-lung bolted from his tent half-dressed, holding a Chinese Mauser. Abdul moved just behind cocking a tommy gun. Tan Chen-te jumped out of his black-and-white tent, dressed only in soapsuds and Astrakan fur cap, and tripped over a tent guy, thereby all but cutting off his own head with the official beheading sword.

"Please do not stab him with our only pair of scissors!" cried Solomon Ma, plunging up like a firehorse.

"Silence!" I yelled, "I am not going to cut short the career of our friend. I only want to give him a haircut."

"God's peace! He only wants to give Dorje a haircut!" cried Solomon to everybody, by now a couple of hundred men crowding around wild-eyed and incredulous.

"I don't believe it! They are enemies! They are always arguing!" shouted the irked Tan, dancing up and down for it was fairly cold for a man in his state.

But I had one friend anyway, a real champ, none other than my late enemy Colonel Ma, who tripped up Captain Tan, grabbed the sword and yelled (as I got it later): "My 'brother' is right! I shall hold court right here! Dorje is guilty! I will behead the Mongol bastard!"

I wasn't altogether sure he was joking either. In the meantime Dorje and I were locked in apparent mortal combat, rolling around on the ground. Then suddenly another voice:

"Prince Dorje is of the Mongol royal blood! You must not do that!" It was Huardamu, a six-foot Tibetan chief, said to be a devout follower of the rites of the Mongol Hutuktus, long-dead prelates at holy Buddhist Urga in Outer Mongolia. "Buddha's thunderbolt will strike us all dead!"

Obtaining the gist of this from Solomon, I gasped out: "I am only giving Prince Dorje a haircut, please calm yourself, Lord Huardamu." I didn't add—"or you'll be next."

The haircut was progressing in spite of all this more or less accurately reported affair; I never had come upon so dirty a fighter. If the hordes of Genghis had the virility of this professor, they would have gone on a little farther and made a clean sweep of all west Europe, adding that savage bit to their world-wide empire, and thereby saving the future American public a great deal on taxes. But I persevered with the true American spirit. The scissors clicked, and the shearing of the royal crest was finally accomplished, and then some.

I broke loose. "You look just like a Mongol version of Rudolph Valentino after a hard night!"

Solomon Ma grinning from ear to ear, held up the polished pot so that the royal Mongol could admire himself.

"I say! This is stupendous!" he wheezed, a bit wild-eyed, "Is that I—?"

He made a wild clutch in my direction, but I was too quick for him, leaping toward the picket line and aboard my horse, and galloping around camp. In a moment Dorje was on his gray mare, hot on my heels.

The upshot of this incomprehensible affair of barbering was that Ma Sheng-lung, with a roar of delight, joined us on his fleet stallion, and soon we were followed at a wild gallop and wheeling in and around the tents, by not only Ma but every man jack in the camp (except Tan who retreated disgusted into his tent) who could find himself a horse or a mule, shooting off guns and laughing so hard that half of us fell off our mounts. The camp looked wrecked, but we all pitched in and got it policed up within a few minutes.

Nearly every morning after that, Dorje would take great care to wake first, so that he could lean over and shout: "Hey! Look out! I'm going to give you a haircut!"

I never failed to come out fighting.

In this holiday mood we began discussing the upper Yellow River, the Hwang Ho of the Chinese, the Machu of the Tibetans. We must learn more of its origins than just its Oring Nor outlet. Maps would be made in detail by our topographers. These other sources—and, so great was the river's volume, there must be a great many—were as yet not all known except by native grapevine filtering into the old Peking Court, or by the questioning of the Tibetans by the German, von Filchner, and Doctor Täfel (I believe his understudy).

Already we had decided that our map-making would be based on the universal rule of using only native Tibetan names. It was alright for foreign nations to favor, for political reasons, China's claims to these wild regions, and do it on improvised, inaccurate maps. This method of mapping was a radical departure from the confusing methods employed currently, as a result of the excellent work done by explorers—such as the Germans, Russians, English, Indian Pandits, French, Chinese, Manchus—each traveler using names of his own fancy, or (if an agent) code numbers, and in his own particular language: thus, a mountain range on today's maps often has as many as half a dozen different names (often spelt differently), instead of one, and no two on the same map! The Germans call the great range dividing Tibet from western Mongolia, the "Richthofen Geb," the Chinese call it the "Nan Shan," while the Mongols, the Russians, the Tibetans, the French, etc., all call it either of these or something else.

Our own policy, suggested in council, was to eliminate all these proud names promoting politics, financial backers, Chinese courtesans, and 32nd-cousins, not to mention just plain friends and prospective scientific and financial future backers; and including even our elimination of Moslem names, and to stick to a scheme so unimaginative as to be entirely workable in the field:—we would adopt the only practicable solution—local Tibetan names, as these are the only ones used today by the people actually living in the country. An explorer, to say nothing of a foreign army, or an advisor, or even an airman, would look damned silly if no native chief could read his foreign maps for him however approved by the experts—and I'll guarantee *he* can't read them. The U.S. Department of Defense air maps, mainly based—as are the General Staff ground maps—on the Chinese Army maps, are absolutely useless for exploration or tactical intelligence operations and battle purposes. No one in Tibet ever heard of the names printed on them.

The Chinese names, which are a species of Romanized spelling of the "Cantonese" (China's political language) style, with dashes, are (as the Moslems explained) mainly extractions from old Mongol. And today no Mongols, even if they lived here, would recognize the bastardized Chinese names. For example: "Oring Nor," seriously printed on these maps, as in the U.S. Air Force maps, is "O-Ling-No-Erh." And the cartographers do it without even printing a smile in the margin. Nor need the British feel too smug, their variants are equally as confusing. Of course there are two distinct seas in the region, Oring Nor and Tsaring Nor. Actually, Oring Nor is called "Tsaring Nor" by the present-day Ngolok inhabitants living on the shores. The Ngoloks suggest (after Dorje and the Secretary had explained the details to them), that apparently the old Mongols supplied the Chinese Imperial Court with second-hand information and got the real names twisted. Today, as always (they insisted), Oring Nor is known *locally* as Tsaring Nor and vice versa.

I now walked to the sea of Ah Shun Gunha (probably seen by von Filchner, though I am not certain), already observed two miles south of Camp 19. This previously mentioned stream branching off from the south bank of the Yellow River, was (at that season) 15 to 50 feet wide, flowing southward, meandering in snake-track loops over the meadow. On reaching the sea I saw that it was covered with thick ice. For a mile along the north shore, this ice-field hung back some 200 yards due to the feeder stream's pressure against the field and the Yellow River's warmer temperature, which caused the sea ice to melt. Now the deduction is that during a May such as this in Tibet, and at this elevation, a flyer (explorer or military) can land a hydroplane in any sea having a sizable stream feeding it. A crack ran through the center of the ice-field, though otherwise this lid remained intact. The ice showed four inches above the water line, a green-white streak, giving an index of approximately a total thickness of 36 inches (or nine times that which is visible).

Up to now we had been traveling through a high, cold country wrapped in a strange silence: there was not the rustle of a leaf, or the single croak of a frog, not the hum of a single insect. But here on Ah Shun Gunha swarmed waterfowl from the equatorial regions of Malaya and India, from perhaps even Ceylon and Hainan, enroute to the Arctic, swarming with a typical racket and agitation of feathers in the open shore-lead, and clouds of gnats hovered above the broad field of dazzling ice. All this spoke of approaching spring.

I found a green mint-sagebrush smelling plant, only an inch high, with little corn-blue flowers having tiny yellow centers, which was blooming in carpets swept clean of snow, announcing that spring at last was coming to the top of the world. Giant goldfish leapt with slapping tails out of the mouth of the feeder stream. Rodents, in their spring flood of millions, popped their little heads out of burrows, and rolled beady eyes in my direction. The tracks of gazelles covered the beach, showing that the upland herds of *whang yang* came here to taste the sweet water of the sea. Fresh water in Tibet is called "sweet" not because it is sweet, but because it tastes so by comparison after drinking the salty waters.

Here, approaching the geographical latitude of central Tibet (though of course we were far east of the center), where the hand of man rests lightly, our hearts were filled with gratitude for life, and we knew the satisfaction of freedom. The grandeur of distance, overhung with a ringing silence broken only now by the calls of migrant birds—hisses, quacks, screams, whistles made clarion in the brittle air, seemed paradise.

I realized there can be no such thing as silence, until it is made evident by sound: the Tibetans know this and go further by saying everything exists as pairs of opposites—black and white, good and evil, etc.

The hills were painted now by the sun's rays, with green sheens on the highest ridge tops, and patches of white and yellow flowers —the primitive flower-colors—were everywhere. White gulls wheeled overhead, tipping in the breeze this way and that, on long, sweeping, pointed wings; their neat black heads darting left and right; their stiff black wing- and tail-tips and powder-blue cambered tops, strumpeting through the air.

Soon after joining me with Dorje, Solomon Ma took a leap into the air, and while scratching around found a small spider on his neck. A moment later his collection box was snapped shut on it. Solomon Ma was chief of the government's biologic and epizootic services for the central Asian province. And still, apparently, another job was the collecting of insects. Dorje, chiding him, was surprised to learn that such "useless idling" (as Dorje called it) had already netted Chinghai's treasury US$100 per pound for certain kinds of feathers; in addition, deer-musk from the sheh chih was purchased from the Tibetan hunters and lamaseries—and when landed in Europe, was (according to him) worth $35 per ounce—the same as gold; dried sheep-stomachs were valued at a king's ransom annually—thousands of dollars; under-wool was among the finest to be had, and the crop was worth millions; grass and flower seeds went to Europe; and even animal hoofs were not to be despised, selling in China, after treatment, as jellies; butterflies brought in another revenue from European collectors, some worth $1,000 each . . . "We want to use everything, and indulge in a great deal of 'useless idling'," ended Solomon Ma, peeking through the ventilation holes of his spider box.

"I'll bet you can't find a commercial use for yak tails," laughed Dorje somewhat smugly.

Solomon's eyes twinkled, and his face broke into a wide, slow grin. "May it please Allah," he began, while polishing his glasses and balancing them on his nose, "on the contrary. It ties in with our policy of freedom of the religions. General Ma Pu-fang exports, annually, thousands of yak tails to America for Santa Claus whiskers."

Our topographers were learning from the Ngoloks that this whole region is known today as the "Star Country," or sometimes as the "Star Lakes Country," so named (according to Tan) because it is covered with seas and lakes "like constellations of stars in the sky." We climbed a hill and saw that the Arctic-like lake on whose fascinating shore swarmed so much wildlife, was perhaps three miles long north-and-south, two miles wide east-and-west. We did not follow its outlet due to a turn in Tibet's quick weather, masses of black cloud streaming overhead, lightning flashing jagged in the graying sky, followed by the crack of thunder. Standing in a rush of wind we contented ourselves with a second best, by tracing, through our binoculars, its channel, curving with deep undercut banks back into the Yellow River after leaving the lake at its northeast corner. By the white light cast from the illumined sky we found perhaps two dozen fresh goose eggs, and when we raced back to camp, the men hailed us with shouts:

"Ah! A fine omelet!" called out Hassan, reaching for our caps.

"May the Holy Father of the Ages, make you fat on these fine eggs," cried Chaharashambe, the head cook, sparks already sputtering from his fire.

"And may He leave a few for somebody besides the cooks!" Dorje and I shouted back above the wind.

Snow began falling, but by midafternoon the snow and electrical displays in the upper regions ceased, and we rode out on a gazelle hunt, amid a clunking rattle of bits, horses snorting, spurs clicking. Highly-bred, nervous Tibetan hunting hounds ran the flanks of our party, riding tail to head, but when gazelles were started we were not successful with the dogs, as the gazelles proved too smart and too fast for them in the hills. As a result, the game was stalked the difficult way—by running low or crawling for what seemed a half a mile, sometimes using elbows and knees, wallowing through wet snow patches and soggy grass sod, before we came up close enough for shooting.

All shots—most of which were clean misses—were made from prone or sitting positions, and with the hinged resting prongs unfolded from our rifles; with his first long shot Tan Chen-te killed a gazelle buck at 300 yards, a long, long shot, but not considered too far a range for that open country. Altogether we finally bagged five. The quarry's skin was covered, at this particular place in early spring, with a thick fur of brownish-gray on back and withers, trimmed with white on the lower sides and flanks, as on the belly, throat, and rump. The animals had a long white-and-black tail scut. And six-inch ears. The horns of the bucks were like corrugated lyres, bending in close to a three-inch gap at the tips, each horn having 21 convolutions. Only grinders of hard flesh were set in the upper jaw, teeth, however, being in the lower. These Yellow River gazelles were small, averaging when dressed, only 25 to 35 pounds on our Chinese pole-type scales. They proved good eating, and we were content until wolves, howling from the ridges, caused a double guard to be set.

There was something sinister in the wolf howls, for as I stood listening in the darkness, I realized they were calling and answering one another—on all sides. Tibet as the Tibetans said had two faces—the kindly, gentle face we had seen that day at the sea; and now its fearful aspect, the face of terror and death. With night all that paradise had turned into a black, fearful region. It was easier now to understand some of the Tibetans' superstitions. I knew we were surrounded, and this strong premonition of danger was final when a scout galloped into camp showering us with gravel as he reined in his horse violently. This Tungan, Ma Liang, shouted:

"Ngoloks! Hurry, they are running off our yaks!"

The guard mounted and took off after him into the darkness. They were back in an hour, saying five yaks had been rustled.

15

Storm on Wambu Gunga

A COMPARATIVELY heavy snowstorm for that region came that night, which prevented the Ngoloks from attempting further stealing. I wondered if I was ever to see one of the great raids about which our men talked frequently; so far we had not been troubled but for a few scattered horse and yak thieves. At midnight I lit a candle in my tent, and began reading from the tattered Bible my mother had given me seventeen years before, when I was leaving home for Dutch Borneo on my first trip abroad. The book had since accompanied me to many parts of the world, but none surely, stranger than Tibet. Colonel Ma waddled over and was soon following my rare example; he bellowed for a quiet reading by the Secretary, from the troopers' well-thumbed Chinese Koran. And there in wildest Tibet, peaceful and content, sat Moslems and a Christian unbeliever together, in the same tent. It was a miracle perhaps that only the Ngoloks and our liking for each other could have brought about.

Every few minutes the Secretary would stop his chanting and glance up, his thin, taut face hard in the soft glow of the candle, listening to the wolf calls in the darkness. Then, as we glanced around at each other, he would resume his reciting, just a little lower if possible. Hearing the Moslem prayers being intoned, the Lhasa emissary, Lobsang Chiempa, wandered over in a neighborly fashion and sat on his heels on a saddle. From his wide, silken sleeve beneath heavy fur robes, he took out a comparatively small Buddhist book about a foot long (some are nearly a yard in length); it was a sacred iron-bound volume from Sakya Monastery, he explained to us in a whisper. His book was not bound like ours, each page being separate and free, the whole volume encased between two pieces of delicately carved camphor wood and bound in two painted iron sheetings.

The pages were hand-made, and of a robin's-egg blue, the Sanskrit written in flowing curlycues in letters of gold, some pages illustrated

237

with illuminated Buddhas, heavens, and flowers. Lobsang Chiempa graciously explained that it was a Sakya lama who converted Kublai Khan to lamaist Buddhism. The Great Khan, who as Emperor of the World soon caused central Asia—the inner core of his strength—to become forever converted, unwittingly brought about the ultimate destruction of his own Mongol military domination over much of the earth's known surface.

Next morning we broke Camp 19 in a flurry of activity, for the cold had driven the Ngolok rustlers west to their tents around Oring Nor (that is, the easternmost sea as shown on the maps). A freezing, cutting wind sliced into us. With regimentals flying from two standards, and a bugle stepping up the pacing of the horses, we strung out over the plain in a formal Moslem order-of-march. Chujeh, leading off, brought the column safely over a pass south of the Yellow River, and then, swinging west, skirted the north shore of the turquoise-tinted sea of Tsu Long Rah. On the crescent-sweeping shores grazed thousands of lyre-headed gazelles. Fog blotted out much of the sea, and so its extent remained undefined on my map. A new snowstorm came in suddenly from the west as we were crossing the high, rolling hills rising to promontories and peaks in that direction. Beyond them lay our destination, the sea of Oring Nor—whose shores Dorje and I now realized were inhabited by Ngoloks.

The storm gathered its power, and burst upon us with full intensity, completely blotting out Tsu Long Rah sea, behind and to our left, until the wind actually howled, and the snow drove horizontally, swooshing over the white stony ground. We kept on in the face of the scourge, weary and disheartened, not daring for even a minute to dismount, turning our faces away from the sting and its serious danger of frostbite. Once Tujeh led down the steep side of a canyon in which we were not long in finding ourselves trapped. Horses whinnied in alarm, yaks were kept in hand only by the continuous snapping of whips and strong Tibetan blasphemy. One of them fell and broke its leg, and as we feared to fire a shot with Ngoloks about, its throat was mercifully slashed.

Somebody found a long rock slide, and climbing out of the canyon by this, we worked along a mountain slope, where the winds kept the snow drifts leveled off somewhat. Twice we wandered blindly into canyons, from which there was no escape, except that of wheeling around and back-tracking out again. The threat of danger from marching over a precipice or a very steep slope was very real. Though we protected our eyes with our free hand, the situation became in my opinion somewhat perilous. Ice formed in clinking clusters on my horse's mane. The big black walked sideways, turning first this way then that, for the wind cut him cruelly. In a —28° C. temperature I nearly froze, and from what little I could glimpse of the others, they seemed in no better condition. We dared not stop, but continued blindly to climb over the mountains still blocking our way into the west. Two hours passed:—our experiences were only a foretaste of more to come. Twice the guides, blinded, wandered off the wrong way, only to be brought up short by a shout as I checked my compass.

After five miles of twisting and turning, back-tracking, climbing fatiguing slopes, plunging down rock slides, we broke out of the region by floundering over a wind-lashed ridge, and lost no time plunging downhill through deep wind-piled drifts of snow. Though belly-deep, we were soon out of the worst of it, and gathering in the remnants that came crawling over the pass. We made a count and found we had lost four pack animals, a mule and three yaks. The half-frozen Moslems led by Solomon gave loud praise:

"Most great is Allah! Our delivery was so decreed from the beginning!"

With the snow shaken out of our banners, we again broke them out. They snapped loudly in silken clouds of blue and white, the many-pointed star of China, gold-bordered, and with red yak-tail tufts dancing horizontally on the lance-heads. Some twenty of us continued downhill and pulled up at a snow-sagging tent fairly bursting with a pack of long-haired Ngolok tribesmen. Their faces were thickly smeared with bear grease, and they were certainly as arresting as any Apache who ever sharpened knife. Dressed in thick sheepskins, stiff with animal blood, they looked like huge, hulking anthropoid apes or the *Dryopithecus*. None of them seemed to be less than six feet tall, and some of them exceeded that. In their belts were stuck knives and swords, and modern rifles probably obtained in battles were carried handily across their backs.

They would probably have bolted had we not surrounded them. One of the men crankily struck out at the head of Ma Sheng-lung's horse with his scabbard-sheathed sword, and under that worthy's rifle butt was sent kicking in the gravel. Before he could rise he was held down at point of a Moslem's bayonet. All about were their bestial, ferocious faces; broad, dirty yellow, thickly-Mongoloid, with cat's whiskers sprouting on chin and upper lip. From their mouths came guttural accents. Even the mules whickered at their smells. There was a strange petulance in their leaping about and in their voices. I rather imagine they were frightened. I spurred in among them, for fear Tan, in the surly mood, was going to shoot the man on the ground. The Ngoloks settled down quite suddenly, staring into my face, pointing at my eyes, and jabbering among themselves. These fellows looked very different from those at Amne Machin Peak.

"They are afraid of your eyes," laughed Colonel Ma (and Solomon) with a chuckling undertone, "They have never seen greenish eyes, and think you are an 'evil eye'."

Their whole manner, though still truculent, changed, and they were presently inviting us into the tent, smiling and cordial. They had seen the caravan following and now beginning to come close. We dismounted and walked in behind the headman. About fifteen of us were handed sour yak milk, which we drank from wild-yak horns a yard in length. The wild yak is incomparably larger than the domestic breed.

I was extremely anxious to study my first Ngolok tent and its contents. A large stone-and-mud stove, about four feet high and five feet long, was standing in the center of this enormous hair tent, placed directly under a long, rectangular hole along the ridge-pole. Yak dung fired it warmly, for it had a hole in the bottom where a skin bellows fit, a boy swinging away at it. Around the walls were any number of hidebound chests; stacks of felts; circular stones for grinding barley into tsamba, which were a foot in diameter and having a wooden handle; firearms—blunderbusses and modern rifles; swords and daggers; coils of hair and hide ropes; sacks of tsamba; piles of dried raw meat; solid lower-walls of yak dung; and a family *zih-da* (shrine) before which a butter lamp stood, completing the picture of this extraordinary dwelling. Though it was savage by most comparisons, to us it looked and felt luxurious.

From out of the storm a strange bombom came into the rather crowded tent; he shook his snow off all over us where we had taken seats on bear rugs, and sat down with a mighty grunt alongside me. This fellow immediately took over, and after some preliminaries told a legend of the great seas lying just west—our objectives. The Secretary translated quickly: During the Lung Dynasty of the "Three Kingdoms," (bombastically deduced between the holy man and the Secretary) there lived three Ngolok brothers. The first was Jalu, the second was Nulu, the third was Choulu. Each of the three brothers owned a lamb. Choulu slept and his lamb was lost. The other two lambs grew up, and became what are possibly the two greatest fresh-water seas—excepting Koko Nor in north Tibet. The first was Jarong, the East Sea; and the second became Nurong, the West Sea.

"And what became of the little lost lamb?" asked Dorje, probably wondering if the wolves had gobbled him up.

"Yap!" sputtered the disgusted Ngolok bombom turning on him fiercely, "The little lost lamb became a small lake between them, called 'Durong.' Today Durong is lost and gone. Poor Choulu!" wailed the bombom, pounding his barrel of a chest till it boomed like a drum.

"Praise be the Lord!" echoed Colonel Ma, whacking a Tungan soldier playfully with his whip. He loved stories of any caliber, and settled himself on a wolf rug. The storm drove by hard outside the door-flaps. I made myself comfortable under a second bear rug, as I knew we were in for it.

But the bombom was wrong on one point, though I anticipate: the little lost lamb, was not really lost, but was eventually found by us on a mapping tour, and immortalized by our Moslem army mapper with the name, "Durong!"

The headman of the tent shuffled up to Ma Sheng-lung and informed him in answer to a curt question, that the Ngoloks of the surrounding hills and rongs east of Oring Nor numbered this season 300 families, and were divided under minor khumbos into family sub-tribes or clans. They were at peace. The pass into the great Oring Nor basin, over which we had just come, is (he said) Wambu Gunga, meaning literally, "Pass Region of Gunga."

The storm outside our black hair shelter increased in fury, whistling weirdly, and so we killed time by talking with the bombom, a rather frightening giant of a man with a massive turban of human hair revealed when he pulled off his fox hat. He claimed to belong to the Red Church, and was a Ngolok by name of Jatm. He was a bestial human mountain, swathed in fox robes worth a fortune.

"What can you do, wise Jatm?" I began diplomatically through the Secretary, who obviously spoke the Ngolok idiom perfectly.

The bombom looked me over from head to toe, focused his blackish brown eyes on mine, flinched, pulled off an enormous boot, played with his gray-looking toes a bit, and sputtered, "Jatm can make rain. Jatm can stop rain. Jatm can call the spirits. Jatm can exorcise devils when he receives scriptures from some great *truku* [priest]. Jatm can tell fortunes by counting beads and casting dice." Here Jatm stopped to dip a big black paw (yes, the same one) into the community meat pot.

"What can you do, 'Evil Eyes'?" asked Jatm, staring hard at me.

Dorje snickered. All the Moslems but the grinning Colonel Ma and Captain Tan looked very serious. These two were enjoying themselves. I paid Jatm a Chinese silver dollar, and suggested he get out the proper scriptures for stopping a snowstorm.

"Jatm can do!"

I was too cold from the storm, still raging outside, to be in a very mystic mood: to me it seemed Jatm only stalled around after putting away the dollar. He dipped into the meat pot again, and swallowed a chunk of yak hind leg that would have gagged a bear. He gawked at my fancy boots and honked his enormous blue nose, a moose-like protuberance. He looked us over, and apparently not struck with what he saw, snorted. He finally decided to settle himself alongside under my own bear rug. And still the wind howled, and the snows whirled in through the opening above the stove, descending upon my red fox skin protected head. Finally Jatm dug up an old boot top from inside his chupa; into this holy receptacle darted a black paw; out came a crumpled piece of pulpy paper.

"How's the weather, Jatm?" I ventured, a little annoyed.

"Jatm can do! One more dollar!"

"No more dollars," I growled and turned my sleeves inside out; we didn't have pockets in our robes. We didn't have any more dollars to waste either.

Jatm looked like he was going to hibernate for the winter.

"Give him a buck, Dorje," I suggested.

"It's a waste of money," sighed the prince, handing over a dollar.

Jatm woke up: Jatm's paw reached high over his head. Ah, I thought, action for a change. But he only dipped it again into the pot, coming up with a slab of horse meat this time that would choke a saber-toothed tiger. Jatm polished that tidbit off with a gulp and a slobber. "Jatm can do!"

Jatm began a chant that might have come up from the belly of a mammoth, stopped, and asked for some milk. When I complained through the sober-faced Secretary, he explained as if to a half-wit, that he was feeding the spirits; but it looked to me as though it was Jatm whose gullet received the benefit. Jatm took out a small bell from his spare boot. This object he held up and tinkled over my head.

"Jatm calls the devils!"

Next he uncovered a human skull decorated with a yak-tail beard, its eyes made from turquoise, its cranium a rattle. This interesting object he held up and jiggled, making a shuffling noise.

"Jatm makes noise!"

Then Jatm lurched up on his feet and went outside to relieve himself. This gave the Moslems an idea, and they too went out and squatted to urinate as was customary with them. Back they trooped into the tent. When Jatm returned he jerked a bear rug out from under Tan Chen-te, whose honest grin turned into a smooth smile. And sat down on it; now he had two bear rugs, Tan's and mine.

"Jatm tired!"

"It's still snowing, wise Jatm," I said, pointing to the hole over-head.

"Jatm can do!"

Again he rattled the skull, rang the bell, looked as if he were napping. The Tibetans, Ngoloks, and Moslems turned their eyes toward each other. All but Colonel Ma and Tan, and I thought they were going to burst any minute so joyful did they seem behind sober faces. Half an hour later Jatm stirred at my knee.

"Wake up!" grunted Jatm.

I glanced up through the hole in the tent. The snow had stopped falling, and wide blue streaks showed in the sky. A minute later we were all outside; and mounting our horses, we went off downhill (the caravan following) into the west, toward an endless sea, now gleaming a turquoise-green to the far horizon.

"Yap!" crowed Jatm, grinning and shaking his skull rattle after us.

16

The Ngolok Peace Treaty

THE CARAVAN clattered on down the hills and over some ridges, hailing Fort Chakar at 2:15 P.M. The fortification was intact, its garrison of fifty Moslems alive and well, and delighted to see us for they were bored stiff. The place rested solidly on a cliff at the eastern edge of the ice-covered sea of Oring Nor. This base, and the fort at Jyekundo far south, represented China's last finger-tip holds in Tibetan territory. But even so, flying above the stone battlements were only Tibetan prayer-flags and a yak-tail standard. Apparently, to flaunt the Chinese flag here openly might raise at this particular time the Tibetans' hackles, for the Moslems posed not so much as conquerors as emissaries and traders.

Our position therefore (due to civil war in China) was more delicate than it would have been in normal times. The magistrate of the district centered in the Bayan Kara mountain range, which widely wedges apart the Yellow and Yangtse rivers in upper Tibet, was named Memamotu. This Tibetan had arrived at the fort only the day before, not having been able (so he said) to penetrate the Ngolok screen swarming around Camp 19 on the Yellow River. Actually, according to some of his men later, he had given us up as lost. With Memamotu was a mounted force of two hundred mercenaries—wild, shaggy warriors, dressed in sheepskins, rifles slung across their backs.

Memamotu, himself a Buddhist, was likewise a hired soldier-politician in the Moslem service of Ma Pu-fang. If I was ever to reach the far western Amne Machins I must study him closely, so believed Dorje. This key to our future was a tremendous man—in height appearing to be six feet three inches, and proportionately wide—dressed in flamboyant red-and-black woolen boots, black cloth-faced wolf-robes, golden brocades and silk Chinese shirt. His hat was of black fox fur having a crown of golden threads woven in the intricate Lhasa pattern of the crossed *dorjes* (thunderbolts). This symbol of "equilibrium, immutability, and almighty power," warned Dorje of an inner loyalty to Lhasa. On his chest woven in gold threads was the Eight-Spoked Wheel—the Tibetan Wheel of the Law, the *Ch'os- 'k'or-bskor*—resting on a lotus throne and surrounded by Flames of Wisdom, representing the Thousand-Spoked Wheel of Buddha, indicating the symmetry and round of the Sacred Law of Dharma. The insignia in its center, the *rgyan-'k'yil*, depicting three whirling segments coupled with the swastika—symbolizing the *Sangsara* (ceaseless change or "becoming")—indicated that Memamotu was high in the Tibetan secret religious (and, of course, political) societies.

I asked Colonel Ma if he could trust this man.

"A single false move, and I will shoot him," growled the Colonel, "I believe he could have reinforced us at the Yellow River."

The Tibetan's mouth was full of gold teeth, which we learned he had obtained in Peking when attending the Court of the former Panchen Lama on his famous visit to China earlier in the century. For some reason I instantly liked this man, and knew we could use him, though I sensed (without any particular reason) it was "politically" unwise to do so.

Also at Fort Chakar were waiting hundreds of taut, grim-faced, mounted and rifle-armed Ngoloks; savage warriors led by huge khumbos. Ma Sheng-lung called in the chiefs, and a palaver was held in the main room of the headquarters, a Chinese-style building inside the inner walled fort. They would not leave their guns and swords outside, and the council was held under full arms by both sides.

"We bring you gifts," Ma said, indicating a chest filled with coin, scarves, and other objects. "But, more important, I bring you a message from the Panchen Lama—the Great White Light!" With that he unfolded my letter from the Kumbum Court and it was read by the Secretary. When he had finished the khumbos strode outside the fort and joined their forces; "We will call a council among the tribes!" With a wild yell they wheeled their chargers and at a full gallop led their cavalry northward along the cliff-shores of the sea.

"Our situation is not so bad," summed up Colonel Ma and Captain Tan, "even though they can call up 2,000 horsemen before nightfall."

Just to be sure, the Moslems mounted machine-guns and a small mortar on the walls, inspected the troops and posted them. We would wait and see what happened.

Leaving the staff, I walked out of the fort and across to the top of the cliff overlooking the sea, for Oring Nor drew me irresistibly. This mystery sea, glimpsed (as I remembered the records in the Lanchow mission) for only a few hours by von Filchner half a century before, was ice-bound, but a shore lead free of ice—extending from a few feet to a hundred—opened and closed with each push of the wind against the pack. A few cracks had burst straight out into the center of the frosty-white sea, whose western shores, owing to distance and fog, were invisible at the moment.

We were safe on this sea side; the fort was well situated for defense on its rocky tongue high above the sea. But I saw—due to easy approach from hills in the east—that it could not stand heavy seige for all of its battlements, entrenchments, dugouts, and outer wall. Between the sea and the eastern wall were tents, hitching racks, radio hut, cook shacks, corrals, adobe quarters for the personnel. On both flanks of the cliff tongue harboring the fort were deep, stony shore bays backed by hills of a pastoral aspect, miles of them, tinged with the early green of spring. To the north and the south, extending along the coast, were sheer cliffs gripping this mighty inland sea in a rock-bound embrace. These massive stone cliffs are of uptilted olive-green shale, and large stones lie on the narrow beaches and under the clear water.

I got out my notebook as I wanted to capture a few details. Two islands were visible; a south one resembling a baby whale with its tail playfully lifted out of the water, bears (according to my pocket compass) 215° from the fort; and a larger one, also whale-like, swims north of it, bearing 235°. It is likely both islands are tips of a submerged chain of hills extending across the sea bottom.

Sliding down a break in the steep cliff, which was made difficult by my bulky robes, I found the sea water in the open lead to be as clear as that in a spring, and sweet to taste. The strike of the shore line on this fort side is northwest-and-southeast. Fort Chakar stood at 4,180 meters (12,736 feet) by Dorje's reading on an aneroid barometer. Variation due to weather would of course make this reading unreliable. The sea's surface, according to von Filchner who, in 1904, reached the east coast in Tibetan clothes, was 4,285 meters (13,056 feet) above sea level. This seemed important as it indicated we were measuring *lower by 220 feet* (the fort was some 100 feet above the water level), and would also measure lower by that figure as applied to Amne Machin. For a cross-check measurement:—our own boiling-point recording at the water level was 87° C., our water taken from the sea not distilled; air temperature was 12.5° C., the weather being clear with few clouds and very little west wind.

Returning to the fort, I was surrounded by hundreds of various Moslem troops, Ngoloks, and Tibetans, and conducted by their chiefs into the back of a hair tent and seated among them on a Lhasa carpet. Local politics lost no time entering our picture of exploration; suffice to say that China, exercising an unchanging policy, wishing to extend her sovereignty into Tibet, was backing Moslem conquest of that country, using Moslems as a "cover" to really take over for her the highly-propagandized so-called "Chinese Dependency." The Sining Moslems were, I realized, a good choice by China, for if at any time disastrous war should break out in Tibet, China could wash her hands and blame the "Moslems"— unruly fellows of the wild northwest! Also, Moslems are far and away the better fighters, when compared with the Chinese—be they Communist or Nationalist. This is my opinion after seeing two civil wars, and engaging in World War II behind the Communist and Japanese army lines; where in the OSS I served with Yen Shih-son, later appointed Premier of China, and Marshal Ku Chu-tung, later appointed Chief-of-Staff of the Nationalist Armies.

Therefore, the three key men—Colonel Ma Sheng-lung, Tan Chen-te, and Memamotu, famed politicians and shock troopers for China, were ostensibly gathered at Fort Chakar under cover of exploration; and were the working tools for the planned Moslem withdrawal from China, and, responsible for the installation of whatever Nationalist forces could be salvaged. Tan and Dorje whispered in my ear that Memamotu was distrusted on religious grounds by the Moslems, and recently degraded, and so we must be extremely careful in using him.

He explained that recently, Memamotu was magistrate of central and south Chinghai (about an eighth of all geographical Tibet), from Fort Ta Ho Pa up to the Tibetan provinces of U and Tsang, and Sikang, which in turn front India and China. When the Chinese Red Army would eventually control U and Tsang, our Moslems would if possible form an alliance with Pakistan (also Moslem), and thus ease Communist Chinese pressure bearing on India. All this was in line with my own objective as explorer; we must obtain through Memamotu, a Ngolok peace treaty, and without delay.

But Rome was not built in a day, and while I waited to bring this matter to the fore, Memamotu reported to Colonel Ma, technically his superior, the current depredations by Ngoloks. We were joined by a very dignified, fierce old giant named Guanju, a lord among the Oring Ngoloks, and a possible future ally. If we could win over Guanju, we might win over the Ngoloks.

"Yes," growled Guanju, quite undisturbed when confronted by Memamotu's news, "Some of my young men grow tired of tending their families and herds, and they raid a little to break the monotony of life."

Such spirited life was too much for Colonel Ma, who fancied himself Sultan hereabouts; "Where?" he asked quietly for once, his cropped head bristling, his hand tipping up his skullcap aggressively over one squinting eye.

"Perhaps here and there," finally answered Guanju coolly.

"Where—Lord Guanju, is 'perhaps here and there'?" asked Ma, appealing to me, then Solomon, in a hurt voice, "Is this not a very indefinite statement?"

Guanju took Colonel Ma in with a quick glance, and smiled faintly, "From thither to yon."

"God's teeth! 'From thither to yon!' 'Perhaps here and there'!"

"My territories are vast," put in Guanju calmly and without much interest, "and as my guest, you must not trouble yourself with small matters."

I chuckled inwardly at the implications. But seeing trouble brewing over the peace treaty, I turned quickly to Tan, and had him ask Guanju the price of tent poles, pointing to a pile of poplar saplings along the tent wall. Tan nodded quietly.

"They cost one ox each," Guanju returned, smiling at me. He turned and fixed Colonel Ma with a hard Ngolok look. "There is plenty of raiding for all." And then he added with a twisted smile, "Including enough for my honored guests." We didn't seem to be getting any place, so we went off to eat at the fort. Guanju fancied our food, and mellowed considerably with a few glasses of ara under his belt.

In the night we discussed our plans for probing in the upper Yellow River regions; for we had been rather more successful with

Guanju than at first thought. Dorje and I arrived at a general picture of the lay of the land, the many problems ahead—especially those concerning the tribes occupying the regions south and west. It was decided to lay on a combination tactic of treaties, trade, and actual armed invasion with support of such Ngoloks as would go along with us. On the basis of this meeting we constructed a skeletal plan, and radioed it to Ma Pu-fang for authorization, and the payment for necessary services and material items.

As for the means of getting abroad, I learned definitely there were no coracles (skin rafts) on these so-called seas and the lakes, such as are said to exist on the Brahmaputra in south Tibet. Even so, next morning we learned there were six islands in the sea, instead of only the two shown on most maps. While following somebody's suggestion that we go out on the ice and look down a hole at the fish (what an idea!) we nearly got ourselves into a jackpot. The sea ice seemed to be oscillating in a clockwise motion, grinding slowly against the cliffs, and snapping warnings along the open lead as we tried to work across to the main ice pack. Suddenly the wind stopped and the lead filled with ice, thus furnishing a precarious bridge. One or two fellows got their feet wet and went home in disgust. A few others however got across. I wasn't one of them, and we had no planks or poles long enough to reach. As we waited, trying to figure out a way across the narrow gap, less than fifty feet at that point, the wind suddenly rose in the west, and the ice pack moved toward us, telescoping against the shore.

Hurrying, we leapt aboard on the main ice field, and found its surface to be smooth enough in places, but creased in others as the ice had been pushed up violently where floe edges collided. This residue had frozen tight, forming long lines some of which were as high as three feet. Sometimes the ridges and roughened areas were formed when two floes crashed, buckled, and slid together, one overlapping the other like playing cards being shuffled. As we walked across the undulating field, a haze rose to meet a cloudy yellowish horizon, obscuring the distant shores and mountains said to lie in the west. Earlier, the Moslems sometimes walk to the islands and find eggs which they bring home for the cook. But the season was too late now, and in order to get ashore we had to wade in, a cold business. Nor did we find a hole down which we could view the fish.

Governor Ma radioed next morning from Lanchow, giving his

assent to our plan. Expenditures, rather a large amount, were authorized. This allowed for the renting of all new yaks, and such pack and riding horses as might be needed. The survivors among the original yaks (and most had come through), together with others supplementing them enroute from Fort Ta Ho Pa, and half our herd of horses and mules, were definitely done in; they must rest at the Oring Nor pastures. The yaks and other stock would then—per our *nela* agreement with the Tibetan tribes in the north—be returned to Fort Ta Ho Pa three months hence, via the regions lying west of our old route. These far west regions, Dorje, Solomon and I now learned, were in the hands of still other Ngolok tribes.

Ho Fa Chung, a locally famed Tibetan international trader, arrived at the fort under escort of a hundred soldiers belonging to Memamotu. It was said his caravans connected much of central Asia; they plied the ancient routes to Tachienlu (in west China), to India, Mongolia and Turkestan, and of course to Lhasa. Whether they did or not, the trader dealt in Chinese tobacco, tea and sugar, silks, powder and lead, gems and ivory, guns and cloth, and a deal of other truck. I photographed Ho Fa Chung, buck-teeth and all, splendidly dressed in crimson brocaded fur-trimmed robes, holding his firearms. He wore a silver casket around his neck, containing a Buddha, and a bandolier of sacred Lhasa hadaks, both of which had been presented by the Dalai Lama. He was from Kanding, in Kham Province, the southeast Tibetan regions called Sikang by the expanding Chinese.

A *kenpö* (priest) down from Lhasa, told my fortune, using red coral beads. He had an enormous turban under his fox hat; I examined this curious pyramid, and found that the turban was fashioned from his own living hair. The holy man was a secretive old fox of whom the Moslems and Tibetans seemed afraid, as he had once foretold the destruction by Ngoloks of a section of Moslem cavalry. He read his beads, but by no amount of good-natured urging could Solomon get my fate from his tight lips.

I thereupon told the kenpö's fortune, which was that he wasn't going to be paid. The holy man jumped up, crying out for all to hear, that Amne Machin would bring about my destruction! I lost no time paying the superstitious old duffer double his usual fee, as I certainly wanted his confounded news circulated no further: Tibetans and Moslems, to say nothing of Ngoloks, might very well be taking his nonsense seriously.

At breakfast, a frugal meal of fish and tea, Abdullah, the regular fort singer, was called into the main assembly room in the fort to perform what was called a *liae*. This seemed to be a Tibetan combination of song and dance. His songs were lyrical and sung to stately, time-established routines—very complicated I should say, and yet quite unlike Chinese or Moslem ones. In lieu of a fan, a luxury in such an outpost, he used his wide sleeve. I was told these liaes were composed for events such as a wedding, welcome, courtship, farewell, war, hunting—much as in our own western world.

Guanju approached, hinting he was working on the chiefs for a treaty. All morning Ngolok horses were led into the fort and put through their paces, and 90 top ones selected by our buyers. They narrowly escaped being sold several old crocks as the Ngoloks had, according to a tipster, blown up their saggy faces with a bicycle-pump obtained at Labrang Monastery near Lanchow. Colonel Ma was amazed and disgusted with human nature.

"Why, they are smarter than I!" he roared angrily, "These Ngoloks steal our sound cavalry horses, and then the bastards sell me their old nags . . . filled with air! God's beard!"

"Allah be praised!" cried Solomon Ma, putting on his spectacles for a close inspection of an old crow-bait's lifted face, "Perhaps we, too, can resell all our culls to the Chinese."

Our blacksmiths set up shop, and the fort compound rang with their hammers striking the iron of the shoes, and their bellows sent up puffs of smoke, cinders and sparks. These particular Moslem blacksmiths used "cold" shoes; they were only shaping the shoes, which—unlike American blacksmiths—they completely cool off in water before fitting. Preparations to get the mapping parties out into the field went on everywhere in a fine bustle of activity. All this was mixed up with singing, hunting, dancing, attempted love-making with the Ngolok girls (apparently without much success), and the showing off of the finished Ngolok horses on the hillside beyond the outer wall gates.

At this time a complete reorganization of the expedition was undertaken; only proven men were selected, and rosters for the different field groups made up; provisions were purchased from the chiefs and packed, instruments tested, small arms inspected and mended by the gunsmiths, ammunition issued, new yak trains obtained and a new devil-doctor hired at $10 per month. As a guild gelong (I believe that was his classification), he wanted $12, but when I told him to go peddle his rain somewhere else, he reconsidered, as he had never had it so good before. The land of the western Ngoloks rang with a new prosperity, and our Moslem gold and silver flowed steadily in a one-way direction.

One day some of our people undertook medical work among the Ngoloks. First, our medicos had to decoy a batch of fifty unsuspecting warriors into the fort, and then slam shut the gates behind them; they had already been disarmed outside on pretense of a powwow, I took a snapshot of this as it was, I believe, the first medical work ever attempted among these remote tribes. Ma Shenglung looked on it as "political." Well, maybe he was right in an offside sense; but the Ngoloks apparently didn't like his politics. Right there the whole show nearly blew up.

When the needles glittered near their bare arms, there was a howl sent up to the gods, and before we knew what was happening, they had swarmed up the ladders to the battlements and dropped twenty feet down to the ground outside, grabbed their stacked rifles and rushed through the gate in the outer wall. Prince Dorje shook his head, and endorsed his entry in the medical journal after first erasing—"Vaccinated 50 Ngoloks," and reentering—"Will try inoculations among the Tsaidam Mongols."

Apparently under Guanju's eye, the four paramount chieftains of the permanent Oring and Tsaring tribes rode into headquarters, presenting me with gifts of yaks and sheep. I divided these food animals among our three magistrates for feeding their men, totaling now about 400 (I think) not counting Ho Fa Chung's. In turn I presented each Ngolok chief with silver and gold. As a sign of friendship they then came up with three cased (unsplit) lynx skins which they presented to Solomon Ma, Prince Dorje, and me. We then caused to be signed our official treaty of peace, and Solomon Ma stamped on a large red Chinese chop (seal). The names of these far west Ngolok Khumbos, important chiefs, and their tribes are:— Gunchuk of the Ratsong tribe; Tsewang of the Metsong; Tsamlu of the Khorkhor; Gelakh of the Urchid. It was said they could mobilize five thousand cavalry.

Hassan awoke me one morning before daylight with, "Arise my master, we ride with God!"

But it proved to be a false alarm; walking outside in a freezing air, I saw that snow was tumbling thickly in fast spirals out of a gray-black vault of sky, and the ground already hidden under a white coat six inches deep. The parapets and battlements were thickly frosted, the exterior works and walls caked with new snow on the west side and packed there by the wind. There was no moving out that day. Further delays might mean trouble with the Ngoloks, for it was said some of the minor chiefs were staying out of the treaty. Tan and the others thought this treaty was not worth the paper used, but I think it impressed the Ngoloks and somehow I believed they would allow us to get about the region and do our mapping.

Sure enough, later, about 7 A.M., hundreds of Ngoloks gathered in and around the fort, and were walking about carrying their bifurcated rifles. Swords were stuck conveniently crosswise into their heavily loaded cartridge belts. I soon learned that the old, hair-turbaned monk from Lhasa had been talking and accusing me of reaching Amne Machin. Colonel Ma and I invited the fur-clad lords into the fort, for a breakfast of hot mutton. We were extremely polite, laughing and joking with them, and eventually the tension eased off. Everybody had a good time, and when they left it was with smiles in their eyes as well as on their lips.

Ngoloks were again soon coming and going, busily engaged with last-minute business necessary for our getting three groups cleared for the field. I had persuaded Ma Sheng-lung to create no contentions among these bloody fanatics, but instead actually to take some of them into our parties; their curiosity alone might outlast the enterprise. Men, together with horses, yaks and pack mules, were at last all in complete readiness, and the storm appeared to be slacking off. We were poised to open the gates and ride out, when a sudden message sputtered over the radio—we were to hold up everything, make no further move until ordered to do so by Lanchow.

Sick at heart and sensing possible failure here, we disbanded the mapping parties. All day and far into the night we waited for orders —none came. We couldn't imagine what was wrong. Dawn opened windy, but the snow was gone; our paper windowpanes stretched over the Chinese-style windows blew out with a pop. To a steaming breakfast of yak ribs, came the most distinguished Ngolok khumbos and our three magistrates—Colonel Ma, Tan, and Memamotu, also the more convivial among the Moslem officers (some of whom were

Colonels), a few Tibetans including the magnate, Ho Fa Chung, and the Lhasa men, Lobsang Chiempa and Sor Dörge.

All went well, and when the Ngoloks trooped out, it seemed we still had their support. Memamotu graciously took his leave of all, and gathering together his 200 retainers, rode out with a clank of arms to the far regions south of Tsaring Nor where no Moslem had yet encroached. His camp was somewhere on the northern spurs of his own Bayan Kara Range. Before leaving, he had led Solomon and me aside and said that I must see him later, as our travels would extend in that direction also, and he would prepare our way among the tribes there. I must come in person: he invited me to visit him in his own camp, and we would fill in that white blank on the government's maps. This extension of our theater of operations was received gratefully by me. At last, at noon, the awaited orders arrived from Lanchow. We could proceed with our plans! But, we were urgently warned to hurry:—the political and military situation in China was fast deteriorating, full retreat from north China had begun under Ma-yuan—whose battle losses were great. Chiang Kai-shek was fleeing south China and intending to hole up in Formosa where he banked on getting protection from the Americans. Seven Communist armies under the shock-trooper, the terrible Lin Pao—whose victories had won most of China for the Communists—were driving at the five provinces under Ma Pu-fang, and trying to destroy his three remaining armies. We must hurry and finish our work in Tibet, and return to Lanchow before its fall. Ma Pu-fang himself wished us good luck.

Outside the wind whistled with a wail across the sea, and it was cold. But we could not afford to wait under pressure of the Governor's urgency, and the Ngolok's untimely restlessness:—we must leave, now!

Thus by 8 A.M., all field parties had radiated out from Fort Chakar (designated as Camp 20). The southern group, of which I was a member, skirted for 20 miles the east shore in a southeastward direction, and then after four hours of fast pacing, turned right toward the west, and rounded the southeastern corner of the sea of Oring Nor. We noted promontories of towering stone cliffs along the sea, holding between them both large and small bays. Beyond the shore the lead was wider here in the south, reaching out as far as 200 yards. Fish flecked the blue-black water (its color changed according to the sky) and ducks, geese, and black swans were everywhere in it. The outline of Oring Nor, as one of the men under Tan mapped it that day, proved to be quite different from that shown on any of our maps. We discovered two very small lakes, scarcely larger than big ponds, off the southeast tip of the sea. The easternmost was fairly round in shape, the west one being a horseshoe in outline with points turned north.

Hit by an electrical storm we took refuge with some Ngoloks; this crashing, booming display delayed us an hour, due mainly to the fact that in these high elevations our guns became dangerously electrified. They were too hot to handle; sparks flew off our hands whenever we dared approach the guns. Our bodies crackled with electricity, which actually frightened the horses. Finally we left the guns stacked on a hillside, and took refuge under felt rugs as rain descended. Thunder crashed all about, with thick bolts of jagged lightning flashing over the sea and among the surrounding mountains, setting the whole country off in white glares.

Flocks of frightened ewes, strange tapir-headed sheep having long, thin hooked noses, had lambed earlier in January, February and March. Their lambs were scampering all over the green hills comprising these southern landscapes. Yaks, however, according to the Ngoloks, calve later—in June and July, and so we saw trotting about in alarm only comical herds of short-yearlings, gangly, hairy, lilliputian yaklets.

This party exploring the southern seas said to lie in the regions adjacent to, and far beyond, the south shores of Oring and Tsaring, consisted only of: 30 saddle horses, 6 pack horses; 12 Moslems, 6 Tibetans, 14 Ngoloks, Prince Dorje, Pao Chang-ching (the Chinese radio chief), and myself.

The Moslems were: *

Mohammed (Magistrate Tan Chen-te)	Tungan	Geographer
Ismael (Yang Shu-jung)	Tungan	Soldier
Abdullah (Ma Chen-ming)	Tungan	Soldier
Rogomane (Ma Yi-hsing)	Tungan	Soldier
Kerim (Tang Fu-hsiang)	Tungan	Soldier
Solomon (Ma Hsien-jui)	Tungan	Political
Yunnesi (Colonel Ma Sheng-lung)	Tungan	Security

* Sining Moslems have two names—Moslem and Chinese. They are included here for comparison with the pure Arabic, Turki and other possible sources.

Abdul (Ma Wei-shan)	Salar	Gunner
Abdul (Ma Hu-chen)	Tungan	Radio
Ladjeb (Han Fu-te)	Tungan	Soldier
Ebrahim (Ma Chin-kan)	Tungan	Soldier
Serje (Ma Ying-te)	Salar	Soldier

We camped a mile or so back of the south shore of Oring Nor, at the head of a spongy turf valley. Tibetan flowers, dwarf pinks and China lilies, patched the ground. In these altitudes the pinks (or so they looked to me) grow only an inch high, though the lilies were normal. ·

A rather incredible Tibetan caravan of yaks plodded by the camp in the evening, and halted just beyond—a truly barbaric sight. The caravan which included Ngoloks, was on a 500-mile trip, heading south to a monastery in Kham, laden with salt taken from the saline lakes 5 li north of Fort Chakar. On this cargo of salt, Colonel Ma's tax-collectors were already busy, a typical move for regaining the wealth poured out for services, horses, yaks, and supplies.

The great yak caravan would return in the fall with cargoes of much-needed brick tea, tobacco (shredded like horse hair), crude sugar, silks, iron, cotton goods, rice-paper and ink, brocades, lead and powder, guns, horseshoes, possibly a little Yunnan opium, and any amount of other assorted merchandise. Nearly a thousand yaks were in this great, lumbering, lowing train, truly a rare and magnificent sight.

In them I saw a practical means for supplying, from Pakistan, our Chinese Moslem army undergoing withdrawal into north Tibet: —yak trains shuttling back and forth from the Himalayan passes fronting Ladakh, Bhutan, Assam, Sikkim and Nepal. Tens of thousands of yaks carrying arms and ammunition, electronic material, agents' printing presses, medicinals, agents trained in guerrilla and subversive warfare. Ma Pu-fang received an outline of the plan two hours later by radio. His answer was almost immediate! Gold was available to promote this idea. We were henceforth to expedite this plan. At one o'clock that morning, in a freezing air, I got to bed dog-tired. I knew now my twin hopes of determining the western Amne Machin Range, and mapping the sources of the Yellow River, were practically certain.

17

The Sources of the Yellow River

WE AWOKE at *torang* time, long before dawn, to find four inches of new snow on the ground. Camp 21 was struck and following Colonel Ma we cut up and over the pass notched in the west end of the valley. On the other side in a glowing sunrise we laid our course across a somewhat desolate space, called by our Urchid scout, "The Hills of Death." Colonel Ma snorted in doubt; whether this was the real name, or one intended to keep us out, was anybody's guess. At any rate we continued on our way. Our heads wrapped in scarfs to protect them from the blasts of sand and the cold, bearing westward for an hour, and then twisting southwest till noon, we finally stopped for tea on a spongy steppe of sod. One of the men dug and found drinking water. A cold northwest wind lashed the barrens, considerably punishing us and the horses.

There was no rest to be found here in the open. Blinded with sand from some nearby desert and shivering with the cold we mounted in something like desperation, riding up and down a series of steep hills—the lower south points of a long east-west range obviously paralleling the south shore of icy Oring Nor which could not be far north. At last we dipped down into a wide barren valley known as the "Wild Ass Plains." Though thirsting for lack of water we entered the plain through countless herds of kyang and a few antelope said to be the *orongo*, and fighting sand and wind emerged on the far side, only to climb up and down more ridges lying in the west, slogging across stark ranges of stony hills, finally to climb up and through a pass, seeing even here all kinds of game high up— kyang, gazelle, bear, and wolf. What were called wild dogs howled on all sides, though I never laid eyes on one of them. The sky was dotted with circling vultures keeping pace, as if expecting us to founder as others had done in the past—men whose bones were lying among those of yaks and horses. Colonel Ma thought these were either Mongols or traders who had been attacked. I was beginning to reckon up our chances for a very unpleasant day, when we struggled to the top pass, and looked over.

Ahead of us lakes were gleaming all about, sparkling in the clear frosty air. Which were salty and which were fresh? With my binoculars I at last made out, beyond all the closer lakes, the long, white, sweeping shores of a sea upon which grazed Ngolok sheep and yaks— thousands of them. We spurred on and came to a large stream, and after drinking, followed it doggedly into the southwest. We hoped it would lead us into mysterious Kolanam Nor, which is on the maps (possibly as a result of Mongol reports), but, according to the Moslems, as yet unseen by an explorer. Kolanam was believed by the Ngoloks to be one of the major "sea feeders" of the Machu (Yellow River), pouring its waters into Oring Nor lying north. Gunchuk, of the Ratsong tribe, had told Dorje of another sea in this direction, and of still others beyond, south of Tsaring Nor; and all these we intended our various mapping parties to examine and place on the map. Of course the Moslems knew of many of these places, but had not necessarily pinpointed them on their military maps. By means of dirt and rock dams thrown across the various outlets at its many upper sources—where the greatest amount of water is consistently obtained—the Yellow River could possibly be controlled (or so believed the Moslems), the waters held in seas or else diverted into empty, dammed valleys. Ma Pu-fang could starve north China, or flood it. Besides Oring and Tsaring, Dorje and I had heard of other seas named Dzurgan, Kutsapo, Aolohuchih, Langkoko.

We learned from a wild young Ngolok whom a savage Guanju scout brought in by his long hair, that our river was called the Kulan (Wild Horse). We followed it upstream through a wide, shallow valley of meadowed terrain spotted with gigantic granite boulders rather resembling (as the others suggested) the figures of men, animals, and eggs. After hours of riding through this country, always working into the southwest, we reached the Kolanam Sea. At the outlet the Kulan was judged 25 to 40 feet wide, averaging, according to the Ngoloks, belly-depth for horses, and flowing swiftly over a rocky bed.

A snowstorm struck and we were forced to take partial shelter in a colony of marmot holes. Suddenly, in midafternoon, the storm stopped and the sky cleared as if by high winds, and we saw revealed immense snow peaks and chains of black-ribbed mountains folded along the entire southwest horizon. These mountains could only be the outlying ridges and spurs of the mighty Bayan Kara system which splits the headwaters of the Yangtse and the Yellow rivers; and the sea must therefore lie due north at their foot. According to their main strike, and their structure, these mysterious mountains were entirely separate from the Amne Machin system paralleling them in the northeast, and were of granite instead of the hard pink stone of the latter.

Afoot we struggled along through seepage bogs close up to the outlet of the Kolanam Sea, which we found located at the northeast corner. A large feeder glacial stream apparently entered the sea from the southwest or south; this we must explore later. By the Ngoloks whom we soon found camped near its beautiful but desolate shores, Kolanam was called Kabla Lham Nor. Von Filchner had reported it, but had not actually seen its waters as he stayed east of us and followed the Yellow River downstream after leaving the east coast of Oring Nor. I would have named it for the German explorer, had not this meant a departure from our mapping system. (Throughout all our travels in the unknown regions, I did not name a single geographical feature in Tibet.) Farther in the southwest, Ngoloks said, was a smaller sea called Wangtsang Jum Nor, another major feeder of the Yellow River. Later we were to reach this one and found that it drained into Oring Nor.

One of the Guanju savages came in, a "long-hair" who said we must come with him immediately. Without explanation he wheeled his horse and we jumped aboard ours and followed. He led us up a draw and over a ridge. Beyond lay a tent village of smoky Ngolok black hair tents. I could hear a bugle made from a yak horn being blown. We were looking to our guns when Gelakh—a mighty-thewed, hawk-faced chief dressed in red brocades and wolf robes, who had visited us at Fort Chakar—ran out and led in my horse to the door of his chari. We were made at home and were soon talking with Ngolok headmen.

I now learned that whenever they can, the Chinese have abolished the tribal and monastic organizations in Tibet, and in their place have installed (as here among these Ngoloks) the inefficient old Soong Dynasty "Bao chia" system. There was something sad in knowing that Gelakh and his Urchid tribe were soon to be leveled in the game of international power politics and trade. The old

Ngolok name, obtained with no small difficulty from Gelakh—and confirmed not at all by Colonel Ma who even denied its existence, saying they were "unorganized savages"—is "Uchi," and on examining its structure, Dorje and I saw that it was a much superior organization to the "modern" Chinese one. Later I talked to some missionaries about this, and they disagreed with me, for the Chinese could do no wrong apparently in their eyes. Still, this was my opinion, and I have not altered it. In fact, few of the experts agreed with anything I remarked upon anyway. The chief's tent was erected over low walls of packed dung, and had a large clay stove in the center. Around this we warmed ourselves, and drank sour yak milk from yak bull-horns.

No islands could be found in the sea of Kolanam, though from the snowy hilltops we used binoculars to study its many square miles of green-flaming ice. A legend was told by Gelakh of a yak-shaped island, which had disappeared under the surface of the water only ten years before. Over the sea floated an unbroken ice field. Along the 30-foot shore lead geese and probably swans swam, and fish flashed and flecked their tails in the clearest possible glacier and snow water. At close range, through this dazzling open mirror could be seen a conglomerate bottom of polished rounded stones fit together as cobbles, and over them swam schools of the large goldfish. Mountains soared on snowy wings in the west and south. (The Chinese maps have such names for the western mountains as La-Mato-Kuo-Yin-Wu-La, So-La-Ma-Wu-La, etc.; while those in the south, one of which was estimated at 17,000 feet, were called, Tea-Fo-Yu-Pa-Yen-Ko-La-Ling, La-Ma-To-Lo-Hai Shan, etc.) The Kolanam Sea and its basin was in my eyes an earthly paradise, and it was recorded on our map that day as one of the major seas feeding the main Yellow River.

At Gelakh's invitation Camp 22 was established at 4,325 meters (13,178 feet), in the midst of a second encampment of Urchid tents, located a mile north of the sea and sheltered in some low, green hills. We had been in the saddle that day for nine hours—such saddle times not including stops for observations or rest—and we were stiff from the cold. It was cloudy that night, but still here in the open light at 9 P.M. The days were lengthening and spring was coming fast. I talked to Dorje about the Mongol's Kutsapo Sea, possibly the Ngolok's Wangtsang Jum Nor.

Intrigued by the possibility of discovering another sea (or lake as you please), he immediately arranged that we go still farther south, though Ma Sheng-lung objected on grounds that we had planned to turn north from here. We won him over mainly because Gelakh reported the "Yellow River" (not the main flow out of Oring, but a tributary of the same name) was in flood, and we could not cross. And so our planned thrust between the mighty seas of Oring and Tsaring was ruled out for the time being, and we were able to extend our work south of Kolanam; far beyond where we had even dared hope to get, for it exceeded the geographical limits set by our arrangements with the Ngoloks.

Gelakh after some hesitation agreed to ride along on the first stage, as at least one marauding band was believed operating in the region. One was particularly dangerous, led by a renegade Khorkhor, half jokingly referred to as a vampire. Some Ngoloks believe that a man becomes a vampire when his spirit formerly inhabited a human body that had been buried in the earth, instead of cremated or fed to animals and birds. Colonel Ma, too long away from Chakar's entertainments and intrigues, wanted to return at once to the fort; but, compensated a little that night by the men's singing (to say nothing of the Ngolok women's), consented to string along to Kutsapo, fearful, actually, that he might miss a chance at bagging the notorious robber. He, too, of course, wanted keenly to increase his own knowledge of these domains claimed by the Moslems. It was very frosty that night and we made down our beds early. In my own corner of the tent, I did my studying in spite of snores, and worked late by the light of a candle stuck on an ammunition case. I had a hunch we would find Memamotu somewhere around the rumored sea.

On arising at dawn we departed from the Urchid camp, following Gelakh who was mounted on a fast red horse, and trotted swiftly out on a south course. At first we skirted the green-flashing icy shores of Kolanam. Then after an hour at a fast clip he bent to the right a little westerly, heading away from the west shore and toward the peaks. For two hours we wended our way carefully along north-south ridges of soggy turf that were sub-irrigated by unfrozen waters, picking our way between small, boggy lakes having diameters of only a few hundred yards or less. They were deep, however, as was learned when one of the men slid in, to come up sputtering, his horse striking out for the bank. We safely crossed a long, low, flat ridge hoping for better ground on the west side, and made for a magnificent and titanic range of snow-polished granite, dead south.

The great Bayan Kara (on U. S. Air Force aeronautical chart: Bayen Kola Shah)—and 90 percent unexplored according to the Moslems! I could scarcely wait to touch its stones with my hand. The range was indeed practically unknown to foot travelers except for the old Lhasa Road from Mongolia which crosses it and is said to have been traveled by Kozlov and other explorers. The Moslems believe the name is Mongol, "Bayan Kara" meaning "Flowering, Rich, Black." I was told Tibetans do not usually name mountains unless sacred to them. Only passes through the ranges are named. Nor apparently is Mount Everest of any particular significance to most Tibetans (at least those in the north), being just another of the many high mountains (all of which shelter gods and spirits); but Mount Meru and Amne Machin are indeed very sacred.

Camp 23 was pitched among Ngoloks at an altitude of 4,440 meters (13,529 feet). We eagerly set out on a tour northward, and after some two hours of difficult riding around and jumping over potholes, approached the sea of Kutsapo (Wangtsang Jum Nor). We found it cupped in a broad alluvial valley, a miles-long ice-bound body of purple water, with tents peppered everywhere along its shores. We then turned south and followed the tributary out from the south shore up to near where it tumbles from glaciers and the permanent snow of the Bayan Kara. The outlet of Kutsapo Sea flows north and joins Oring Nor on its southwest corner. As I have noted, there were those among us who believed the damming of such seas could control the Yellow River, and form a most important irrigation project, comparing with the Nile and Colorado systems. In my opinion this was not practical for several reasons, including the best—not sufficient labor.

Memamotu's noisy camp was found in a gorge on the banks of the feeder. Scattered about were perhaps a hundred Ngolok black tents, and a score of white mushroom-shaped Mongol yurts of felt, and two or three of the huge blue flower-tents used by Tibetan aristocracy. 180 Tibetan troops were stationed here, free-lance guns of Memamotu's. Surly outguards led us up to a yurt, which we entered after opening a red-lacquered door decorated with a cloth having a figure of the Dhyani Buddha Vairochana, embraced by his *shakti*, or divine spouse, the Mother of Infinite Space.

Within, this yurt was something of a surprise, being rather luxuriously appointed and furnished, and warmed with a brass brazier.

For the first time I saw sparks of open suspicion fly between Colonel Ma and Memamotu. We were soon talking, and learned that no other seas of any size existed in the south or immediately across the Bayan Kara. Memamotu relaxed somewhat and, calling for our horses, we were soon riding along a new river, the Oroko, flowing north to feed Oring Nor. (In Chinese this would be O-lo-k'o-Ho.) Returning by nightfall—and none too soon, for high winds began moving off the heights of the southward white granite, black-stained peaks—we safely reached camp. Four yurts were assigned to us (audience, mess, radio, soldiers'). In the evening, with the wind beating against our felt shelters, I rode with Dorje to the great black tent of Memamotu, and found him sitting sad-faced before a golden Buddha.

He joined us and we quietly had milk-tea Tibetan churn-style. Apparently the Moslems had left him alone purposely, so that he would lose face with his people. We were soon speaking of religious matters, always the foremost subject to the devout Tibetan. In addition to having traveled to the Asian countries, Europe and America, Memamotu's knowledge of profound Tibetan matters was great.

Next morning at Memamotu's invitation, Dorje and I rode to a still more southward headquarters, finding here his main tents at a valley-head enfolded in the cliffs of the breathtaking granite-canyoned Gala Bon Zon, "Residence of the Chieftain Mountain," which rose almost sheer in the background of the camp for certainly 3,000 feet. His audience tent was a roomy Tibetan yak-hair chari of about 45 by 25 feet; with a 10-foot stone and clay stove in the middle. Hanging over the range were copper kettles. Around the walls were neatly stacked fuel dung, meat in leather pouches, a silver casket, ivory images, bales of furs, cases of ammunition, painted saddles, pack-racks, rich as well as ordinary clothing and coarse sheepskin chupas, packets of salt, bridles, kegs of gunpowder, chests of Tibetan medicines compounded in the medical colleges of the Lhasa district, rich blue carpets from U, a chest of coins including golden louis, Maria Theresa pieces, Spanish gold pesos, English guineas, Dutch florins, even a few ancient Greek coins with the head of Alexander the Great. . . .

A shrine with 108 brass lamps glowed before a golden Buddha backed by stiff tapestries having golden threads. A few jade pieces were also seen. Outside, rising above the tent, was a high mast streaming and snapping with hundreds of prayer-flags, others flying from stays stretched out to the four cardinal points. In a yurt (or *ger*, which I was told is proper Mongol, "yurt" being bastardized Russian) was spread for us what was probably a yellow Maralbashi carpet. About were rare Tibetan books faced and backed in cloth-bound wooden sheafs, all within easy reach of a skin-covered divan. On the wall hung a tiger pelt, another of leopard; good rifles of London workmanship; and a silver-chased, hand-tooled Belgian shotgun; alongside of which were antique *objets d'art*.

Overcome by curiosity, Colonel Ma and Captain Tan galloped into camp riding a pair of newly-purchased stallions bought from raiders returned home from out of the west. The *Depön* (General) Memamotu, Dorje and I, had been sipping thick rose-wine, carving a duck and chucking the scraps to his hounds, laughing, and reading a Tibetan agent's report on a supposedly Pan-Islamic mullah who had recently declared a very localized *jehad* against the Nationalist Chinese and led a pro-Communist insurrection north in Kashgaria; we had also been doing a spot of map work. There was one subject upon which he would not discourse: Amne Machin. Our genial host now rushed out to invite the Moslem officers into the ger and soon, with them seated at the glowing brazier, began royally to entertain by calling in a Kirghiz lutist. This musician finally finished singing a love song through his nose, when who should happen along as if by accident but Solomon.

Memamotu again rushed out and hailed the newcomer as a long-lost brother. On returning Memamotu glanced across in my direction and smiled obliquely, possibly grateful for this opportunity for patching his differences with the all-powerful Tungans: Moslems whom I suspected would not be all-powerful very long unless they utilized Memamotu and through him made their peace with Lhasa.

Prince Dorje had been a very good friend of Henning Haslund, the Danish explorer of Mongolia, only recently (he believed) shot from ambush attempting to get into Tibet from Afghanistan. He now told us an amusing story told him by Haslund of the Swedish-German Hedin expedition to Mongolia and High Tartary—Sinkiang. Given an assignment to measure accurately the distance between

two Turkestan cities, one of the Chinese topographers attached to
the expedition, finished his job in a remarkably short time. Asked
by Haslund, who was also a member, how he had accomplished the
impossible, the Chinese answered condescendingly that he had
counted the telegraph poles strung between the two oasis-cities, measured the distance between two of them, and multiplied.

"Ingenious!" we laughed unanimously, to Dorje's disgust.

We were invited to stay for an early lunch, and accepted with
alacrity for the contrast would be considerable between Memamotu's
table and the primitive food we had known for weeks on our expeditionary *yu-li*.

The *purba* bowls were of polished birch ringed with silver, cups
of old burnished silver, and chopsticks of walrus ivory. Tibetans
maintain connections with the Buddhist tribes of Siberia, and
through them obtain ivory and other Arctic Sea valuables. The
power of Buddha is far-reaching, the secret societies, it was hinted,
even reaching into the very heart of the Soviet Socialist Republics.
Sophisticated Tibetans who have traveled to China, often keep ivory
chopsticks and occasionally serve various Chinese-style chopped
dishes. Food prepared by our host's *machen* (chef), who had once
faithfully followed his master from Tibet into India, and thence to
Europe and Peking, was exceedingly tasty. We particularly delighted
in the reputed baby bees, imported from Yunnan, and fried in honey.
To please our devout Moslems, we were served with *tukash* (I believe it was called), an unleavened Turkish bread.

While chewing on wild duck I learned that Memamotu's status
was actually that of a political exile, a Lhasa nobleman who was a
member of one of the sixty ruling families of Tibet. He had followed the fateful fortunes of the late Panchen Lama, who, he believed, was poisoned. Memamotu was now a religious follower of
the new Panchen Lama's Kumbum clique, which is considered by
both Tibetans and Moslems to be pro-Chinese, and so he claimed to
be ostracized from U and Tsang as a Tibetan turncoat who favored
Chinese conquest of the country—either Nationalist, or, should fate
decree, Communist. However, I rather gathered the Moslems at bottom considered him loyal to Tibet.

He said that bighorn sheep were plentiful in these forbidding
mountains. He believed Tibetan sheep were often killed by wolves,
bears, and snow leopards. However there were few wild yaks due to

the importation of repeating rifles. Scattered over the plains and mountains of Tibet, we had already seen hundreds if not thousands of the enormous white skulls of wild yaks, the fate of the herds written in bone and horn, as was that of the American bison a century ago.

Candied Irkistan melons were brought in; a long-bearded Tarim Turk waited on us, moving silently as a Persian cat in his long, curly-toed, silken slippers. Other servants were Tibetans, and these wore red wool robes and heavy white stone bracelets, while great looped silver earrings hung from their left ears. A big, hairy, vicious "lion dog" from Lhasa was ensconced here—not unlike an Old English sheep dog—and when I heaved his heavy bulk off my foot which was going to sleep, got nipped for my pains. The Tibetans keep many fine breeds of dogs, of which they usually take excellent care, being unique in this respect among Asians. But nearly all these well-kept dogs seem to have a vicious streak in their make-up.

We returned to our own camp that night, and in the early morning—still protected from the rumored Khorkhor robber by Gelakh—we returned north across the valley, and eventually set up Camp 24 five miles east of Kolanam Nor, where we found the camp of our old Lhasa friends, Lobsang Chiempa and Sor Dörge. They had left Fort Chakar and were now bound for the inner provinces, through this morass south of Oring Nor, hoping by the more circuitous route to get away quickly into the far west—as far away as they could manage from the Ngoloks. Possibly due to our treaty the Oring and Tsaring tribes had granted them safe passage, but beyond the valley they could give no guarantee. We were very stiff and cramped, having ridden hard through a thawing semi-swamp for thirty miles, and thence weaving along the outlet of the Kulan River to this place on its squishy sod banks.

Some of my aches disappeared after I had bathed in the icy water of the Kulan and changed my clothes. Our Tibetan friends entertained us in their gorgeous tents with bells tinkling in the breezes. Here we saw tsamba made "hygienically" (observed Sor Dörge) in a queer-looking sheepskin bag. Held in the hands, the small bag, not much bigger than an oversized mitten, magically rolled out sausages of tsamba. It was the only mass-production machine I had seen in Tibet. The one in the British Museum, so our friends informed us, delighted at our wonder, cost the British £100. I didn't openly express my own wonder at this stiff price; but any tsamba bag even rumored to be worth £100 was sure to heighten our interest. The bag is called a *tongu,* meaning "skin-bowl." These veterans of the Tibetan spaces—Tan and Colonel Ma—had never heard of a tongu, and were so intrigued that sausages of tsamba were soon being squirted by the colonel at random all over the tent. When one disappeared down a serving woman's dress, it was certainly high time to get on with other curiosities.

Prince Dorje had stayed on a few days at Memamotu's; the Tibetan intriguer was now a trusted friend of us both. Dorje and he would discuss some various Tibetan customs and other matters of interest. Remaining with Dorje was the Secretary, Chutsu Tsereng, who would escort the prince back to Fort Chakar. The Secretary had given loyal service all the way from Fort Ta Ho Pa up to the very approaches of Amne Machin, and now southwest to the Bayan Kara. I should add, it was he who escorted Major I. Tolstoy during the late war on his splendid journey from Jyekundo to Tangar.* I saw to it before leaving Bayan Kara that Chutsu Tsereng was rewarded for his services, which delighted him, and of course his followers, all top men of many races and religions.

Memamotu had resigned from the Moslem service, and would soon strike his tents and line out for Lhasa; with him would go a message from me to the Dalai Lama. It was my hope that Ma Pu-fang and the Dalai Lama could together somehow find a means for countering the Communist occupation of Tibet; or failing that, could work together clandestinely after full occupation had been carried out. Memamotu assured me that the Dalai Lama was long ago aware of my presence on the Machu. The plan for not only withdrawing the remnant of the Moslem armies into Tibet, before their complete destruction by the Communists, but for supplying them from Indian Moslem bases, had been fully developed. Frankly, though a capitalist without capital, I hate Communism—and, as a citizen of the United States, I saw no valid reason why, in a private capacity, I should not help the anti-Communist forces here to continue their fight. They—the Moslems—would be the only effective armed forces having natural resilience, standing between the Communists and India.

---

* See Tolstoy's article, "Across Tibet From India to China," in *National Geographic Magazine,* August, 1946.

I was squarely in central Asia, knew the possibilities latent there, and was personally acquainted with the basic issues. Ma Pu-fang would turn from the defeated and discredited Nationalists under Chiang Kai-shek, and cooperate with the whole Moslem block of nations westward to the Atlantic—and a militant movement could be initiated by him in Cairo through the entire anti-west Moslem world against Communism, which in their true Moslem hearts they fear.

In Tibet Memamotu would spread rumors among the Ngoloks, and other peoples, that the expedition was returning to Sining and would not make another journey to sacred Amne Machin.

In our Kulan camp the Lhasa men's prayer-flags were planted in a spirit of amusement before our audience tent on a bronze-headed lance shivering with wind-blown tufts of dyed yak tails, and a yellow flag embellished with black Buddhistic characters. That night we gathered in Colonel Ma's flower-tent with our officers and men, together with the Lhasa people and their two beautiful wives. Unlike most women of the Orient, Tibetan women are on an equal social footing with men, and freely mingle in their company. Many travelers have gone out of their way to call Tibet the world's most backward country, and its people the dirtiest. But it is my sober opinion that Tibet is among the most civilized of nations, and, though the poorer classes could certainly use a bit of soap, the inhabitants seemed the most generous, polite, and in every way cultured people, that I had ever seen anywhere. And that goes for Europe and every other region I have traveled in. Missionaries, commercial organizations, politicians, travelers looking for the bizarre, and many others, are responsible for most of the false beliefs held about Tibet, and that is because most of them would like to break down the barriers of the country and install themselves there.

Tan Chen-te brilliantly danced a wild Tungan sword dance, and afterwards when all was quiet, we leaned back contentedly, while the two *Cham-kushos* (Lady Excellencies) charmingly sang and danced for our entertainment.

That irrepressible extrovert, Colonel Ma, was not long in crowing about his own prowess in the Tibetan dance, and soon was grandly flourishing his golden toothpick while dancing a saga called (according to him) "Inexperienced Young Hunter and Wise Old Bear." It was the funniest performance imaginable, for the burly Ma surprisingly was an artist, and by the time he had finished with the expression of the happy old bear lopping over the horizon, Solomon and I were rolling in the aisles, so to speak.

"God's peace! I was not that good!" bellowed Colonel Ma with a black glare, "And now—Clark-ah must do a Tibetan dance. . . ."

Not all the dogs were Christian infidels, I wanted very much to tell him. Well—I did a Tibetan dance, "The Wooing of the Tiger and the Unhappy Monkey."

Everyone was most considerate and grave throughout this horrible dance, but I thought Colonel Ma would have a spasm and expire on the spot as he rolled over his saddle rug, and it finally became necessary for Abdulla to assist him back to his divan, from whence he had rolled with such unseemly mirth.

"It wasn't as bad as all that," I told him when I had given the monkey the *coup de grâce*, which sent him rolling off his couch again—"May the Good God bless you, even if you are an unbeliever!" he finally managed to gasp out.

I was soon dozing from the fatigue of our long ride, and finally retired to my own tent though the others stayed on, singing and dancing.

18

Oring Nor's Ice Pack Breaks Up

IT WAS not yet daylight when I wakened from the cold.
The sounds of singing told me the party over at Colonel Ma's was still going on. I dressed and walked against a stiff wind over to the big tent and was soon talking with Solomon and Lobsang Chiempa, about Dorje's recent findings of an ancient pre-Buddhist "White" cult. The Tibetan added but little to our knowledge, and that apparently with no great enthusiasm. However, he did admit its existence, though puzzled and curious about how we had learned of it in this largely secretive theocratic empire. He was not long in changing the subject to certain deposits of gold, thinking that gold was the one subject always fascinating to the foreigner. In this news of gold deposits Solomon in particular was interested, as it was already being mined throughout Chinghai on a contract basis, miners working for a licensed labor-contractor who in turn was legally obliged to turn his gold into the Moslem forts for supplies. Tens of millions of dollars worth of the yellow metal was being recovered annually. It was this gold that was financing our hypothetical scheme for supplying the retreating army.

Nor would Lobsang Chiempa discuss for long "Pönpo" ("Black Cult") magic. First—for clarification of the religions and sects—there are the two major churches: Seima of the Panchen Rim-poche; Ngongma of the Tsogchen Rim-poche. Then follows the unknown White Sect; and in addition, Pön—making four in all. The Pön followers pronounce the six sacred syllables backwards—thus "Om Mani Padme Hum," becomes in the mouths of the Black Bones priests, "Hum-Me-Pad-Ni-Ma-Om." All their sacred texts and canons on magic are read backwards. The Pöns worship the "Main Wheel," and the mystic symbolic ideas behind "Black Bones Magic": they harm their clients' enemies but bear no witness; they cause rain to fall or to stop; and they can control temperatures; their priests may levitate in air as ordinary men do in water. All this is what Lobsang Chiempa believed to be true.

As to further details supplied by our Tibetan friend:

When clouds are present, the Pön priests will mix skimmed milk and tsamba together, which they wrap in a sacred written formula, and bury in the earth. Rain begins to fall soon after. A lama oracle of Derghlet *gompa*, well-versed in scriptures, is able to show "hell and heaven" visually to his audience of monks or of laymen. Secret drugs are known to Tibetan holy men, especially to *geshe*, of whom there are a hundred such medical professors in Tibet; but this "vision" is not induced by the use of drugs. Our companion conceded it may be mental, autosuggestion, or mesmerism. It definitely exists, whether physical or spiritual. The worldly Lobsang Chiempa believed that the "Black" priests practice the dread *chöd* ("walk of the dead"), and have communications with the spirits of the dead on the "Bardo plane" soon after death and following for 49 days: many such things he had seen and heard. He knew of a lama who had spent 38 years on a single experiment, and who had traced back through his memory, delving into the subconscious mind in the deepest of meditations, five human reincarnations. These births had been steadily upward toward enlightenment, though incarnations go downward also into lower forms of life such as animals over eons of time. All this of course follows the West's more or less proved theory of evolution, and that every effect must have a cause, every cause must have an idea, and every idea must have a will:—and so back to to Primitive First Cause.

Dawn began lighting the eastern horizon when Lobsang Chiempa finally summed up thus:

"Some people can breed fine horses. Some people can visualize and assemble an automobile. And some people can do these mystical things. Again, a truly great painter or musician can do both—he draws on the physical and on the spiritual."

Swiftly we struck camp on the double, and at 5:10, bade goodbye to our good Lhasa friends and their wives, and turned our horses toward Fort Chakar. The bleak Wild Ass Plains were safely crossed in a freezing wind that was perishingly cold. For hours we reined to left and right through potholed turf beyond, dodging holes filled with ice and water, and then rode through tang country of yellow sand dunes that melted in the wind before our eyes, half-blinding us. Once one of the horses suddenly balked, refusing for a few moments to continue; the Ngolok riding him became frightened, believing the animal had seen a ghost. We actually had to back-track and circle this place. All Tibetans, even the wild Horpa tribes northeast of Lhasa, and the Gya-de tribes east of us, are convinced that horses have this instinctive gift; they watch them constantly for indications of ghosts and "idea spirits," so that propitiation may be made at the next wayside *gyatse*. It is just one of those things the traveler must contend with. Arguments will avail him nothing but ridicule and desertions.

Later we found before us hundreds of frozen and unfrozen lakes and ponds, all flashing in the sun: such bodies of water, if salty, are easy to determine from a distance as they do not freeze over except in very low temperatures. Green pebbles paved the ridges to the north, and over these latter we climbed, headed east. There was much game that day, including a gigantic mastiff—probably a Ngolok outcast—which Colonel Ma and I took to be a bear, and both shot at. The range was excessive, about 500 yards. When we missed by quite a few feet, the sand popping around it in little jets, and the dog streaking out across a hillside, we could see what it was; our faces were completely gone for the rest of that day. Each laughingly accused the other of yelling "bear!" first, and of shooting first; but I think it was about an even break.

After ten fast, dreary hours in the saddle, we approached Fort Chakar, only to run into one of the few really trying experiences of the whole expedition. While yet a few miles south, we were suddenly struck by a windstorm from the west. The force of the wind rose steadily until it ranged past at a velocity of perhaps seventy miles an hour. Dust, snow, and chunks of ice sliced sideways into us, stinging our faces. Even with goggles I could not keep my eyes open for more than a few seconds at a time. We froze. It was the worst storm we had yet encountered in this land of what may well be the world's worst winds. The sea-ice began ponderously moving and then all at once, with terrific grinding sounds, as if the world were disintegrating and about to come apart, the ice-fields began piling up right under us to our left. We were riding along the crest of a cliff when it hit. Ice fields miles long broke asunder with a rending screech under the wind's pressure. At moments we were completely deaf.

Wide leads suddenly opened out from shore—the thin, cold air filled with noises as if heralding doom itself—splitting straight out as far as we could see for miles into the haze suspended in streaks over

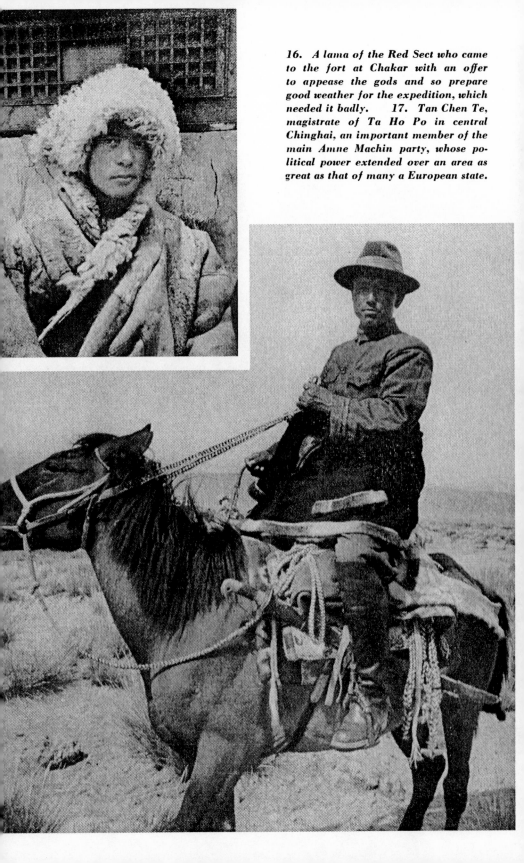

16. *A lama of the Red Sect who came to the fort at Chakar with an offer to appease the gods and so prepare good weather for the expedition, which needed it badly.* 17. *Tan Chen Te, magistrate of Ta Ho Po in central Chinghai, an important member of the main Amne Machin party, whose political power extended over an area as great as that of many a European state.*

18. *The head lama of the Panchen Lama temple at Tsaidam, a jolly old man who royally entertained the expedition.* 19. *One of the expedition's Tibetan sharpshooters, showing how the rifles were steadied against the two-prong rests: these men seldom missed their mark.* 20. *Ma Wei Shan, former bodyguard of Ma Pu-fang's son Ma Yuan, shown plotting our course to Amne Machin from the camp south of Ta Ho Po.* 21. *A friendly Ngolok chieftain of the Oring-Tsaring area west of Amne Machin, who presented welcome gifts of yaks and sheep. Behind him lies ice-covered Oring Nor.* 22. *A Tibetan scout resting on the way to Amne Machin: he is happily carving up gazelle and wild sheep meat, which he will eat raw.* 23. *Moslem radio crew of the expedition, detached for this work from the northwest Chinese Nationalist armies seeking a safe retreat in [northeast] Tibet.*

24. *A surveying party taking observations on Amne Machin from a point 25 miles away: explorer Leonard Clark is on the right.* 25. *Part of an armed escort near a Tibetan obo. Prince Dorje is on the white horse second from the left; on his left are Solomon Ma and Ma Sheng-lung: all important members of the party.*

26. *The party on the north side of Amne Machin peak, the main peak lying behind the long ridge. This photograph was taken at very close range. The man in black coat and glasses at right is Solomon Ma.*

27. *Ngoloks camped at the foot of Amne Machin, with their herds, and prayer flags raised above the tent. The man seated is a lama.*

28. *A striking view through the Kuder Hills east of Tsaidam Swamp, showing camel train of the expedition under close guard because of robbers in the area.* 29. *An elaborate Tibetan obo perched atop Tsebagase Mountain midway between Oring and Tsaring Seas. The man is Tan Chen Te.* 30. *Armed Moslem escort crossing the headwaters of the Yellow River south of the rugged Amne Machin range.*

31. Ma Sheng Lung, magistrate of South Chinghai and one of the important men on the expedition. He is shown with a hunter's bag of gazelles, whose throats are cut to make them fit for Moslem consumption. 32. A group of Ngolok chiefs from Oring Nor, south of Amne Machin. Usually hostile to all explorer's parties, these Ngoloks were friendly, bringing welcome gifts of yaks and sheep.

the turbulent sea. The whole field of sea-ice for fifteen miles west, was physically shoved relentlessly toward us, over enormous boulders twenty feet above the water and shore line. Boulders weighing tons were wrenched off the cliffs, and these smashed down on the ice below. At one place we were blinded with sand and hail, and our horses, frightened by these forces of nature, scattered—some of them bolting as horses sometimes do in a fire.

A whole tent village of the Ngoloks flew away under the wind's fury, herds of yaks and sheep were scattered and running in every direction over the hills, only a few being driven into gullies by their herders, who were waving their cloaks in desperation. Many of the Ngoloks simply threw themselves on the ground and hugged mother earth, their prayers lost in the wind. Colonel Ma, Captain Tan and I finally rounded up our scattering party, and drove it ahead at the trot with whips falling on reluctant animals. It did no good to yell threats or warnings, for not the slightest sounds came from our lips —so loud was the roaring of the wind and the breaking of the ice. Typhoons experienced during fourteen crossings of the Pacific seemed as breezes compared to this upland cataclysm of the elements.

We made our way north, however, and an hour later somehow reached the gates of the fort. Even the sentries had left their protected posts to escape the fury. When the bars were at last thrown down, we rode into the compound, I for one grateful to be still among the living. For an hour we remained half-blinded in our rooms; our nostrils and mouths gritty with sand, our faces and limbs cold and stiff. I had frozen the left half of my face, but by carefully warming it, and moving the hard skin gently for two hours, I brought back the circulation. Tan wanted to rub snow on it, but I would not allow any such foolishness. Apparently the Arctic is not the only place in the world where this old woman's remedy exists.

Some bad news awaited us. One of the mapping groups in the northeast had been ambushed and all its horses stolen. Riders had been sent out to bring them in.

Having—due to rivers in spate—failed in part to reach the region between the two seas of Oring and Tsaring, we at once began preparations for a ride north around Oring Nor (the sea on which Chakar was located), hoping to be more successful from this direction. These were the two great seas referred to by the bombom, Jatm, in the Ngolok tent below Wambu Gunga pass which we had crossed after leaving Camp 19 on the Yellow River. Further, the north side of the eastern sea, Oring, had not been mapped as part of this was a section of the region allotted to the party which had lost its horses. After reaching the area between these two great seas, and mapping it, we would return to the main Yellow River spillway out of Oring Nor, reunite with our whole party—new mercenary Tibetans and mostly all new Moslems from the garrison—and start across the unknown midway junction lying between Amne Machin Peak and the Kun Lun, hoping to come out at the eastern end of the Tsaidam Swamp. We expected Dorje in soon; and would not leave for the north for a few days, as I wished to take him along. Another mapping party sent southeast had returned safely and the work in this direction declared complete.

Next afternoon the wind returned. Fascinated, we watched the display of these natural forces, and the annual break-up of the Oring sea-ice, by establishing ourselves on the headland below the fort:—the high winds began twisting the pack this way and that, opening and closing the leads at will, breaking and grinding down the fields to floes and brash.

This was not the controlled power of an explosion, it was nature gone wild. The Tibetans believe that the earth was conceived in a "fire mist," and that from its whirling atoms all matter, life, ideas and instincts, have come; here at Oring Nor, one of them pointed out that some day the earth would disintegrate in a like manner, its parts eventually reforming to start all over again in space. Some of our faces became gray with just watching, feeling, and hearing it; and I think the first real fear on the expedition was felt by many of us then, not because of any physical danger that might overtake us —for we could escape to the stone walls of the fort—but the fear of the apeman when saber-toothed tigers roamed the earth, the fear coming from realization of our absolute human helplessness before the powers of space.

Even so, preparations continued in the shelter of the fort for sending out the last mapping party north and west between the seas. For myself, I now intended leading this detachment to a point midway between the Oring (the eastern on which we were based) and the Tsaring (lying west of it) seas, and mapping the area. As said before, while the Ngoloks apparently reverse the names of these two great seas, for our purposes I have retained the names used on the world's maps. There should be no confusion here. This meant we would have to follow the coast of Oring Nor in a northwest direction, and ford the flooded headwaters of the Yellow River where it spilled from Oring Nor on its tortuous way across China to the Pacific Ocean. Then we would swing west along the shore, and finally bend south to a mountain reported formerly to Dorje by Gunchuk, the Ratsong chief, to rise high between the seas.

More yaks must be brought in for the great Tsaidam trek: new yaks and new horses, and also some of those Ngolok mules said to have been raided from caravans the previous fall. The old train of which Dorje, Solomon and I had been so proud and careful, was virtually destroyed; except for a few of the stronger riding horses, it was a wreck. Verification came after much haggling with the Ngoloks, that those few yaks and horses still remaining sound would be kept on at Oring Nor during the coming summer months to feed and rest. Some Ngoloks with Moslems would then attempt to drive them north to the Ta Ho Pa Tibetan tribes in the early fall before winter set in. The labor with heavy packs on the hurried way from Kumbum and Fort Ta Ho Pa; the strain of climbing steep, icy passes; the poor, late-winter grass; the freezing winds and storms; the depredations of wolves and robbers; the bogs and salty drinking water; our slaughtering of them for food; the heart-straining elevations encountered week after week with no respite—each had taken its toll. As for the personnel, most of the original men also badly needed a recuperative period, as well as morale rehabilitation. The majority must be left behind, and fresh Chakar garrison troops eager for adventure would fill their places. Guanju was lending us a few scouts, as trouble was anticipated from the northern Ngoloks unknown to me and possibly (I could never learn for sure) even to the Moslems.

One day, suddenly, when the air was breathtakingly cold and still, another windstorm broke loose, sweeping banks of clouds in from the misty heart of the western solitudes, where they streamed in across the wrecked Oring Sea. The clouds rushed in fast, tearing themselves on the gleaming peaks of far-distant snow ranges silhouetted against a cold, metallic, rain-washed sky; the booming open ice-leads of the shattered sea began suddenly to flash an eerie, phantasmal, fiery-green flame, while the yet unbroken floes and the finer brash became sparkplugs radiating a dazzling ice-fire of white, blue, red.

At this time several strange bomboms from Lhasa, and other various categories of magicians, soothsayers, and monks, rushed importantly into the fort where I had taken refuge from the wind. They handed Solomon and me the customary blue gauzy-silken hadak. We presented each with a scarf, which was received in the Tibetan manner across outstretched hands; and also to them went gifts of medicines. The novelty of these last, and especially the idea that such a queer looking fellow as myself knew anything of medicine, delighted them no end. As a *geshe* among the Ngoloks, I had already become known for the size of my bandages and the bitterness of my pills. Everybody in Tibet knows medicine is not effective unless it tastes bad; and so mine (I probably should say Dorje's) were spiced with bitter Chinese compounds. I was in turn presented with various concoctions, one being a "love potion," all of which—including those compounds likely to be poison—were carefully wrapped by our medico and his helper and labeled for later study. I had about as much use for a "love potion" as an Eskimo for an icebox, and this aphrodisiac was likewise filed for research.

We showed the holy men illustrations from a recent copy of the little-known Tibetan account (printed in Lisbon in 1626) of the Portuguese priest, Antonio de Andrada (1580-1634)—one of the world's greatest adventurers—who was the first European in Tibet: the priests were delighted, pointing out that the costumes of that day were so far as they could tell practically identical with those in use today. Whether these were from originals I do not know.

Our radio informed us that Governor Ma Pu-fang was now, officially, Chinese *Tupan*—Commander-in-Chief for China and her "dependencies." This meant—to me at least—that a "goat" had been chosen by the Nationalists for the inevitable fall of the provinces of Chinghai, Kansu, Ninghsia, Sinkiang, Chahar; of North and Northeast Tibet, Inner Mongolia all the way east to Manchuria, Turkestan, all the provinces of northwest China—a vast empire possibly as large as the United States, now suddenly placed under the Crescent of the Prophet. My original deduction that Ma Pu-fang was the natural eastern hinge of world Islam had been justified. This Nationalist ultimatum, however, automatically made Governor Ma—a man almost unknown in Europe and America (which had a

Chiang Kai-shek fixation)—the prime target for Communism in Asia. Hence his great peril, and my fear that his ultimate defeat in China was certain; a fear based on a close study of the radioed situation and the order-of-battle on both sides, and on due consideration of the political, economic, and morale factors involved.

On our exploration work alone now depended whether all China's bases and its armies would be lost on the mainland. Many of the Moslem leaders, and particularly Ma Pu-fang, were on the Red "Death List." And so we continued planning—our long-range view being to save as much of the cream of the fighting men as possible. It was apparent that thousands must be sacrificed deliberately to save these others; and during the last four days before the fall of Lanchow, 8,000 Moslems died bravely while their comrades got safely away into Tibet. We schemed to save at least 30,000 mounted infantry, to transport them into Tibet, to feed and supply them—for eventual underground use against the Reds again.

At one of the tents pitched inside the outer wall, Ma Sheng-lung presented Dorje (who had returned), Solomon and me each with a silver-tipped bearskin robe for the trip west. Also pairs of felt-lined Lhasa boots having black and red wool sides embellished with blue and white maltese crosses. I lost no time pulling mine on, for they looked warm, if gaudy. As the colonel scratched his shaved head, with a pleased look spreading over his big red face, he grunted contentedly and passed over pieces of sizzling liver which he speared with an old bayonet off the coals of the brazier. I took a book out of my robe and with Solomon's help read aloud to him Dorje's Chinese-English *Arabian Nights*. These old stories seemed fitting to our own 20th-century travels. They delighted Ma, especially those not generally circulated in English because of their outrageous risquéness. He especially liked the naughty one approximately en-titled: "The Beautiful Princess and the Affair of the Keyhole." This bawdy tale of what can happen when a woman is not trusted, but is penned up as most Moslems pen up theirs, sent him into howls of laughter; he held his sides and rolled around on the tent's carpets, scattering pots and soldiers every which way, and squealing with joy, finally catching his breath and bellowing—

"May the good Lord preserve me!"

Colonel Ma then gathered us all nearer—Dorje, Solomon Ma, and all the other officer Mas—to tell delightful Tungan stories that matched Scheherezade's for ribaldry; and, like that talkative lady's, they had no ending, each being an anticlimax reminding him of a new one. He would roar for all Oring Nor to hear, but with a stamp of exaggerated modesty on his gleaming face:—"Now, friends! You take Aladdin . . . there was a boy! Ho Ho! God's teeth!" He would clear his throat, narrowing his eyes on us as if he thought we were not sufficiently overcome with delight at what was in the offing.

He apparently was not always pleased with what he saw on our faces, for he would scowl and sulk like a primadonna, pull out the gold toothpick, and lapse into silence. He had taken to wearing a dilapidated old European felt hat, a most jarring object when worn with Tibetan boots and a velvet robe, and this he would either jam down on his ears or fling across the tent. But bursting to tell his story he would finally get on with it, and after a few flourishes at his enormous gold teeth (said to be gold caps on good teeth!), he would condescend to proceed: "Now, there was a boy! . . . that Aladdin!" His head would wag mightily, his whip would lash out at a nodding soldier, "But! . . . I, Yunnesi!—Ma Sheng-lung!—when a mere boy!" Here he would roll his eyes toward the top of the tent as if hoping to read an idea there, "Did, once!—find a more precious treasure! . . ."

Even Prince Dorje would raise his nose out of his work, usually some old Tantric manuscript, or his dog-eared copy of Goethe's *Faust*. But all of Colonel Ma's treasure hunts always ended up with one of his numerous enemies getting away with the swag, and he, himself, getting lost among the silken curtains of some narrow-minded potentate's harem.

The day arrived when our preparations were concluded, our stories exhausted; there was nothing left but to get back to work!—the Tsaring Nor mapping section wound up its last-minute affairs.

I would next see Colonel Ma and the main Tsaidam expedition at the Yellow River spillway up north. Tan and I, together with Solomon Ma and Prince Dorje, planned to evacuate the fort before dawn of the day following, and would try to reach Gunchuk's mountain in a single day—100 li (50 miles). A temporary arrangement with the nomadic Ratsong tribe had been worked out, and couriers were out notifying all the clans in this western region of our coming.

19

Exploring Two Seas

IN THE COLD semi-darkness of dawn, the Tsaring Sea party streamed out of Fort Chakar to the beat of hooves. Once clear of the gates, we found ourselves marching against a quartering gale on our left while following the northwest slant of the coast of Oring Nor, soon passing around wide-sweeping, desolate bays. Below the cliffs, the pack-ice, which had frozen tight since the great storm, was grinding together under pressure of the night wind, and sending up a considerable racket. The sky gradually changed over from a dark blue to a hazy lapis as the sun's rays shot upward over the Amne Machin Range, lying unseen in the east.

Rocky headlands had to be traversed above the sea, where we picked our way through cautiously. Travel in Tibet can hardly ever be compared to pottering about on a bridlepath, but this place was more in keeping with tradition. We followed a Ngolok path, slippery with ice, strung between and along cliffs that sometimes fell away into the sea below, and the wind continued. We shivered even in our thick sheepskin robes. My legs and feet soon felt wooden with the tense cold.

Some of the bays had rock, sand, or pebble beaches, which as we rode along became plainly visible in the dawn; but the going continued rough, the beaches often being gouged by blocks of ice pushing relentlessly, sliding inland with the power of bulldozers. Full daylight at last broke when we had nearly reached the northeast corner of the sea. In a silvery mist, incandescent as a frosted electric light globe, we passed a salt lake on our right, where Ngoloks by the hundreds were already collecting salt off the white crust lying over the water's surface. A larger lake was passed still farther north, just over a hill. These two lakes supply salt to west China, through southeast Tibet, now called Sikang (sometimes Sikong).

Black, snow-streaked stone ranges were now streaming diagonally northward, lying off Oring Nor's northeast "corner"; these mighty ranges were separate from the main Amne Machin Range and were called by our Ngolok scouts, "Amne Kor." The name will be found on no existing maps. Von Filchner crossed east of them till he hit the Yellow River (while he was going south from Sining) and then followed it up to the outlet, from where he went down the east coast of Oring Nor. The Amne Kor rise to over 16,000 feet and are named on Chinese maps the A-Mu-Na-K'u-La Ling. On the far side, in a northeast direction would lie our old Black Sea (estimated at 45 miles airline).

Any extension of Amne Machin Range through this junction between Amne Machin Peak and the mighty Kun Luns is marked variously on the world's maps as "Ugutu Mountains," "Ha-La-Chai-Shan," "Burchan Buddha," "Marco Polo Geb," "Amnyi Machen," "Amne Matschin." . . . The range is called in Tibet by no other name but "Amne Kor." This mighty stone structure had a definite strike of southeast-to-northwest, offset to the east by several miles, but generally following parallel with the slanted east coast of Oring Nor.

At the northeast tip of Oring Nor, through a well-defined channel cut through a gravel beach, on a 90°-angle corner of the sea, there flows easterly, across a broad plain bordered on the south bank by low hills, the mighty Yellow River. We forded our horses across its hard gravel bottom. The water was clear, cold, and as sweet to the taste as spring water. It was 45 feet wide at the spillway, the very narrowest part, where the current was too swift and deep for our horses to ford safely. We had no trouble crossing the outlet 200 yards below, at a place 200 feet wide. Fish—big goldfish—jumped in the mouth of the Yellow River.

A hundred yards to the west, resting on the sea, was the ice-pack, its leading edge composed of a dazzling green ice, now, quite incredibly, rotting under the sun's terrific impact in this rarefied and dry air. Strangely, even during daytime on the Tibetan tableland, you can practically freeze one of your hands if you hold it in the shade, while at the same time the other hand will become sunburned if you expose it to the sun. Geese and Mandarin ducks nested on the meadow. Herds of gazelles and kyang grazed unconcerned. These last shook out their tails and raised their heads to stare at us a few moments as we closed the distance, before herding together and moving off across the wide *tang* desert-plain of sand just north toward Amne Kor.

We measured at various places the speed and depths of the Yellow River, and then reined into the west, hugging the north shore of the sea which was a jumble of icy blocks. We steadied on a compass point varying between west and southwest. Two hours beyond the Yellow River we pulled up to rest the horses, which had been pacing almost steadily since leaving Fort Chakar. At this time a drenching rain sluiced down from the gray sky, our first of the trip, then turned suddenly into hail. Driven hard before a wind, came curtains of silvery hail with the sun full upon it; when the icy storm hit us we shivered with the cold, and, being caught in the open, mounted and rode on. So furious were the blasts of wind that the horses quartered away from it, for the ice-stones stung them badly. This icy blast was followed abruptly by a session of burning sun, and then terrific heat for us who were bundled in furs, which brought out steam in spiraling clouds off the turf of these high, barren, northern hills. All this country was fascinating and, in a storm setting, strangely dramatic. In the northwest, behind the north-south hills running down into Oring Sea, could be glimpsed white peaks, hiding we knew not what. Tan said snow was always on their summits. The army map carried the name Meng-Ko-Cha-Su-T'u-Wu-La. Directly north of Oring Nor were two peaks estimated at approximately 17,000 feet, in a range called Ha-La-Chai Shan. Such peaks, of course, were higher than any in the Alps. The peaks themselves, according to our companions, have no names.

After only a few minutes respite, cold weather again settled down along the coast. We found some scattered wild kyang dung, and after a few attempts with frosted fingers finally got a fire started in the lee of an obo. This belonged to the migrant Ratsong tribe. Its warriors sometimes killed strangers on sight (said one of the Moslems) and even other Ngoloks. All this talk of killing struck me as overemphasized since we had been only worried by a few horse thieves to date. But for the moment we had other worries—we were simply *freezing*, the temperature had dropped to −13° C.!

As was customary, we had left the fort without eating, and were hungry, and so against the foot of the stone obo we dumped out a leather bag of raw, cold ribs and chunks of meat. While carving away on this, and eating, the temperature warmed and it began raining again. Then as suddenly the rain froze in midair into hailstones, a high wind sending us into fits of shivering: our hands and faces turning blue within a matter of minutes. The wind's fury increased in step with its velocity and began rending the sea-ice lying off a hundred yards on our south side, sending up grinding noises that echoed against the blue-black slate cliffs just below. Not long after the sun burst out again, and we were being blistered. We were soon shedding our sheepskins. This sun quickly burned off the skim of white hail covering the ground, the moisture ascending swiftly to the skies in twisting streamers.

But the hot weather did not last long. During a short, violent and cold storm-flurry—in a freezing mist—I was forced to remove my sunglasses as their metal rims "burned" my cheekbones and irritated my frostbites. Without their protection I was blinded in a wind filled with flying crystals; but the batlike Guanjus—after stomping out the coals—led us through the driving mist, forward along the rims of cliffs above the sea, calling out warnings whenever someone wandered too close toward the brink. All this north side of Oring was fairly straight, with no bays at all, though we rode along cliffs descending sheer to the water and ice—usually 100 to 200 feet below. Nor were any new islands seen along this coast either.

Swarms of insects, loosened by the first spring heats, came out—strangely, no mosquitoes; but plenty of ants, common houseflies, and spiders. Black gnats bothered the horses, buzzing and stinging as they apparently laid their egg hatches in the animals' nostrils. The horses swished their tails, for we had to let out the knots; champed their bits, tossed their heads and the reins, stomped their hooves and whinnied nervously. But all this did little good; the gnats and flies swarmed around in clouds.

Pale-greenish leads were opening in the sea's ice-fields; in these narrow stretches of open water, fish flashed gold and silver, and waterfowl—mostly geese and duck—played and fed to a strange medley of hisses and quacking. Later as we marched during another short but violent storm, electric displays accompanied by thunder, which incredibly followed all these other atmospheric disturbances, were flashing all around. At the moment we were riding along a narrow sand dyke separating by a few hundred yards a small lake from the main body of the sea: Oring Nor was a deep royal purple on our left, while the small inland lake—about two miles long—was a bright sea-green on our right. Each body of water flashed its completely different color at us, in a fantastic manner suggestive of flames running over water.

Tan and I asked Gunchi, the chief scout, what caused this, and he answered, "Lords, the Gods are watching us and making the way very beautiful."

But not all was beautiful; for in a few minutes, Gunchi reined aside and pointed to a ridge. On its crest were a hundred horsemen, standing silently and watching us. As we must pass within a hundred yards of their rifles, Tan said:

"We must retreat back to the Yellow River."

"Wait," I answered as he reined around, "Let us try a little farther."

Before he could object, I went forward, the whole party following, and continued along Oring Nor's icy shore. Soon we turned around a sharp corner—the northwest corner of the sea—riding over crunchy gravel banks into the southwest. We passed directly under the horsemen and were soon riding along a coast formed of deep bays with massive stone headlands. Two hours later we finally crossed several hills lying inland, and safely reached a point directly west of Fort Chakar, which—with difficulty owing to the distance—we picked up in our glasses across the shattered ice. We were now halfway down the west shore of Oring Nor! The first stage of our mission was accomplished.

After 10½ hours in the saddle we pitched Camp 25 on an open plain at 5:45 P.M. There was no use trying to hide, as Ratsongs were seen on the northern hills a mile above. We were located midway between Oring Nor and an isolated small mountain having two peaks, one standing erect at each end of a long, sagging snow-saddle. The summit of this mountain was our immediate objective. From it the whole of the west country would be revealed as on a contour map. Hail, snow, thunder and lightning burst upon camp most of that night, and my tent (shared with Solomon and Dorje) was flattened on the ground by the wind's impact.

We were so tired, wet, and beaten down, that we didn't even get out of our beds to raise the tent, but lay under the sodden canvas which flopped about over us, though we were warm enough and anything but short of air. Dorje and I almost prevailed upon Solomon, who couldn't sleep either because of the racket and weight, to get out of his warm bed and fix the tent's poles, but at first he couldn't find his glasses in the darkness, and when we located them for him he became wide awake and of course, changed his mind.

Why should he do all the work out in the freezing wind while we lay in our beds and directed him?

"Because you, Solomon, are much stronger than we," said Dorje.

"Yes, and your skill is greater," I added.

We almost had him on the move, but not quite. We finally gave up arguing; so to hell with it, let her blow and be damned.

Next morning in the dawn's cold gloaming, Tan Chen-te came running over, his boots crunching in several inches of new snow, exclaiming:

"The Lord's mercy on them. They are frozen to death!"

Foul creatures, we lay quietly, snickering under our wrecked tent, wondering what would happen. The Tibetans, Moslems, and Ngoloks rushed around outside with what sounded like considerable cries of concern, and when the tent was finally raised off us, and Tan saw our grins, I really thought he was going to blow his black Tungan version of a fez. He actually looked worried, and my heart softened toward him a bit. Dorje, however, pointed out that he was probably only concerned about what to do with our bodies, since as the ground was frozen hard and he couldn't possibly have buried us, bad luck might have visited him. But for all Tan's cynicism, the expression on his taut face proved that he was not such a bad fellow after all.

With dawn breaking out of a yellow sky, we crawled out, dressed and saddled up; and as the scouts of the strangers made no move toward us, we were soon trotting across the plain toward the white mountain. Riding through bands of orongo antelope, I studied it for an easy way up; it was steep and frosty—snow- and ice-sheathed all the way from its base to the tips of the twin peaks. It was called by our Ratsongs—"Tsebagase," which means, "Mountain God Between the Two Seas."

Now all our half-dozen men in this party were top riders, and our horses trained in mountain climbing. Still riding, we began quartering the stomach of the god, a slippery, rocky slope, and after many panting halts, during which we and our mounts breathed in jets of steam, finally climbed up to the rocky pinnacle jutting on the far side—the Tsaring Nor west side. Our altitude in camp had been 4,485 meters (13,666 feet), and was now more than 15,200 feet. We had climbed about 1,500 feet above camp. Tibet lay like a map unrolled at our feet; we were halfway down the narrow neck separating Oring Nor (lying in the east) from Tsaring Nor (in the west) . . . quite possibly, in their way, among the most beautiful seas on earth.

Tsaring Nor, according to my pocket compass, was lying a little north of west; and was the higher in elevation of the two great seas, its waters supplying the main Yellow River by flowing eastward first into Oring Nor. Tsaring was ringed by rather high mountains, clifflike in places, and snow-covered—completely majestic. Since to my knowledge they have no names in European languages, the Chinese ones will have to suffice. To the north, lying east and west, rose the Meng-Ko-Cha-Su-T'u-Wu-La; to the west, and extending north and south, the So-Lo-Ma-Wu-La; immediately to the south, the Kuo-Yin-Wu-La hills; and farther south beyond these, the Bayan Kara.

This sight alone was worth all the trials I had gone through since leaving home on the other side of the globe; a civil war, endless red-tape and bickering with suspicious Chinese officials, finding a backer, disappointments, failures, sickness, trying to live out of a suitcase, intrigues, war-planning, dodging agents interested in my work in World War II, trying to live on what few dollars I had gotten into China, bad food, delays of weeks, cold, and finally the long hours of for the most part dreary riding that had melted into endless days.

The reader of a traveler's journal, of course, gets a thumbnail picture compressing all the best adventures, landscapes and the like, and is spared the (to the traveler) seemingly endless hours of humdrum living during which absolutely nothing occurs. If only the armchair traveler knew that his evening's enjoyment was in reality spread damned thin over the long trail of the real traveler, I doubt if many such records would ever see the lamplight.

But here it was—at last! Here was the heart of the new base for China's defeated mainland armies.

Hills radiated below us from star-shaped Tsebagase, sweeping their sharp points out from the culminating summit where we stood in a tearing wind, in long, downward-curving ridges of browns and yellows, with snow plastering their gullies from top to bottom where their points were fixed in the surrounding plain. I realized that we gazed upon the mighty junction of three Eurasian continental mountain systems—Kun Lun, Amne Machin, and Bayan Kara!

Closer at hand, the only life seen on Tsebagase was a very large bird perched on a cliff just below. We could not identify it, nor had we seen one like it before; the plumage was of a dark brown, mottled with splashes of yellow, surmounted by a cream head and a wide-ruff neck. The great bird did not fly away until I tossed a stone to frighten it, for Tan was getting ready to shoot the poor thing and we had no way properly to prepare the specimen in the cold and wind.

We got busy, and with cold-numbed fingers sketched detailed charts of both seas, Oring—eastward, Tsaring—westward (for uniformity in this record we have placed them according to common foreign usage); showing bays and such major islands as were visible to us. A detailed description of the surrounding country was also taken by Solomon. Dorje noted there was no trail such as shown by the Chinese maps to exist between the two seas. A strange lake was lying near Tsaring's close east shore, extending to the base of our perch off its northwest ridge foot: it was called Durong Nor, said Gunchi.

"That must be Choulu's lost lamb," I chuckled to the others, calling above the wind.

"What—?" shouted back Prince Dorje anxiously, his pen poised above his map, "Do you feel alright?"

"Sure, I feel fine; why?"

"Drop the subject, old boy."

"But don't you remember Jatm, that Ngolok bombom below Wambu Gunga Pass, after the snowstorm?"

"Never heard of 'Jatm' . . . what's 'Wambu Gunga'? . . ."

A snowball caught him a moment later on the ear; and then he remembered: "Oh, you mean that crazy legend—sure, sure."

Back to our mapping: The great Tsaring Sea was sketched on the maps as a third smaller in area than Oring. It was wider east and west than Oring, but not so wide north and south. Two islands were said by the Ratsong to exist; but I saw only one alongside a curtain of hail, and marked this in the center of the sea; it was quite large and fairly flat. Simultaneously, over the entire enormous landscape spread around the sea, were going on various weather shows: hailstorms, snow flurries with bright sunny patches between and shafts of sunlight sunk fast in the earth. Deep purple shadows lay among the towering white mountains ringing the horizon. Here and there streaks of black indicated shadowed canyons and valleys. Dazzling blues and greens reflecting off seas; whites and rock-yellows flashing from peaks and glaciers were everywhere. The new islands reported at Chakar were marked for Oring Nor, likewise headlands, bays, and feeder rivers and streams.

Tsaring Nor, a deep Mediterranean-blue (at the moment) was completely clear of ice, and was—in spite of the circling mountains— a possible seaplane base for aircraft, even this early in the Spring. Looking around in the opposite direction, eastward, we saw that the main source of the Yellow River at the Oring Nor outlet bears directly northeast from Tsebagase Peak. This whole heartland of the headwaters region of the Yellow River, was photographed (by Solomon), noted, mapped, and certain features sketched. The entire pattern for the Moslems' flood-control idea of the Yellow River—the key to the northern half of China, in peace and war—lay exposed before them.

Buffeted by blasts of wind we cinched our slackened saddle girths, mounted, and rode carefully through whirling snowflakes along the slippery rim of the summit. I imagined this might be among the first mountaineering exploits accomplished in Tibet on horseback. I bowed my head at what my mountain-climber friends such as Edwin Marth, a guide who had climbed the Matterhorn over a hundred times, would think of such unorthodox business; but after all, I was not a mountain-climber, only a vagabond who liked to do most of his wandering on the seat of his pants. After I had found the mountains, my friends, including Marth could climb them on their hands for all I gave a damn.

Through the storm we made out an extensive square-shaped *mani-obo* (a double-barreled word coined for the occasion). Dismounting we found that it measured 12 by 12 feet, and was surmounted by the 30-foot mast of a tree trunk. Only Buddha knows how that mast ever got on a 15,000-foot mountain top in treeless Tibet, for we hadn't seen a tree since climbing out of the canyon below Fort Ta Ho Pa. But there it was, held upright by rope stays secured to the four corners of the Buddhist world symbolized in the shrine. From the stays hung hundreds of cotton flags—mostly white and yellow—with prayers painted on each of them. This sacred stone structure was 5 feet high on its shortest side, and up to 8 feet high on the lowest side—for the base was irregular, though the top level. The foundation was of rough uncut stones, while the top half was quite possibly made up of some thousands of carefully arranged sheafs of flat *mani* stones of green and red native slate.

Tibetan Sanskrit, the painted pictures of Buddhas, the Wheel of Life, various animals including elephants and tigers, yaks and sheep; demons, heavens, and hells—all were chiseled on them, comprising by far the most elaborate obo we had yet encountered out of many hundreds so far seen. One slate, standing upright in a niche, was carved in bas-relief, and delightfully painted with palm trees and crocodiles; swinging from a temple was a monkey, his tail curled over a golden bell. Buddha sat in the center of the sun, and men played in the mud near the animals and yet appeared to be afraid of them.

The winds rose to a thin whistle, the snow flew thick and fast all round, and the horses stomped their impatience. To the mast were bound tightly with thick cords a rusty gun and sword, a turquoise-studded saddle, a whole horse's skin stuffed with wool, its shrunken head fitted with an agate eye (the other was missing); a bundle of robes and boots, a lance, baskets of dried raw meat and tsamba, and several other objects. One of these was called a death-mask or *spyang-pu*—a rag with the painted effigy of the dead person, showing the sacred mirror, conch, lyre, vase with flowers, and the holy cake. In the Tibetan cremation funeral rite a paper spyang-pu is burned in the flame of a butterlamp, and by the color of the flame is determined the after-death fate which the deceased has met. This has been an "air-funeral," however; and the ghost-mask, the spyang-pu, remained for us to see. The face was that of a middle-aged warrior chief. The whole pile looked like a Viking's funeral—except that the boat and flames of the latter were replaced here by the mountains and elements of the air.

All this was fascinating and I had forgotten that my hands and feet were threatened with frostbite until Gunchi, very agitated due to his belief that our horses were seeing a *yid-lus* (perhaps a thought-body), remarked curtly that the obo was bad for us, and intended by the lamas for the use of the Mountain god.

The driving snow increased until three inches of it lay on fur hats, and now the seas and valleys below were blotted out. Solomon thought we had done a month's work in a single day; the maps were finished and put away. The wind blew against the peak, lifting the snow off the rocks and obo, and driving it straight into our robes. Threatened with freezing we had to leave; we picked our separate ways down the mountain toward camp, each man believing he knew the best route—scrambling and sliding, leading our shivering horses. These were sure-footed as goats, leaping from rock to rock, skating down icy inclines. Everybody safely reached the flat at about the same time, though we were scattered along for half a mile. We mounted and trotted the remaining couple of miles to camp. When the storm lifted I got a bearing on the obo, barely visible atop the nearest peak, and found it to be west southwest from camp in the center of the plain.

As a scattering of Ratsongs were gathering on the north hills, camp was struck. While doubling back to join the main expedition supposedly coming up the east coast of Oring Nor to the rendezvous at the Yellow River outlet, we stopped and collected grazing grasses and various other botanical and geological items, in all of which our Moslems were interested. For a time the Ratsongs rode along in the north, keeping abreast of us, and then left. I was not sorry, as their march got a little on our nerves, though a pair of machine-guns were carried on the saddles of two of our men.

Tiny lizards, only a few inches in length, were everywhere, their first day out apparently, for none had been noted before. They scampered underfoot, the horses shying at first. These were the only reptiles we had seen in Tibet. Skirting back along the north shore of Oring Nor, we became so hot from the sun's heat that we periodically pulled off our robes, even going bare-skinned down to our pants; but whenever the moody wind came up we lost no time getting them on again.

On the north bank of the Yellow River, after six hours of cantering, we came upon Colonel Ma's camp—a sizable and clamorous settlement of tents, yaks, horses, soldiers, Tibetans, Ngoloks, dogs, and sheep. The Colonel had established Camp 26 according to plan. He was eager to see our larger plans translated into action, being sure as always that all China was soon to be lost, and that, if complete disaster was to be avoided, we must act without error. Therefore, he had decided to accompany us in person from Fort Chakar into the northern regions lying between us and the Tsaidam Swamp.

In his tent he informed Solomon and me that no treaty had been secured for these regions, and that we would have to take our chances with whatever tribes we might find there. As for natural obstacles (about which we asked), he said with a snort he did not know whether we could get on past the cliff-faced mountains of the Amne Kor, and for all he knew the seas up there, if any existed, might be "salty and poisonous."

We thought Colonel Ma summed up the situation perfectly when he finally got down to brass tacks:

"Good God, Clark-ah and Solomon! If we can't get through—we can always die can't we?"

20

Across Amne Kor

WHILE in Sining we had heard that bands of Hussacks had invaded north Tibet and massacred the western Mongols of Chinghai (or Tsinghai, if you prefer the Chinese). And now Sining wished us to find out if any of the outlying Mongol Leagues and Banners had survived intact, and if so, what were their strengths, Order-of-Battle, armament, and leaders, political and military. Our findings in this matter (that is here in the south) had been so far a blank. Apparently all Mongols in the regions we had traversed were gone—vanished; either driven out or killed. I heard that Mongols were farther east, but I saw none of these. In the regions northwest in Tsaidam, we might learn of their state when and if we could get there after crossing the wide mountainous area separating Oring Nor from that swamp.

To sum up the situation and our chances: the expedition was now considerably altered to fit the new circumstances—it was smaller and more compact. Besides our two magistrates' tents, we had seven others; audience, Tan's men's, radio, my own (shared with Dorje and Solomon), Colonel Ma's soldiers', and two for our Tibetans. All other tents had been left behind at Chakar. A completely new herd of pack and saddle yaks, some new mules and horses in addition to the best of the old ones, were now in our possession. These totaled approximately 200. A small band of sheep had come along also, and these were being used by the Tibetans for packing; later, as we should require them, they would be killed and eaten; as Colonel Ma pointed out, we had no way of knowing about current game conditions ahead as the sea Ngoloks either did not know, as they insisted, or would not tell us.

Early in the night at intervals, hail and thunder and lightning came, and then at 2 A.M., snow descended in blasts against the tents. Next morning in darkness, we reluctantly bestirred ourselves at four o'clock, to face the night in a temperature of —24° C. There seemed nothing to be gained by waiting at the Yellow River, as scouts reported the clans were gathering in Ratsong territory. However, Colonel Ma said they were not after us, but perhaps preparing for a foray toward the west. Camp was struck with cold hands, but finally, at five sharp, we swung into our saddles, beginning a ride which would last for hours on end directly across the wide up-slanting tang plain extending flat-surfaced but tilted slightly (the high side in the north). By 9:30 A.M. we found ourselves close up to the south flanks of the gaunt Amne Kor. Behind lay a curdled sky.

Our altitude on the tang at this northern edge was said by Solomon, I believe, to be 4,300 meters (13,102 feet), only 46 feet higher than the sea. This seemed too low to me, but I record it here for what it may be worth. Part of the way had been through a windy, freezing snowstorm; we were very cold and forced to dismount and walk considerably in order to keep from freezing in the saddles. Instead of moving in from the west, which was normal, the wind's direction had shifted and was coming down out of the Amne Machins lying east and southeast (direction due to downward curve in the range). Above it swept at times along the cliffs with a whistle, moving across the ice wedged in crevasses of the barrier of the Amne Kor extending before us in the north and along our right side. There was something ominous about that range of mountains, and what lay on the other side.

Under the Kor we had a strengthening breakfast while sitting crosslegged on saddle carpets spread on the windy open tang. Food was of frozen mutton, a few wild goose eggs gathered on the way and boiled, and mugs of hot tea mixed with yellow-greenish butter. We were half-starved and this breakfast tasted good. Such tea remaining in the copper pots was given to several of the horses, and it seemed to revive them.

The Amne Kor, in all its cold beauty, loomed ominously over our campfire; a black, snow-streaked, icy, jagged range with sparkling cliffs falling away for thousands of feet in long, clean-shattered curves bending into the dirt of the tang. The Chinese military mapmakers know this range as the A-Mu-Na-K'u-La Ling. Peaks rising as white cones in the west were judged by our people at between 18 and 20 thousand feet high, though I don't think they go to those heights in spite of the very steep appearances and low and heavy snow on them, this last due likely to the present snowfalls. Other far-distant mountains glimpsed through clouds separating for a moment beyond, indicated the presence of still other peaks, and the permanent appearing snow-lines seemed very much lower on two of them. Dorje wondered if they were the eastern end of the Kun Luns. Very likely they are, though possibly being spurs or fragmented and isolated mountains and ranges entirely separate. Such problems are for the surveyor and not for the scout—and we could hardly be considered more than that. The surveyors of future generations will have plenty to do in such regions.

South of the whole range revealed on our side stretched wide sloping plains, containing isolated, cliff-sided tablelands of a reddish color, and still others of a rich brown dirt of sedimentaries—possibly the pulverized residue of the stony spurs flowing from the black rocky mass of the Kor. The plain on which we sat was covered with a growth of submarine-like flora—heads of cabbage-looking mosses, tufts of waving grasses, lichens and various cucumber-looking nubbins, stars, and other plants: and these were of many colors.

Men and officers seemed considerably preoccupied; how could we ever cross this barrier of the Kor? "Let us return to Chakar. . ." some mumbled among themselves.

Colonel Ma and Captain Tan thought there must be a way through, for a trail was here somewhere. In front of our resting place, immediately north, and striking east-and-west, were reared two massive, red sandstone ridges carved up like the sides of the Grand Canyon by water and wind. Behind these perfectly stupendous edifices blocking our way lay another obstacle, a fantastic ill-omened mountain.

This mountain was shaped almost exactly like a dead, petrified dinosaur of the big-bodied, long-necked type known as *Brontosaurus*. Its small reptilian head and long, fat neck stretched straight out into the west toward our left, and directly away from the high-arched, slate-colored, black-ribbed and altogether grotesque body. It took little imagination to see that the shoulders were there, looming in cliffs; the lean, shrunken ribs, the back with its fringe of horns, the reptilian tail. I made a rough sketch of it, Ma and Tan deciding that we must cross over the Amne Kor at this very place. We would shape a course over the low-lying neck at a point midway between shoulders and head resting upon the earth.

I called for my black horse, and when Hassan led him to the fire, swung aboard and reined north toward this mountain in the Kor.

I walked him slowly and in about ten minutes I could hear the caravan coming up behind. We were now at the basement stone walls of the two red mountains. Things looked better from this angle; I turned left, and a quarter of a mile beyond came to a narrow canyon: into this, hundreds of feet high on both sides, I now turned, accompanied by a Tibetan for guide. The column streamed along just behind, heads down, mens' hands tucked inside their robes against a sudden flurry of snow. The canyon's floor increased its upward pitch, but at last after an hour we broke clear at its head, and before us lay the neck of the mountain. Marching along with deep puffs of steam blowing from its heads came the column, with sporadic zigzagging jabs requiring all its mettle, moving slowly upward alongside the dinosaur's neck. There was a trail alright, but most of it must have washed out the winter previous.

Our good luck did not hold. A new hard-driving snowstorm struck at this dangerous place, here of all possible places. The air turned brittle with crackling frost, and driven by a whistling wind which beset us from the northeast off the Kor. Puffs of steam blew out from the flaring nostrils of the beasts; the yaks' ribs heaved for want of more air in their lungs; the horses' hooves dug into the slippery, shifting rubble for footholds: as they clawed up the steep gradient of the mountain's neck they lurched forward in short desperate stabs as only horses and yaks with their Tibetan stamina could possibly do.

Even for my mount, now called "Alashan" for short, the way was rough. Some years ago I once saw a Mexican while hunting bring his horse down a 45-degree slope, but even he, I am sure, would have considered the way difficult. A mountain climber would no doubt have rated it all just so much duck soup, but we were hardly in that category—merely soldiers, a handful of Tibetan tribesmen, and a couple of wanderers trying to get somewhere and find a warm, dry camp. And so if the way seems over difficult and a bit dramatic, you know why. And as we rose higher into the blasted sky the course became ever steeper and wetter. The clatter of the flat, downward-sliding shale seemed never-ending. Occasionally a horse and its rider would fall and slide a bit downhill with a rattle of stones. One man rolled for a hundred feet before coming to a stop against a bench of boulders; incredibly, he recovered his horse, mounted, and maneuvered it back on his level into the long line of steaming animals. The Kor, we saw at such intimate range, was composed of a dark green slate with (as I recall) outcroppings of a hard lighter-green stone. And up this we crawled, kicking toeholds, a rider and horse now and then falling and getting up, cursing, cutting our feet (a few walked) and hooves on the brittle stones, but always going up . . . up.

An hour later, Colonel Ma, Dorje and I stood on top of the neck; here was a pass at 4,750 meters (14,473 feet), the aneroid reading taken in a freezing gale of snow. It was undoubtedly the lowest possible place to cross over the range; even so, this point was about as high as Mount Whitney (14,496 feet), the highest mountain in the United States. Here we found a thin trail probably used by Tibetans and Ngoloks.

The long far-away rumbling of a stone avalanche, caused by the snow weighting a steep shale slope, warned us to be careful. The main body comprising this particular mountain of the Kor on our right was blotted out. Underfoot the way was so very bad that we finally decided, when joined by others, to space ourselves and animals well apart to prevent slides, and proceed slowly downhill at a tangent. We started down behind Tan. Men, horses and yaks stumbled and slid downhill through a darkening day, a few falling to their knees on stones, skidding across steep icy patches. Occasionally a cry, probably a curse, came out of the snowstorm, horses snorted, even a yak moaned now and then. But always the column felt its way down foot by foot, or even inch by inch; some of the men crawled on their knees over dry patches.

Driving snow caked thickly on my goggles, and from time to time I risked frostbitten hands in cleaning off the icy layer. I personally had a very bad time of it in the broken shale on this northern descent. A few times I wasn't sure I could go a step farther. My Tibetan boots, unwisely worn that day for warmth alone were of the soft-soled variety, a kind of soft moccasin type suitable for riding. I found myself walking on the sides of bruised feet, through shattered shale. We finally reached a bench, one of the officers bugling the somewhat scattered party together.

While we rested the wind and snow lifted from time to time for a minute or two, and what we saw before—or rather below us—was enough to make me think twice if not three times. What looked like practically a sheer cliff dropped off into a canyon, and we were

huddled on a bench somewhere topside of it. How we were to get
down Allah only knew: our straits seemed so desperate that I could
think of nothing to do but laugh and whack Colonel Ma playfully
with my whip, and shout above the wind:

"Why you old Moslem yak, look where you've led us."

He laughed in glee and soon had the whole party joking and
craning its necks for a way down. Evidently we had lost the native
trail. I don't mind saying these men were a hell of a lot tougher and
more experienced in such places than I was. Tan came alongside,
grinning, motioned for us to get started, and shouted orders at the
men. Soon we were moving like centipedes off that narrow shelf,
and on to a slanting rubble wall, below the right fore-shoulder of
Kor. The sharp rocks underfoot were even sharper as we descended
into the canyon. Slowly, slowly, we went down, myself mostly on
my rear, and some two hours later found ourselves jumping off a
boulder into the very bottom V in the head of a narrow, miniature
Grand Canyon. About ten men were ahead of me. This slot proved
jumbled and clogged farther down from recent rock slides. Overhead, strung like a necklace of vari-colored beads along the slope—
and all but invisible through swirling snowflakes—were about fifty
men and animals, the others, should they still be with us, being
blotted out higher in the storm. I mounted with the others and rode
on down the canyon, but after a hundred yards we had to dismount
again, and feel our way among the boulders; the gradient became
steeper and rougher and I could hardly make any way at all, dropping behind and plugging along as best I could over rock piles and
through snowdrifts, and rocky stretches slippery with ice.

The snow melted on the horse, and icicles were hanging from his
mane. The only thing that kept me going at all was stopping once
in a while and cursing a blue streak. I was damned near frozen, and
my feet felt as if cut off at the ankles. The black horse would cock
his ears forward and neigh, at those up ahead of course. This never
failed to bring a laugh, and I would start all over again. At one
place I waited for some others, and saw that one horse had a split
hoof. The going improved and I finally got into the saddle. We
continued on into the north through the canyon; for hours on end
we were practically blinded by snow, and very cold.

But Colonel Ma said there was no stopping in this avalanche
trap under even these circumstances. Men and animals stumbled

along through the bottom of the darkening canyon, until finally its walls expanded outwards and we emerged on a 200-foot-wide gravel bed gouged out by ice, meandering in riverine loops northward. To left and right jutted skyward rock peaks around seventeen thousand feet above sea level. Many were of a curious red-brown, others being black; their summits suddenly shining as the westerly sun burst through a hole in the storm and, for a moment, struck the higher snow-fields and glaciers.

We stopped and Camp 27 was finally set up after much oh-ing and ah-ing, on a wide bench on the right hand (east) side, some few feet above the dry glacier bed. Snow was still falling as the clouds had closed and the storm had returned. The bench was part of a seepage and covered with a foot of new snow, which was mushy and clinging. Our feet were soon wet. When a lull came in the snowfall, somebody let out a yell—and pointed up toward the east. Wondering if the mountain was falling on us, I glanced up and instantly saw nine bighorn sheep about 500 yards away, standing on a slope rising directly alongside camp on our flank.

Bomba and two other Tibetans dropped their tent-pegs and grabbed their guns, and started out toward the game. I stood aside and watched; carefully the hunters screened their approach behind a jutting pinnacle. As they climbed the steep slope, I suddenly saw a movement far above them: still other sheep were coming into view, bunching under a very high cliff a good quarter of a mile above the nine animals already marked down. Hassan brought binoculars, and we counted off by bunches over 500 sheep in that single band. Dorje joined us, and right there on the spot, started work on the first natural history faunal report to come out of the Amne Kor, undoubtedly the western extension of the Amne Machin Range as von Filchner had believed.

The snowfall continued to hold off: later, with camp established for the night—the fagged men resting around the fires (they preferred several scattered ones to a single big one)—and scouts out watching for Ngoloks or other tribes, I joined the three hunters. At 250 yards I shot and killed a young ram. This made a total of three sheep with the pair Bomba and his men had already secured. My feet felt better after that, and there was still plenty of light. Late that afternoon I hunted alone among the lower regions of the snow peaks and cliffs on this eastern side of the canyon. Game was plentiful, and varied, as indicated by the animals themselves or by their tracks:—gazelles ranged high in this altitude, as did yaks, bears, foxes, wolves, asses, and herds of musk-deer. All about were coveys of partridges. Large rabbits, fat as butter, hopped everywhere. In the air—rare as it was—were eagles, hawks, and vultures, scouring the cliffs. I was sitting on a bench over a willow thicket when I glimpsed something in the brush, and a moment later got a quick shot at a musk-deer as it snaked through the cover, but missed, though the range was only a hundred yards: no excuse but the best possible one —I just missed.

Sitting on the bluff, I studied the lay-out of the country. The first fold in the Amne Kor's south range, which we had crossed, sheers off rather steeply as I have indicated, footing in the dirt plains on the south, Oring side, tilting up grandly as a major watershed. But the range breaks up on the north side into stony chains of peaks, short spurs and ranges, single mountains with deep canyons between, everything scrambled up all which way but maintaining a general strike (when all of them are considered in bulk) into the northwest. The basic rock is a hard jade-like green stone, while other extrusive rocks alongside are composed of a hard, brittle, yellow-brown stuff. A bright-orange cliff-like wall some two or three thousand feet high, drew me off the bluff to its base across the canyon, but it turned out to be the green stone covered over with a microscopic fungus; other rocks and slides were also covered with the growth, as well as by other kinds of moss. A few willow thickets in which we scrounged for firewood in the absence of dung, grew in the deep detritus of broken stone, gravel, and the little soil lying at the bases of the stone towers.

I returned to camp happy if half-frozen, and very winded. The slack air-pressure, and insufficient oxygen, seemed to tire me quickly. To our game bag of three sheep, had been added a buck musk-deer —luckily shot by the head cook from camp as it was standing in the nearest willow patch. At 6:15 that evening, a warm wind forged up the canyon, and with it came a drizzle of rain. Nothing worse could have happened, said Tan, not even an earthquake.

The snow melted fast. We soon found ourselves camped in a pool of slushy water. We were certainly uncomfortable but better off than if we had pitched camp in the glacier bed below, which was now becoming a racing torrent. Summer was fast reaching out over

Tibet; it was mainly in order to evade this very difficult season of
thaws and bogs that we had planned our late-winter start from
Sining. The temperature mounted, and the lowlands ahead were
becoming saturated. Thus with more winds, which would accompany the warmer airs, we could expect an even colder and more
difficult time of it than heretofore. By nine o'clock that night we
actually got so warm we had to remove our sheepskin robes and put
on woolen ones. By ten o'clock we had to get back into the wet
sheepskins as a downdraft off the snow peaks set in and nearly froze
us.

With the sound of the ice in the torrent alongside and just below
camp there was little sleep that night. With dawn we saw that the
flood was very likely going to overflow our shelf, and we had to get
out. The tethered animals were packed, and the whole caravan
plunged into the edge of the torrent which reached halfway up the
horses, and practically covered the yaks and their cargoes. With ice
and chunks of snow in the river we were soon not only wet but
cold. Keeping to the shallower parts of the run-off bed, Tan led
the way; the canyon still meandering north toward the Tsaidam.
Later, at 8:30, we broke out of the steep-walled canyon and moved
across a muddy, mile-wide plain and then headed into another
steep-sided valley.

We were now flanked on both sides at fairly close range by ice
and snow peaks. As we waded through the flood water I found time
to observe that a rather amazing amount of big game was about. It
seemed every few minutes we would spot a bear or a hunting wolf,
herds of musk-deer, kyangs, gazelles, bighorn sheep, or foxes. This
must be one of the last unspoiled big-game paradises remaining in
Asia. Once at a considerable distance on the right-hand slope above,
somebody made out what appeared to be wapiti—believed by some
to be the ancestor of the North American *Cervus canadensis*, called
elk in the United States. It is said the European variety may also
be descended from these deer.

We continued wading on into the north. While riding through
a light hailstorm, just after fording a turbulent muddy river called
the Longjod, which flowed northward, one of the soldier's wolf-
hounds, while racing up and down our flanks, suddenly put up a
large cat. It bounded into the air over a bush and vanished. Most of
the men, though fairly wet in spite of the much vaunted buttermilk

process of waterproofing the sheepskin chupas, were eager for the chase: half the caravan yelled in glee and jammed spurs to its horses, splashing through a net of shallow streams, going through half-melted snowdrifts, charging up gravel banks, smashing through willows—racing at breakneck speed—streaming after the yipping hound now following at the heels of the quarry. I lost no time joining in, all my hurt feet, misery, aches, pains and wetness forgotten.

The valley had widened here to about a mile, and over its floor we pounded, throwing mud behind us. In about ten minutes the cat winded and came to bay in a shallow gulch. Yellow-eyed it sat back on its haunches (there is no treeing a cat here due to lack of trees), and glared and snarled at the hound. That astute hunter stood back and wisely howled for assistance. As we galloped up the men joyfully rode around the pair in what Dorje explained was the Mongol *kurultai;* the horses dancing and snorting at sight and smell of the cat. Now in any other country I suppose the cat would have been shot, but not here, for the kurultai is a form of knightly jousting.

The first man on the scene had been Abdul (another Abdul), a very handsome younger brother of Colonel Ma whom we had picked up at Fort Chakar, and this Moslem soldier now threw himself off his rearing mare and deliberately launched himself, bare-handed, into a flying-tackle at the snarling cat. Man vs wildcat! I had often wondered how a man "who fights like a wildcat," really fights. For a full minute we could see bits of man and cat cartwheeling around on the muddy ground, tumbling over and over—first the cat on top, then the man—a coughing snarl coming from the furious beast and an occasional howl coming from Abdul's lips. His face was cut up and bleeding, his clothes partly torn in front.

I was absolutely certain Abdul's intestines would be ripped out by the cat's hind feet, and that we would have a sewing job on our hands that night; but Abdul hung on and, finally, emerged holding the cat by the scruff of its neck. He only half dragged it off the ground, for it was five feet long and rather heavy: and then I saw that it was a super-kind of lynx.

The hunter slipped a noose around the lynx's neck and, knotting it to prevent slipping and choking, remounted his skittish mare, and led the cat along in our midst. At first the tawny, brown-spotted animal had to be pulled along, but finally she (for such it was) decided to cooperate, and it was amusing to see the horses ride along-side as it lopped along, sniffing, snorting, half-bolting, rearing on their hind legs as if to strike it, and obviously enticed by the novelty of danger (however slight) represented in the unsheathed claws and bared fangs.

We rode through a prickly dwarf forest of wet, stunted conifers some five feet high, then into thick patches of gnarled willows, and plunged finally into a deep rushing stream of flooding muddy water. Soon we joined the caravan, still plugging miserably along. In one of the many canyons beyond, terraced crisply as a model relief map, and banded with strata of bold earth-colors, volcanic in origin, we at last stopped exhausted. That day according to Solomon we had lost 1,500 feet of elevation, and the grass was partly swept free of slush and snow by winds coming through several steep-walled av-enues of dreary canyons. Tibet is not supposed to have any active volcanic mountains, but these ragged, colored ranges and peaks above seemed active, and we determined to find out for sure. We were now sandwiched between the Amne Kor and the Burchan Buddha mountain system. Farther northwest the Burchan Buddha Mountains form part of the rim lying along the south margin of the 200-mile Tsaidam basin. The mountains above camp were called (by our Tibetans) the Tsagan Horga. This is of Mongol derivation. They are not on any map known to me, and even our Chinese mili-tary maps had no names for them.

Camp 28 was established in "Red Water Plain," at an elevation of 3,695 meters (11,261 feet). We were now at the junction of four rivers—a rarity in Tibet. I say "a rarity in Tibet," because that high, basined country is the eternal land of lakes and seas, but not often of really long-flowing rivers (except those big ones already men-tioned, and those channels containing the run-off of the summer thaw). The eastern river could only be the westward-flowing outlet from Tossun Nor, the Black Sea, on the far, eastern end of which lay the ashes of our old base camp lying northwest of Amne Machin Peak. Our old Camp 12 on the Black Sea now lay 50 miles south-east.

This river flowing from the Black Sea into the west proved once and for all that Tossun Nor was not tributary to the upper Yellow River northeast of Amne Machin Range, as some in the past had believed, but that its overflow runs westward towards inner Tibet, and contributes to swelling the waters of the Tsaidam sink. The Tsaidam, one of the great marshes, lay in a basin at a reputed 2,730 meters (our maps appeared to vary), between the Kun Lun, Altin Tagh, and the Nan Shan—the mountains forming in part the north geographical boundaries of Tibet against Sinkiang and the Mongolian desert.

I went hunting with a strange Ngolok camped near. Bareback we swam our horses through two flood streams and after dressing headed westward into the color-banded region of hills and mountains. Soon we left our animals due to rough terrain, and tied them to a willow clump. The Ngolok went ahead and I followed through some badlands. No active volcano was found, but an hour later, puffing in the rarefied air, we approached a steaming mineral spring flowing from under a reddish bluff. I leaned my rifle against a rock, and knelt to wash myself as hot water was a rarity on the trail.

At this moment the Ngolok fired his rifle at something beyond in a flat, and I glanced up to see a leopard moving between some high tufts of salt grass. I grabbed my rifle but was too slow to get in a shot, for it disappeared.

We had accidentally approached the leopard upwind to where it was very likely lying in wait for a bighorn. Plenty of sheep tracks showed in the game trail we had followed. No doubt these animals were drawn to the salty minerals encrusting the rim of the spring. We had seen any number of the skins of the *ounce*, the Tibetan snow leopard, a long-haired, whitish-gray, mottled type. But the leopard just seen was one of the black spotted tawny Asian type known as *Felis pardus,* identical to the African variety. Their skins can be purchased in Lanchow at fifty Chinese silver dollars.

We began chucking rocks into the grass patch, and when it ran out I fired, leading too far and missing the shoulder but striking the head. It leapt into the air, but was not long kicking as the Ngolok ran forward and shot it in the ear. He removed the skin and we headed for home. The Ngolok later said leopards do not go farther south than the Amne Machins, and so probably the few found here range in spring and summer southward out of Tsaidam and the mountains farther north of that swamp.

Snow began falling gently, and under its cover we managed to stalk a few gazelles grazing on a snow-free meadow, and a buck was killed. Later the Ngolok also shot four rabbits, and while he carried the gazelle meat I killed a "snow chicken," a very large Tibetan ptarmigan. This bird was the first seen by me and the largest game bird (other than the big water fowl) identified, being the size of two ordinary pheasants. The head was gray and chicken-like, with yellow eyes, black and rust-mottled neck-ruff, chest splashed a red-brown-gray patchwork. The worn spurs were only half an inch in length, the legs orange, white under-wings, white under-tail. It was two feet one inch in length from beak tip to tail tips, or the same from beak to feet claws. The Tibetans call this king of ptarmigan, *kumo*.

The Moslems sometimes talked about them, but no real evidence of tigers was found in this region, though a few may exist, as the Ngoloks knew of them. No white hunter, I believe, unless possibly Russian, has ever killed a Central Asian tiger; Sven Hedin, on one of his first expeditions, obtained the skin of a tiger in Sinkiang after it had been trapped by a herder. Poison imported from Russia apparently has cut down their numbers everywhere in recent years. The late famous hunting brothers, Colonel Theodore Roosevelt and Major Kermit Roosevelt, while hunting many years ago in Turkestan, failed also in their efforts to secure one. However—if any hunter wants to try for this unique trophy, there is real evidence of its existence, as Prince Dorje's father had killed eight tigers in Alashan, west Gobi, and the regions adjacent. But the real tiger country of China is, of course, and of all places, Fukien Province on the east coast.

A detailed examination of the region showed the junction of Camp 28 to be definitely the meeting and departing place of four rivers: the Longjod coming in from the south after flowing off the north watershed of the Kor; the Norjong entering from the west, said by the Ngoloks to head in a western sea of that name; the Dong Chu meandering in from the east after spilling out of Tossun Nor— and finally, the three collected rivers joining and flowing northward as one very much larger, called the Yughra. None of these names will be found on any map. The Yughra is marked on Chinese maps as entering the Tsaidam, and is called the Shi-shi. This would seem to be the main river system draining the junction of mountains west of the Amne Machins to the Tsaidam. We learned that much of this span is a summer feeding range for Ngoloks, though far west of the federation's supposed pasturage lands.

In the evening following the hunting trip, a wild-looking, sheep-skin-robed band of sixty Ngoloks moved in on us, camping along-side: seeing our strength and Moslem willingness to use it, they became surprisingly friendly for Ngoloks. As Colonel Ma called a powwow at the main fire and we cut chunks off raw meat, eating it in one of the Tibetan styles, the headmen told us their tribe was called the Hashu, a small unit consisting of 200 family groups. Our interest increased when the chief mentioned a rinderpest cure known to them. The importance of such a rumor should not be tossed off. It is a curious fact, our people had found, that only the herds in Tibet are free of this scourge. Whenever an outbreak occurs—note this carefully—*it is immediately curtailed and cured* (according to the Moslems).

Nor is the Tibetan method one of slaughtering, burying, and burning, such as is practiced elsewhere over the world, thereby destroying valuable animal assets to the tune of many dollars. Untold British and American treasure has been, and is being expended on trying to hit upon some cure for rinderpest; but the Tibetans here, and at other places, told us they have the answer. Our epizootic chief, Solomon Ma, was obtaining reports on the animal resources of Tibet; for weeks (I now learned) he had been working on this particular problem of rinderpest. Suffice to say, that the secret lies in a five-day cure for infected animals: and that a preventative can also be given. Clotted blood of gazelles, specially treated apparently, is obtained from a certain lamasery in Sikang (Kham), and fed by mouth to infected animals. Needless to point out that should the Moslem's hunch be correct, the wealth of the Tibetan mines would be as nothing compared to finding this cure for rinderpest.

Anthrax, believed Solomon, can also be cured in Tibet. I remarked that perhaps anthrax was unknown in Tibet, and some of the Moslems answered smiling that they had once introduced infection into a Tibetan herd, and then stood back and actually seen the lamas clean it up. Although I was interested, the Moslems would talk no more about either cure, so this is all I know of the matter.

Orders were issued to pack and get under way by dawn. We would follow the new river, knowing it would lead into the Tsaidam. And so after a good night's sleep, in the flush of dawn we gathered and had a solid breakfast in Tan Chen-te's tent. Roasting over a bed of coals on the floor were pieces of bighorn sheep, gazelle, and the rabbits and ptarmigan. Snow was falling again, and already 8 inches deep, coming down faster by the minute. And this in a rising temperature. The ground was wet underfoot. With yells and cracking of whips the caravan started moving along the river's right bank. Yaks left muddy tracks all over the slushy patches of snow. Horses plunged into run-off bogs, wading through mud. Many animals in the train bawled or moaned unhappily. There was nothing but mud, mud everywhere under the snow, the worst ground yet encountered. The colonel said we must exert every effort to get down to lower elevations, as only a few of the wiser animals were pawing off enough snow to get at the scanty vegetation. Many others were slowly starving. The tragedy was that even should we find grass and stave off starvation, we would merely be exchanging that fate for one of bogging down deeper in the mires which he warned must be inevitable.

We got out of Red Water Plain, and on a northeasterly heading the train was eventually clattering along over firmer ground, following a rocky canyon floor through which flowed the turbulent Yughra. We stuck to the mud and gravel banks whenever possible, and when forced in by closing walls of rock or rubble slides, took to the river itself, fording or even swimming as chance would have it: we soon found rough going when confronted by very high cliffs and steep slopes, the canyon footing choked with boulders. Across this detritus we made our way.

While fording precariously at one place in the river bed, trying to extricate ourselves from a narrow canyon, we saw at close quarters on the left side, a single kyang jack standing on a point of red stone, and across the river a bighorn ram poised on another. They seemed to be staring at each other silhouetted like statues. In spite of our worries, and the swift, icy water, the whole caravan glanced up, every man captivated by the beauty of the spectacle. Afterwards it seemed strange that no one reached for his gun, for to see game was to shoot with most of us, and this though we needed meat, our only food now but tea. The train yaks, sheep, horses and mules, were too thin to retain much strength in their meat. The last tsamba had been fed to several failing horses in the pass country. And we had over a hundred hard-working, half-starved men to feed at this time. The bighorn pointed the way for us along a shelf above the water, and we finally broke clear of the river and reached it, eventually to find a safer place below the walls.

As the river bed widened from time to time, flocks of very tame pigeons were everywhere on the narrow but lush meadows, and other game birds thrashed from under our feet and hooves—birds such as partridges, doves, and red and blue pheasants, most of which were nearly always in sight, and almost always heard.

Obviously we were getting down into milder altitudes, working our way slowly off the escarpment of the inner Tibetan Tala. On a map I marked the entrance of a rift, a sheer-walled, half-mile-wide, ice- and water-gouged valley, coming in from the west, now fairly dry, but later it would constitute the gravelly bed for a torrential spring flood draining the mountains comprising the western regions out toward the Kun Luns. I shivered, and not from the icy water, knowing if a rainstorm hit now, we could be swept away—for no escape was possible in such a trap. I spurred on a little faster. Another hour went by, and another rift gouged in from the east, a stone gutter with peaks high as Mount Blanc's. We moved faster, watching the darkening skies all the while. Brown mountains and rust-colored peaks, brilliantly color-banded, presently rose on all sides. We had broken clear of the trap, and none too soon—the clouds clashed in the mountain tops, and torrents of rain fell—turning the region into a series of torrents. It was easy to understand how the Tsaidam swamp was formed.

Strung out along a slope we halted and watched, not anxious to move for fear of starting slides. When the deluge stopped, we worked our way along the side of a mountain, and by midafternoon the majority of the animals were heaving with fatigue. The string of weary wanderers stopped in a small meadow in Yughra Canyon, and set up Camp 29. To insure good drainage this was placed on a ridge just under a black-banded mountain of cliffs rising in the west. Peaks were everywhere, thrusting their heads into the clouds, the lower slopes miles wide and glinting with ice and snow. But in our cozy valley were crocuses, various flowering shrubs, willows popping with balls of silky cotton, and green conifers unbelievably high and splendid—four feet high, these trees! Fields of buttercups, dwarf snapdragons, yellow-blossoming broom—whole mountainsides of it.

At our fire many of us gathered, and Prince Dorje entertained with stories as usual, one of which was about a general in Kansu Province (where Lanchow is located). This general, a powerful semi-independent warlord, had ordered a million-dollar electric power-plant to be constructed, sending to Shanghai for a European engineer. On arrival the Swede engineer found there was not enough water-power available in the desert, so he recommended that the general mine coal, which was plentiful, and make steam. The general answered with great anger that he did not want "steam," only "electricity!" . . . and promptly fired the engineer.

With early evening the skies turned black and a drizzle fell, a penetrating rain that soaked us practically to the skin. Clinging fogs and intermittent winds chilled us. This on top of the fact that we had forded the Yughra River some twelve or fourteen times and wet all the pack loads including our bedding, clothing, and every personal item we possessed. The rain caught us with these things strewn all over camp, on every tent line and bush. Films set out to dry were now soaked anew, and 53 rolls of negatives ruined with cloth dyes had eventually to be thrown away. Luckily some others had been placed in an empty tobacco tin and taped, otherwise the entire lot would have been lost. But such were the fortunes of travel.

21

Tsaidam Swamp

THERE was a lull in the storm and all was quiet. Then winds came whirling off the peaks, and in a starlit night we found ourselves outside the tents trying to save what was left of camp, now scattering over the meadow. Standing in the middle of a pretty good gale and its wreckage, Colonel Ma began sounding off like a bull yak with a willow caught under its tail. Now what in hell, I thought. I stopped pounding on a tent peg, to glance around. There was no great amount of old rain water flooding through the canyons. But as his bellowings increased in volume, I dropped the rock being used for a hammer and got my rifle. Many of the others stopped their work in surprise; men ceased running about to stare outward into the gloom wondering if perhaps Ngoloks were attacking; or a wall of water moving down on us; or a mountain toppling over; or just what. . . .

Imagine our astonishment when it turned out to be only a call for Colonel Ma's orderly to come—and remove his hat! It was certainly an indication of how far-stretched our nerves had become.

There was no sleeping that miserable night, for the bedding was soaked. With morning's first flush we were off, as flights of hoopoes indicated our approach to low, lush regions where Tsaidam sun, rain, and warmth were combining to grow feed for them along this great flightway. Later we left the hoopoes and entered "magpie altitudes." We were working to produce a table of altitudes, determined approximately by species of birds; this (I hoped) to be used by anti-Red guerrillas having no instruments for calculating elevations. It was found that different Tibetan birds may be so catalogued, and altitudes above sea level calibrated roughly. On mountain tops, however widely scattered, we had often found birds of the same kind, while none of that type existed in either lower or higher elevations.

In the same manner, and largely because of necessity, I had worked out a storm-warning "machine"; by getting some ingenious character to calibrate the vibrations of a certain cricket, it was found that an adequate warning of change in weather could be had. All this, and more, was a source of interest and amusement, as, like most people over the world, these Tungans and other Moslems erroneously believed that Americans, especially, could not operate effectively unless furnished with the latest scientific instruments. It might perhaps be of interest that during the following year, I was in Kalimpong north of Darjeeling in India, and offered my services to the Tibetans. If they would give me command of the army, I would undertake, not the halting of the two Communist field armies invading Tibet from Lanchow and Szechwan, but would attempt their destruction. The seven Tibetan emissaries then enroute to New Delhi, refused, meeting instead the Chinese Communist delegation and handing the country over without a fight. Their main objection to my plan was that I could not give them modern arms and other material, not realizing that this would only have led to their certain defeat and the burning of the temples (which was their main worry).

Twenty-three of our yaks were now bleeding at the nostrils, from which long clots hung. While talking with their drivers, I saw that the yaks' nostrils had been pierced with iron skewers, some a foot in length, this so their laboring, possibly dilated hearts, would not burst the arteries due to strenuous work and the change in elevations. They lost no animals that night from this bleeding treatment, the drivers insisting the operation was necessary, cruel though it seemed.

With nightfall it was said we had made good some 15 miles, and as we pitched the tents for Camp 30 a crisp yellow crescent moon sailed out in a sea of deep blue ether. Under this sky with its flashing galaxy of red and white and blue stars, our rough Moslems, led by Abdul, devoutly spread their saddle rugs, and, facing Mecca—which lay thousands of miles westwards beyond the uplands of Tibet, the plains of India, the deserts of Arabia—cried out as one man in adoration of the Merciful and Blessed Lord of the Universes. For their Lord's grace, bestowed from heaven on us, they were grateful, and further, showed that gratitude by praising some more exalted force than themselves, their own earth-bound egohood. The beautiful prayers ended with—"There is no god but God. . . ."

As these *hui hui* Moslems of evil reputation rose from their rugs, a sound of humming came to the ear, and then "Om Mani Padme Hum!" floated out in answering chanted waves from the Tibetan

and Ngolok camps. The rattle of a priest's drum, and the jangle of
caravan bells on the necks of the quietly grazing animals, spelled
contentment for us on that glorious blue, star-shining, moon-illu-
minated night. It is during moments such as this that the traveler
receives wages for his work.

Solomon Ma came along and together we entered our tent, where
I dictated the usual daily reports (which he put into Chinese); this,
so that should anything happen to me, all information would be
available to Ma Pu-fang. This duty consumed not less than an hour
each night, exhausted though we might be, and whenever we missed,
two hours or more spent at this job on the following night. For
weeks on end, sometimes far into the night clear up till near dawn,
this task hung like a millstone around my neck. Solomon laughed
happily as we finished: waving his precious papers, and squinting
at me through his thick spectacles, he remarked—"Footnotes on a
continent!"

By daylight we broke camp, after first thawing out before a cheer-
ing fire of willow twigs; our reduced caravan of originally 200 animals, now only 168 (some had dropped out with Ngoloks to attend
them back to Oring), carefully picking its way through the canyon,
in narrow dark threads, along the shadowed roots of peaks. Yak
drivers sitting hunched on their saddle yaks snapped their whips,
others giving that curious duck-quacking sound. Whenever a pack
animal fell and could not rise, riders moved over to it, and dismounting, lifted the horse, yak, or mule bodily back on its legs.

Slipping and sliding over patches of ice and mud, our direction
northeast, we patiently twisted and turned like a crawling snake in
the very bottom of the deep canyon. Later, our narrow way still
meandered along, and due to the steepness of its rock walls, a mile
high in places, we had several times to take to the muddy river, and
ford across to the opposite bank. This happened time and again.
The water was running straight off the glaciers overhead, and in the
channel it was usually horse-shoulder-high even at the shallowest
fording places. We were, at times, practically frozen and seldom
stopped shivering. And these tortuous places were found only after
the most careful searching. When animals were swept off their feet
they had to swim for it as best they could; four yaks and their valuable loads of fuel dung, sticks, and hides (some trading had been
done with Oring Ngoloks) were lost in a single rapid: submerged

in deep pools below, the drowned bodies did not reappear, believed due to the heavy packs anchoring them to the bottom.

By midmorning we swung 90° left, heading into the west. A very large herd of kulan, or kyang, being chased by that same wolf-hound—quite sharp after baying the lynx, created a never-to-be-forgotten sight. Certainly a thousand of the fleet, orange-brown kulans started a thunderous stampede rearwards parallel to the caravan train, keeping only two hundred yards off our right flank, the wolfhound running after in full voice.

The surprised kulans—for the stallions are said to be wolf-killers —at first had gathered together and then started off slowly, but soon crowded on more speed, lining out with flying tails behind their leader. Slowly the fleet animals began to out-distance the hound. And then suddenly, and without warning, a thousand kulans leapt out into space, and hit the Yughra River, jumping straight out from the brink of an embankment, and coming down splashing. Then the whole herd swam across and emerged on the far side, where it climbed out. Here the herd stood and gazed back over its shoulders at the baying hound, now standing ridiculously alone on the opposite bank. We could almost hear the kulans snorting in derision, as they threw up their heads, switched their tails, and trotted off.

While fanning over a gravel flat, and in order to shake a few kinks out of my horse who was cutting up a bit, I galloped in a short race against Kerim's big buckskin, and in doing so kicked up a human skull. Colonel Ma, riding just behind, reined in and looked the skull over, saying it had a bullet hole through it and was a bad omen. To still his tongue, I reached down and picked the object up by hooking an eye-socket with the front-sight of my rifle, and a few hundred yards beyond, balanced the skull atop an obo.

A Tibetan beggar-monk camped here told Tan than Ngoloks had raided into the Tsaidam the fall before and had used the canyon as a line of retreat, killing what few people they found. When questioned, our Ngolok guides confirmed this, and added that it was the limit of the raiding grounds in the federation's northwest quarter. Tsaidam Swamp could not be far off!

Next we saw through binoculars a party of strange peacock-plumed riders out hunting gazelles with gerfalcons. The birds were far too small for the game, and as they dived the fleet animals merely ran into brush where they were safe. And soon after we began seeing camels as we rode through the most easterly spurs of the Burchan Buddhas, surely a lost paradise. These snow ranges fell off northwards, comprising the southern rim of the Tsaidam—a wide blue plain in the distance. On every ridge and in sheltered canyons were groves and forests of giant tamarisks, thick burly trees. Riding under their spreading limbs which were loaded with cooing blue pigeons, we were soon among *gers* (yurts), whole colonies, spread through the forest aisles and over the meadows like big, round, white mushrooms, wrapped in thick felt blankets bound tightly to willow frames. Smoke poured out of their domes. Suddenly I realized these were Mongols! The last of the Tsaidam Mongols. . . .

Dorje and I were excited being among these true sons of Genghis Khan, once proud conquerors of the most civilized parts of the earth, still living by their ancient warrior code, the Yasse (the Mongol Law of the Steppes).

Here, under a hill crowned with a great globe-shaped obo, rising skyward like the dome of a planetarium from which hung thousands of prayer-banners on high masts, were Mongols plowing behind camels—a strange sight. They were everywhere, these semi-settled nomadic Mongols—who had learned agriculture from the Rong-pa Tibetans. Surprisingly, they were dressed as Tibetans, in sheepskin chupas and black yak-leather boots. Being Buddhist Mongols, and therefore hating and fearing the Sining Moslems, they did not approach us as we streamed along.

At 3:40 P.M. we were greeted at Fort Shan Je Te (pronounced: "Shen-Re-Day") by its skull-capped Moslem commandante, the seemingly 6-foot-6-inch Colonel Ma Dei-bio (which is as close as I can spell it). He was a burly, hoarse-voiced, fierce-looking Tungan of perhaps 250 pounds of meat and bone, inherited by Ma Pu-fang from his father, the former Governor Ma-yuan, who (so they said in Sining) had stopped the expeditions of around thirty different would-be explorers.

"God has kept thee well," he said piously, holding his huge hands before him bowing a gracious *salaam* and stroking his long black beard; "Ma Pu-fang—a thousand years of life to him!—has informed us you were coming."

Ma Dei-bio as practically Amban (Viceroy) for South Chinghai, under the former Tungan governor, had had a hand in a bloody punitive expedition against the Ngoloks which destroyed 480 families, some of whom were said to have been bound in leather and thrown into the Yellow River where they perished. He wore a long, ground-sweeping, black, so-called "modern-style" Chinese overcoat with high stiff military collars. His fort was new, constructed of high, beaten-clay walls and enclosing gray baked-brick houses with double-decked verandas in the Turki style. Its massive iron-studded, wooden gates were reinforced by heavily-armed Moslems, and two enormous stone Chinese lions. This fort marked China's westernmost important permanent garrison in Tungan Tibet.

With giant, jolly, red-faced Ma Dei-bio, we had dinner while sitting crosslegged on thick-napped Yarkand rugs. We ate from bowls of Chinese porcelain, and with bone and ebony chopsticks. After such astonishing chinoiserie luxury, we stretched out on the carpets, for we had been in the saddle for nine and a half hours. The shrewd-eyed Commandante Ma Dei-bio was impressed with our ultra smartness, and said so a couple of times. We finally confessed that we had covered our real paucity by ingeniously stopping ten miles out, while the entire troop bathed in the river, shaved, and all of us who had them (including the Tibetans), had changed from old sheepskins into robes of black, blue or red, not forgetting our best silk sashes, our shiniest boots or most gaudy Tibetan footgear and spurs, daggers and sidearms, our swords and other gauds and accouterments. And—above all—the bugles and banners. The horses, too, had been curried and rubbed down glossy, and fresh double-knots twisted into their tails.

I doubt whether, except perhaps in Arabia and India, such splendor could be found in many places today. Ma Sheng-lung's robe was of knee-length Kashmiri blue velvet, edged with a four-inch silver band; very high black polished Russian Cossack boots, red silk sash with a four-foot tail falling behind in pleated folds, from which sash hung a sword and poniard. After removing his red fox Tibetan cap, his headgear was a white Moslem skull-cap. He rode his white stallion, purchased on the Yellow River, and was indeed a sight for all his soldiers to admire, and to follow anywhere with a wild yell!

Tan Chen-te had ridden a big, dancing, liver-colored stallion, and he was as elegantly dressed in velvet as Colonel Ma, but (as usual) in browns, tans and black, trimmed with gold. For some reason he always wore a blue silk sash. My own robe was a very dark

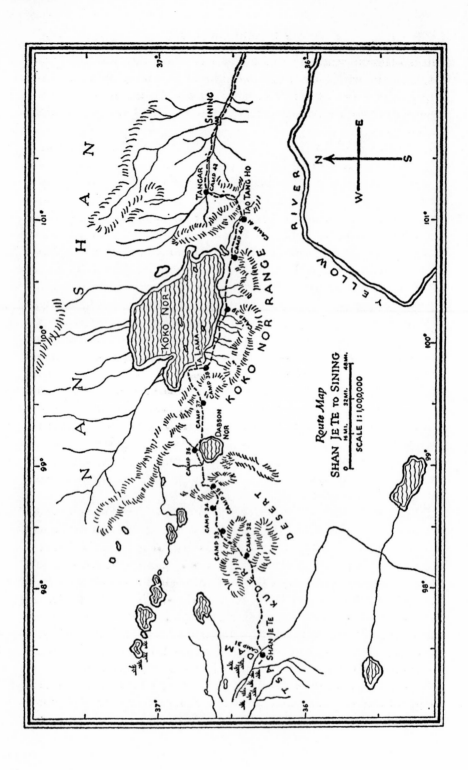

Route Map
SHAN JE TE to SINING
SCALE 1:1,000,000

red (a blackish red), my Lhasa boots of black and red wool sides embellished with blue and white Maltese crosses, my sash black silk; headgear of red fox Tibetan style; arms, a pistol and Tibetan dagger, and I rode Alashan, certainly one of the greatest stallions in central Asia.

Our column of hui hui, followed by our Tibetans and Ngoloks whose dress-clothes outshown our own, had entered walled, flat-topped Shan Je Te behind wind-stiffened banners, through a scattering mob of gaping Mongols and Tibetans, at a fast triumphant clip, bugles flourishing our arrival, arms clashing, spurs jiggling, our brightly dyed yak-tail fly-swatters flicking out at the clouds of flies and mosquitoes falling on us from out of the town and swamps. And we came singing. . . .

Lying stretched out on Colonel Ma Dei-bio's carpets, it seemed we had again demonstrated something. At least Colonel Ma thought so, and expounded that in modern armies—and he had fought over much of central Asia and in China—too much attention was being paid to materiél, to firepower, to manpower, to stationary posts, and too little attention was paid to campaigns of movement, and especially to morale, that kind of morale sparking his own troops. His face shining, he told us there was a fervent energy in his soldiers of Islam who were holding at bay a nation of 5,000,000—themselves famed fighters. In former years the regular Chinese infantry, though guided as always by guile, had never been able to accomplish what his few hundred Moslems were doing. There was certainly considerable fire in this patriotic smoke.

It was true that there was in them a joy and a pride in soldiering not found today in slogging, half-sleeping, motorized infantry, going into battle with a quite often sick, half-yellow feeling in their guts:— bookkeepers and factory hands, farmers and students, turned momentarily into reluctant killers. These few Moslems alone had beaten back large forces of Tibetan cavalry, who in turn, though outnumbered, had defeated Chinese infantry many times:—these same Chinese who were said by officers of General Stilwell's staff to be the world's greatest soldiers. But the Chinese themselves are not fooled, hence their use of the Sining Tungan Moslems.

"If the Moslem peoples of central Asia ever join with the Russian Reds, all the armies of the West cannot take Asia!" cried Colonel Ma Sheng-lung, "You must awaken your people in America to this fact. That we want to be their friends, and fight with their help before it is too late!"

"You forget we Americans have a navy, and an air force."

He stared at me as if I were a child who had stepped on an egg, "You will be unable to beat even the rabble of China! Your casualties will be enormous!"

"Where?" I asked, smiling condescendingly.

"In easily defended Korea, or elsewhere . . . it is coming soon—with the fall of Ma Pu-fang!"

I argued no more, for I too knew that the mode for land war in Asia was changing; I had seen less than 300 American guerrillas tie up more than a million Japanese battle-infantry in China, while two of our guerrillas alone had probably destroyed as many railway locomotives and rolling stock as had the combined British and American Air Forces based on the mainland of Asia, and at a cost of only $1,500 as against a cost of untold millions of dollars in operations, support, and the subsidizing of the Asian countries. There was only one way that man, the ever stubborn, ever learned, and it must always be the hard, bloody way. . . .

In Shan Je Te it was hot, much too hot for us who were long accustomed to the cold air of the uplands, and our horses were swishing their tails at the insects. On a tour of inspection we saw that two hundred Khoshoit Mongol families were settled here in large, square, clay-brick houses, and felt gers which were pitched in many of the courtyards of the town. A forest of masts fluttering with flags stood above flat rooftops and in the walled courts everywhere. Hundreds of tall, thin poplar trees were also here, planted in long ranks by Ma Dei-bio, a wonderful green to our eyes so long accustomed to the yellows, whites and blacks of Tibetan landscapes.

Nearby was a Mongol lamasery in the Tibetan castle style, over which an incarnated god-abbot presided, said to have been formerly a lama in the court of the old Urga king-priest. This king-priest had been blood descendant of Genghis Khan; the living Buddha, Hutuktu, Bogdo Gegan, God and Emperor, Prince of the Four Mongolian Khalka Khanates. He was now replaced by the economic-minded, baggy-pants, brief-case-carrying warrior commissars of the Soviet Socialist Republic of Outer Mongolia. The aged follower of this fantastic Urga prince, apparently also a hutuktu, a living Buddha, sent a messenger saying we must come to see him. He was

far too feeble with age to leave his temple; and as he was preparing
for death and *Khorva* (Magical or Illusory Show), and reincarnation,
this was indeed an honor.

Our tents were pitched alongside the fort in a grove of small
trees, and equipped with Chinese paper lanterns. Solomon, Dorje,
and I had—for courtesy's sake—to take over the colonel's private
quarters within the walls of the fort. We couldn't find Fort Shan
Je Te on the maps, so while joking about it with our astonished
host—who fancied himself holding down Ma Pu-fang's west flank
in Tibet—we marked the fort and town in with bright red ink on
our new military maps.

Snakes had to be watched for. I nearly sat on a small green one
in the grass among the tents of Camp 31. Evidently they were coming out of the Tsaidam, searching for rodents and birds among the
drier gullies of the Burchan Buddha. Mosquitoes were bad, never
a minute free of them, and being accustomed to the pests we and
our livestock suffered accordingly. Even so, we began at once cata-
loguing all things Mongol. The general situation, while known to
Sining, needed timely details to complete the picture. Sir Charles
Bell, the late British political agent, an authority on Lhasa and a
very able observer, had noted he had heard of the existence of
Mongols in Tibet. But since the diplomat had not been permitted
far out of Lhasa (where in 1920 he was the first European ever to
be officially invited by the Tibetans), he could add little to verify
or refute the rumor. Undoubtedly, many of these Mongols, particularly east of us, were the residue of former Mongol invasions
launched in the direction of Lhasa; and Leagues and Banners, together with Arrows, are today represented more or less intact—
though the ancient tribal systems are now destroyed in Soviet-
dominated Outer Mongolia. These Sining Moslems said the fiercest
of the Soviet's shock infantry used to stop the Germans at Moscow
and Stalingrad, had been Mongols.

However, Dorje learned that during the past eight years the Moslem Hussacks (or Khyber Khasaks) had indeed come into Tibet from
Sinkiang across Nan Shan, and had been responsible for pogroms
among the Buddhist Mongols and running off stock, many of these
Hussacks later reaching the safety of the home Khyber country with
their booty. We now learned it was the belief of local Moslems that
eight thousand Mongols had died in these massacres, as the Chinese

Nationalist Government had disarmed them. I had no way of checking such figures of course, in fact my friends seemed very reluctant
to discuss this. Later in Lanchow, mentioning the Hussacks to the
missionaries, they had not heard of any such raids and did not believe
these had occurred. At any rate, a few stray bands of Hussacks were
apparently still in the region, killing and looting what few people
fell across their path. Ma Dei-bio's forces, of course, had been
stripped for the fighting in China against Lin Pao.

As a result of Chinese intriguing and Hussack raiding, few Mongols, except in the Nan Shan mountains and south of them, are left
today in north Tibet, and it was Colonel Ma's opinion that practically none exist in the Tsaidam. For hundreds of years this has
been a favorite Mongol stamping-ground.

The expedition felt the low altitudes, as we were down to somewhere around a mere 8,000 feet. Physical laziness and sluggishness
of mind now cropped up among us. Gone, however, was the nausea
from those who suffered high-altitude sickness, and gone, too, sleepless nights due to lack of sufficient oxygen. Our thumping hearts had
been too long overstrained, though no one seemed to suffer a dilated
heart. Because of the mosquitoes, which set us itching without rest,
we fled within the fort, to a second-story room having a paper-
windowed balcony where the low-flying pests were not so numerous.

A *shanag*, probably second cousin to the Eskimo *shaman*, a Mongol "Black" Pön priest of atavistic sorcery, came and worked to eliminate the mosquitoes; whether it was his magic, or his incense, we
could not determine—but the mosquitoes practically left the rooms.

Colonel Ma held a conclave in one of the rooms and decided to
find a herd of new pack horses and about 40 fresh remounts. Yaks
were considered too slow in these low regions. He scoured the countryside and secured in exchange for our worn yaks, several cattle-
oxen—they being combination pack animals and also broken to haul
the enormous two-wheeled carts in use here.

The Beile, introduced as a prince of the 3rd rank, chief of the
local Mongols, presented to us, after much formal talk, a few sheep.
With the Beile came the Merin (Mongolian magistrate) and the
Khuruldei (Council of Chiefs)—their own laws intact since the Khoshoit sacking of Lhasa in 1637. The Mongol *darkhans*, hereditary
craftsmen, sent a good saddle. I rather imagine these titles are merely
used by the Moslems in a social sense and do not imply power.

The expedition in turn dispensed medicines for these surviving Mongols. It also gave forth with plenty of free advice on how to run their affairs, a prerogative of Chinese government agencies in such regions. A cake was sent to the fort by the hutuktu, this as I recall being made of rice, raisins, brown sugar and *tsao,* a kind of dehydrated reddish date.

At the tents we indulged in our first afternoon tea, with Dorje presiding, plying ourselves with rock sugar and *yuan* (nuts, brown-colored and marble-like in shape). Later, after going over practical plans for the trek east to the great sea of Koko Nor, and marking waterholes on a map, we rode to a rich man's house. At the doorway of the pounded earth building, the crude wooden doors themselves plastered with the Chinese papers printed with some sort of devils in ancient classical costumes (as seen in Sining and all these towns); and as polite guests, each of us tried to salaam his neighbor in ahead of himself. This was necessarily accompanied by a stroking of the beard, and those of us who were clean-shaven pretended we had them. Since each guest insisted he was more humble than his fellows, our anything but grand entrance ended up practically in a wrestling match to see whose friends would have the honor of going in first. Tan Chen-te and Colonel Ma Sheng-lung jerked each other around, most politely of course, in and out of the doorway, finally joining and propelling me to the place of honor at the back of a foot-high table resting on a dais.

On carpets we settled ourselves crosslegged and began to crack and eat watermelon seeds. The customary quiet but elegant speech from the host followed more or less in this manner:

"Dear guests, beloved brothers, honorable sirs—having descended from heaven, you graciously honor me by coming to my poor, miserable house. For my honor, you eat of my disgusting food. For my honor, you sit on my shabby carpets. For my honor, you break your teeth on this tough mutton. Praise God."

Later we crossed over to Colonel Ma's tent, and listened to the breeze moving through the trees. We drank Chinese tea with white blossoms floating on the top of painted cups. We also discussed more plans for obtaining transport and riding animals. But the Hussacks had really impoverished the country, stripped it almost clean. Further, our party was obviously a drain on the local economy and we must clear out soon; and so more agents were dispatched into the countryside. A radiogram from Governor Ma urged us to hurry. Hurry back to Sining! Three hundred thousand troops had been lost to the Reds, who were victorious everywhere in Inner Mongolia, Manchuria, North China, northwest China, Turkestan.

In the starlit evening as we were being entertained by a traveling troupe of Khotan musicians and dancers, in the grove strung with paper lanterns, a Tibetan scout galloped in, reporting to Tan that some horses had been bought from Mongols; *but,* a pack of robbers —probably Hussacks—had attacked and stolen them. The Mongols wanted very much to regain the rustled horses, and at the same time strike a blow at the last Hussacks before they could cross over Chang Tang to the India-Afghan frontier. But all this was beyond our resources.

22

Entertained by a Hutuktu

WHEN a white man serves under the banner of an Oriental chieftain, "face" is the all-important consideration, and he must do everything in his power to build this up and to preserve it. Without face, you are ineffective, paralyzed; your chief servant can very often make you or break you: for important men check on you through him, using their servants as a means of contact.

Next morning after our receiving the news of the robber Hussacks, I was wakened in the fort of Shan Je Te, by the foghorn booming of the ten- or twelve-foot silver and copper ceremonial bassoons being blown at the lamasery. Since we have not gone into the matter of "face" and how it is sometimes built, perhaps this is as good a place as any. Hassan, the faithful servant, entered my kang-equipped bedroom, and playfully flogged off the serving men who were gathering, and brought *sung-pang* tea—believed to be a medical herb and an aid to digestion—and a brass bowl of steaming mutton. Hassan served notice to all, as usual, that he personally, would attend to matters. He wore that morning, a new Turkish cap of curly-black karakul, a robe of dark blue wool and shining black boots said to have been lifted off the corpse of a Red Army Russian officer killed at Khalkin-Gol, called today in Moscow "The Bain Tazagan slaughter," when Zhukov destroyed the Japanese Sixth Army in Mongolia, just prior to World War II.

Hassan beckoned the fort servants to approach closer now that I had begun to dress. He became extremely grand in manner: he deemed it advisable personally to assist me in cinching up and arranging every fold of my robe. But after due consideration he relented a bit, and allowed the others to assist, somewhat; these men were half a dozen regular servants belonging to the quartermaster department.

Hassan barked a command, calling up a man to stand at attention and hold up a mirror. Another held the hot-water basin. Another held comb and brushes. Another a towel. Thus on that morning the shaving operations required the assistance of four valets, not counting Hassan, and this though I wished to shave myself, not desiring a barber, who would want to scrape my eyelids, ears and tongue according to custom.

At last, with shave and honor properly attended to, Hassan bowed me out to the veranda. Below in the court were any number of children, Mongol, Moslem, and Tibetan, and as Dorje and I descended the stairs and walked among them, they sang and made salaams, handing over a shredded wildflower or two probably snatched along their route here. They had come for vaccinations, and when we ran out of vaccine that morning due to our past too liberal policy among the upland Tibetans, they went away happier than when they arrived. So far apparently we had used up, or issued for eventual use, thirty small cases containing many inoculations and drugs. Solomon sent the children away with smiles and promises to send back medicines from Lanchow: this, eventually, he did, in spite of battle conditions there.

In learning more about the Mongols, and something of Mahāyana (The Higher Path), I compared it as best I could with Ceylon's Southern School, Hīnayāna (The Lesser Path), which I had already read something of in that island while with the OSS. With the best interpreter of Mongolian, Dorje, and a Tibetan called Damchu, I called on the old Hutuktu of the lamasery. Dorje did not think him a real hutuktu, but that the locals called him that out of respect. This high-walled temple lamasery, and its inner compound, were banded horizontally by broad stripes of red, white, and black; I was told its wide double doors must be entered from the "sacred side" —the east. We wended through Shan Je Te's narrow streets, and at the gates of the lamasery found watchdogs chained loosely to wobbly posts. They barked with their usual ferocity.

We edged past and walked by obos; at the far end of a long rectangular court of *dugans* (temples), stood a 7-foot-high prayer-paper furnace, belching acrid smoke. Walls and courts were everywhere, painted in classical scenes beloved of the lamaists; explained as exalted Buddhas and Buddhasatvas sitting in the mysterious lotus position, their hands held in the secret code-signs. These spiritual attributes of the Cosmos are positioned so that the hip joints are dislocated, contemplation fills the stilled mind which is centered on the White Light, and the Buddha is presumably hearing only the sounds of the Life Flux and the Generating Universes—part of his own bloodstream no doubt—echoing in the psychic inner ear.

Crowds of Mongols in tall peaked hats and sheepskin chupas, and also Tibetan Drök-pas, prostrated themselves on the ground, others doing penance by measuring their lengths around the temples, moving clockwise in their circumambulation. Mongols in passing through the main court, were spinning various prayer-mills a few of which were tall as a man. Two of these barrels were painted with gods in their Fearful Aspect, and were on both sides of the doors opening into the hall of contemplation, study, and worship. The few missionaries who have seen central Asian temples (missionaries are seldom permitted in Tibet), hate them, calling the gods "Devils and Idols," but to those possessing slightly more information (such as Dorje's) and possibly more detached and less-hardened hearts (perhaps such as mine), and who realize even superficially what profound ideas are symbolized here, find a feeling very often of what can only be described as "goodness."

Dorje, Damchu and I entering, found inside the main hall—itself a beehive of activity—a forest of red-lacquered pillars, upholding painted ceilings hung with "rainbow" prayer-flags, and painted banners called *than-Kas*. Rows upon rows of low dais for the chanting monks were extended parallel in long ranks, and red carpeted. Unlike most other temples in the East, those in Tibet and Japan are clean, and in Tibet are entered on bare feet. Crosslegged on golden thrones were giant as well as small deities, gods and devils of many hues and colors—explained as Aspects of Divine Consciousness. There were numerous different Buddhas, besides those brass ones most familiar to the West: green Buddhas (Amogha-Siddhi), yellow Buddhas (Ratna-Sambhava), blue Buddhas (Samanta-Bhadra), red Buddhas (Amitabha), white Buddhas (Vajra-Sattva). Each apparently presides over one of the Five Elements (Kingdoms) of Water, Air, Earth, Fire, Ether. Buddhas are symbolical, say the lamas, not idols to be worshiped: they are mystic symbols only, as symbols are used in higher mathematics, to enable the mind to grasp the profound ideas of the Unborn-Undying. Except to the masses, there are no personal gods in Northern Buddhism, no real anthropomorphism.

A library was here of sacred volumes with wooden backs, patinaed from constant use, some block-printed in black ink, others hand-painted in letters of gold, having silken yellow tabs. *Dörje* sceptres (thunderbolts) and *dilbus* (handbells) lay on the altars, symbolizing Method and Wisdom. Dorje explained it is generally thought that the exoteric similarity of holy objects, mass, confession, etc., existing between the Catholic and Buddhist churches might be due to early Nestorian missionaries. The sacred numeral "7" is used not only in Christian doctrine but in Buddhist as well. But this "borrowing" neither he nor I believe to be true; for the priest-historian Ashvagosha wrote in the first century A.D., which indicates Northern Buddhism to be fundamentally the same then as it is now. In fact, primitive Christianity due to Indian missionaries in Alexandria and elsewhere, had borrowed much of its doctrines and symbols from not only the Greeks but also the East, and actually accepted Reincarnation—later ruled out by the established sects brought together by the eastern Romans! This last edict was issued in 553 A.D. by the Second Council of Constantinople. The Trinity and the Incarnation are also possibly borrowed. There is known to me in India a sect worshipping Jesus whom it is claimed studied in India seven years, and while this one is Moslem, Tibetans say the Sermon on the Mount is pure Buddhism. The tomb which this sect guards, is believed by them to be that of Christ, who rose to heaven in spirit but whose body was returned to India. This Moslem tradition is reinforced by an exactly similar tradition in Tibet, where manuscripts relating in great detail to the Indian years of Christ are extant today. The West of course, and Christian tradition itself, has no knowledge of the life of Christ between the age of twelve years and thirty.

Monks were going about the temples dressed in red and yellow togas; all of them marshaled by the red-gowned Chötrimpa, the provost, wearing a yellow Grecian helmet and carrying his mace of authority. Some monks were placing lotus incense, slabs of cooked meat, and containers of butter before the images—a phase of the Holy Communion of the Buddhist Trinity. I had a fleeting impression that here, in the 20th century, was ancient Egypt and Rome, Greece and Babylonia, Chichen Itza and Sheba. Schopenhauer, considered by some to be the West's foremost philosopher, believed after much study that only the Vedas (from which Buddhism stems) holds the true riddle of life, man, eternity, and the knowledge of God. Yet, even today—and who has not talked to many such!—are men who call themselves enlightened, who would destroy the objects then before me, even as did the Spaniards in their *autos de fé* at the temples of Peru, Mexico and Yucatan. What wouldn't we give to possess the lost books of the Maya—philosophy, religion, mathematics, and medicine.

Other priests were beating circular, flat drums with swan-necked drumsticks. The *löb-pon,* professor of doctrine, chanted endless dogma from his texts. In other halls, behind doors fastened by heavy brass locks, were being conducted secret rites; and no man except of the lamahood—guardians of the Mysteries—could enter. Such priests I was told are believed by the Mongols to die to all outward appearances for as long as 21 days, except for a single warm spot on the top of the head. Another was said, in his psychic body, to be able to walk on water. These miracles I doubted, but they are believed in completely by not only Mongols but Tibetans.

Symbolic objects, many of very ancient Shamanistic origin, were crowded into the temples: as I recall there was a zoo of stuffed animal skins—such as yaks, cows, cats, dogs, birds, leopards and such; on precious trays were insects, some real, others of metal or stone. And there were *garudas* (Horned Eagles) with human-bird bodies, having two human-like arms, eagle wings and feet. Another, one out of many idols, was the Great Glorious Buddha-Heruka, three-headed, the right face being white, the left, red, the central, brown; embraced by the Mother, Buddha-Krotishaurima, her right hand clinging to his neck and her left putting to his mouth a red shell filled with blood. All were apparently symbolical of the Will behind nature, the senseless Will manifesting Itself through evolution culminating in the brain of man, so as to acquire ultimate realization of Itself on the Wheel of Life, and the eventual disappearance of matter into the Knowing First Cause.

Upstairs, through painted halls of red, green, yellow, white and blue, on which were executed exquisite bouquets of celestial flowers, we were taken quietly by a deputation of monks to a smaller shrine. Here was the Hutuktu, a very old man with the face of a mummy, sitting at the naked feet of the Maidari Buddha. This golden deity caught my attention, for it was very lifelike: the beautiful half-smiling Buddhist king of heaven, obviously half-man, half-god, seated so humbly on his throne, and yet so splendidly robed in brocades and white and red silken embroideries. A curl of incense rose before the wise, gentle face, contributing to the illusion of animation.

After bowing to the Hutuktu, I draped across the thin hands a hadak—emblematic of the rainbow; and then we withdrew. At the door I hesitated in the shadows thrown by the butterlamps which rested on the floor. Near the living God were shelves of rectangular books of sky-blue paper (made in Lhasa) marked with letters of gold. To look at them it was necessary to unwrap the cloths in which they were wrapped. The old lama would soon leave behind his ancient shell, to be reborn in an embryo that would become a child and succeed him as Hutuktu, making himself known to the searching lamas by selecting from many objects certain ones that had been dear to him in his former incarnation.

Downstairs we moved through the temples and listened to the spinning of *chörlos,* the hum of prayers in the halls and outside courtyard, the clashing cymbals, long flutes, ancient shaped drums—all of which, when even momentarily idle, are wrapped in sacred scarves before being set aside by the priests. Several Mongol women wore witches'-hats, peaked sharply and a foot high, around which were bound rims of fur. A few wore turquoise and coral (the colors of "Space" and "Fire") over long brocaded gowns, but most were poor and had the chupa. Their hair was braided tightly into a fine net of tiny pigtails. Hanging from this net, swinging pendulant to the ground, were cloth trains, clanking with large bowls of solid silver. Surprised by the weight, I found these hair braids are false, being of yak hair, and are fitted cleverly over the real hair like a crown. This was learned when Damchu gave a playful pull on the pigtail of a pretty Mongol girl who was placing a silver bowl of wild iris on the altar before a Buddha.

She turned and smiled, lifting the crown of tiny braids off her head so as to show it to us. Her mother moved in, spoiling Damchu's research program. When we left I placed an offering on the main altar of Chenrizi. The Hutuktu was said to have contacts, direct or indirect, in Outer Mongolia, Inner Mongolia, Lhasa, India, perhaps even to the rim of the Arctic Ocean, Russia, China and Siberia . . . if so, he was not so isolated in mid-Asia as one might suppose.

In the afternoon we and the officers attended a dinner of many courses, in a "great" Shan Je Te house. After the feast of roasted camel and rice cooked in mare's milk, our host petitioned the two contented magistrates, Colonel Ma Sheng-lung and Captain Tan, asking, in the time-honored manner, for a favor. It seemed that a soldier of Colonel Ma's merry troop must very soon marry his one and only beloved daughter, and take her to Fort Chakar.

The colonel listened gravely: finally he roared, waving his golden toothpick—"Allah's kindness on all the pretty, gentle females! His fire and brimstone on all the ugly, sharp-tongued ones!"

"She is very beautiful, very gentle," protested the father, while leading out his daughter, and holding aside the green silken veil worn by Chinghai Moslem women. And indeed, she was very beautiful and very gentle, in looks, but who—as Tan pointed out with a shrug—could tell her temper unless he had lived with her.

"By the Lord's shadow, this great honor is not for me," roared Colonel Ma.

But the father became even more persuasive, and suddenly dropping his voice, gave out with more timely details.

"Mohammed has no punishment good enough for this rascal of mine—Ma Liang!" bellowed Ma, but looking very pleased with the alleged potency of his follower.

Finally, after much stalling, all right then! He, Ma Sheng-lung, a man of justice as all the world knew, would not only make the girl happy with her husband, but he would personally stand all expenses for a wedding feast. Liang was poor and had no family, therefore he, the colonel, would act as legal father. All this apparently was according to Moslem law, or at least local custom. There would be food such as Shan Je Te had never seen, horse races, war games, sword dancing, the house-to-house calling on dear friends, and the singing of love songs!

"But, dear friend, all this will cost you a fortune," warned the cautious Tan, with a smile.

"Never mind!" cried Colonel Ma happily, now that his face was established and the honor of his troop saved, "I will hold court and fine somebody!" Never have I seen him look so virtuous. Further, no soldier of his could go around seducing the females of the land and building up the population without his, Ma Sheng-lung's, personal blessing. The weeping father stroked his beard at such good fortune descending upon his house. I must explain that, while in China soldiering is considered a low job, here in north Tibet it was held the most honorable of professions, and the sons of the best

Moslem families were anxious to serve under the famed colonel. At that time I learned that four of the richest men of the Tsaidam were the fathers of four of our private troopers. No wonder their arms were of the finest, their horses, saddles and robes those of local princes.

I realized something was going on behind the scenes, but what this was I did not know. Dorje bent an ear to the conversation and further enlightened me. Colonel Ma shifted himself; "God has momentarily blinded me, after eating all this good food!" He shoved the skullcap over one eye, and thrust out his gold teeth and big chin. "Settle on me, as father, a dowry of fifty saddle-horses! And I'll take this wench off your hands!"

So that was the game; as "father" he figured he was entitled to a dowry. Tan and I glanced at one another and grinned; our friend was managing all right. This time, the father of the girl—who had known about the lack of family and had hoped to get off easy—really wept. Papers would be drawn up, the settlement being about a third of the horses asked. With Tan's wink, I realized Ma was richer by a free meal, several horses, and had landed besides a fine bride for one of his men. And I shall never forget the father's anguish, when under questioning by Ma, the girl said she—of course!—was a virgin. We rolled over the carpets laughing till it was necessary for an orderly to fetch the colonel and help him mount his horse, for now a messenger had come to take us off to yet another feast, at the lamasery. As we rode through the mud-walled streets, Captain Tan congratulated our friend on his success as a father. The colonel answered with a faint smile—

"Brothers . . . God alone is great. He invariably watches over His simple soldiers."

The Hutuktu was ready in his temple. Greetings over, he told us he was born a Tibetan, and named Chutang Danzig Namja, and raised—as we had heard from the Moslems—as a Mongol in Urga. Entertaining us in an anteroom, he told that in Soviet Russia were still many Buddhists. . . .

There was a seventh man present (besides Tan, Ma, Solomon, Dorje, the lama and I), our layman host, who was to serve us at the feast to come; he was introduced as the paramount Tibetan Pönpo (Lord) of Shan Je Te, his name—Jang Ba Sak. He was believed to be a member of the Dalai Lama's intelligence service for Turkestan and northwest Tibet, and so to Jang Ba Sak I said our aim was to proceed direct to Sining. This seemed to please him, and we were led upstairs to the throne room, a red-lacquered hall, and presently seated with ceremony at a Chinese table. A few moments later, just opposite in a red chair, was placed the living Buddha—Chutang Danzig Namja, gowned in sumptuous robes and silks. Massive silver butterlamps burned between us and the Buddha dominated the scene. Colonel Ma, very alert, estimated each lamp to contain hundreds of new catties of silver, all together a king's ransom—that is, an ancient king, not an impoverished modern one. Strangely enough, and a contradiction of most Moslem history, the only part of China and the Chinese "empire" where religion was really free (Ma Pu-fang subsidized Chinese and Moslem temples and the Tibetan Panchen Lama, and I believe has even donated to the Christian missionaries in Sining—at least he allows them to operate) was in this Moslem northwest.

I do not know of any American having been entertained by a lama said to be an Hutuktu, though very likely some scholar will one day point out to me the errors of my ways. A cloth embroidered with blue and white lotuses was laid on the ebony table; several courses passed over it. There were no Chinese chopsticks. Our table service was of Mongol two-pronged silver forks, and 10-inch silver knives with blood-red burl handles from grape roots bedded in solid Arctic ivory—famous knives made at Dalanor, in Chakar, Inner Mongolia. They had been sent to the living Buddha by a prince of the Ordos Desert Mongols—said to have been among Genghis Khan's shock-troops in his conquest of China.

When we took our leave of the living Buddha servants followed with bowls heaped with black rock-sugar, nuts, melon seeds, bricks of tea, and cuts of sheep and yak meat. There were also packets of "human head" tea wrapped in green paper, candied melon rinds from Hami, pale-green raisins from Turfan, red rose wines from some other place, fowls such as ducks, pheasants, pigeons, black-skinned chickens. But of horses there were none.

That night a message came from Ma Pu-fang. Tibetan Moslem plans must be completed for an immediate withdrawal out of China; including estimates on the opening of possible caravan routes between India and High Tartary. With the victorious Communists now sealing off coastal south China all of the south, west, and south-western provinces would fall. The northwest provinces and the "dependencies" under Ma Pu-fang would definitely also collapse, either before or soon after the others, it made no long-range difference. I guessed only an overland road from south to central Asia (and none existed for Moslem anti-Red forces!) could keep any of the troops intact and fighting a *jehad* near this heart of World Communism. I began that rainy night to draw up military and political plans for submission to Ma Pu-fang in Lanchow—now his central headquarters. These included not only methods for facing the Reds in the localized region of China proper, but international patterns for an underground attack on the Soviet Union itself.

Based on what we had learned in Tibet, plans were made to salvage 30,000 crack veteran Moslem soldiers. Today this army constitutes the only effective Asian anti-Communist force available in central Asia. It seemed to me, as I worked in the rain, that exploration had come a long way since the days when it was necessary only to pick up a few flowers and press them in a book. At a time like this, the modern explorer in central Asia, unless he is a specialized scientist or a collector should be a combat political and military tactician. He must not only observe; he must act. With China lost, there was only one thing to do; see that Ma Pu-fang became the eastern hinge of the world Moslem block, and that Turkey became the western hinge. I must suggest to the governor that he make a pilgrimage to Mecca—and then continue to Cairo and Turkey, for the solidifying *within* of the generally anti-West Moslem peoples. He was said to have a house in Pakistan (a Moslem country), and from here agents could direct the means for supplying arms and essentials to his forces in Tibet. On this army and any of the Chang-Tang Tibetans who might join, would depend the fate of India and ultimately all Asia to the east of that country.

It was now clear that eight years before a thousand destitute Hussack families had trailed across Nan Shan and penetrated the Tsaidam Basin; and only last year did the main force return to Sinkiang. The Hussack raids against the Mongols had left only a remnant of these people, and these absolutely stricken and impoverished. The Chinese Nationalist Government did nothing to protect them during the fatal eight years, as the Hussacks were well-armed and stronger than the government's western forces.

A single Mongol herdsman lost overnight a thousand horses—the source of his Arrow's livelihood. (An "Arrow," or "Sumon," is a subdivision of a "Banner," or "Hoshun.") The Hussacks are fanatic Mohammedans, professional killers, speaking a Turki dialect; they are ger dwellers when here.

In spite of the Hussack massacres, the Moslems said twenty-six Mongol Banners, however fragmented, still exist today in north Chinghai (Tibetan—Amdo.) This "Banner" designation is the same as that authorized by the Manchu emperors, who craftily scattered the feared Mongols to the far rims of the Celestial Empire.

23

The Desert of Mok Hor

WE NOW gathered together a mixed caravan of our old animals and what few new ones we had acquired —pack and saddle horses, yaks, camels, oxen and mules, and drove this hodgepodge east across a river in spring spate. This was called the Jagharu, thought by Dorje to be the main eastern Tsaidam feeder, Mongols guiding us through the several deep channels of swift water. Colonel Ma Dei-bio, his black overcoat slapping like a storm cloud, forded the river only to lose his footing and nearly drown. Somebody fished him out, getting him to the farther, east, bank, which infuriated him. He was assured that Allah rules every man's fate, and after lending him a tall camel to get back across the torrent and return to the fort, he bestowed blessings, stroked his beard, and left with a growl. We set our course northeast, using a road.

This we soon left and following a trail under a deep violet sky of clouds we began climbing into a mass of hills called the Kuder, which were, until the coming of the Hussacks, one of the richest Mongol ranges in Tibet. On our right stretched the snow-girted Baga Aman Range, while north, on the left, streamed the white flag of the Ikhe Aman Mountains. (These are local Mongol names and are not likely to be found on any foreign map.) In the Kuder were clouds of mosquitoes; and as we rode ever higher we prayed for a breeze to stir out of the blue haze of the westward Tsaidam at our backs, and drive the pests back into the grass where they bred.

Spring flowers were perfuming the air. Tibetans, Moslems and a few Mongols sang lustily as the caravan rattled along against the base of cliffs or trailed through canyons, listening gleefully to the resounding echoes of a hundred lusty voices. They sang sagas of war and love, local songs that were epical, wild, and strange, underlined with a sure streak of beauty: among them I recall were—*Jyekundo Dancing, Heroes of Three Nations, Kashgar.*

Still climbing the caravan traversed the steep, ever-mounting hills, and finally, with a tremendous digging in of muscle, bone and tendons, and considerable wheezing, crossed the cedar-forested summit—leaving behind the vast, empty, rich grazing grounds of the vanished Mongols whose skeletons alone now peopled it. Eastward stretched a high, dry desert, gleaming white in a pall of dust. This we must cross. Leaving the pack train to follow our trail, many of us hurried on downhill: miles farther we emerged on a broad, gray-earthen valley. An oasis appeared, and being under irrigation, the air was everywhere thick with mosquitoes. Unless other oases were enroute, this would be the last before entering the Desert of Mok Hor, probably a local name.

"We must wait in this village," said Tan, "consolidate the caravan, strengthen it, and learn about present water conditions ahead."

To shake off a few of the stinging pests, we trotted into the small caravanserai of Tsagan Ussu (White Water), a rather dismal, ramshackle place with clay walls and more bearded, skull-capped men than Mongols and Tibetans. We dismounted at the headquarters, marked by a flag, our yak-tail swatters whipping the air and, we hoped, the mosquitoes.

It was 5:40 P.M. and we groaned with gladness as we stretched our legs, for the day across the Kuder had been hard and (in our clothes) scorching hot. Tsagan Ussu proved dusty and stinking; it was a link of the north Tsaidam caravan road to Sinkiang, from whence roads led to Persia, Afghanistan, and Kashmir in India. Along its single vulture-infested street, littered with a few bones and much manure, stood any number of camels, yaks, oxen, mules and horses, the lead animals belled. Some were being watered, other relieved of their packs of wool, silk, grains, ores, and all the cargoes of this most remote region in the Orient.

Bitten by mosquitoes and fleas all that night, we were compensated next morning when Tsagan Ussu's leading citizens—a black-gowned Chinese merchant, a skull-capped Tungan, a fur-capped Tibetan lama, a button- and peacock-plumed Mongol, a turbaned Turki, a Sart without a hat but wearing carpet slippers—came and for the most part gravely stroked their chins and presented a sheep from each of their peoples. The cooks lost no time cutting the throats of the sheep and getting them into pots over a fire, for we were starved. Our elevation was 3,135 meters (9,552 feet), and we designated this camp as "32." It was pitched away from the flea-crawling buildings, and in a walled park shaded by rows of young pines, poplars, and willows. The park was cool, and with carpets scattered about in the shade of the tents, was endurable. A ditch flowed through it and from this we slaked our thirst, and dipped cooking water.

Complications set in; a Tungan messenger who had ridden all yesterday and all night without halt except for changing horses, galloped in on a sweating horse from the magistrate of Tulan, in whose *hsien* (district) I now learned we were. In the message—a red-bordered square of rice-paper—were flowery greetings, but no information about water in the desert or about transportation. Then came a radio from Lanchow ordering Colonel Ma back to Fort Chakar on Oring Nor to prepare for receiving the retreating army. Tan Chen-te would ride with my party east to Koko Nor, the Blue Sea, and then on to Sining, the terminus of the expedition. And we must hurry before the Communists got there!

While others scoured the oasis for pack animals, I pulled off my clothes and soon had a bucket brigade of hot water extending from the campfire to my tent. Word got around that Americans must be dirtier than other people, as this one was always washing.

Tsagan Ussu's population squatted around on its carpet slippers, sucked loudly on its Chinese hubblebubbles, and took in the sights. "By the Beard of the Blessed Prophet! That foreigner must be preparing for his *hadj* (pilgrimage to Mecca)!" Dorje, I suspected sometimes, did not give a literal translation, but one that amused him. Anyway, he and Solomon, Tan and Colonel Ma were soon at it themselves.

That night among the trees (they were only a few feet high) a Mongol youngster danced the legendary *Flying Crane Dance;* another the *Nomad Dance; The Shepherd's Song* was sung by the daughter of a Tibetan merchant, and it set our feet to twitching. Various Moslem musical instruments were brought out, and a beautiful 18-year-old Turki girl swathed in a green veil, sang *A Lover in Autumn,* and then her heavily painted eyes and lashes peering over her veil, she handed me an armful of red roses. This last would have been a calamity anywhere but among Moslems.

At dawn a deeper spell of heat descended from out of the desert, to hold the town in its grip. We nearly suffocated—wool padding was jerked out of Chinese military jackets and pants. Linings were ripped from robes. The thermometer shot up to 108° F. in the shade; Chinese fans were at a premium in the mart. Finally, the *ula* transportation arrived, supplementing our own—this ula train being of horses, mules, dzos, camels, carts pulled by *laung*—a queer-looking oxen. This ancient ula system is undoubtedly a hardship, compelling farmers and herders to pay off their tax arrears by supplying the government with transportation, and in addition accompany the animals and care for them. Regardless of custom, I paid out hard silver dollars, though Colonel Ma winced.

At midnight this crazy circus-looking caravan started ahead into the desert, led off by some thirty camels, and half our men. The rest of us went to sleep. At dawn the bugle sounded, and Ma Sheng-lung and his gay blades—Tibetan and Moslem tribesmen—all singing, escorted us for the last time, through the dusty street of Tsagan Ussu and its buzzards. Beyond, on the edge of the desert, the men of both parties galloped in a circle, while Colonel Ma, Dorje, Solomon and I dismounted. He was silent, though smiling in the dusky light; and in shaking hands "foreign style" I palmed into his hard right paw, the jack-knife which I had once presented him, and which he had returned during our feud at Camp 16 east of the Amne Machin peaks.

He gasped in surprise (though I had supposed he had forgotten it) and without looking, dropped the knife into his boot top. In his own palm was already held (and it was my turn to be surprised!) the golden toothpick I had returned. He grabbed me by both shoulders, and two big streams of water ran down his weather-beaten face.

"I am sorry about the Amne Machin camp," he said.

And I wanted to say, "Never again will we hunt together, tell stories together, eat yak and sheep meat together, laugh together . . ." but did not.

A moment later after bidding Dorje and Solomon goodbye, Ma Sheng-lung walked away and leapt into his saddle, and touching spurs to the white stallion, raced for the town, his cavalcade streaming after, firing their guns into the air and shouting such farewells as—

"May God keep you always, Prince Dorje and Solomon and Clark-ah! May your stars shine brightly!"

With Tan, Abdul, and the Secretary leading off, we rode east across the wind-stirred, dusty tang, the daylight showing white dots here and there which launched upward on wings to become cranes. Our horses, already sweating, moved along in a canter; at 9 o'clock Tan made a swing left into the northeast, and at 10:30 reined abruptly north to enter a desert valley gray with mosquitoes. A seepage was found here but no water. The column threaded through dry sand dunes dotted with brush, scrubby, thorny stuff, and clumps of dry spear-grass. The sun turned coppery. A yellow haze was smeared in a ring clear around the horizon, which merged into a blue disk of sky. A wind came up like a blast from an open furnace and the blue melted to a reddish copper, as the sands danced and sent dust skirling into the upper regions.

As we penetrated deeper into the desert, we rode along slower, for the horses were lathered in their fear of the clutching sands. These sands must have once been the bed of an ancient *nor*. Hours later we rattled across a very small stream clogged with algae, and followed it into dunes, where it finally sank into a bog, ending its existence like so many others do in the center of this queerly inverted heart of the earth's largest continent. Although the tracks of the pack caravan were at times wiped out by winds, we still were able to follow or to take short cuts and intercept them. Yellow dunes rose in waves and ridges all around, many being 30 to 50 feet high at their crests, perhaps drifting forward (though some may be stationary) like Juggernauts before the Tartary winds, senselessly obliterating everything in their path—valleys and streams. Soon the tracks would likewise be buried, and all trace of our passing erased forever.

A camel was found, abandoned; then two very thin old horses, their throats cut. We hurried on. Mirages sprang up in thin wavering lines—"idea lakes," Damchu called them, shimmering with a cool blueness between groves of tall trees, inviting puddles of shadows at their feet; but we reached them to find only empty desert and dry sand whose very sight burned my throat. Without warning the tracks turned right, and we entered an oasis set in a wide wash, slit with irrigation channels into which we waded gleefully, drinking the muddy water and splashing each other like a lot of kids. Had the camel train not turned into this oasis we would have by-passed it. The horses stomped, riling the water, tossing their wet lips and neighing, a few kicking out and nipping handy necks.

A man dressed in white pants closed at the ankles, a short jacket bound with a red sash, and a kind of turban on his head, came sliding down a sand cliff. He stroked his beard and said the place was very small, and called Sharia Ha (Pine Tree), immortalizing, apparently, a wind- and sand-blasted knot clinging to a crack in the side of a cliff. "Much worse lies ahead of you," he said, "Your caravan is safe. You must rest here."

While jumping the ditch of water farther on, my horse slipped and lurched forward, falling short, and stumbled. I checked his fall, swinging my right leg over the saddle pommel and his neck, intending to slide off the left shoulder so he could extricate himself from the bog. At that moment, Alashan heaved up, tossing me head over heels into the brush beyond. For a moment I lay stunned, and on moving, thought my shoulder might be broken. But the only damage was to my pride, a rotted headstall hair rope held in my hand, the bursted $2 box camera at my belt, while I and the carbine, carried on a sling across my back, had also parted company. Tan cleared the ditch in a long jump, and pulling over, chided me. He caught up the horse, and I was soon mounted.

Several houses presently appeared—large and flat-roofed, protected by walls of pounded clay. The people were Mongols, growers of *ney*, the hardy Tibetan barley; old settlers here who are being driven off by the Chinese, who for a "squeeze," obtain "legal" ownership from the hsien magistrates. The Sharia Ha Mongols are thus recognized only as squatters on their own lands, now, of course, the new Chinese owners' property. Since not much has been written about the Tibetan Mongols, I should add that to keep from starving—for they have forgotten the nomad culture and would perish on the steppes —these desert Mongols usually stay on as laborers, their own women sometimes serving as concubines. Should summary justice be carried out against such legalized robbery, or revenge be undertaken, swift punitive measures are dealt the Mongols, as I learned from one of them. We had lunch (tsamba) at one such "Chinese" house, with Mongol servants—dirty and ragged. On the altar, placed before the bearded Mongol god, Tsagan Oborgon (Protector of Pastures and Flocks), was a bowl of desert flowers, perhaps a silent plea for divine justice; for gone were the red-blooded laws of Genghis Khan's Yasse, gone forever since the Chinese invasion of Koko Nor (Chinghai) in north Tibet.

Tan sent the caravan out into the desert to make camp. And while the others rested on a kang and tried to keep the flies off, and because I could no longer stomach the arrogant Chinese, I walked through fields of wild iris. The iris, which brings gladness to the color-starved eye and joy to the heart, is called by the Mongols "Little Daughter."

Nearby and close to a wrecked temple, on the north side of the houses, in an east-west line, loomed four giant sentinels of the dead, *soboroks* (the Mongol *chörten*). We had not seen anything like them before. The Tibetans build their great burial stupas in a round shape, somewhat like a top inverted, but these soboroks were square, and set astronomically, their twin faces turned southwards toward Lhasa, and northwards toward Urga. The multiple roofs were of three tiers, the widest being twelve feet along each side, and stacking up from large to small. On top were set 6-foot wooden spires, with the sacred emblem of the cupped moon, sun and flame.

Inside, visible through windows, were 4-inch tablets and cones of clay having patterned buttons and molded Buddhas. The clay is said to be made from the deceased Mongols' ashes. There must have been thousands of these tablets, objects which would one day likely confound archeologists, as today do the tombs of Ur and Babylonia.

I joined the others, who were wearily napping on their carpets, and soon we rode on to occupy Camp 33. It lay beyond in the desert, the tents glowing a welcome as night settled. Feed-crunching files of tethered camels, horses, yaks, mules, and oxen were already established between the tents. The wagons had been drawn up in a circle, as protection.

There were now with the expedition 240 animals: 34 oxen, 29 cart horses, 22 pack horses, 20 mules, 32 camels, 83 saddle horses, and a few remounts. Personnel had been trimmed at Sharia Ha to a 22-soldier escort, 40 Sarts and nomadic Turki of different tribes, quite a few of our old Fort Ta Ho Pa Tibetan tribesmen, and 30 new Tibetans—mostly Tanguts. Tanguts may very well be the descendants of mysterious Khara Khoto, Kozlov's famous "Black, Dead City" in West Mongolia (Black Gobi). Kozlov believed the desert "had swallowed them" some 600 years ago. Our Tanguts said their legends stated that some of their ancestors had indeed been driven out of Khara Khoto by a Chinese army, but that the survivors reached Koko Nor (or Ch'ing Hai), the Blue Sea. Here Dorje and I would soon see the Tangut tribes intact!

Gathered round a brush campfire, Solomon Ma, Abdul, the Secretary, Tan, Tujeh, Lord Huardamu, and all the others who were not on guard listened to a typical story of the Tibetan deserts. We had spread ourselves comfortably while gazing at the stars, enjoyed a full round of stories of hunting, fighting, and lovemaking. Finally Prince Dorje spoke, his face lit by the fire, filled with dignity and a touch of pride:

"In the mid-1700's the Manchus came out of China and killed 600,000 Öret Mongols, surprised in Inner Mongolia; thus began the Chinese pogroms against my people, still being carried on for the ultimate extermination of the Warrior Race. Having destroyed the Mongol South Wing they then, by decoying allies with intrigue and gold, took over all Sinkiang from the weakened Mongol West Banner—held by the Torgut Horde, my own, actually the 5th Khanate. Later they seized the other four Khanates, in Khalka, which today is Red Outer Mongolia.

"The Torguts—those who escaped the massacres of the Chinese—gathered together, and moved across the face of central Asia into Europe. Previously, it had been a Torgut who, having conquered the Tatar Hordes beyond the Urals in Russia, swore allegiance to the Czar of the Russias, by licking his knife's edge and placing it against his throat, and whom Russia then trusted and launched as their cavalry commander against the Turkish Empire in Constantinople. Under him the Torguts fought and defeated the Ottoman Empire—and its African, Arabian, and Middle East confederation of Moslem nations and races. These Torguts held, alone, the entire Moslem front penetrating Europe through the Balkans, thus allowing Russia to put down internal chiefs and to consolidate her feudal rear areas—forming what is today Red Russia. Two hundred and fifty years ago these Torguts smashed the feared Charles XII of Sweden, Europe's strong man.

"In 1771, 400,000 Torguts prepared to leave Russia by a ruse, learning from spies that Russia would now destroy them, though they—still Buddhists—had loyally served for generations. 'Bloody' Catherine [The Mongol name for Catherine the Great] then sent against them her Cossack armies, killing 300,000 men, women, and children. But in the end, 'Bloody' Catherine lost the campaign, for though her armies pursued the Torgut Horde clear across south Europe and Asia to the deserts of Sinkiang, she had forevermore lost for Russia the support of the true Mongols. She had killed 300,000 but 50,000 still lived. Today, the Western Banners of the Torguts rest in their gers to attack in revenge the Slavic masses of the west. Clark!—the Red Army in Russia uses hundreds of thousands of northern Mongols. Why do you not go among the free West Mongols, and see in them the means for bringing about the fall of Red Russia?"

"I think the White House and the Pentagon should decide such matters," I answered.

"But they know nothing of the situation!"

"Forget it. Right now we are working on Amne Machin and the Moslems, remember?"

That night we rested comfortably, for there were no alarms, only a wolf or two. We struck camp at 8 A.M. next day, waiting late for a fog to burn off the desert, and finally rode at a slow pace into a white eastern sky. The pack train (including the big carts) had not been sent ahead as the desert seemed to hold some vague threat, about which Tan and the others would not speak. I suspected robbers, for invariably raiders and stock thieves were denied by them, as reflecting on the Moslem peace preservation program. It was usually only by Dorje talking to one of the underlings that anything of this kind was learned. I rather suspect we had been subject to more rustling forays than I knew about.

My face, previously frostbitten, was in poor shape due to mosquitoes in the Kuder hills and Tsagan Ussu. Skin was peeling off and no amount of protective United Nations' white-zinc ointment would help against the desert's wind and sun. Finally I bound a black silk scarf around my head, cutting eye-holes and a mouth-hole —scaring a few Tibetans passing west, if not easing my pain very much.

Sand . . . sand . . . sand—after two hours of trudging through the clinging stuff, word came in that robbers were riding far out along our flanks. We hurried on. There was no question of stopping to fortify ourselves against possible attack. We had to have water. Many of the animals, especially our old stock, were already weakening. Our guides said there was water and we had nothing to worry about.

All this hot desert region through which we trudged lay southwest of Koko Nor. Underfoot was a crusty, saline, sometimes sandy, white-glaring mirror sparsely covered with a low, spiny brush. Solomon thought this would be bad country to fight in, offering little protection. We continued—camels moaning, yaks grunting, some packs rattling and making a considerable racket. Several times in rougher country Tan took precautionary measures, but instead of the robbers cutting in and charging, as was quite often customary according to the men, only kyangs scurried away from our line of march, and gazelles flashed signals as they jumped away under thin spirals of white dust. It became plain to some that the robbers were banking on our not finding sufficient water for so large and awkward a caravan. The Secretary warned that sometimes waterholes are found poisoned. . . . As I think back on it, he may have meant poisoned from chemicals in the ground.

While going ever deeper into the desert that afternoon, half-asleep in the saddle from the impact of heat and fatigue, wearily swishing off horseflies and gnats, two strange Tibetans were found checking on our strength and movements. They were watching from a ridge overlooking an old trail we were at the moment following. One of our flankers had luckily crossed their tracks; and instantly taking their trail, he approached them from the rear, shooting one fellow in the back of the head (so he said) and capturing the other. This one was led along on the end of a rope attached to a saddle cantle.

A scout was sent forward to the top of a low hill. He cantered back saying he had seen the water; we dodged north and camped on a stream called Sha Liu Ho (Sand Willow River), its shallow bed gleaming with mica. As the animals and men drank, Dorje and I saw that this stream flows not into the nearby Koko Nor, our objective yet fifty miles away, but westward toward Tsaidam basin. This westward-flowing river is called Mek by the Tibetans, and in crossing the desert they always try to find it. At this season its dusty banks were loaded with blooming red-bud bushes. No fish could be found in the riffles; we had hoped to add a few to our boiled camel and yak. The game trails of bighorn sheep and musk-deer angled sharply back and forth across the steep, barren slopes of high ridges standing bleakly about Camp 34, whose elevation (3,545 meters, 10,820 feet) made it cold at night. Just south rose "White Cedar Mountain," while north stood Sharza (Lead Mountain), a source for Tibetan bullets. (These are local names and will not be found on any map.) Even here in the north, this region except in a general way, remains for all practical purposes largely unexplored. While the maps often show great detail, much of it has been supplied by natives and even they did not necessarily themselves set foot or eyes on the minor geographical and other points labeled.

That night Tan's scouts were out in strength, as a full moon rose to illuminate the rather narrow gulch. Signals warned that, though the band following had been tricked by our sudden maneuver, it now very likely lay about on all sides. Guns fully loaded, we waited out the night (sleeping in relays) while the animals rested, but no attack came. Abdul remarked that sometimes a caravan will be followed for days, and then for no apparent reason, those following will just vanish. Such bands may be after stock or even hope to get possession of the cargo. They may be comprised of Tibetans either local or far-ranging, Mongols, any number of tribes from Sinkiang, even mixed elements such as army deserters, or just plain down-and-out tribesmen of any race, looking for stock they can steal or eat. They are not necessarily professional robbers at all, though there are plenty of these too.

Two hours before dawn the men silently loaded the train, both animals and carts, and Tan moved it out past one of the strangers' campfires, staying in the bottom of a wide, dry gulch; a mile past he turned north after an hour of slow, cautious going, moving fast now through washes and canyons barren except for a few stunted bushes and spiny clumps. The region was a desert more on the Nevada type, with hills culminating in stony points. A few vultures began to circle overhead, a sure pointer for those behind. No water was found in the bottoms of washes. Because of this it was feared we had to cover that day about a hundred li (50 miles). We had started off in a freezing night, but as the hours slipped by, the dry air turned to a shimmering heat.

After ten o'clock, Abdul's binoculars picked up a party hanging on our left flank. Being mounted and unencumbered by carts, yaks, and other slow baggage animals, they moved easily. The hours crawled by—eight of them, and still no water. It was now blazing noon. A Sart scout said that a water-hole lay in this region somewhere. Thirty-two of the slowest animals were cut out and abandoned, their packs shifted over to carts and these thirty-two various carriers would be returned to the west by their owners, who would go north and then west. The last seen of them was going up a side canyon on our left. They seemed glad to be rid of us, robbers or no robbers. We moved just as slow however. It was midafternoon when the camels and horses scented water. . . .

We scouted ahead to enter a canyon, and a Sart announced that it was the water called "Bandits' Well." We followed him to a mud-hole lying in a desert gulch, and soon animals and men were drinking the muddy water. Scattered about were what had once been the corpses of men: twenty-six of them. The curious thing about it was that, according to these local men, none of these had been shot; every man's throat had been cut from ear to ear. Tan said they had been miners on their way to Sining. He did not know who had killed them, except that Moslems of some tribe had probably been responsible.

In this place the caravan rested, the men scanning the ridges about for any movement. Our doggers' plan was apparent now—we were too strong to attack, but should we have missed finding the water-hole, we might have perished in the desert. That was their main chance. The camels rested quietly, chewing their cuds and spitting a vile-smelling greenish saliva, but the oxen and yaks bawled once in a while and riled the water-hole until it became a soup. This water was rotten-smelling stuff, but drink it we did.

The prisoner, who claimed to be a poor hunter, was now turned loose with a warning for the band to keep clear; the would-be robbers were moving in all around, and a few sat in the open on a high ridge over Camp 35. We counted about 400 in the band, undoubtedly Tibetans from off the Tala. The order was issued not to fire on them unless attacked, for that would certainly provoke a battle.

A council was held. Tan fearing to stop at this place too long—for due to lack of water, these wild and thirsty characters would be forced to move in—we pulled out in the cold of night after first (on the spur of the moment) mounting four machine-guns and spraying the ridges. Quite a racket can be made in a canyon with four machine-guns, and apparently the strangers were impressed. None came out, and with yells and whips cracking, the caravan was driven north into the desert, heading for a point off the northwest shore of Dabson Nor (sometimes Datai-dabasu, or any number of other names).

Some of us wrapping our heads in scarfs to cut down the amount of dust we must breathe till late next day, we scattered the fighting men and were soon threading in and out of desert passes, lining across flats and traversing easy hillsides. Several times an alarm was given along the line that robbers were close, and so alternately we would move forward, halt, scout, move . . . peering into the starlit darkness. Tan finally figured to hell with it, that he knew the main Tibetan party was back at the water, and these were only a few out to grab off a horse or what they could.

At 1 o'clock we halted, drew up on the top of a ridge, dismounted, and rested for two hours. Cargoes were adjusted, and fifteen animals unloaded and turned loose in the desert, as they were too weak to proceed farther. And that was the last we saw of the Tibetans, for undoubtedly they gathered them in. All was quiet under the stars, much of the desert a shining white, a smell of night-moisture on the salt-dust, the whispers of men moving off on routine guard, others working among the animals, or resting.

Herding together the largely ragged train, we started out once more, moving slowly and taking advantage of easy terrain. After dawn we emerged above a flat, hazy basin—perhaps twenty miles across—which blinded us with the reflected sun's rays striking upward from the salt-pan of its floor. Gleaming in the center was Dabson Nor, an emerald set in a ring of white salt.

The camels stretched their heads forward, and they and the oxen and yaks moved a little faster, apparently feeling the moisture in the air, as a breeze blew across the flats toward us. When I yelled at a mule turning off to graze on a bush, I found I could only croak and my lips were cracked. The way was downhill, and eventually, under all our urging, the whole train—horses, camels, laungs, yaks, mules, and even men raised their heads a little higher out of the dust, and trudged forward. There still lay before us a long ride, nostrils filled with alkaline dust, eyes aching from the glare. And we were thirsty; the canteens empty. While descending toward the sea an hour later, some of the riding horses began going lame; we had to dismount and lead them. The sun rose higher, the heat held fast, and our feet sank into a soft alkali and salt *tuffa*.

With burning feet we at last approached the upper, left-hand side of the basin, and saw scattered over it the camels of Mohammed Ali, whom we had last seen months before in Narda on the edge of Gomei Desert. These camels enquiringly raised their foamy muzzles out of a stream called the Dabson River; and in it was to be seen a trickle of water! Laughing men and excited animals closed the distance and sandwiched together along the west bank in their eagerness to get at it. Salt water that burned our throats like fire!—yet we drank, washing our mouths and spitting out the warm salty stuff.

Camp 36 was pitched a few hundred feet beyond, for we ached in every bone and muscle from weariness. After an hour's rest, we set out on foot among the thorny clumps scattered over the desert all the way down to the sea still miles away, to dig up roots called *fu yen* (bitter salt), according to Solomon a famous Chinese medical substance. This root grows only in the deserts hereabouts, and is a very valuable pharmaceutical item in China as a curative for various ailments including common colds.

East of camp, humped high along the distant skyline, were long snow ranges lying between the Tibetan plateau and the great Nan Shan Range north of Koko Nor. These were the South Koko Nor Mountains, the easternmost extension forming the south dam of the vast sea of Koko Nor, on whose northern bastion lay the mighty snowy peaks of the Nan Shans—the northern geographical border of Tibet. Our next leg was to cross this lofty range of the South Koko Nor Mountains and reach the shores of the Blue Sea.

Even by 5 P.M. the temperature inside our tents was stifling, 108° F., and so we lolled around on carpets spread outside on flat brush piles in the scanty shade cast by the high carts. Later, in the cooler night, the stars appearing close, we rejoiced, for we had been sizzling all day. Mohammed Ali joined us, and our friendship with the Tungan giant was resumed. By ten that night, the camp was again all abustle, as the cargo train, after a brief rest, must depart at three in the morning to escape part of the heat expected on the next stage of the march. We packed our personal saddle-bags in order that this caravan might take them along. In the light cast from thorn-bush fires and the stars, we examined some camels, showing them off around camp, finally selecting several to relieve our own burden carriers of their galling packs. The best of Mohammed Ali's riding camels, dark-brown with taffy streaks, had upstanding, solid humps, indicating their good condition. When trotting, these camels held their tails curled tautly up over their backs exactly like a Husky dog. We obtained thirty of the woolly Bactrians, to be used for lightening loads and by our Tibetans and Tanguts, some of whom had been set afoot after turning loose some animals and returning others back home while enroute here.

The last of us departed from camp at 5:15 in the morning, in a streaked black and red sunrise, and widely circled the salt sea in a clockwise movement, finally settling on a course due east:—on this we held fairly steady. On the far (east) side of the basin we began moving through salt-grass where Mongol camels and sheep grazed on all sides. Springs were found, and from these our mounts drank deeply. The water was salty, but safe. Fields of blooming iris—a dark blue—swept against the horses' hocks. For twenty miles these flowers lay in almost a single bed.

We came to the tents of a few Mongol herdsmen. These shelters stood about like the skin summer tents of the Siberian Samoyeds, having a dais of earth set at the back, over which skins were strewn to form a communal bed. The Mongols ran away at our approach, thinking us to be robbers, but Prince Dorje called out assurances of our peaceful intentions—and that our guns were for protection only. These wild-looking, skin-clad people finally gathered around, and eventually sent riders out on ponies to let other Mongols know of us.

A few hours later, herds of hundreds of yaks could be seen out on the dazzling salt crust bridging the sea. They were being loaded with salt by the Mongols. These Dabson Nor Mongols are lamaistic, ger dwellers; their headman Beile Torja, an old and disillusioned man. His tribe had dwindled from a hundred to only 30 families in recent years. They had been disarmed by order of the Central Government, having (according to gossip among the men) been marked for extinction, due to the Chinese historical hatred of the Mongols, and wish to seize their holdings. Of the 26 surviving Mongol Banners of Chinghai, this 30-family clan is the last remnant of the former mighty Koishoit "Left Wing Banner" which came to Dabson Nor in the Ch'ing Dynasty, so Torja and Dorje figured (about 1640). They had sacked Lhasa, and while returning to Mongolia, had been cut off by Chinese armies, and so settled here—losing contact with the main council of the Khans. Many tribes have raided Tibet from the north, including Dzungar in 1721.

All Dabson Nor formerly belonged to these Koshoits, and from its salt beds they had extracted a good livelihood, and had abandoned raiding. But now they worked without pay for the new owners, the government. Their poverty was quite appalling. In

Torja's ragged ger, one of the forty round felt gers standing about, Prince Dorje and I drank cool milk of a particularly fine flavor. It was explained that, first, fermented grain is put into fresh yak or camel milk, and set aside to stand two or three days; the result tastes not unlike buttermilk. None of our proud Moslem conquerors would condescend to enter the ger, and so sat on their horses, their gullets remaining dry, while we took our leisure inside.

In Torja's ger, a lamaistic shrine was standing against the felt wall directly opposite the doorway. Brass cups holding water were lined on the altar before the brass Buddha. Prayer-lamps of butter were lit. There was little butter for the god, Torja explained, only enough to show reverence and none to eat, as the tax collector had taken all that very morning. The stove in the middle of the ger was more elaborate than that of the Tibetans. Stored around the white felt walls were old, tooled saddle-bags, cases of hide bound in metal, camel harnesses, yak saddles and heaps of yak dung.

Prayers were now said to the Lord Buddha. Then our Mongol hosts, and their wives, whispered that the feared Tungans were harder taskmasters than even the Chinese before them—if that could be possible. With clockwork regularity a Moslem holy war swept through Chinghai every third of a century, and Torja felt another was about to break. He had only one old musket to defend the tribe.

We were faced with a long ride, and so regretfully left the Mongols and outside found the tribe gathered to bid us good-bye. The women in their long sheepskin robes, colored boots, and peaked hats, sang a song of spring to us. Standing among the colony of gers were a score of masts from which hundreds of prayer-flags fluttered. Against a background of lowing camels and yaks and moaning prayer-mills operated by wind, we felt as if time had reverted back to the Great Khans. Solomon took a picture with his camera.

At 3:45 P.M. we changed course, and turned our camels and the other train animals outward, away from the basin and headed for the lowest notch in the snow-capped South Koko Nor Range. While riding thus east through rocky valleys waving with wild flowers, alternate stony ridges, and grassy upland slopes, we saw our first Tibetan snake since leaving Tsaidam. It was only 18 inches long, a mottled brown, with a narrow neck and a flat ugly head. The reptile was cold and did not move much, merely crawling into the top of a thorn bush. The horses were not afraid, for having been raised in the highlands they knew nothing of snakes. We didn't hurt the snake but rode on.

After thirteen hours of riding we pitched Camp 37 during a cold drizzle, at an elevation of 3,350 meters (10,207 feet). The air turned cold, —14.4° C., and the drizzle increased to a downpour that drummed on our tent tops all through the night. The camels and the ox wagons did not come in that night, having bogged down in mud, though the mule pack-train arrived long after dark, mud-streaked, weary, foot- and back-sore. These big black Tibetan mules are magnificent; they packed nearly 300 pounds that day (mostly cargo obtained from Tibetans and Ngoloks), and yet had been moving gradually uphill since three o'clock in the morning—18 hours before we had struck clean snow-water!

We were wet to the skin, and because of more storms in the offing there was no stopping to rest. Again our direction was eastward. The old caravan trail (now a military road) led us for 60 li up and down, and across the range; the first 5½ hours through green, rolling, curiously rounded earthen mountains having stone crests—almost Peruvian Andean in appearance. Later, peaks with snow and ice lay on all sides, and in between were wide-reaching spaces holding herds of yaks, horses, and sheep. This was Tangut country, perhaps Kozlov's lost tribe. It was among the finest ranges in all Asia for grazing, Tan Chen-te believed, marveling, though at 12,000 feet elevation. Using the main road we climbed to Dzahase Pass, at 3,750 meters (11,426 feet), the lowest notch at least in the mountains immediately about. At last we stood on top of the range, and under us in the northeast lay fabled Koko Nor, the Blue Sea.

Wonder and delight was expressed by Dorje, Solomon, and me as we gazed at that intensely blue expanse of water, so blue the Mediterranean seems pale beside it: this was one of the largest seas in Tibet, if not the largest. One of the finest passages in all Sven Hedin's fine works describes it. Even the most hardened among us thrilled to the idea that the regions about were only partially mapped as to details, though the country was very well known in a general way.

24

Koko Nor—The Blue Sea

WHEN the scattered cavaran had joined together on the snowy summit, the bugle was sounded and we left the heights and, mostly on our tails (for we made short cuts off the road), slid down the steeply pitched slopes of the South Koko Nors to the southwest corner of what may well be the most fascinating sea to be found anywhere. We camped on a green turf-meadow called Ta-lama (Big-lama), half a mile south of the coast. An encampment of Tangut black hair tents was scattered eastward along the coast as far as binoculars (from the foothills) could reach—perhaps 30 miles. Our tents were raised on the north bank of a river marked on our Chinese military maps at the Ta-lama Ho (Big-lama River); but the Tanguts who were soon riding into camp called it "Stanach Ma."

As I have said, there are details unknown about this strangest of seas; ethnology, natural history, and geography being somewhat obscure in spite of its relative closeness to Tangar. Therefore, though our story—in all its geographical, political, and other ramifications—concerns the finding and penetration of legendary Amne Machin, I don't see how we can overlook the opportunity (as laymen) to learn something of this fabulous paradise sea. It has been calculated as being 65 by 40 miles. Islands lay before us, including Kozlov's and Sven Hedin's famous central island of monks. By pocket compass, bearing 65° from Camp 38 was a row of shark-toothed white rocks, guano covered, only a few miles off the beach. All native peoples call them "White Rocks."

The central island was reached by the Russians at the beginning of the century and though quite a few travelers have been here, not much detailed descripiton has been left. Missionaries had frequently, even in recent times, come to these shores, but mostly to gaze and then return to Sining. The central island is known today variously by Chinese as "Hai Hain Shan" ("Mountain in the Middle of the Sea"); by Tibetans as "Zurgnon" ("Head of the Sea"); by Däde, high-elevation Mongols, as "Kuisui" ("Navel of the Sea"). These local names have not been recorded outside, as far as I know. In winter the island lies about a day's trek over the ice-fields. No skin boat or raft is to be found on the Blue Sea—for its waters are sacred. Only Kozlov's party went to the central island in their own boat, and set off fireworks still remembered by some of the resentful Tibetans. Tan knew the story of the expedition and related it to me, even mentioning the Russians' great joy and firing of rockets and fireworks.

Through binoculars we made out, on this central island which so captured Sven Hedin's imagination, an obo, and what looked like a shrine. Hedin gives few details though he vividly and dramatically describes the life of the monks there. Here, where they have gone to escape (according to Dorje and the Tanguts) the "fury of the world and the strife of Endless Becoming," lived a few mystics and lay-hermits. This most isolated of ecclesiastical retreats lay on a bearing of 70° from Ta-lama, at an elevation figuring 3,150 meters (9,598 feet), and is a long, smooth, treeless, humped porpoise of an island, with a hill on its north end. Of this mysterious isle of which so much is heard in Shanghai and Tibet, in India, and even in far-away Singapore and Java, a Tungan now said quite seriously, that "a thousand monks lived there in golden temples!" Actually, the number varies from year to year. A Tangut chieftain told that from two to five persons usually live there, sometimes more; and that quite a few men while crossing over from the mainland on the winter ice, are lost when they disappear down the cracks during sudden storm. When food does not reach the island, the inmates starve, and others take their places. The golden temples are really caves. An old Tibetan woman is there now: she arrived on the island fifteen years ago, and has not returned to the mainland. This devout *a-ni* was still alive when last heard from two winters past. Her only desire had been for a holy book; food she did not desire, as "the birds feed her." Probably, we reasoned, with the eggs they laid there, and the fish that gulls and cormorants undoubtedly dropped on the island. We gave up all idea of rescuing her when Tan said she would only despise us, and the attempt bring trouble.

We took our maps and climbed the mountains back of camp; from the peaks we espied a very large, flat, green island, not shown on any of the maps in our possession. It lies north and is called "Hai Sse Pi" ("Spleen of the Sea") by the Sining Moslems, and lies in the northwest quarter of the sea. The Tibetans call it "Tserwa Re" ("Spleen Mountain"). Dorje thought Hedin and Kozlov may have missed it: for when a low haze lies over the surface of the sea, the island would not be seen even from the circling mountains. A Tangut legend has it that one of Genghis Khan's generals buried the loot of Russia on it. I personally do not believe it, for the loot of Russia undoubtedly reached Karakorum.

In the evening, as we were hungry for a change of diet, we fished in the river by using blankets for nets, but with no luck as the fish were too nimble, the water too clear, and we ourselves too awkward; then we tried hook and line, but there was so much running around and splashing and shouting that we still had no luck. And, finally, in disgust, by standing on the steep 10-foot-high banks and throwing big stones down at the fish, we stunned 32 of them, some exceeding two feet in length, none under 14 inches.

We were lucky to find them, for according to the Tanguts the fish run up the rivers to spawn at a time corresponding to our May, descending to the sea by September. Tan, on seeing our enterprise, hooted with skepticism, but afraid he was missing the fun soon began calling for the beheading sword (a most useless object lugged all the way from Sining). In a few minutes this hardened skeptic, too, leapt zealously into the rushing waters—crying the Moslem version of "If at first you don't succeed, try, try, again!"—and soon managed to slice up several fish already stunned by our rocks. We yelled in anger, and finally he went after his own fish, presently getting the hang of it, cutting a few big fellows running up stream through the shallower riffles. He was soon slashing so wildly, laying about to left and right, that he must soon decapitate someone. We gave him a wide berth thereafter, and let him recover his own fish. Our Tibetans and a few Tanguts cleverly placed their hands under the banks, catching the fish by their gills.

By night three toothless varieties were heaped at the campfires: a "golden fish" 18 inches long, with a gorgeous bright yellow-orange mail coat, beautiful as a trout. Another was of a dark green color, having yellow-mottled sides, its fins a yellow-orange, golden eyes fixed in a long, narrow, bony head—and was called "sand fish." The third was a flashing herring-like fellow of greenish-yellow, having a fine trout head—a few of this kind being speckled with black. Dorje remarked at dinner that Kozlov had had the honor of scientifically naming these beauties, but we were having the opportunity of recording the native names and also the fun of eating them.

"If only Ma Sheng-lung were here!" laughed Dorje, looking very wise.

"God's teeth! You mean, 'yu!' only 'yu!' " piped up Solomon Ma. We missed Colonel Ma and soon after this sally, went off to our tents to busy ourselves with maps, notebooks, and reading for pleasure.

At midnight an urgent radiogram came in from Governor Ma, warning us to get a move on. The reverse was fast developing; Mayuan's armies were in full retreat fairly close to Lanchow, and wholesale defections had occurred in those of Ma Hung-kwei, the Moslem governor of Ninghsia Province (northeast of Kansu and in Inner Mongolia). All the loyal Chinese armies everywhere must now be lost, I saw; consequently, the best units from these of the north must be withdrawn without delay toward the inner Moslem orbit of Chinghai and away from China proper—drawn westward, in the geographical and psychological direction of Moslem Afghanistan, Persia, and Pakistan, and based on central Tibet. This message heralded a political and military crisis for the entire Asian picture, and not just for China alone, which, in my opinion (though even today I am probably alone), was merely a side-show. The Communists were laying down two storm armies, estimated at 250,000 veteran combat infantry, in a pincer drive fed from two bases: Black Gobi, and Sian —at the strategic bend of the Yellow River.

I had once operated there with Yen Shih-son for five and a half months, behind the Yellow River Japanese Army lines, and so knew the geographical, political, and military situation. The points of those two Red armies, I reasoned, would meet *between* Sining and Lanchow. Both Red swings in force were too far north and south to mean anything else. This evaluation meant that not only would the Northwest Provinces of China fall soon, but also that the Communists would sweep on into the west and take over North Chinghai at the same time! Since no aid had come from the Central Government fleeing to Formosa Governor Ma must extricate as many top troops as possible from Kansu Province. The governor wanted immediately to know the situation in Tibet. The answers were worked out, the code work attended to, and the messages sent out on our short-wave radio. However, Tan decided that the expedition must rest another day or two on the meadows, for the animals were very lean and weak from past hunger and overwork.

My black horse, frisky as ever, was shod anew next morning. First, he was thrown and held in order to do the job; a long rawhide rope was tied—as is the unique Moslem fashion here—in a loop around his shoulders. This was explained as necessary, for he was big and powerful, and fighting mad. The two ends of the rawhide were cleverly passed between his fore and aft legs, and again carried around behind his two hind hocks, then brought forward outside his hooves, and inserted through the shoulder loop. Thus it did the stallion no good to snort and bite, buck, or rear and strike. Three husky Moslem blacksmiths on each side pulled steadily on the two thongs, until finally, the fighting stallion's hind legs slid forward. Now he was pushed over from a kneeling position, to lie helplessly on his side; eight men pinned him down, two holding his head as he was still trying to bite. Thus—by perhaps this cleverest of all methods known to horsemen anywhere in the field—he was shod.

Koko Nor is a salt sea, though its waters are quite drinkable. An old Tibetan pönpo rode in with his medieval retinue and after greetings and tea in my tent, told us that over 100 streams and rivers fed the Blue Sea. Another chief who arrived claimed 108 streams, but we recalled that this number was a favorite Buddhist one, and so made a slight allowance in our estimate. The river lying about 70 miles east, the Tao Tang Ho (Reverse Flowing River), was the one we had already crossed weeks before south of the Sun and Moon Mountains, and from which the Moslems obtained fish by trampling them with horses and camels. This Reverse Flowing River is famous in China, but actually there is no reversal of the law of gravity—the strange lay of the land and mountains along its course merely give it an odd, uphill appearance. Thus it looks like an outlet, but actually is just another feeder; there are no outlets flowing from the Blue Sea. We must reach this river before turning north towards Tangar.

Chinese, Tibetans, Tanguts and even Moslems, make annual pilgrimage to Koko Nor, elaborate ceremonies being undertaken to honor the lake's spirit. Every third year is said to be marked for an important sacrifice to this ghost, attended by Tibetan lords, High lamas, Mongolian princes, imams of the Church of Islam and even Black Bones magicians. Governor Ma Pu-fang himself has attended. At this time the Black Bones, followers of Pön, may demonstrate the control of weather. From what I was able to gather, they believe that *mantras,* words of power, are the keynote to any particular body of atoms, and that each organism has its own vibratory rate though it be the sun or a rain cloud. When this rate of vibration is known, the organism can be disintegrated, or even created. The ancient Greek theory of music appears similar to this Tibetan conception. What a pity none of the Greeks ever described the rites and theories known as the "Greek Mysteries." The power lies, the Black Bones claim, in control of the sleeping Goddess Kundalini. This is the Serpent Power, based in the spine. As the outer air vibrates to the priest's mantra, the vital airs (*prana-vayu*) are set in motion. The Goddess responds in tones of divine music causing it to ascend from her "throne" in the spinal Root-Support Psychic-Center to stages of other Centers above, until the music fills the head, the Lotus of a Thousand Petals, heard now by the Higher Buddha who responds through the "Law of Cause and Effect." There are no "miracles" among Buddhists, for, unlike Christians, Moslems and the others, they operate on theories only now being called by science "The laws of Natural Forces."

According to Tanguts, the Blue Sea usually freezes over by mid-November and does not break up until April. Later I was told by Bishop Haberstroh in Sining, whose Roman priests after some 400 years around Lanchow know a great deal more about many phases of Tibet than I could ever know, that the natives say that to secure fish, they cut a hole in the ice-pack, and build fires around the edge. The fish are attracted to the glow, leap out toward it, and are frozen on striking the ice. It is said that this is also done in Siberia, though I still remain a bit skeptical. Then, with morning light to guide them, the fishermen merely have to collect the frozen fish (which have died an "accidental death") by tossing them into baskets lashed to yaks and horses. These Koko Nor fish are said to be an important commercial item in the markets of Tangar and Sining, though the Tanguts do not eat them on religious grounds. Probably a hungry Tangut would do so, and to hell with his chances for heaven.

Near camp and along the shore, casting their fleeting shadows over the meadows, were yet other fishermen—many crying eagles, fishing-hawks, gerfalcons, ducks, geese, swans, gulls, cormorants, shore-waders, and other kinds of birds unknown to me. While watching these we followed the coast, and a mile and a half northwest of camp, found a very large foam-flecked obo partly submerged, resembling in size and shape a surfacing submarine.

One Tangut legend of the sea's origin says that long, long ago, before the tribes came here from Black Gobi, there was once on the north side a famous golden-roofed lamasery called "Golden Mountain Temple." A well formerly existed in these olden times on a plain below the lamasery. A traveler came one day from the "Black City" of Khara Khoto; now this man was a Khara Yasse, (Black Bones), a noble and a follower of higher Pön, sorcery, and magic. Of course the lamas did not know this at the time, or they would have set upon him and entombed the fellow in a cave or cell, where he would have died a "natural" death. This stranger went one day to the well and "forgot" to replace the lid over the coping of the well, and its waters being forced up through the earth by a devil's hand, overflowed, and so was created the Blue Sea! Golden Mountain Temple, with all its golden roofs, was submerged.

Today (according to the natives living here), on the shores of Koko Nor live four groups called Tanguts: they are organized into four tribal sections, each having 1,000 families. By this division they get the most out of the pasturage. In the southeast sector of Koko Nor Basin are the Chambre; in the southwest, the Duschua; in the northwest, the Wonshdeh; in the north, the Gong Tsa.

Our camp was thrown into a considerable excitement. The paramount lords of this mighty federation galloped into camp after some had traveled a hundred li to see us. Their scouts—alert for friend or enemy—had brought word of our approach out of the Tsaidam. With these dignified men, beautifully garbed in fascinating robes, came gifts of live sheep.

They were made welcome on our best carpets. An old man told us that the lamaseries of the Blue Sea include: in the north, Gong Tsa Gompa—70 monks under a high lama; in the northeast, Sharong Gompa—30 monks. Most "lamaseries" here, however, are merely tents, and their priests usually on the move. The Tibetans of the Blue Sea go to Kumbum very frequently, and make long pilgrimages to Lhasa, Shigatse and other places. However, all Tibetans (as well as the Tanguts) are great travelers; it being no very uncommon event to talk with men who have been to Urga in Outer Mongolia, Manchuria, China, Lhasa, Sikkim, Nepal, and Ladakh—all of them separated from one extreme to the other by many hundreds of miles.

For a man to travel even today from New York to Chicago and beyond by cart (not to mention camel or yak caravan), would certainly be considered a hardship; but in lamaistic countries such an expedition over regions quite often robber-infested and under complicated political and military circumstances may be said to be common.

Tracks and sight of game in the mountains near camp gave Dorje, Solomon and me something of the cross-section of wildlife inhabiting the Koko Nor region: these were bighorn sheep, antelope, gazelle, wapiti, bear, musk-deer, ass (kulan or kyang), possibly horse, wolf, fox, leopard, snow-leopard, lynx, barking-deer. Tracks indicated there may be many other kinds of big game. As to Prjevalsky's famous wild "horse," I saw none anywhere in Tibet, though animals were two or three times pointed out in the far distance, said to be "horse" and not "ass." But I cannot vouch for their existence here at Koko Nor, or at any other place. Nor did I see any of Dr. Sven Hedin's "wild camels"—though the natives have stories concerning them. Dorje thought old horns found in native camps were of argali. Tigers may exist, but if so they are extremely rare, and probably cross over from the Gobi during poor game seasons. The elk too are scarce, their horns being in demand by the Chinese drug trade. I saw four sets of antlers, bound in cloth, and on a mule being led possibly to Tangar.

While sitting around the campfire listening to gulls and breakers on the beach, and toasting pieces of fish on willow sticks, one of the chiefs told something of the secret code signs used by caravaners and hunters. Quite a bit, according to Dorje, has been made of them by early explorers. These codes were supposed to be so highly secret that only special initiates could follow them. In this region today the Tibetans, especially Drök-pas, do use signs over swamps, mountains, tang, steppes, and possibly in other different kinds of confusing terrain, but they are not "secret" in the exact sense formerly meant; they are secret only to outsiders (foreigners such as Mongols, etc.). Trail-wise Drök-pas, Chang-pas, and even any number of Rong-pas —such as hunters, robbers and herdsmen, probably know most of these signs.

When asked how the fishes got into the sea of Koko Nor, a serious-faced old chief answered with dignity, "A favored sea has fish, does it not, Sir? Likewise, man has his fleas, does he not, Sir?" Here he glanced around the tent for confirmation: "The fish didn't fly here, nor did they walk. Then there is only one answer. The whole matter of fish, Sir, is destined by Fate . . . the Plaything of the Gods." He must have been a wonderful politician.

Here as elsewhere in Tibet, we heard of the "Snow Men," a race of creatures believed by Tibetans to inhabit the more inaccessible parts of their country. This is apparently not merely one of their legends. They actually believe in the existence of what seems to be a troglodytic race of "apemen," saying that barefoot tracks up to a foot and a half long can be seen, and that these giants are hairy, use stone weapons, and sometimes kill men though they more often confine their raids to stealing yaks or sheep. Prince Minchur Dorje, who has been in Lhasa, called on me in the Lanchow mission, and said his and Prince Dorje's father had once maintained a lama in his retinue who had been captured by four of the Snow Men, and brought to a high camp in which there were several women and children, all clad in crude animal skins. The shelter was a cave, bones scattered over the floor as in a wolf den. A fire was in use outside, and over this only sign of civilization was "burned" their game that night. The word "burned" he felt was interesting, for Tibetans boil their meat, and normally do not roast or broil it. And they sometimes prefer meat raw. The lama stayed five days, and then escaped one night, finding his way back to the Mongol camp in Alashan. I believe Prince Minchur said the place of the Snow Men was somewhere up in the higher Min Shans. That would place it somewhere east of the Amne Machins. The Roosevelts mention seeing tracks in snow, tracks believed by their native bearers to be those of "Snow Men." Mount Everest climbers have reported seeing such tracks, and, I believe, even the creatures themselves. Personally, I have made no decision concerning them, as I have not made a search; but it was just as well not to tell the pönpos of my inner doubts, as these would be resented.

Solomon Ma and his helpers, always busy with various collections, and I, found riffles of tiny shells on the sandy beaches of this sea, but no large shells. The sea appears to be rising, encroaching on the fine grass turf, for old shell banks or wind-stacked saline deposits are absent, and grass grows down tightly to the narrow beach itself.

Now rested and strong enough for another go, the pack and draft oxen, yaks, camels, mules, and horses were turned back toward the Tsaidam, and with them went their owners or keepers. A second detachment consisting of drivers, troops, craftsmen, interpreters, technicians, and servants—including Sarts hired in the west—were returning south to Colonel Ma in Fort Chakar (some diverting to Fort Ta Ho Pa). Of the expedition there remained now only a few big carts drawn by horses, and 20 pack horses and mules; there were 22 mounted Moslem riflemen, 40 armed and mounted Tibetans.

Both discharged groups, containing men who had started in Kumbum—who were traveling on fast horses and compactly organized for protection—were paid off in silver and not in goods which was customary. Gifts and provisions were added to see them safely home. Their elation was touching—farewells were said, and yells came from the Tibetans:

"Aros! Shihu!" ("Hello-Goodby! Friend!")—as they wheeled their horses away from camp and departed.

Streaming out from our tent poles, and clattering in the sea-wind, were their presents of yak-tails and the flat bones of animals having prayers inscribed on them.

Before leaving, the hui hui Moslems—some of whom had followed our fortunes from Kumbum to the Black Sea and Amne Machin, and thence to Fort Chakar, across Amne Kor to Fort Shan Je Te, and now up to the Blue Sea—came to our tent, where Dorje, Solomon and I sat in accordance with etiquette, one by one to bow and say such things as:

"May the Merciful God protect you, Clark-ah, from the evil-eye."

"May the Merciful High Lord bless you with many sons."

"Friend—come to fight with us against the Communists!"

"Ask God's help, and all your wishes will come true."

Among the last came Hassan. "God's blessings!" cried my protector and friend, shaking hands.

And to all of them we would say: "God go with you."

These men too left in a rumble of hooves on the road west out of Big-lama. Tan's order was given and the expedition started up the main road, the lead-bell on a white mule tolling the way into the east.

25

Homeward Bound

CAMP 39 that night placed us somewhere on the sea's mid-southern shore, though we had marched all day. Sometimes we stayed on the road, and other times we left it, especially the horsemen. While fording innumerable creeks and rivers flowing off the South Koko Nor Range into the sea, Dorje counted that day 40 fishes per minute running upstream to spawn. A total of 100 streams entering the sea would add up any way you figured to a considerable run of fishes over the four-month's season, and indicate a virtually untapped source of food.

After a good rest that night we were again on our way at 4 A.M., marching along the road through the night, or silently over a soft, springy turf, strung out under the wheeling stars. The fall of easy breakers on the shore alongside our left, and the call of sea birds, lulled me into a peaceful state of mind. I don't recall anything of interest until 1 P.M., when we began marching through a whole nomadic tribe of Drök-pas, living in hundreds of black charis—people grazing their herds, and not doing much of anything at this paradise of a sea. We spread our tents over the turf to dry out the rainwater (for it had rained in the night and sprinkled during the morning), so as to lessen the burdens. Pigeons fluttered from a clear sky and played at our feet over the blue canvasses, tumbling around in their scramble for a handful of barley, the last bit of our feed.

Again we mounted, whips cracked over the ears of the cart horses, wheels screeched as they turned slowly, a few horses snorted and danced, men whistled and yelled—and we were on our way again. Once I rode away from the column (without yaks it might more properly be called that) and walked my horse silently along the emerald south shore, listening to the breakers combing over the sand and gravel stretches. Once I pulled up and went swimming. A cluster of Tibetan tents was close by, and people ran out of them to watch. I remembered hearing in Sining that two French explorers (whose names I have forgotten) had gone swimming on the shore closest to Tangar, their bullet-riddled bodies later being found on the road by soldiers. Apparently, or so believed the locals, they had been warned by the Tanguts to stay out of the sea, and had paid no heed. As I lay in the cold salty water I saw all about purplish, sharply-crested mountains, one of them fantastically covered with red snow—and the sea, an apple-green that day, was over 150 miles in circumference, a swimming pool large enough for the gods. Red snow, incidentally (as explained by Dorje), is peculiar to Tibet, and is a phenomenon having to do with a microscopic fungi. Colonel Ma had once mentioned it at Chakar, but I had paid no attention to him. When thunder began in the mountains, and lightning turned the sea white, I dressed and trotted after the caravan, now rolling and nodding along a couple of miles east—hot, dusty, half-asleep, each man thinking of money, or glory, a friend or an enemy, or what we were going to eat that night, or (very probably) wishing he had a woman between his legs instead of a horse.

For weeks we had had very little tsamba (which I had learned to like), about twice a week, and not much tea—only meat, meat, and more meat—mostly yak and a few times horse—but most of it tough and stringy, and little of it fat. Pack sheep had proved tough as gristle. Gifts from the natives and wild game helped out, but it was little enough for the stomachs of such an expedition. We were lank, most everyone tough as barbed wire, but whenever gusts of wind came from the sea, I felt that we would be blown right out of our saddles. Solomon, Tan Chen-te, and I cut off from the right flank of the column, heading for a herd of some 200 gazelles. A mile out we dismounted, leaving our horses with orderlies, and crawled forward, keeping low and shoving our rifles ahead of us, for some 200 yards. We reached a point about 250 yards from the herd, now alert, aimed through a few spears of grass, and fired:—two gazelles jumped into the air and fell down in a leap. We walked up to them and after Tan had performed tsai, with a wink, we leaned against the carcasses to rest. I pulled off my boots and wiggled my toes which were cramped from the stirrups.

The orderlies were approaching with our horses. "My friend," began Tan, glancing at me, "Soon we will not hunt any more." There was actually a note of regret in his smooth voice. I couldn't believe this hard, cynical character could feel anything toward another but an inward contempt. His only humility in the past, had been to refer to himself once, as (according to Solomon) "God's footstool."

"The Lord will keep you for many more hunts, High Footstool," I answered with a grin, Solomon doing the honors.

The tall captain rose and tossed the gazelles behind our saddles— for the horses were being led up—lashed them, and without another word galloped off with a laugh toward the lumbering caravan, now a few miles away in the distance.

That night an old tribesman came into Camp 40, gossiping and pointing out that the green grass underfoot dries in October, and snows begin falling in November. We decamped at dawn and rode with little rest until 8:10 P.M. During 15 hours we actually made what I was assured was a good 90 li (45 miles), riding past scattered black tents, and through herds belonging to the Tangut Chambres. The tribe extended also through a long valley, in which flowed the Tao Tang Ho. We left the sea and followed it on the right side. Several times we had to beat off mastiffs which came out. Finally, one of the mules had its belly cut or snagged by the fangs of a dog, one of a pack. Several tents were near. Tan got so angry at these dogs that he whirled his horse toward them, drew his saber—carried under his left leg—and dismounting, advanced toward the pack on foot. The dogs were momentarily so surprised at seeing a stranger actually daring to approach them, that they fell back, barking savagely. The caravan pulled up, and watched, some men unslinging their rifles. Several Chambres were now running into their charis. If they came out with guns, we might be in for it.

Tan approached the closest tent at which ten Chambre bucks, wrapped in sheepskins, stood insolently, hands resting on broadswords, rifles being slipped off their backs to rest on the thong looped over the right shoulder. Temper and anger are hard emotions to figure out. The Tibetans say there are three symbols defining man—a pig, a cock, and a snake: the pig typifies Ignorance; the cock typifies Desire-Attachment; the snake typifies Anger. They are the base of all man's calamities. Dorje and I rode slowly toward Tan, afraid he might be set upon, and in the resultant mêlée we could not fire without hitting him. The dogs by this time were recovering from surprise, and were circling, crouching, baring their fangs, and howling. A Chambre spoke up, and one of the dogs launched itself at Tan. . . .

I dug in my spurs, then checked the horse's pace.

Tan's saber point flicked upward with a glint of light, and the dog ran itself through from throat to belly. Another dog, heavier though not so tall as a wolf, leapt on its companion and began tearing at it. Tan walked toward the Chambres, but as none came forth, he spun on his boot heel and leaping on his horse, rode off at a clip into the east toward Fort Tao Tang Ho.

Abdul reined alongside and explained to Dorje that the Koko Nor region was divided into zones falling under three administrative hsiens, and this corner had been at one time under Tan Chen-te; had he been attacked by the Chambres, a punitive Moslem expedition would have been put into the field against the tribe. In such a totally heartless manner are affairs arising from foolish incidents often settled in this country.

In this region, farther north, a German they called Major O. S. Hermann—regarded by the Moslems as a very gallant and brave officer—once attached to them as a Central Government advisor, wished to try his hand at exploring; and had had his feet frozen as a result. Abdul said that with both feet amputated, Hermann later commanded a German tank column in World War II. He asked if I knew this officer, and I had to tell him the world outside China was a pretty big place, and that ordinary Americans and German tank officers had very little in common, usually, except for possibly taking pot shots at each other. He pretended to be horrified, "You should love one another, you are all Christians!"

Dorje chuckled and we rode on laughing. A bugle sounded ahead, and with flags flying we rode into Fort Tao Tang Ho. We were greeted by Ma Ching the commandante. That night we rested on our old kangs—the same used on the wintry southbound trek to Fort Chapcha. From here, Camp 41, it was only a day's travel north across the Sun and Moon Mountains to Tangar.

Next morning we left and crossed the mountains to Tangar. Camp 42 was pitched at the rest-house in the grove down in the valley. In spite of martial law prevailing, a feast was held here by Magistrate Wong Wei-chung, our former host. Next day we passed hundreds of foot soldiers and some horsemen trailing west toward Tangar and Tibet. They looked mauled by the Reds, and yet were all that remained in the northwest of a free China.

As we approached Sining's towering gray brick walls, our escort broke into the last trail songs—*The Flying Crane Dance, Everywhere is the Perfume of Peonies* and a final change, accompanied by the firing of guns while riding at a gallop, *When Can We See Our Friends Again?*

Reports were completed and delivered. We called on the smiling Panchen Lama at Kumbum, and saw the "Devil Dances" at the annual festival, "Sunning of the Buddha"—during which priests, in magnificent costumes and masks, are said to become *gurtums* instead of men, and with the spirit of incarnated gods in them, dance their fearful religious ballets. Afterwards we received the Panchen Lama's congratulations. In not so many months he would head for Lhasa . . . at the head of an army, all right—the Chinese Communist Army!

Solomon Ma, Dorje, Tan Chen-te, Huardamu and I, later joined by the Secretary and Abdul, had a farewell dinner in the park beyond the river outside Sining's walls. And then I said my farewells to all these friends and to Bishop Haberstroh and to kindly Polish Father Cvick who was dying from tuberculosis, and to Deputy-Governor Gow of Chinghai—now promoted!

In Lanchow Dorje and I found the Communists very close: we hurried day and night—his Amne Machin elevation computations were completed after collaborating on barometric readings with the National Institute of Science; maps and other types of reports turned in, one of which dealt with Hong Kong's findings on our geologic specimens—including petroleum, gold, tungsten. . . . From Solomon's hand, Governor Ma Pu-fang received at his Northwest Political Headquarters plans covering withdrawal of three Moslem divisions into Tibet; and their support. From the governor in turn, I received a letter of thanks and congratulations covering our findings, and the locating and measurement of Amne Machin. The expedition's affairs were thus closed.

Communist pincer columns were moving in fast from the Gobi lying north and from south Kansu, the west infiltration converging at the junction already foreseen between Sining and Lanchow. Moslem withdrawal from China proper by trucks began—heading out of Lanchow west into Chinghai. Other units were fighting rear-guard actions, and it was said by the Moslems that 8,000 men died holding the Reds while planes came up from the coast. These planes were delayed four days due to weather. During this time word came that my black horse Alashan had been killed in battle. I said good-by to

my old wartime friend, Malcolm Rosholt, General Chennault's airline advisor here; and also good-by to my Swedish friend Gus Söderbom, without whose good will there could have been no expedition
into Tibet much less to Amne Machin.

On the fourth morning, the thirteenth of August, (six months
since arriving from Hong Kong on February 18th) Governor Ma
sent for me; I packed in ten minutes: Bishop Buddenbrock was
gone—said to be praying in the cathedral—and I could only leave
him a farewell note; also a quick scribble to Prince Dorje who had
left a short while before to take refuge with Mongols in Alashan;
and then I bade my old Moslem comrades good-by at headquarters,
and last of all Solomon Ma (for whom I pretended I must first find
his spectacles before he could shake hands). And then I took rick-
shaw to the airport. Governor Ma Pu-fang was leaving with his staff
of fifty for Canton via Chungking, to make final arrangements with
the Chinese government concerning his defeat and the Tibetan
Army. From Hong Kong he would go on pilgrimage to Mecca, in
Arabia . . . thence to Cairo.

Watching the governor climb the ladder into the plane, I wondered if Amne Machin had cursed him like all those others!

> "I've lost Britain and I've lost Gaul,
> I've lost Rome, and, worst of all,
> I've lost Lalage . . ."

But, unlike Caesar, Ma Pu-fang had not lost Lalage—he had an
airplane full of Lalages following, all in green veils. With him too,
eventually in other planes, were 600,000 ounces of gold.

When the plane had taken off Governor Ma asked me (through
Solomon who had boarded the last minute) to go with them to Cairo
(since I had been there before), and become a "friend and purchas-
ing agent" for the army. I calculated that if custom prevailed, I
could net approximately 10 per cent of that 600,000 ounces. I said
I would join him. Officially I was not permitted to fight Communists, but I felt that my country would have no objection to my
settling down to the quiet life of a businessman for a change.

Solomon and I whiled away the time talking about Amne Machin
and our friends. Oddly enough, the thing that he remembered most
was those days when we had a steady marching wind on the cheek.

Selective Index of Names

Other titles in the Equestrian Travel Classic series published by
The Long Riders' Guild Press. We are constantly adding to our
collection, so for an up-to-date list please visit our website:
www.thelongridersguild.com

Title	Author
Southern Cross to Pole Star – Tschiffely's Ride	Aime Tschiffley
Tale of Two Horses	Aime Tschiffley
Bridle Paths	Aime Tschiffely
This Way Southward	Aime Tschiffely
Bohemia Junction	Aime Tschiffely
Through Persia on a Sidesaddle	Ella C. Sykes
Through Russia on a Mustang	Thomas Stevens
Across Patagonia	Lady Florence Dixie
A Ride to Khiva	Frederick Burnaby
Ocean to Ocean on Horseback	Williard Glazier
Rural Rides – Volume One	William Cobbett
Rural Rides – Volume Two	William Cobbett
Adventures in Mexico	George F. Ruxton
Travels with A Donkey in the Cevennes	Robert Louis Stevenson
Winter Sketches from the Saddle	John Codman
Following the Frontier	Roger Pocock
On Horseback in Virginia	Charles Dudley Warner
California Coast Trails	J. Smeaton Chase
My Kingdom for a Horse	Margaret Leigh
The Journeys of Celia Fiennes	Celia Fiennes
On Horseback through Asia Minor	Fred Burnaby
The Abode of Snow	Andrew Wilson
A Lady's Life in the Rocky Mountains	Isabella Bird
Travels in Afghanistan	Ernest F. Fox
Through Mexico on Horseback	Joseph Carl Goodwin
Caucasian Journey	Negley Farson
Turkestan Solo	Ella K. Maillart
Through the Highlands of Shropshire	Magdalene M. Weale
Wartime Ride	J. W. Day
Across the Roof of the World	Wilfred Skrede
Woman on a Horse	Ana Beker
Saddles East	John W. Beard
Last of the Saddle Tramps	Messanie Wilkins
Ride a White Horse	William Holt
Manual of Pack Transportation	H. W. Daly
Horses, Saddles and Bridles	W. H. Carter
Notes on Elementary Equitation	Carleton S. Cooke
Cavalry Drill Regulations	United States Army
Horse Packing	Charles Johnson Post
14th Century Arabic Riding Manual	Muhammad al-Aqsarai
The Art of Travel	Francis Galton
Shanghai à Moscou	Madame de Bourboulon
Saddlebags for Suitcases	Mary Bosanquet
The Road to the Grey Pamir	Ana Louise Strong
Boot and Saddle in Africa	Thomas Lambie
To the Foot of the Rainbow	Clyde Kluckhohn
Through Five Republics on Horseback	George Ray
Journey from the Arctic	Donald Brown
Saddle and Canoe	Theodore Winthrop
The Prairie Traveler	Randolph Marcy
Reiter, Pferd und Fahrer – Volume One	Dr. C. Geuer
Reiter, Pferd und Fahrer – Volume Two	Dr. C. Geuer

The Long Riders' Guild
The world's leading source of information regarding equestrian exploration!
www.thelongridersguild.com

Printed in the United States
33449LVS00003B/22